CONTAINING MULTITUDES

Poetry in the United States since 1950

Twayne's Critical History of Poetry Studies

•

Alan Shucard, Editor
University of Wisconsin-Parkside

CONTAINING MULTITUDES

Poetry in the United States since 1950

FRED MORAMARCO
San Diego State University

WILLIAM SULLIVAN
Keene State College

Twayne Publishers
An Imprint of Simon & Schuster Macmillan
New York

Prentice Hall International
London • Mexico City • New Delhi
Singapore • Sydney • Toronto

Critical History of Poetry Studies
Containing Multitudes: Poetry in the United States since 1950

Fred Moramarco and William Sullivan

Copyright © 1998 by Twayne Publishers

Twayne Publishers
An Imprint of Simon & Schuster Macmillan
1633 Broadway
New York, NY 10019

Library of Congress Cataloging-in-Publication Data
Moramarco, Fred S., 1938–
      Containing multitudes : poetry in the United States since 1950 /
  Fred Moramarco and William Sullivan.
          p.   cm. — (Twayne's critical history of poetry studies)
      Includes bibliographical references and index.
      ISBN 0-8057-1647-5 (alk. paper)
      1. American poetry—20th century—History and criticism.
  I. Sullivan, William J. (William John), 1937–   . II. Title.
  III. Series.
  PS325.M67   1998
  811'.5409—dc21   97-36476
                                                                                              CIP

This paper meets the requirements of ANSI/NISO Z3948–1992
(Permanence of Paper).

10 9 8 7 6 5 4 3 2   (hc)
10 9 8 7 6 5 4 3 2 1 (pb)
Printed in the United States of America.

Do I contradict myself?
Very well. . . . then I contradict myself;
I am large. . . . I contain multitudes.

Walt Whitman, *Song of Myself*

· Contents ·

Preface   ix
Acknowledgments   xv
Chronology   xxv

ONE
Lost Worlds: Midcentury Revisions of Modernism   1

TWO
Exploring New Terrain: Self and Community   37

THREE
New Maps for Contemporary Poetry   73

FOUR
The Poetry of Place   122

FIVE
"A Whole New Poetry Beginning Here":
The Assertion of Gender   163

SIX
Turning Inward: The Poetry of American Men   195

SEVEN
Borderlands: The Diversity of American Poetry   245

EIGHT
Restoring Whitman's Vision: The Anthologies of the Eighties   314

Notes   329
Selected Bibliography   346
Index   355

· *Preface* ·

This volume concludes the journey through the dense thickets, myriad paths, and diverse cities of American poetry begun by Alan Shucard in *American Poetry: The Puritans through Walt Whitman* and continued by Shucard with Fred Moramarco and William Sullivan in *Modern American Poetry: 1865–1950*. What we have attempted in each of these volumes is to provide something more than a mere chronicling of names, books, and achievements. We have tried to present a *reading* of our poetic heritage that recognizes the simple reality that poems can only be read and experienced one at a time and that poets, despite the tendency of university professors to group them in schools and movements, write individually.

The first task to confront us was the problem that faces every writer, whatever the subject matter: what to put in and what to leave out. In this volume particularly, the decisions surrounding that task were difficult, since many of the poets we have written about are still living and there is no widespread consensus on what constitutes the canon of American poetry since the 1950s. In fact, the current *Directory of Poets and Writers* lists more than 4,000 poets writing in the United States today, and this includes only those who choose to be listed in the directory.

The contemporary generation may in fact be the first generation in American history in which substantial numbers of poets actually make a living teaching and writing poetry. This is in sharp contrast to the modernist generation of the earlier part of the century in which nearly all of the major figures sought their income elsewhere: T. S. Eliot was a banker, Wallace Stevens an insurance executive, and William Carlos Williams a pediatrician. So although a very large number of people may identify themselves as professional poets, there is the simple reality that in any given period of literary history, only a handful of poets really survive the test of time and are read a hundred or more years later. Between the many thousands writing and publishing poetry in the United States today and the handful whose work will be read in the year 2100 (if anyone at all is still reading then), we opted for a manageable middle road that includes detailed commentary on the work of about sixty poets. Who the handful of survivors will be is anybody's guess, but we risk the assertion that they will be found—barring the discovery of an Emily Dickinson who kept her work hidden from the world's view during her lifetime—among the poets included here. This said, however, we are certainly aware that a whole other book could be written merely surveying the notable poets we were unable to include in this volume because of time and space considerations. That book would include commentary on Josephine Miles, Karl Shapiro, David Ignatow, May Sarton, Melvin Tolson, Edward Field, Ed Dorn, Paul Blackburn, Lawrence Ferlinghetti, Isabella Gardner, Maya Angelou, Larry Levis, Donald Justice, William Meredith, June Jordan, Paula Gunn Allen, Howard Nemerov, Amy Clampitt, Alan Dugan, John Hollander, and many more.

Once we agreed on the general scope of the book—about sixty or so poets born before 1950 who had published at least three books of poems by 1990 or in some other way played an essential role in the making of contemporary poetry in the United States—the task remained to "chart the terrain" of the poetry of the United States by looking at it from several different perspectives and constructing "maps" based on each of these perspectives. We began our literary cartography by outlining different philosophic and aesthetic values that the poets at midcentury either shared or reacted against.

William Sullivan, in chapters 1 and 2, charts the significant modifications of modernism by the "middle generation" of poets who came of age prior to the literary revolutions of the late fifties and sixties and wrote under the still dominant shadow of the great modernists. Beset by both personal and public traumas, Weldon Kees, Randall Jarrell, Robert Lowell, Elizabeth Bishop, Theodore Roethke, Stanley Kunitz, and John Berryman often experienced a debilitating sense of loss. In creating poems that confronted these traumas directly, they played an important role in the creation of an intensely experiential and personal mode of poetry. Muriel Rukeyser, Gwendolyn Brooks, Robert Hayden, Richard Wilbur, Denise Levertov, and Robert Duncan push beyond the sense of a "lost world" and discover the possibilities and satisfactions of "the things of this world." Their perspective is often social or collective; they speak for more than the isolated self, and they are engaged with the political and economic issues of the time. Questions concerning race (Hayden), gender (Rukeyser), race and gender (Brooks), ideology (Wilbur and Levertov), and sexual preference (Duncan) are discussed more freely than ever before, and this new emphasis foreshadows the concerns of a later generation who would take these distinctions further and develop a whole poetics based on one or more of them.

In chapter 3 Fred Moramarco identifies the new mapmakers of the contemporary period—poets like Allen Ginsberg, Adrienne Rich, Sylvia Plath, John Ashbery, Frank O'Hara, Robert Creeley, Robert Bly, and James Wright—who redefined poetic values and ushered in the revolution in taste and style that characterizes the poetry of the second half of the century. These poets, although vastly different in style and outlook, created collectively a "contemporary" poetic voice. Whether that voice was passionate and emotionally intense (Ginsberg and Plath, for example), whether it was whimsical or eloquent (O'Hara, Ashbery), whether its primary concerns were political (Rich) or linguistic (Creeley), or whether it sought to revolutionize poetic imagery and explore deep inner psychic states (Bly and Wright), it was innovative and revolutionary.

In chapter 4, Sullivan takes the map metaphor quite literally by first looking at the creation of a truly national mode of contemporary American poetry, in which every region of the nation finds poetic expression. He then explores the importance of place in the poetry of William Everson, William Stafford, Thomas McGrath, A. R. Ammons, James Dickey, Maxine Kumin, Mary Oliver, and Gary Snyder, noting how these poets record the various regional landscapes as well as the spiritual and redemptive qualities of nature. This belief in the sacredness of the land and its replenishing powers remains a persistent theme despite the predominantly urban character of late twentieth-century American life.

Moramarco, in chapters 5 and 6, explores the degree to which gender has shaped the contemporary poetic landscape. He chronicles the assertion of gender in contemporary women's poetry through the work of Anne Sexton, Audre Lorde, Marge Piercy, and Sharon Olds, among others, and locates the gendered aspects of male poetry as well by exploring the work of Galway Kinnell, W. S. Merwin, Mark Strand, Philip Levine, C. K. Williams, Donald Hall, and others.

Then Sullivan celebrates the expansion of ethnicity in American poetry that occurred from the midsixties onward. Chapter 7 travels across the borderlands of contemporary poetry and discovers the birth and growth of multicultural poetry as well as an amazing richness and diversity of styles and language. Poets like Imamu Amiri Baraka, Lucille Clifton, Sonia Sanchez, Etheridge Knight, Michael Harper, and others create a vital African-American poetics that draws from a cultural heritage too often suppressed by what is often called the "mainstream" culture. Other ethnic voices are heard in this chapter as well: Latino (Corky Gonzales, Alurista, Bernice Zamora, Gloria Anzaldúa), Native American (N. Scott Momaday, Leslie Marmon Silko, James Welch, Simon Ortiz, Wendy Rose), Asian American (Lawson Fusao Inada, Janice Mirikitani).

Finally, Moramarco concludes by chronicling the anthologies of our poetry that appeared in the 1980s and demonstrated more than ever the richness and diversity of the poetic landscape. This chapter looks at some of the "movements" and trends that emerged in the eighties.

We hope this survey will demonstrate that contemporary American poetry, far from being a remote, academic, esoteric pastime, reflects the vastness and variety of America's people in a way that is closer to the spirit of Walt Whitman's vision than it has ever been before. In the preface to *Leaves of Grass* Whitman speaks of Americans as having "probably the fullest poetical nature" of any nation on earth at any time because we are not "merely a nation but a teeming nation of nations." He speaks of America's diversity as its strongest asset and looks forward to a time when poets will be able to rise to "the gigantic and generous treatment worthy of it." It is hard to retain Whitman's inspiring optimism at the end of a century of devastating violence, and yet in another sense Whitman seems to be speaking directly to all of us in the late twentieth century, when his words seem more prophetic than ever, when his vision of a multicultural America is a reality that is finally beginning to be acknowledged.

This volume embodies Whitman's vision of the United States as a country whose strength and uniqueness are its pluralism, a trait Whitman celebrated and expressed in his own person and in the originality of his poetry. He prophesied an America rich in the variety of its cultures and people, not a "melting pot" that homogenizes all of its citizens but a mosaic that expresses its beauty in a multitudinous assortment of patterns. Whitman's America was, like our own, an America filled with paradoxes and contradictions. Our title comes from his famous pronouncement: "Do I contradict myself? /

Preface

Very well then . . . . I contradict myself; / I am large . . . . I contain multitudes."

While our poetry has always contained contradictions and multitudes, literary critics and historians have too often valued only a canonical Anglo-American poetry characterized by the mastery of conventional language and the conveyance of received wisdom. They have not paid enough attention to the many poetic voices of America's many peoples. This survey includes poets who were educated on the streets of the inner cities and barrios or ghettos and even in prison, as well as on the vast plains of the Midwest and in the courtyards of Harvard; it finds the poetry of work and struggle as compelling as the poetry of detached social observation; and it recognizes that poets write as men and women with diverse cultural backgrounds that shape the language they speak and write, rather than as "universal human beings." We hope this "poetics of inclusion" helps to move us closer to recognizing and assimilating the uniqueness of the poetry of our place and our time.

· *Acknowledgments* ·

Grateful acknowledgment is made to the following for permissions to use material as indicated.

Excerpts from various poems, from *The Selected Poems*, Expanded Edition by A. R. Ammons. Copyright © 1987, 1977, 1975, 1974, 1972, 1971, 1970, 1966, 1965, 1964, 1955 by A. R. Ammons. Reprinted by permission of W. W. Norton & Company, Inc.

Excerpts, from *Self-Portrait in a Convex Mirror* by John Ashbery. Copyright © 1972, 1973, 1974, 1975 by John Ashbery. Used by permission of Viking Penguin, a division of Penguin Books USA, Inc.

Aunt Lute Books. From Borderlands/La Frontera: The New Mestiza © 1987 by Gloria Anzaldúa. Reprinted with permission from Aunt Lute Books.

The LeRoi Jones/Amiri Baraka Reader by Amiri Baraka. Copyright © 1990 by Amiri Baraka. Used by permission of the Publisher, Thunder's Mouth Press.

Black Sparrow Press. Excerpts from William Everson, "A Canticle to the Waterbirds" in *The Veritable Years: 1949–1966*.

Black Sparrow Press. Material from *Medea the Sorceress, Emerald Ice,* and *The Collected Greed 1-13*. Copyright © 1966, 1970, 1984, 1991 by Diane Wakoski. Reprinted with the permission of Black Sparrow Press.

Blue Cloud Quarterly, for excerpts from "Builder Kachina . . ." in *Blue Cloud Quarterly*. "Three-Thousand Dollar . . ." and "For the White poets who would be Indian" in *Academic Squaw* by Wendy Rose.

Acknowledgments

Michael Blumenthal. Excerpts from "The Hearts of Men," in *Against Romance* by Michael Blumenthal. Copyright © 1987 by Michael Blumenthal. Used by permission of Viking Penguin, a division of Penguin Books USA Inc.

Georges Borchardt, Inc. Excerpts from M. S. Merwin's "The Undoing," "The Pencil," lines beginning "There is no season," lines beginning "I dreamed I had no nails," "Finally," lines beginning "When my father," "Berryman," in *Selected Poems*.

Broadside Press for quotations from Sonia Sanchez, "blk/woooooomen/chant," "Poem for etheridge," "answer to yo/question," and "A Letter to Dr. Martin . . ." in *we a baddDDD people* and "Malcolm," "to all brothers," "to all sisters," and "to blk/record /buyers" in *Homecoming*.

Celestial Arts: Excerpted from *Shedding Silence* copyright © 1987 by Janice Mirikitani. Reprinted by permission of Celestial Arts, P.O. Box 7123, Berkeley, CA 94707.

Lucille Clifton. Excerpts from *Good Woman: Poems and a Memoir, 1969–1980*, copyright © 1987 by Lucille Clifton. Reprinted with the permission of BOA Editions, Ltd., 92 Park Ave., Brockport, NY 14420.

Curtis Brown, Ltd. Quotations from the poetry of Maxine Kumin are reprinted by permission of Curtis Brown, Ltd. All rights reserved.

Darhansoff and Verrill. Excerpts from "Old Cracked Tune," "For the Word Is Flesh," "Night Letter," "Father and Son," "Journal for My Daughter," "The Testing-Tree," "The Layers" from *The Poems of Stanley Kunitz: 1928–1978* and "The Long Boat" from *Next to Last Things: New Poems and Essays* by Stanley Kunitz.

Doubleday Publishers. Excerpts from "The Rose," "Feud," "Lost Son," "Four for Sir John Davies," "I Knew a Woman," and "What I Can Tell My Bones" in *The Collected Poems of Theodore Roethke* by Theodore Roethke.

Acknowledgments

Ecco Press. From "Elms," © by Louise Gluck. From *The Triumph of Achilles*, first published by Ecco Press in 1985. Reprinted by permission. "A Fantasy" © 1990 by Louise Gluck. From *Ararat*, published by The Ecco Press. Reprinted by permission. "The Deviation" © 1980 by Louise Gluck. From *Descending Figure*, published by The Ecco Press. Reprinted by permission. From "Santa Barbara Road," "Privilege of Being," and "On Squaw Peak" from *Human Wishes* © 1989. Published by The Ecco Press. Reprinted by permission.

William Everson. Excerpts from "Outside this Music" and "The Vow" in *Residual Years: Poems 1934–1948* and "The Scout" and "The Black Hills" in *Man Fate: The Swan Song of Brother . . ."* by William Everson. Copyright © by Jude Everson and the William Everson Literary Estate.

Faber and Faber. Excerpts from "Children of Light," "In Memory of A. Winslow," and "To Peter Taylor" in *Lord Weary's Castle* by Robert Lowell; "The Beautiful Changes," "October Maples, Portland," "A Dubious Night," "Love Calls Us," "The Undead," "On the Marginal Way," "Advice to a Prophet," "On Freedom's Ground," and ". . . Etruscan Poets" in *New and Collected Poems* by Richard Wilbur.

Reprinted by permission of Farrar, Straus & Giroux, Inc. Excerpts from *The Dream Songs* by John Berryman. Copyright © 1969 by John Berryman. Excerpts from *Collected Poems: 1937–1971* by John Berryman. Copyright © 1989 by Kate Donahue Berryman. Excerpts from *In the Western Night: Collected Poems, 1965–1990,* by Frank Bidart. Copyright © 1990 by Frank Bidart. Excerpts from *The Complete Poems: 1927–1979* by Elizabeth Bishop. Copyright © 1979, 1983 by Alice Helen Methfessel. Excerpts from *The Complete Poems* by Randall Jarrell. Copyright © 1969 by Mrs. Randall Jarrell. Excerpts from *Selected Poems* by Robert Lowell. Copyright © 1977 by Robert Lowell. Excerpts from *Day by Day* by Robert Lowell. Copyright © 1977 by Robert Lowell. Excerpts from *Axe Handles* by Gary Snyder. Copyright © 1983 by Gary Snyder. Excerpts from *Poems: 1963–1983* by C. K. Williams. Copyright © 1969, 1988 by C. K. Williams. Excerpts from *Above the River: The Complete Poems of James Wright* by James Wright. Copyright © 1990 by Anne Wright.

Four Walls Eight Windows Press. Excerpts from Ted Berrigan, "Things to do in Providence," and Andrei Codrescu, "Au Bout du Temps," in *Up Late: American Poetry since 1970*, edited by Andrei Codrescu.

Acknowledgments

Excerpts from "The Days" and "Maple Syrup" in *The Day I Was Older* by Donald Hall. Reprinted by permission of the author and Story Line Press.

Donald Hall. Excerpts from "Eating the Pig" from *Kicking the Leaves*.

HarperCollins Publishers, Inc. Excerpts from Robert Bly, "A Man Writes," in *Selected Poems*. Excerpts from Sylvia Plath, "The Manor Garden," "Lady Lazurus," "Lorelei," "Cut," "Childless Woman," and "Daddy," in *The Collected Poems*.

Houghton Mifflin Co. Excerpt, from *The Avenue Bearing the Initial of Christ into the New World*. Copyright © 1953, 1954, 1955, 1958, 1959, 1960, 1961, 1963, 1964, 1970, 1971, 1974 by Galway Kinnell. Reprinted by permission of Houghton Mifflin Co. All rights reserved.

Houghton Mifflin Co. From "Under the Maud Moon," *The Book of Nightmares*. Copyright © 1971 by Galway Kinnell. Reprinted by permission of Houghton Mifflin Co. All rights reserved.

Houghton Mifflin Co. From *Love Poems* by Anne Sexton. Copyright © 1967, 1968, 1969 by Anne Sexton. Reprinted by permission of Houghton Mifflin Company. All rights reserved.

Houghton Mifflin Co. From *Live or Die* by Anne Sexton. Copyright © 1966 by Anne Sexton. Reprinted by permission of Houghton Mifflin Company. All rights reserved.

Houghton Mifflin Co. From *All My Pretty Ones* by Anne Sexton. Copyright © 1962 © renewed 1990 by Linda G. Sexton. Reprinted by permission of Houghton Mifflin Company. All rights reserved.

Houghton Mifflin Co. From *To Bedlam and Part Way Back* by Anne Sexton. Copyright © 1960 © renewed 1988 by Linda G. Sexton. Reprinted by permission of Houghton Mifflin Company. All rights reserved.

Houghton Mifflin Co. From *Transformations* by Anne Sexton. Copyright © 1971 by Anne Sexton. Reprinted by permission of Houghton Mifflin Company. All rights reserved.

Acknowledgments

University of Illinois Press. Excerpts from Michael Harper, "Corrected View," in *Images of Kin: New Poems*, Urbana, 1977.

University of Illinois Press. Excerpts from Michael Harper, *History Is Your Own Heartbeat*, 1971.

Excerpts from various poems, from *Collected Poems of Robert Hayden* by Frederick Glaysher, editor. Copyright © 1985 by Emma Hayden. Reprinted by permission of Liveright Publishing Corporation.

Lawson Fusao Inada. Excerpts from "I Told You So" from *The Buddha Bandits Down Highway 99*.

From *When One Has Lived a Long Time Alone* by Galway Kinnell. Copyright © 1990 by Galway Kinnell. Reprinted by permission of Alfred A. Knopf, Inc.

Philip Levine. Excerpts from "They Feed They Lion," "One for the Rose," and "Sweet Will" from *New Selected Poems*, Knopf © 1991, and "Asking" from *Seven Years from Somewhere*, Atheneum © 1979.

"The Woman Thing," copyright © 1973, 1970, 1968 by Audre Lorde, from *Chosen Poems: Old and New* by Audre Lorde. Reprinted by permission of W. W. Norton & Company, Inc.

Reprinted by permission of James Welch. From *Riding the Earthboy 40*, Harper & Row, 1976. Copyright 1971, 1976 by James Welch. All rights reserved.

Reprinted by permission of William Matthews. Excerpts from *A Happy Childhood*. (New York: Atlantic Little Brown, 1984).

Thomas McGrath poems from *Selected Poems: 1938–1988*, © 1988 by Thomas McGrath. Reprinted by permission of Copper Canyon Press, P.O. Box 271, Port Townsend, WA 98368.

From *Selected Poems: 1946–1985* by James Merrill. Copyright © 1992 by James Merrill. Reprinted by permission of Alfred A. Knopf, Inc.

Acknowledgments

Reprinted by permission of Janice Mirikitani: Excerpts from *Time to Greez: Incantations from the Third World*, edited by Mirikitani, Glide Publications, San Francisco, 1975, and *Awake in the River: Poetry and Prose*, by Janice Mirikitani, Isthmus Press, San Francisco, 1978.

N. Scott Momaday. Excerpts from *The Gourd Dancer*. Published by HarperCollins.

William Morrow and Co. Excerpts from *Before the War* by Lawson Fusao Inada.

University of Nebraska Press. Excerpts from *The Collected Poems of Weldon Kees* by Weldon Kees.

New Directions Publishing Corporation, for lines from Denise Levertov, *Candles in Babylon*, copyright © 1966, 1978, 1979, 1982 by Denise Levertov, and *A Door in the Hive*, 1989; for lines from Gary Snyder, *Turtle Island*, copyright © 1974 by Gary Snyder; for lines from Robert Creeley, *Mirrors*, copyright © 1983 and *Later*, 1979; and for lines from Robert Duncan, *Selected Poems*, copyright © 1968, 1987 by Robert Duncan. Used by Permission of New Directions Publishing Corporation.

James Wright, excerpts from "A Blessing," from *The Branch Will Not Break*, © 1963; "In Response to a Rumor that the Oldest Whorehouse in Wheeling, West Virginia, Has Been Condemned," from *Shall We Gather at the River*, © 1968; "Many of Our Waters, Variations on a Poem by a Black Child," from *Collected Poems*, © 1971; "At the Executed Murderer's Grave," from *St. Judas*, © 1959.

James Dickey, excerpts from "Chenille" from *Helmets*, © 1964; "The Sheep Child" from *Falling, May Day, & Other Poems*, © 1982; "Slave Quarters" from *Buckdancer's Choice*, © 1965. Philip Levine, excerpts from "In a Grove Again" from *Not This Pig*, © 1968. Wesleyan University Press by reprint permission from the University Press of New England.

University of New Mexico Press, for lines from "Rainy Mountain Cemetery" in *The Way to Rainy Mountain* by N. Scott Momaday.

Acknowledgments

Northwestern University Press. Excerpts from "Southern Road" in *Collected Poems of Sterling Brown* by Sterling Brown.

From *Collected Poems* by Frank O'Hara. Copyright © 1971 by Maureen Granville-Smith, Administratrix of the Estate of Frank O'Hara. Reprinted by permission of Alfred A. Knopf, Inc.

University of Pittsburgh Press. Excerpt from "The Sisters of Sexual Treasure" from *Satan Says* by Sharon Olds, © 1980. Reprinted by permission of the University of Pittsburgh Press.

From *The Gold Cell* by Sharon Olds. Copyright © 1987 by Sharon Olds. Reprinted by permission of Alfred A. Knopf, Inc.

From *The Dead and the Living* by Sharon Olds. Copyright © 1983 by Sharon Olds. Reprinted by permission of Alfred A. Knopf, Inc.

Permission to quote from Simon Ortiz's poetry granted by the author. The poetry appears in a 3-in-1 compendium of his work, *Woven Stone*, University of Arizona Press, 1992.

From *Circle in the Water: Selected Poems* by Marge Piercy. Copyright © 1982 by Marge Piercy. Reprinted by permission of Alfred A. Knopf, Inc.

From *Available Light* by Marge Piercy. Copyright © 1988 by Marge Piercy. Reprinted by permission of Alfred A. Knopf, Inc.

From *Stone Paper Knife* by Marge Piercy. Copyright © 1983 by Marge Piercy. Reprinted by permission of Alfred A. Knopf, Inc.

From *My Mother's Body* by Marge Piercy. Copyright © 1985 by Marge Piercy. Reprinted by permission of Alfred A. Knopf, Inc.

University of Pittsburgh Press. Excerpts from "Cell Song," "Hard Rock Returns to Prison from the Hospital for the Criminally Insane," "For Freckle-faced Gerald," "He Sees through Stone," "The Warden Said to Me the Other Day," "The Violent Space," "As You Leave Me," "Haiku 4," "My Life, the Quality of Which," "Feeling Fucked Up," "Con/Tin/U/Way/Shun Blues," "Belly Song," "The Stretching of

Acknowledgments

the Belly," "On the Birth of a Black/Baby/Boy," "The Idea of Ancestry," and "A Poem For a Certain Lady on Her 33rd Birthday" from *The Essential Etheridge Knight* by Etheridge Knight, © 1986. Reprinted by permission of the University of Pittsburgh Press.

Laurence Pollinger Limited. Excerpts from "The 90th Year" from *Life in the Forest*; "Pleasures" from *Collected Earlier Poems*; "Matins," "Two Variations," "The Altars in the Street," "City Psalm" from *Poems: 1960–67*; "In Memory of Muriel Rukeyser," "Candles in Babylon," "What I Could Be," and "Talking to Oneself" from *Candles in Babylon* by Denise Levertov. U.K. and Commonwealth Rights.

Princeton University Press. Excerpts from *Sadness and Happiness* by Robert Pinsky © 1975.

Random House. Excerpts from *The Collected Poems of Frank O'Hara* by John Ashbery.

From *Collected Early Poems: 1950–1970* by Adrienne Rich. Copyright © 1993 by Adrienne Rich. Copyright © 1967, 1963, 1962, 1961, 1960, 1959, 1958, 1957, 1956, 1955, 1954, 1953, 1952, 1951 by Adrienne Rich. Copyright © 1984, 1975, 1971, 1969, 1966 by W. W. Norton & Company, Inc. Reprinted by permission of the author and W. W. Norton & Company, Inc.

From *The Fact of a Doorframe: Poems Selected and New, 1950–1984*, by Adrienne Rich. Copyright © 1975, 1978 by W. W. Norton and Company, Inc. Copyright © 1981 by Adrienne Rich. Reprinted by permission of the author and W. W. Norton & Company, Inc.

From *Your Native Land, Your Life: Poems by Adrienne Rich*. Copyright © 1986 by Adrienne Rich. Reprinted by permission of the author and W. W. Norton & Company, Inc.

From *Time's Power: Poems, 1985–1988* by Adrienne Rich. Copyright © 1989 by Adrienne Rich. Reprinted by permission of the author and W. W. Norton & Company, Inc.

Wendy Rose. Excerpts from "Half-breed Cry," "Robert," and "Yuriko" from *Halfbreed Chronicles* by Wendy Rose.

Acknowledgments

William Rukeyser for excerpts from Muriel Rukeyser, "Mediterranean," "Night Flight: New York," "Prose Statement," "In Letter to the Front," "Don Baty," "The Draft Resister," "Welcome from War," "Open the Gates," "Ajanta," "The Poem as Mask" "The Speed of Darkness," and "The Hostages" from *The Collected Poems*.

From the book *Homegirls & Handgrenades* by Sonia Sanchez. Copyright © 1984 by Sonia Sanchez. Used by permission of the publisher, Thunder's Mouth Press.

Charles Simic. Excerpts from "Description." Reprinted by permission of George Braziller, Inc.

Gary Snyder, excerpts from "Soy Sauce" in *Axe Handles*.

Selections from the poetry of William Stafford are from *Stories That Could Be True* (Harper and Row, 1977), copyright © 1977 William Stafford. Reprinted by permission of the Estate of William Stafford.

Sterling Lord Literistic, Inc. Excerpts from *Rivers and Mountains* by John Ashbery and excerpts from *The Complete Poems* by Anne Sexton.

Mark Strand, excerpts from "Violent Storm" and "Elegy for My Father" as well as "Keeping Things Whole" (entire poem) in *Selected Poems*.

From *The Continuous Life* by Mark Strand. Copyright © 1990 Mark Strand. Reprinted by permission of Alfred A. Knopf, Inc.

Quincy Troupe, excerpts from "River Town Packin House," "Blues for Delmar Does," "Skulls along the River," "River-Rhythm Town," "Up Sun South of Alaska," and "Ode to John Coltrane" from *Skulls along the River*.

Yale University Press. Lines from "Artemis" from *Beginning with O* by Olga Broumas.

· *Chronology* ·

This chronology is a highly selective compilation of major events in the world of American poetry and of titles of important individual works of poetry published between 1950 and 1990 and discussed in this volume.

1950 Gwendolyn Brooks, *Annie Allen.*

Charles Olson, "Projective Verse," a seminal essay in the development of the new poetry.

1951 Adrienne Rich, *A Change of World.*

1952 Lawrence Ferlinghetti and Peter Martin open the City Lights Bookstore in San Francisco.

W. S. Merwin, *A Mask for Janus.*

1953 Charles Olson publishes first segment of *The Maximus Poems.*

1954 Wallace Stevens, *Collected Poems.*

1955 Allen Ginsberg reads "Howl" at Gallery Six in San Francisco.

Elizabeth Bishop, *Poems North and South—A Cold Spring.*

1956 John Ashbery, *Some Trees.*

John Berryman, *Homage to Mistress Bradstreet.*

Allen Ginsberg, *Howl and Other Poems.*

1957 Richard Wilbur, *Things of This World.*

Evergreen Review begins publication.

San Francisco Judge Clayton Horn clears *Howl* of obscenity charges.

1958 Stanley Kunitz, *Selected Poems.*

Theodore Roethke, *Words for the Wind.*

The Fifties magazine, edited by Robert Bly and William Duffy, begins publication in Pine Island, Minnesota.

Chronology

1959   Langston Hughes, *Selected Poems*.

Robert Lowell, *Life Studies*.

W. D. Snodgrass, *Heart's Needle*.

Gary Snyder, *Riprap*.

Wesleyan University Press establishes Wesleyan Poetry Series.

1960   Randall Jarrell, *The Woman at the Washington Zoo*.

Weldon Kees, *Collected Poems*.

Sylvia Plath, *The Colossus*.

Ann Sexton, *To Bedlam and Partway Back*.

Donald Allen edits *The New American Poetry*.

1961   Hilda Dolittle dies.

Leroi Jones, *Preface to a Twenty-Volume Suicide Note*.

1962   Robinson Jeffers and E. E. Cummings die.

John Ashbery, *The Tennis Court Oath*.

Robert Bly, *Silence in Snowy Fields*.

Robert Creeley, *For Love*.

Muriel Rukeyser, *Waterlily Fire: Poems, 1935–1962*.

William Stafford, *Travelling through the Dark*.

Donald Hall edits *Contemporary American Poetry: An Anthology*.

1963   Robert Frost, William Carlos Williams, and Theodore Roethke die.

Sylvia Plath commits suicide in London, age 31.

Gwendolyn Brooks, *Selected Poems*.

James Wright, *The Branch Will Not Break*.

1964   John Berryman, *77 Dream Songs*.

Denise Levertov, *O Taste and See*.

Robert Lowell, *For the Union Dead*.

Frank O'Hara, *Lunch Poems*.

1965   T. S. Eliot dies in London.

Randall Jarrell killed in automobile accident.

Elizabeth Bishop, *Questions of Travel*.

Chronology

Paris Leary and Robert Kelly edit *A Controversy of Poetry*.

Dudley Randall establishes the Broadside Press to publish African-American poets.

1966 Delmore Schwartz dies.

Frank O'Hara killed in automobile accident on Fire Island, New York.

Robert Hayden, *Selected Poems*.

Sylvia Plath, *Ariel*.

Theodore Roethke, *The Collected Poems*.

1967 Carl Sandburg and Langston Hughes die.

Robert Bly, *The Light around the Body*.

James Dickey, *Poems: 1957–1967*.

Rudolfo Gonzales, *I Am Joaquin*.

Anne Sexton, *Live or Die*.

1968 Galway Kinnell, *Body Rags*.

Mark Strand, *Reasons for Moving*.

Diane Wakoski, *Inside the Blood Factory*.

Paul Carroll edits *The Young American Poets*.

1969 Jack Kerouac dies.

Imamu Amiri Baraka, *Black Magic: Collected Poetry, 1961–1967*.

Elizabeth Bishop, *Complete Poems*.

John Berryman, *The Dream Songs*.

Randall Jarrell, *The Complete Poems*.

M. Scott Momaday, *The Way to Rainy Mountain*.

Richard Howard, *Alone with America: Essays on the Art of Poetry since 1950*.

Stephen Berg and Robert Mezey edit *Naked Poetry: American Poetry in Open Forms*.

1970 Charles Olson dies.

Michael Harper, *Dear John, Dear Coltrane*.

Chronology

1971   Lawson Fusao Inada, *Before the War.*

     Galway Kinnell, *The Book of Nightmares.*

     Frank O'Hara, *The Collected Poems.*

     James Welch, *Riding the Earthboy 40.*

     James Wright, *Collected Poems.*

     Dudley Randall edits *The Black Poets.*

1972   John Berryman commits suicide in Minneapolis.

     Marianne Moore, Kenneth Patchen, and Ezra Pound die.

     A. R. Ammons, *Collected Poems.*

     John Ashbery, *Three Poems*

     Allen Ginsberg, *Poems of These States: 1965–71.*

     Philip Levine, *They Feed, They Lion.*

     Janice Mirikitani edits *Third World Woman.*

     American Poetry Review begins publication in Philadelphia.

1973   Robert Lowell, *History, The Dolphin, For Lizzie and Harriet.*

     Adrienne Rich, *Diving into the Wreck.*

     Sonia Sanchez, *A Blues Book for Magical Black Women.*

     William Stafford, *Stories That Could Be True: New and Collected Poems.*

     Mark Strand, *The Story of Our Lives.*

1974   Anne Sexton commits suicide.

     John Crowe Ransom dies.

     William Everson, *Man-Fate: The Swan Song of Brother Antonius.*

     Philip Levine, *1933.*

     Gary Snyder, *Turtle Island.*

1975   John Ashbery, *Self-Portait in a Convex Mirror.*

     Robert Hayden, *Angle of Ascent: New and Selected Poems.*

     Adrienne Rich, *Poems: Selected and New.*

     Duane Niatum edits *Carriers of the Dreamwheel: Contemporary Native American Poetry.*

1976   W. H. Auden, *Collected Poems.*

     Elizabeth Bishop, *Geography III.*

Simon Ortiz, *Going for the Rain.*

Bernice Zamora, *Restless Serpent.*

1977 Robert Lowell, *Day by Day.*

Lowell dies from a heart attack in a New York taxi.

1978 William Everson, *The Veritable Years: Poems 1949–1966.*

Audre Lorde, *The Black Unicorn.*

Muriel Rukeyser, *The Collected Poems.*

1979 Elizabeth Bishop dies.

Stanley Kunitz, *The Poems of Stanley Kunitz: 1928–1978.*

1980 James Wright, Robert Hayden, and Muriel Rukeyser die.

Sterling Brown, *The Collected Poems.*

Sharon Olds, *Satan Says.*

Mark Strand, *Selected Poems.*

1981 Simon Ortiz, *from Sand Creek.*

Sylvia Plath, *The Collected Poems,* edited by Ted Hughes.

Anne Sexton, *The Complete Poems.*

Sherri Morega and Gloria Anzaldúa edit *This Bridge Called My Back: Writings by Radical Women of Color.*

1982 Kenneth Rexroth and Richard Hugo die.

Robert Creeley, *The Collected Poems.*

Galway Kinnell, *Selected Poems.*

Maxine Kumin, *Our Ground Time Here Will Be Brief: New and Collected Poems.*

Marge Piercy, *Circles on the Water: Selected Poems.*

1983 Gary Snyder, *Axe Handles.*

Mary Oliver, *American Primitive.*

Elizabeth Bishop, *The Complete Poems: 1927–1979.*

1984 Robert Duncan, *Groundwork: Before the War.*

Allen Ginsberg, *Collected Poems: 1947–1980.*

Philip Levine, *Selected Poems.*

Robert Pinsky, *History of My Heart.*

Adrienne Rich, *The Fact of a Doorframe: Poems Selected and New, 1950–1984.*

Chronology

1985 John Ashbery, *Selected Poems.*

Louise Glück, *The Triumph of Achilles.*

Robert Hayden, *Collected Poems.*

Wendy Rose, *Halfbreed Chronicles.*

1986 Robert Bly, *Selected Poems.*

Etheridge Knight, *The Essential Etheridge Knight.*

1987 Gwendolyn Brooks, *Blacks (Omnibus).*

Lucille Clifton, *Next: New Poerms; Good Woman: Poems and A Memoir 1969–1980.*

Gloria Anzaldúa, *Borderlands/La Frontera: The New Mestiza.*

C. K. Williams, *Flesh and Blood.*

1988 Robert Duncan and Raymond Carver die.

Robert Duncan, *Groundwork II: In the Dark.*

Thomas McGrath, *Selected Poems.*

Donald Hall, *The One Day.*

David Lehman establishes the annual series, *Best American Poetry.*

Carl Moss and Joan Larkin edit *Gay and Lesbian Poetry in Our Time: An Anthology.*

1989 Sterling Brown and Robert Penn Warren die.

Frank Bidart, *In the Western Night: Collected Poems, 1965–1988.*

Marie Harris and Kathleen Aguero edit *An Ear to the Ground: An Anthology of Contemporary American Poetry.*

1990 Gerald Stern, *Leaving Another Kingdom: Selected Poems.*

1991 Adrienne Rich, *An Atlas of the Difficult World.*

John Ashbery, *Flow Chart.*

Philip Levine, *What Work Is.*

1992 Audre Lorde dies.

Sharon Olds, *The Father.*

James Dickey, *The Whole Motion: Collected Poems, 1945–1992.*

Denise Levertov, *Evening Train.*

Mary Oliver, *New and Selected Poems.*

Marge Piercy, *Mars and Her Children.*

Chronology

1993　William Stafford dies.

Audre Lorde, *The Marvelous Arithmetic of Distance* published posthumously.

A. R. Ammons, *Garbage*.

John Ashbery, *Hotel Lautréamont*.

Mark Strand, *Dark Harbor*.

Wendy Rose, *Going to War with All My Relatives*.

1994　Robert Creeley, *Echoes*.

Allen Ginsberg, *Cosmopolitan Greetings*.

Mary Oliver, *White Pine*.

Galway Kinnell, *Imperfect Thirst*.

Philip Levine, *The Simple Truth*.

Lucille Clifton, *The Book of Light*.

Simon Ortiz, *After and Before the Lightning*.

Wendy Rose, *Now Poof She is Gone*.

1995　James Merrill dies. *A Scattering of Salts*.

Adrienne Rich, *The Dark Fields of the Republic, Poems 1992–1995*.

John Ashbery, *And the Stars Were Shining*.

Stanley Kunitz, *Passing Through: The Later Poems*.

Sonia Sanchez, *Wounded in the House of a Friend*.

1996　Denise Levertov, *Sands of the Well*.

Gary Snyder, *Rivers and Mountains without End*.

Maxine Kumin, *Connecting the Dots*.

Sharon Olds, *The Wellspring*.

Lucille Clifton, *The Terrible Stories*.

Quincy Troupe, *Avalanche*.

1997　James Dickey dies.

Allen Ginsberg dies.

Robert Bly, *Morning Poems*.

· ONE ·

Lost Worlds:
Midcentury Revisions
of Modernism

"O world so far away! O my lost world!"
—Theodore Roethke, "Otto"

"How shall the heart be reconciled to its feast of losses?"
—Stanley Kunitz, "The Layers"

Major midcentury poets like Randall Jarrell, Robert Lowell, Elizabeth Bishop, Theodore Roethke, and Stanley Kunitz, born in the first
two decades of the twentieth century and at the center stage of
poetry by the fifties, inherited the heaviest of burdens. Not only did
they work in the shadows of their towering predecessors—T. S. Eliot,
Wallace Stevens, Robert Frost, W.H. Auden, E. E. Cummings, and
William Carlos Williams, who were still publishing important
work—but they were not free to carry out the modernist creed of
making poetry new. By now classical modernists such as Allen Tate
and New Critics such as John Crowe Ransom had already defined
modern poetry and restricted both its vision and its aesthetic practices. Modern poetry, they believed, should acknowledge human fallibility, the perplexing nature of existence, as well as the decline of
Western civilization and the singular value of art and tradition in a
decadent age. It should be ironic, impersonal, complex, allusive, and
carefully wrought. As if this cramped predicament were not enough,
the American poet was becoming more isolated, less tied to a com-
placent audience rapidly turning to mass media for its culture.

History was equally unkind. By the end of the 1950s, these poets
had witnessed the Great Depression; two world wars; the Holocaust,
which resulted in the death of more than 6 million Jews; the dropping of the atomic bomb on Hiroshima and Nagasaki; the firebombing of cities in Germany and Japan; the specter of totalitarianism in

Stalin's Russia; the intrigues of the Cold War; and, at home, the rise of the security state, McCarthyism, and the injustices of racism. The decade Robert Lowell characterized as "the tranquilized *Fifties*"[1] offered little hope for a "brave new world."

In addition, the poets' lives were often as bleak. Most of the major midcentury poets suffered either a personal or psychological loss in childhood that threatened their sense of identity, belonging, and well-being. Given their private and public histories, many fell victim to various addictions, psychological breakdowns, shattered relationships and marriages, and extremely disruptive lives. A disproportionate number actually committed suicide. They were, seemingly, a cursed generation who had been born in the worst of times. Having lost their connection to a secure, comforting world, they struggled to write well and honestly and—literally—to remain alive in a hostile environment.

Out of this struggle came some very significant poetry that is often overlooked as readers pass quickly from the modernists to what Donald Allen called, in an important anthology, *The New American Poetry*. A closer look at these middle-generation poets reveals a group of artists who courageously faced the dislocations of their public and private lives in a manner more direct and more linked to contemporary events and to actual life than that of such classical modernists as John Crowe Ransom, Allen Tate, and Robert Penn Warren. For the new generation there is much less obliqueness, less insistence on "objective correlatives" (Eliot's term for poetic language that corresponds to particular emotional states) and corresponding myths and allusions; in place of these modernist literary values there is more emphasis on directly confronting the particulars of existence. These poets not only test the classical modernists' insistence that poetry must flee from the personal but actually move closer to what would become a central strain of contemporary American poetry: an insistence on the primacy of personal experience. As they wrote more candidly about individual experience and personal history, they also explored the possibilities of a more prosaic diction and less rigid rhythms than their predecessors had used. Their difficulties were many and often overwhelming; they are not to be seen as the last vestiges of a self-satisfied but exhausted movement but as a bridge to new territory in American poetry.

As James Breslin illustrates in *From Modern to Contemporary*,[2] earlier strains of modernism may have come to "The End of the Line";

however, in vision and form, a number of the midcentury poets pushed ahead, retaining what they found valuable in the earlier modernist models but also creating their own poetic worlds and constructs. The result, viewed after the heat of the battle between perceived traditionalists and innovators has cooled, is a body of work that is often moving and, presumably, lasting.

WELDON KEES (1914–1955)   Although Weldon Kees was one of the most talented artists of his generation, he was, according to Donald Justice, "one of the bitterest poets in history."[3] Yearning for an earlier America of boundless optimism and hope, Kees never felt at home in the contemporary world. Born in Beatrice, Nebraska, a typical rural American small town, Kees went on to the University of Nebraska, where he became a contributor and reviewer for *The Prairie Schooner*. His career as a short-story writer peaked in 1941 when Edward J. O'Brien dedicated his *Best Short Stories, 1941*, to Kees. Kees, however, was already moving from fiction to poetry and in 1943 published his first of three volumes of poems, *The Last Man*, which was followed by *The Fall of the Magicians* (1947) and *Poems: 1947–1954* (1954). A fourth volume, *The Collected Poems of Weldon Kees*, was edited posthumously by Donald Justice (1962, revised 1975). Blessed with many gifts, Kees was also a highly respected literary, music, and art critic for *Poetry* magazine, the *Nation* and the *New York Times Book Review*. His articles on abstract expressionism that appeared in the *Nation* remain important introductions to America's most important modern art movement, and Kees himself became an accomplished abstract painter, exhibiting with the likes of Hans Hoffmann, Willem de Kooning, Jackson Pollock, and Robert Motherwell. When he left New York for San Francisco in 1951, he turned to jazz, writing piano compositions and scores for a number of experimental films.

As talented and versatile as Kees was, however, he could never identify with what he thought were the false values and illusionary pleasures of contemporary America. In 1955, Kees, depressed by his country's betrayal of Whitman's vision of a just and democratic nation and exhausted by his futile attempts to weather the harshness and violence of contemporary America, committed suicide by jumping from the Golden Gate Bridge into the cold waters of the Pacific.

To read Kees is to experience directly and honestly the sense of loss, bitterness, and despair that many of the midcentury poets experienced. Writing with a detached and bitter voice, he often worked in set forms like the sestina, the fugue, the villanelle, and the round, and employed traditional rhyme and meter. His language and rhythms create a tenuous balance between a number of polarities: between the lyric and the prose poem, between the commonplace and the world of the imagination, between objective reality and expressionistic vision. His poetry, read, as Donald Justice insists, in its entirety, has an incremental effect on its readers as it slowly and subtly draws them into the emptiness of existence and into the struggle of the poet to recover his lost dreams and escape from his nightmares. We must, he writes, quoting Hawthorne in the *Marble Faun*, be willing to explore "those dark caverns into which all men must descend, if they would know anything beneath the surface and illusive pleasures of existence" (87).

Hope and happiness prove to be mere illusions, and glimpses of Kees's lost worlds occur in a number of his poems. In "Place of Execution," for example, he asks: "Where are the marvelous cities that our childhood built for us, / With houses unlike those that we have come to know, . . . ?" (164).

In "For My Daughter," the speaker contemplates the inevitable corruption and death of his infant child: "The night's slow poison, . . . / Has moved her blood." He initially rejects these bitter thoughts, "These speculations sour in the sun," but then concludes with a line that shocks and dismays: "I have no daughter. I desire none" (14). Whereas Yeats in "Prayer for My Daughter" wished his daughter to be sheltered from the world's corruption, Kees concludes existence is so meaningless that the desire for children is futile, for we are cut off forever from a world of innocence and peace, "Never to enter innocent and quiet rooms" (19).

It is a dark, apocalyptic vision voiced quietly but insistently in such poems as "Fugue," where Kees assures us, "Light will fail, / . . . Falling night / Will cover all" (36). As the title of his second volume, *The Fall of the Magician,* implies, the world of childhood dreams, magic, and visions does not survive into adulthood, but few are willing to confront the bleakness of the life that remains.

In "Travels in North America" (*Poems: 1947–1954*), Kees's fine use of satiric detail captures the objective reality of a barren, commercial, and violent American culture. The poem shows that Kees is one of our early ecological prophets, presenting image after image of a devastated environment. When he nears Los Alamos, the birthplace of the atomic bomb, he records the horrors of the Atomic Age, the culture's embrace of annihilation, and ends with his own sardonic reaction to this horror: ". . . We meant / To stop, but one can only see so much. . . ." (115).

The human journey, Kees suggests, may begin in hope, for "Journeys are ways of marking out a distance, / Or dealing with the past . . . / Or ways of searching for some new enclosure in this space / Between the oceans" (117). But regardless of the road taken, all our travels and dreams inevitably lead us to "towns that smell of rubber smouldering" where "the skies are raining soot" (116).

Within this desecrated landscape, which mirrors the interior of the soul, Kees's characters and his own wounded self wander. Four poems center around a person named Robinson, who suggests E. A. Robinson's bleak outlook. Although Robinson seldom appears in the poems, he mirrors Kees's portrayal of contemporary existence, a solipsistic, isolated existence in which a hostile, impenetrable, and violent world offers no redemption, connections, or answers. So "Robinson alone provides the image Robinsonian" (59).

The details or "Aspects" of Robinson's social life are reminiscent of Eliot's "Waste Land"—an empty existence, marked by superficial relationships, empty polite talk, sordid love relationships, and outward signs of prosperity and well-being "all covering / His sad and usual heart, dry as a winter leaf" (129). Although Kees insists that we will never escape this empty life—"Never to enter innocent and quiet rooms," never to discover a "bright Jerusalem,"—he does recall moments in his childhood when innocence and serenity existed, and sometimes even tries to regain entry into that world. In "1926," for example, the speaker remembers a time when he did not know the tragic, violent side of existence and recaptures a sense of home and security:

> I did not know them then.
> My airedale scratches at the door.
> And I am back from seeing Milton Sills
> And Doris Kenyon. Twelve years old.
> The porchlight coming on again.
>
> (104)

It is also clear that he wished and at times even believed he could escape the raging winter storms of life. As expressed in such poems as "Salvo for Hans Hofmann" and "Turtle," Kees's hope was to find relief from the hellish heat of contemporary life in his art and nature, but he firmly believed that he lived in a vapid, destructive culture. The question whether he is, as Justice claims, "among the three or four best [poets] of his generation" (vii) awaits posterity's judgement.

RANDALL JARRELL (1914–1965) Randall Jarrell appeared destined to become a leading member of the second generation of classical modernists and, like Alan Tate, a "man of letters." His ties to the Fugitive poets, a group associated with Vanderbilt University and the *Fugitive* literary magazine, a leading modernist publication, were many. He was born in Tennessee and received his B.A. and M.A. degrees from Vanderbilt University (1935, 1939), where he studied under John Crowe Ransom, Donald Davison, and Robert Penn Warren. He published in the *Southern Review* (edited by Warren) and was encouraged by both Warren and Tate. When Ransom moved on to Kenyon College, Jarrell was quick to follow, and it was here that he met another young admirer of the classical modernists, Robert Lowell.

However, in both his criticism (*Poetry and the Age*, 1953; *A Sad Heart at the Supermarket*, 1962; *The Third Book of Criticism*, 1969) and poetry, Jarrell ranged far beyond the perimeters of classical modernism. Central to his approach was an insistence that poetry acknowledge, confront, and capture, in appropriate language, the particulars of the present world. Echoing Wordsworth, he argued and demonstrated, like Walt Whitman, Robert Frost, Langston Hughes, and William Carlos Williams before him, that poetry should not reach for an elevated form of language but rather should capture the real rhythms of speech. In his emphasis on the everyday particularity of contemporary life and his use of a prosaic line, Jarrell, like Lowell, attempted to move poetry closer to prose. He wrote a novel, *Pictures from an Institution* (1954) and edited five volumes of fiction. This commitment to prose clearly influenced his practice and criticism of poetry.

As a critic, this led him to fault poets who failed to record contemporary life accurately and to imitate the rhythms of actual speech. In Jarrell's view, for example, W. H. Auden's work lacked both substance and power because it had degenerated into mere poetic rhetoric. By contrast, Jarrell praised Whitman, Frost, Marianne Moore, and Williams for dealing directly with life and capturing it in compelling language. He was admired and feared for his acerbic wit and wisecracks as he lashed out at verse that did not live up to what he considered to be the potential of poetry.

Jarrell's critical ability to draw blood delighted his readers; by contrast, his highly supportitive and ardent campaign to win the day for Whitman, Frost, and Williams brought about not only a reappraisal of these poets but also an examination of the nature of modernist poetry and its importance. As Leslie Fiedler observes, his critical work enabled Jarrell to free both "himself and *his* readers from the literary canons of his own time."[4]

As for his poetry, Jarrell first drew praise for his striking war poems, which capture the physical and spiritual losses of individuals entangled in the destructive and amoral war machinery of the state. Speaking from the grave in "Losses," a member of an American bombing crew tells how he and his fellow crew members in bombers "named for girls"[5] were instructed to destroy cities they had only recently read about in textbooks and to kill people they had never seen. Dispirited by the indifference and injustice of the mass bombing of civilian targets, the men's "lives wore out" (145). Reduced to being functionary cogs in a machine, they had no recourse but to accept the maps and orders given to them and to burn the cities. In the last lines of the poem, with an imaginative switching of speakers, the devastated cities ask seemingly unanswerable questions: " 'Why are you dying? / . . . why did I die?' " (146).

Speaking from the grave, the ball turret gunner bitterly remembers that horrific moment he was taken from his mother and "fell into the State" (144). Encased in his ball turret, which is attached to the belly of a bomber, he sees himself as both animal and helpless child, who is trapped in the womb or tomb of the state. The "dream of life" (144) is over. Killed in action, the gunner recognizes how little his life meant to the state and therein provides the reader with one of the grimmest images of the military machine: "When I died they washed me out of the turret with a hose" (144).

Although criticized for overly emotional or sentimental content and too irregular and rough a line, Jarrell's poetry provides a touchstone for his generation. James Dickey declared, in an essay first published in 1956, that Jarrell's poems embody "the feel of a time, our time, as no other poetry of our century does." They present "the uncomprehending stare of the individual caught in the State's machinery: in an impersonal, invisible, man-made, and uncontrollable Force. . . . Now *that* is our time. It is humanity in the twentieth century."[6]

Jarrell continued to portray this sense of loss, insignificance, and meaninglessness in his later works, often in monologues featuring an aging woman who suffers from a sense of emptiness and a growing desire to rejuvenate her life. One of the most striking examples is "The Woman at the Washington Zoo," the title poem of the 1965 volume that brought Jarrell a National Book Award. In that poem, the woman acknowledges that she has wasted her life as a functionary in the Washington bureaucracy. Most devastating to her is the realization that no one is even aware or concerned that she has lived a colorless existence. That, it seems, is expected. Her life, she now realizes, is less meaningful than that of the animals at the zoo. To her, they appear more vibrant, have fellow cellmates, and, most important, are neither responsible for their entrapment nor conscious of their impending death. In desperation she asks a caged vulture to step forth as a man, her "wild brother," and restore her vitality: "change me, change me!" she pleads (*Complete Poems,* 215, 216).

In his last volume, *The Lost World* (1965), Jarrell adopted an autobiographical stance, reconstructing his childhood in California, where he had lived with his grandparents. Working from letters from this earlier period of his life, Jarrell records his youth, with particular emphasis on his physical and imaginative growth. Like Wordsworth, who recorded the growth of his imaginative and intellectual life in *The Prelude* and other poems, Jarrell recounts the inventive games he played, the many fanciful books he read, and his warm and supportive relationships with his grandparents and aunt. Like Weldon Kees, he expresses his desire for a world free of pain and tragedy. Sometimes his memories are so vivid that they seem to come alive as he recounts them; for example, his recollection of his "tall, brown aunt" (288), who took him to the home of the man who owned the Metro-Goldwyn-Mayer lion, takes his breath away. In this world, there was no wound or doubt that could not be "mended" by reassuring adults, our "comforters." Childhood, to Jarrell, is "the end of our good day" (293). As in Dylan Thomas's "Fern Hill," it is an Eden that time forces us to leave. However, memory and language can create poetry, an ideal realm that transcends change and decay, and this becomes a possible antidote for loss and pain.

But psychological problems overwhelmed Jarrell. In February 1965 he was hospitalized with a "nervous breakdown." Memories and poems were not enough; prescribed drugs only increased his psychological despair. In October of the same year, while walking on a highway, he was hit by a car; the driver claimed Jarrell deliberately walked into the path of the automobile. A brilliant career was cut short and America lost a most talented poet and critic, truly a man of letters. In Robert Lowell's words, he possessed a "noble, difficult, and beautiful soul" and was the "most heartbreaking . . . poet of his generation"[7]

ROBERT LOWELL (1917–1977)   Robert Lowell's sense of loss is both cultural and personal. His illustrious ancestors included a prominent clergyman, an astronomer, a president of Harvard, and the poet James Russell Lowell. His mother's ancestors, the Winslows, included the Puritan patriarch Edward Winslow and the Revolutionary hero John Stark. However, Lowell believed that his parents and his patrician class had squandered their legacy and plunged into a state of ineffectiveness and disintegration. In *Life Studies* (1959) Lowell's father, a naval commander and later an unsuccessful businessman, becomes the pitiful symbol of the decline of a once illustrious class, and his mother, Charlotte Winslow Lowell, emerges as a dominating, frustrated, narrow-minded woman who displays little love or support for her son. Lowell, in fact, would conclude in his last volume of poems, *Day by Day* (1977), that he was an unwanted child. Unlike Kees and Jarrell, Lowell is unable to remember an idyllic past. Whether it be in "91 Revere St.," Lowell's prose autobiography, or the poems in *Life Studies*, one can find only pain and disillusionment as Lowell reveals the shrill and angry disputes of his parents. "I felt," he writes, "drenched in my parents' passions" (*Life Studies*, 19).

Estranged from family and class, Lowell rebelled and began his search for a personal and cultural context that would provide both meaning and love. He discovered poetry and adopted a number of poets as father figures. Richard Eberhart, his poet-teacher for five years at St. Mark's School (Southborough, Massachusetts), for example, befriended Lowell and nurtured his interest in poetry. At Harvard, however, Lowell was unable to find the support he needed. Robert Frost did read his poems, but after a brief meeting and a lesson on poetic compression, he coolly dismissed Lowell. At home, his quarrels with his parents were intensifying; he struck his father, an act that would haunt him throughout his life and enter into a number of his poems. It was clearly time to leave New England.

With the aid of Ford Maddox Ford, he met Allen Tate, one of the leading classical modernists. Lowell camped on the Tates' lawn in Clarkville, Tennessee, in the summer of 1937, and that fall he transferred to Kenyon College in Ohio, where he studied New Criticism, a literary movement that emphasized a close reading of texts and saw the poem as an art object. He also studied the classics with John Crowe Ransom and Tate. The disillusionment Tate and Ransom felt with the modern world, their belief in classical values, and the centrality of art and poetry became Lowell's new cultural context. His new "family," headed by Tate and Ransom, also included two classmates with strong literary interests, Randall Jarrell and Peter Taylor, a fiction writer. In 1940, Lowell graduated summa cum laude in classical studies. Following the example of Tate and novelist Jean Stafford, who was Lowell's first wife, he converted to Catholicism, an act that illustrated his break with his heritage. Lowell's early work, written while he lived with Allen and Caroline Gordon Tate, appeared in *Land of Unlikeness* (1944) and *Lord Weary's Castle* (1946). The 1946 volume included many of the poems in his first volume and received the Pulitzer Prize for poetry, an award that established Lowell as one of the leading poets of his generation. In addition, his refusal to be inducted into the armed services in 1943 in protest over the firebombing of German cities brought him national notoriety. He was sentenced to a year and a day at the federal prison in Danbury, Connecticut, for his act of defiance and was paroled after serving five months.

Lord Weary's Castle, centered on World War II, dramatizes and contemplates the fall of America and God's displeasure with and just punishment of America for its loss of spiritual values and its amoral pursuit of money and power. Apocalyptic in vision and Catholic in doctrine, *Lord Weary's Castle* also echoes the thunderous jeremiads of Jonathan Edwards, warning us that we are "Sinners in the Hands of an Angry God" and must return once again to God. The title, taken from an old ballad, tells the story of a mason (the Creator) who built a fine castle for Lord Weary (humanity), 'But payment gat he nane. . . .'[8] A covenant has not been kept, and as Lowell examines American history, he discovers many broken covenants. In "Children of Light," for example, he recalls that "Our FATHERS wrung their bread from stocks and stones / And fenced their gardens with the Redman's bones" (34). Like Nathaniel Hawthorne, he is haunted by the sins of his ancestors, such as John and Mary Winslow, who along with the other "Indian Killers" are buried in the King's Chapel Graveyard in Boston (60–61). Even his childhood idol, Arthur Winslow, is viewed as a fallen man whose spiritual salvation is, at best, in doubt. In his elegy "In Memory of Arthur Winslow," he visits his grandfather's grave in Dunbarton, New Hampshire, and tells Arthur that "I came to mourn you, not to praise the craft / That netted you a million dollars" (27).

Because sin abounds, Lowell concludes that only a terrifying punishment can bring redemption, and this becomes the function of World War II. "To Peter Taylor on the Feast of the Epiphany" concludes:

> Peter, the war has taught me to revere
> The rulers of this darkness, for I fear
> That only Armageddon will suffice
> To turn the hero skating on thin ice
> (52)

The strongest poem in *Lord Weary's Castle*, "The Quaker Graveyard in Nantucket," again focuses on the breaking of a covenant, namely our stewardship of the planet. Because of our greedy exploitation of God's creation, which Lowell describes in a series of violent verbs that record the dismemberment of a whale for profit, nature is at war with us as we are at war with ourselves. The death at sea of Warren Winslow (Lowell's cousin) during the war becomes a personal and cultural sign of the repercussions of our sinful ways. This violent and apocalyptic world can be redeemed only if we return to adoring Mary and Jesus.

Lowell's poetry in this phase adopts not only the Christian vision of T. S. Eliot and Allen Tate but also many of the tenets of classical modernism. The language and imagery are extremely dense and complex, and the poetry is replete with religious, literary, and historical allusions. In addition, Lowell displays his craftsmanship in his mastery of metrical verse and rhyme. It is a mode of poetry that Tate and John Crowe Ransom could and did applaud.

However, there are signs of things to come in this volume. Because Lowell, like the other poets discussed in this chapter, drew heavily from personal experience, his early work is private as well as public. We do learn of his family, even receive a glimpse of his coming to blows with his father in "Rebellion," and experience Lowell's religious conflicts in "Colloquy at Black Rock." Lowell's packed lines also indicate a tension between control, an important value of the classical modernists, and the need to express one's personal anguish.

Lowell's next important work, *Life Studies* (1959), would be the volume in which he temporarily resolved these tensions, discovered a new voice, and, in the process, made legitimate the break from classical modernism. By 1957, Lowell had concluded that his poetry to that point was "distant, symbol-ridden and willfully difficult."[9] Inspiration for change came from a number of sources. He began to correspond with William Carlos Williams, whom he had abandoned as a model in the thirties when he turned to Tate and Ransom; Williams encouraged him to seek a new style and in some ways became Lowell's new poet/father figure. Elizabeth Bishop also presented possibilities in her more prosaic yet carefully crafted poems—a bridge between the formalism of Tate and Ransom and the openness of Williams. W. D. Snodgrass, one of Lowell's students at the State University of Iowa, provided yet another model for personal poetry in poems like "Heart's Needle," which deals with the pain of "losing" his daughter through divorce. In addition, Lowell, in reading fiction, began to think of novelists such as Flaubert as providing prose models of clear, precise, and natural language for his new poetry. He was also aware that a revolution in style and taste was already underway, led by Allen Ginsberg and others, and that his Christian and classical modernist creeds were becoming anachronistic.

When Lowell, the heir of Tate and Ransom, published *Life Studies* in 1959, the literary world was shocked. In the very first poem, "Beyond the Alps," Lowell not only abandons his Catholicism—"I left the City of God where it belongs" (*Life Studies*, 3)—but also employs a prosaic diction and structure that ushers in a new Lowell, a new voice, one more comfortable with the vernacular: ". . . even the Swiss had thrown the sponge / in once again" (3). Absent is the fiery Catholicism, the apocalyptic vision, the overloaded line. In its place is a more relaxed line and voice—a cooler, more detached, at times breezy, at times tragic, and at other times humorous voice—that registers Lowell's more sardonic, weary vision of the world he inherited and the life he led. There are few aesthetic or ideological buffers here to compromise his steady, hard gaze at the reality of his life.

This "study" of his life, whether in his prose autobiography "91 Revere Street" (included in *Life Studies*) or in his family poems, is painful. The study becomes no more pleasurable as he explores his adult life. In "Memories of West Street and Lepke," he reevaluates his decision in the forties to become a conscientious objector— "Ought I to regret my seedtime? / I was a fire-breathing Catholic C.O." (85); he ruefully recalls his mental breakdown and hospitalization in "Waking in the Blue," where he finds himself among the "thoroughbred mental cases" where "each of us holds a locked razor" (82); confronts his memories of a broken marriage in "Man and Wife" as well as his dire psychological state in "Skunk Hour."

As Lowell studies his life, past and present, and his likely future, he is forced to confront its value and worth. By the time acute readers such as John Berryman came to the concluding poem, "Skunk Hour," they sensed that Lowell was not dealing with artifice but was actually assessing whether he should continue his existence. The poem renders a sketch of Castine, Maine, its deterioration from a pristine refuge for the patrician class and a working fishing village to its current status as tourist town, where the "fairy / decorator brightens his shop for fall" (89). Lowell's psychological decline is deeper. He relates a voyeuristic experience in which his speaker drove to a hill where lovers park and transformed the lovers into sunken ships who "lay together, hull to hull" (90). In Lowell's mind Eros (love) is transformed into Thanatos (death). It is at this point that the narrator confesses that "My mind's not right"; and echoing Milton's Satan, he concludes, "I myself am hell" (90).

In "Skunk Hour," Lowell's speaker has reached the nadir of his journey into darkness; his very will to live is threatened. He is totally alone, there are no creeds to save him, and there are no human relationships that give meaning to his existence. Then the speaker, who has been standing on the back steps of his summer cottage contemplating the town's fall and his own descent, notices a family of skunks parading down Main Street in search of food. The mother is defiant and determined, a nocturnal creature who can live off the scraps of existence. She becomes a model for his own survival, a creature who "will not scare" (90).

After *Life Studies* Lowell moved with his second wife, Elizabeth Hardwick, and their daughter, Harriet Winslow Lowell, to New York City and became involved in the political events of the decade. In 1962 he traveled to South America, and in 1965 he found himself at the center of political controversy when he declined an invitation from President Johnson to attend a White House art festival because of the country's involvement in Vietnam. Two years later, as recorded in Norman Mailer's *The Armies of the Night* (1968), he participated in the march on the Pentagon. In 1968 he was an active supporter of Eugene McCarthy's bid for the presidency and an admirer of Robert Kennedy. By 1970, disillusioned with the public sphere and American politics, he had moved to England and was teaching at the University of Essex.

Lowell's poetry in *For the Union Dead* (1964) reflects his engagement with contemporary public issues of his time. The tone is often one of doom and disillusionment. There are startling images of the desecration of the environment in "The Mouth of the Hudson," a terrifying sense of doom in "Fall 1961" as the world moves closer to nuclear war; a clear sense of the corrupting influence of Washington, D.C., in "July in Washington," and an evocation of the political upheavals in Brazil and in "Buenos Aires." But, Lowell also reveals a longing to recapture America's lost land and ideals: "but we wish the river had another shore, / some further range of delectable mountains."[10]

The title poem of this collection, "For the Union Dead," is one of Lowell's greatest achievements. It fuses past and present, biography and history as successfully as any contemporary American poem. Its seventeen four-line stanzas provide structure and order without being overly formal or rhetorical, and the imagery is sharp and highly suggestive. Lowell contrasts an age of heroism and ideals with the present world of commerce, where the only monument to World War II is "a commercial photograph" of a Mosler safe that survived the bombing of Hiroshima; where black school children are still blocked from entering public schools; where the Boston Common and the statehouse are undermined by the spread of parking garages; where nature gives way to "yellow dinosaur steam shovels" and "giant finned cars nose forward like fish" (72). "The ditch," or death, Lowell warns us, "is nearer" (72).

Lowell's work in the late sixties and early seventies, beginning with *Notebook 1967–68* (1969) and continuing through his several revisions of that volume, are more experimental and difficult to assess. His turn to Williams and the public realm clarified and extended his poetic vision, but he now wished to go beyond the realistic photograph or sketch and begin to filter reality through the transforming mind and imagination of the poet. His model here was

Wallace Stevens, and he adopted Stevens's idea that "things as they are" would inevitably be changed as they interacted with the poet's imagination. For this reason, Lowell's work in the late 1960s and early 1970s became more abstract and expressionistic.

In addition, he retained an ambition to write a long poem that, as many American sequences do, would be a song or epic of the self. He had in mind John Berryman's *Dream Songs* and Ezra Pound's *Cantos*. Lowell's personal life as well as history itself would be, he hoped, made to cohere, through the unifying mind of the poet. Lowell's initial attempt at this sequential mode, *Notebook 1967–68*, revealed the difficulties of such a task. The inclusion of very private autobiographical material often recorded in an abstract, expressionistic style, as well as a seemingly random ordering of the poems (arranged in the order they were written) produced a volume that many found formless and indecipherable. Dissatisfied with the results, Lowell published an expanded and revised edition entitled *Notebook* (1970), and in 1973, with the invaluable help of Frank Bidart, made a major revision by breaking the work into three separate volumes. His domestic poems, dealing with his life with Elizabeth Hardwick and their daughter, as well as his extramarital affairs and fears of aging, were published separately in *For Lizzie and Harriet* (1973). The rest of the poems from *Notebook* were once again revised, new poems were added, and the material was then arranged chronologically and published under the new title of *History* (1973). As Lowell confesses in his prefatory note: "My old title, *Notebook*, was more accurate than I wished, i.e., the composition was jumbled."[11] The third volume, *The Dolphin* (1973), which won the Pulitzer Prize for poetry, focused on the end of his marriage to Elizabeth Hardwick, his affair and eventual marriage to his third wife, Caroline Blackwood, the birth of their son, Robert Sheridan, and their life in Kent, England.

Both *The Dolphin* (1973) and *Day by Day* (1977) return to Lowell's personal history, and in both volumes he moves closer to a more successful marriage of life and art. The scope of both works is much smaller, as he literally moves from examining historical figures and events to contemplating the day-by-day emergence of his present life. The first volume is often celebratory, as he discovers in his life with Caroline Blackwood a sense of renewal and regeneration at a time when both the public and private realms offer no meaning and when the specter of aging and death loom ever larger.[12]

Day by Day can be read as a companion piece to *The Dolphin* in that it completes the Caroline Blackwood narrative. But more central to this work is the theme of survival, which for Lowell means the ability to live day-by-day despite the absence of love and the realization that death is near. And as Steven Axelrod points out, Lowell is the naked poet in this volume who does not hide behind symbolism, rhetoric, or subject matter.[13] It is his most personal and honest volume. In it he explores his distant past, his parents, the lives led by his generation, his recent past, his continuing bouts of depression, his hospitalization, and other highly personal matters, all in an attempt to survive, for art has now come down to the question of survival, a means of getting well. Lowell ends "Unwanted," for example, by asking: "Is getting well ever an art, / or art a way to get well?"[14]

In addition to Lowell's directness, there is also a breakthrough in terms of style. Prior to this volume, Lowell had adopted a loose sonnet form and metrical line; here, however, he employs a line that seems more in keeping with the values of Charles Olson's idea of projective verse, which stresses open form and lines based on the breath of the poet during the process of creation. Lowell's late poems visually record his breathing patterns as he becomes winded and weakened by his failing heart. "Our After Life I," for example, describes how Lowell informs Peter Taylor: "After fifty, / the clock can't stop, / each saving breath / takes something . . ." (22) The lines marvelously echo the sense of enervation, the struggle to survive, the gasp for air that one senses in the poem. Form and content become one.

In "Epilogue," the poem that concludes *Day by Day*, Lowell discovers within himself that *"The painter's vision is not a lens, / it trembles to caress the light."* Yet he worries that there is little light or vision in his work, that all he managed to capture were "garish" snapshots, "paralyzed by fact" (127), and he fears that his work failed to illuminate either his history or ours. However, in both *The Dolphin* and *Day by Day*, Lowell has managed to preserve and illuminate existence, to record new discoveries and joys as well as losses and struggles, and this was his ultimate goal, for what was true for Lowell, as he writes in "Epilogue," is true for all of us:

> We are poor passing facts,
> Warned by that to give

each figure in the photograph
his living name.
(127)

ELIZABETH BISHOP (1911–1979)   Elizabeth Bishop, a native of
Massachusetts, suffered the death of her father when she was still an
infant, the permanent institutionalization of her mother when she
was five, and the loss of her adoptive home, Nova Scotia, the following year when she was taken back to Massachusetts by her paternal
grandparents. Dislocation marked Bishop's life thereafter as she
moved about, living not only in Florida but also in Brazil for some
fifteen years with her lover Lota de Macedo Soares. That relationship
ended tragically when Lota died in 1967—most likely a suicide. In
addition, Bishop was hospitalized a number of times for alcoholism
and asthma attacks. Yet there is little direct complaint of a tragic existence in her four volumes of poetry (*North & South*, 1946; *A Cold
Spring*, 1955; *Questions of Travel*, 1965; *Geography III*, 1976; and two
Complete Poems 1969, 1983).

It was not until she published *Geography III* that she directly
revealed what seemed to be the purpose of her long and distinguished career as a poet. All of her poetry, she exclaims in her unforgettable villanelle "One Art," is directed toward mastering "the
art of losing," for "so many things seem filled with the intent / to
be lost . . ." and we "Lose something every day."[15] Abandoning her
previous refusal to be personal in her poetry, Bishop begins by
recounting the easily acceptable loss of her house key, then moves
on to the more emotional loss of her mother's watch, her "three
loved houses," her "two cities," "two rivers," and a "continent."
These losses are painful, but not one is a "disaster," for "The art
of losing isn't hard to master." However, when Bishop moves from
the loss of material possessions to the loss of a loved one—the "you"
(Lota perhaps) in the poem—she is forced to rethink her claim that
"losing isn't hard to master," for "it may look (*Write* it!) like disaster"
(178). The rhyme of "master" and "disaster" rings in the reader's
ear and suggests the melody underlying all of her work. Disaster
is ever-present, but art, a product of the mind and imagination, can
re-create the world and, if not master, at least, create beauty and
order out of tragedy. This villanelle, for example, a difficult form to
master, becomes a means of countering the disasters of existence. As
it is to Frost, the poem to Bishop is a stay against confusion, a means

of creating lasting beauty out of our momentary and imperfect existence.

Poets as diverse as Randall Jarrell, Robert Lowell, James Merrill, and Mark Strand all attest to Bishop's considerable poetic achievement. She was a "poet's poet," and her work was constantly lauded by her peers. James Merrill called her "our greatest national treasure."[16] She consistently demonstrated her ability to work comfortably in what can be confining and artificial forms for less talented poets: "A Miracle for Breakfast," for example, is a finely wrought sestina; "Roosters" contains forty-four triplets of two, three, and four stress lines; "The Burglar of Babylon" is a successful ballad; "Visits to St. Elizabeth's" recounts her visits with Ezra Pound in the form of the nursery rhyme "This Is the House Jack Built"; and, as mentioned, "One Art" is a villanelle. What is common to all these poems, in addition to their artfulness, is that in one way or another they all deal with the disasters of existence. Art and disaster, then, form a dialectic in Bishop's work—one in which the aesthetic quality of the poem lightens the heaviness of existence.

Bishop's artistry acts as a foreground that often dominates or masters a darker midground and background; her skillful use of imagery, for example, counters the personal and tragic nature of her work. The detail, the sights and sounds are so exact, alive, and complete that the reader is often satisfied to stay on the surface of her poems and enjoy her presentation of the world. She painted (especially watercolors), and paintings are the subject of a number of poems (such as "Poem" and "Large Bad Picture"). In discussing the "dollar bill" size painting of her great uncle, she, like Lowell, marvels at the ability of art to capture life: "art 'copying from life' and life itself, / life and the memory of it so compressed / they've turned into each other. Which is which?"(177). This marvelous mimetic quality is apparent in "At the Fishhouses," in which she ponders the sights and smells of the Nova Scotia fishhouses she knew as a child:

> The big fish tubs are completely lined
> with layers of beautiful herring scales
> and the wheelbarrows are similarly plastered
> with creamy iridescent coats of mail,
> with small iridescent flies crawling on them.
>
> (64)

The scene remarkably comes alive with colors, texture, and movement.

However, as Bishop stresses in "Questions of Travel" (93–94), to ponder and to study the history of a place is as important as seeing and hearing its sights and sounds. This reflective side of Bishop and her imaginative powers transform literal reality into a symbolic internal landscape and create a correspondence between the inner and outer worlds. In "At the Fishhouses," for example, she moves from describing a lovely, rural Nova Scotia scene to the contemplation of the ocean, which is a "Cold dark deep and absolutely clear, / element bearable to no mortal." It is "indifferently swinging above the stones, / icily free above the stones, / above the stones and then the world" (65). The sea is seen by Bishop as a transhuman realm of absolute knowledge that we can only imagine in our limited existence as mortals.

To see, to hear, to imagine, to ponder, to study history, to create art are various means of living in an imperfect, inexplicable world in which we can only raise questions—for everything usually remains blurred and inconclusive; only the sea is absolutely clear. Once Bishop is expelled from her world of certainty and innocence, she cannot find her way back to the lost world. She travels and she explores, but *"the choice is never wide and never free"* (94). So she questions whether she should have traveled at all and whether she will ever find a place she can call home. *"No. Should we have stayed at home, / wherever that may be?"* (94)

This feeling of homelessness or alienation is addressed directly in Bishop's "In the Waiting Room," which appears in *Geography III* (1976). Prior to the appearance of this poem, her search for a home was registered less directly, through her use of personae, her depictions of objects, places, and animals (a technique learned from her mentor and friend, Marianne Moore), or, as in "Man Moth," her use of surrealism, a style of writing she adopted after her travels to France in 1937. Bishop, "In the Waiting Room," however, speaks in her own voice and focuses on what was to be a central event of her life: the time she became conscious of her individuality as well as her humanness and imperfection.

The setting is Worcester, Massachusetts, where she lives with her paternal grandparents after the institutionalization of her mother, who never recovered psychologically from the death of her husband. By the time the poem opens, Elizabeth has already lost her father, will never see her mother again, and has been separated from the Bulmers, her maternal grandparents. She has also left behind Nova Scotia, the land she loves, where the "beautiful pure sound" of Nate, the blacksmith, "shaping a horseshoe"[17] drowned out the cry of her deranged mother. The year is 1918, the season, winter. Bishop is almost seven years old and about to experience her initiation into the world of human imperfection and suffering, an event that takes place in a dentist's office where her aunt is being treated.

Elizabeth is "In the Waiting Room," reading a *National Geographic Magazine* that features images of a volatile and hellish world of volcanoes, "black, and full of ashes," as well as cannibalistic natives, "Babies with pointed heads . . . [and] naked women" whose "breasts were horrifying" (159). It is a side of life the innocent Elizabeth has not experienced; her aunt's pain becomes her pain as the terror and chaos of native life enter her consciousness: "I-we-were falling, falling." The overwhelming fear is that she will not stop falling until she falls off "the round, turning world / [and plummets] into cold, blue-black space" (160). Although the abyss, or nothingness, is the ultimate threat, the alternative—to accept one's human identity with all its imperfections and foolishness—is not a happy one. If she is "an I," "an Elizabeth," she is also "one of them"—a fact that seems without reason and meaning to her. She can only voice a series of unanswered questions as to how or why this has happened. However, she does know that pain and loss await her. This new awareness threatens to plunge her "beneath a big black wave, / another, and another" (161).

But in the final stanza she reenters the world at large, a world at war (WWI), but one that she clings to in order to escape the void. It is the world she will imaginatively explore in her travels and in her poetry, but always with the knowledge that it is never a disasterless world; her voice is now that of the modern poet deeply aware of human tragedy, but never wallowing in self-pity.

Bishop's constant search for moments of beauty and joy to pit against the calamitous nature of existence is especially poignant in "The Moose," from *Geography III*, in which the journey through life is symbolized by a bus ride from Nova Scotia to Boston. The bus travels west through the rural countryside and into the fog, night, and moonlight of "The New Brunswick Woods." In the back of the bus, "Grandparents' voices" recall the "deaths and sicknesses," the tragedies of life, agreeing with a "peculiar / affirmative. 'Yes . . .' /

... 'Life's like that' " (172). Life as well as its tragedies are affirmed in "a half groan, half acceptance"; and it is at this point that the moose appears, a female moose, "Towering, antlerless, / high as a church." She is "grand, otherworldly." The speaker asks "Why, why do we feel / (we all feel) this sweet / sensation of joy?" (173).

In addition to presenting the moose as a symbol of female joy and otherworldliness, Bishop also renders female subjects who are the victims of a social order that lacks compassion and denies joy and beauty to the oppressed. "Pink Dog," for example, makes use of a comic, if at times sardonic, tone to describe a female, hairless, pink dog with scabies who lives by her "wits" while hiding her nursing puppies in the slums of Rio de Janeiro, Brazil. The speaker asks this "poor bitch," if beggars and the undesirables are thrown into the river, "what would they do to sick four-leggèd dogs?" (190). If the dog is to survive, she must, the speaker explains, be in tune with the celebratory air of Carnival, a festive occasion in Rio de Janeiro—for "Carnival is always wonderful! / A depilated dog would not look well." So "Dress up! Dress up and dance at Carnival!" (191).

This dialectic between celebration and oppression is rendered subtly and artistically in Bishop's poetry. She insisted that she not be identified as a "female" poet because such separation of the sexes, she believed, "was a lot of nonsense" (Schwartz, 322) and lessened the import of women poets. And she remained silent about her lesbian relationships. However, as a number of feminist critics have claimed, Bishop's poetry resonates with the voice of the outsider, which, as Adrienne Rich indicates, can be associated with her own sense of isolation and exile as a woman and lesbian during the 1950s and 1960s.[18] Her work also sharply depicts the violence and destruction of a male-dominated society. In "Roosters," for example, she depicts the barnyard cocks as proud tyrants who "brace their cruel feet and glare / with stupid eyes." Dressed in their "green-gold medals" they plan "to command and terrorize the rest." As for the wives, they "lead hens' lives / of being courted and despised" (35). In contrast to the joy, beauty, and serenity that the female moose brings to a weary world, the roosters fall into a bloody battle in which the fallen are "flung on the gray ash-heap" (37). It is yet one additional facet of the richness of Bishop's work that she speaks to both the formalist and the feminist critic, and it is this richness of form and vision that ensures

Bishop her stature as one of our most accomplished post–World War II poets.

THEODORE ROETHKE (1908–1963)   Theodore Roethke's parents, Otto and Helen Marie, were the proud owners of a successful flori-cultural business in Saginaw, Michigan, that included twenty-five acres of greenhouses within the town boundaries as well as a stand of virgin timber and game preserves in the country. It was a world where young Roethke experienced the ordered and cultivated world nurtured by the mind and hands of his German-American father, Otto, along side the wonders of the natural world, the wildlife in the field and woods beyond the greenhouses. Like Wordsworth before him, as a young boy Roethke experienced a mag-ical realm as a prelude to his entry into the mundane adult world. In this garden, this sea of greenhouses, Roethke was part and parcel of the primordial world of plants and animals. Later in his life, Roethke would acknowledge that this world was "both heaven and hell, a kind of tropics created in the savage climate of Michigan, where aus-tere German Americans turned their love of order and their terrify-ing efficiency into something truly beautiful."[19] But as a child neither the darker side of nature nor the domineering aspect of his father seemed to threaten him. This was Roethke's childhood paradise, his heaven on earth where ". . . flowerheads seemed to flow toward me, to beckon me, / only a child, out of myself."[20] Father and nature, spirit and body transported the young boy out of his separate ego and physical existence into a transcendental union and identity with all that lives. "What need for heaven, then / With that man, and those roses?" (197).

This heaven on earth vanished in adolescence, when Otto died and left Roethke without a spiritual or earthly guide at a time when he was beginning to become aware of and confused by the changes in his sexual and psychological identity. Now he was beset by phys-ical urges that filled him with guilt and shame, and he severed his ties to the natural world. He was also beginning to lose the gift of intuitive thinking as he became more rational and was drawn into the world of human aspiration and frailties. A new awareness of death, human imperfection, and separation meant that the garden was gone both literally and psychologically, and as with Adam before him, expulsion was painful and lasting: "O world so far away! O my lost world!" (217).

Once expelled from his earthly garden, Roethke found life difficult. He continually experienced psychological, financial, and professional insecurity. The Great Depression forced his withdrawal from the Harvard Graduate School and made it impossible for him to secure a tenured position at a college or university. At Lafayette College, after teaching classes, coaching tennis, and running the public relations office, he was let go for financial reasons. Recurrent manic-depressive states continued to make it difficult for him to find and hold onto a teaching position. In addition, throughout his career, Roethke was obsessed with the need for recognition and fame. He became his own promoter, carefully noting every publication and professional honor. It was not until he secured a life-long position at the University of Washington in 1947 that Roethke seemed to escape the financial insecurity, if not the psychological hazards, that haunted him for so many years.

As Roethke proclaims in "Open House," the title poem of his first volume of poetry, published in 1941, his heart is filled with "anguish, anger, rage, and agony." The personal declarative lines do include the world "love," but it is the sense of pain and anguish that dominates the "language strict and pure" (3) in this and most of the poems in this first volume. The poems depict Roethke as attempting to transcend the limitations and "sins of the flesh and the sins of past mortals," for "Corruption reaps the young" and "The spirit starves / Until the dead have been subdued" (4). Roethke sees this as a "feud" with our human inheritance, and his task is to somehow go beyond the "devouring mother" (death) and the "father's ghost" (guilt and corruption) (5) and use poetry as a fusion of spirit and word to regain lost innocence.

Although he is occasionally drawn to nature in his early poems, Roethke's main goal is to deny his physical and instinctual urges so as to reclaim his spiritual identity. In his later poetry he would radically change his means of recapturing this lost world, but his quest to regain a sense of oneness with his physical and spiritual world was life long, a quest that links Roethke to the visionary tradition of such American poets as Walt Whitman, Hart Crane, E. E. Cummings, and Robinson Jeffers as well as to Weldon Kees and Randall Jarrell (discussed above). Roethke, in fact, emerges as one of America's strongest visionaries, a poet of intense personal feeling whose work is marked by the presence of compelling literal and figurative imagery, moving and varied rhythms, meticulous craftsmanship, and a unique blend of traditional forms and bold innovative techniques. Roethke learned the importance of craft and modernistic techniques from Eliot, Yeats, and other modernists, but he employed them or went beyond them for his own visionary purposes. Some of his boldest techniques appear in *The Lost Son and Other Poems* (1948) and *Praise to the End* (1951). In the greenhouse poems of *Lost Son*, he recaptures a sense of unity with the natural world. The greenhouse, to Roethke, is a world of growth and renewal where a cutting from a plant, for example, is nurtured until it manages to root itself in new soil. In his two-part poem "Cuttings," Roethke identifies with the cutting in its struggle to survive, "to put down feet" and to gain "a new life" (35). The barrier between the botanical world and the human world dissolves as the speaker physically partakes in the process of transplantation. Here there is more than a rhetorical use of figurative language; what the cutting experiences, the speaker experiences, and the reader enters a mystical realm of experience akin to Thoreau's experience when spring comes to Walden Pond.

Even more startling than the greenhouse poems, however, is the title poem of *Lost Son* and the companion poems in both *Lost Son* and in *Praise to the End*. Here Roethke merges psychoanalysis and poetry as his speaker plunges into his unconscious to revisit the onset of his life as a "Lost Son." As he explains, he must first go backward in time and development to free himself from the past in order to go forward. Once he dives into that "dark pond" he encounters and vanquishes the obstacles and obsessions that block his passage to spiritual renewal. Each of these poems, Roethke explains, "is a stage in a kind of struggle out of the slime; part of a slow spiritual progress; an effort to be born, and later, to become something more" (*Craft*, 37).

Roethke knew he faced a very challenging structure in this surreal and dialectical series of poems. He must, he wrote, "keep the rhythms, the language 'right,' i.e., consistent with what a child would say or at least to create the 'as if' of the child's world" (41). He must also be willing to face up to genuine mystery. His language must be compelling and immediate: he must create an actuality. He must be able to telescope image and symbol, if necessary, without relying on the obvious connectives: to speak in a kind of psychic shorthand when his protagonist is under great stress. "He must be able to shift his rhythms rapidly, the tension. He works intuitively, and the final form of his poem must be imaginatively, right" (42).

In *Lost Son*, the speaker overcomes the horrors of death, guilt, and shame by returning to his father's greenhouses, where the will to live is revived. Here "Frost melted on far panes; / . . . Even . . . the bent yellowy weeds / Moved in a slow up-sway (*Poems*, 54). The spiritual self previously buried in his unconscious announces, "It will come again. / Be still. / Wait" (55).

The companion poems in *Praise to the End* (1951)—the title of which is taken from Wordsworth's *Prelude*, Book I—complete what Roetkhe calls his "spiritual autobiography beginning with the very small child" (*Craft*, 58, 59). As indicated by the title of the final poem, he shouts, "I Cry, Love! Love!" as he ecstatically announces that the night of despair has passed and "proclaim[s] once more a condition of joy" (*Poems*, 88).

Roethke's quest after *Praise to the End* moved beyond a renewed love for the physical world; inspired by his love of Beatrice O'Connell, an Irish student he met while teaching at Bennington College and married in 1953, he went on to compose some of the finest love poems of this period. "Four for Sir John Davies," which appeared in *The Waking* (1953), is perhaps his finest. His reading of the Elizabethans (including Davies's "Orchestra") and Yeats, as well as his marriage to Beatrice, became the stimuli to break what had been a dry creative period and to write a moving and witty love poem in the stately and cadenced rhythms of Yeats. In the poem, he overcomes his earlier fear of the flesh and discovers that "The flesh can make the spirit visible" (102). As in Whitman and the modern visionary poets, the body is now celebrated as well as the soul, for "Who rise from flesh to spirit know the fall: / The word outleaps the world, and light is all" (103).

"Four for Sir John Davies" reveals Roethke's new appreciation of the body, the feminine principal, that dark mysterious side of knowledge that appears richer and more complex than a child's innocent union with nature, and this theme is continued in the sixteen love poems in *Words for the Wind* (1958), including the wonderfully witty and romantic "I Knew a Woman," in which Roethke proclaims, "These old bones live to learn her wanton ways: / (I measure time by how a body sways)" (122).

As Roethke's bones and body aged, however, he had to confront the specter of his own death, and it obviously threatened his newfound paradise with Beatrice. Initially, he explored this new theme indirectly. In the poem "Meditations of an Old Woman," for example, the speaker, modeled after Roethke's mother, who died shortly before the composition of the poem, voices her bitterness and skepticism but also her visionary and celebratory views of life. She was, Roethke wrote, "a gentle, highly articulate old lady believing in the glories of the world, yet fully conscious of its evils" (*Craft*, 58). The mode of organization, the alternating themes of alienation and affirmation echo the structure of his earlier volumes and no doubt correlate with his own vacillating attitudes toward mortality. The speaker remains perplexed, ambivalent in the last of the mediations, "What Can I Tell My Bones?," for "It is difficult to say all things are well, / When the worst is about to arrive" (*Poems*, 166). Yet the speaker transcends rational doubts, affirms her belief that "God has need of me," sees the revelatory nature of the landscape, and moves into the sun-filled fields where her "spirit rises with the rising wind" (167).

Roethke's last volume of poems, *The Far Field* (1964), posthumously published and winner of the National Book Award in 1965, approaches the fear of death directly and comes closest to showing Roethke completing the quest for his lost world, where nature, humanity, and spirit become one. In "North American Sequence," the journey motif is employed to depict the poet as an explorer in search of "A body with the motion of a soul" (182). In addition to speaking in his own voice, Roethke moves from the measured lines of poets such as Yeats to the more expansive a lines and catalog techniques of Whitman and Jeffers. Throughout the volume Roethke uses a highly textured physical setting to evoke a spirituality in which all of nature becomes a metaphor for the soul. By the time Roethke completes his journey to "The Far Field," "the windy cliffs of forever," he has learned "not to fear infinity" (194). At the end of the poem he is about to enter the sea, a symbol of the spiritual realm, and there the "lost self" will be found. The doors of perception open, the gates of wrath have been passed, and the speaker knows, as did William Blake in the eighteenth century and his visionary followers, that "All finite things reveal infinitude" (195).

For Roethke the quest to rediscover that lost world of innocence, purity, union, and happiness was all, and it inspired him to compose a body of visionary poetry that is uniquely his own.

STANLEY KUNITZ (B. 1905) In 1935 Theodore Roethke arrived at Stanley Kunitz's doorsteps with a copy of *Intellectual Things* (1930),

Kunitz's first published volume of poems. In that volume and those that followed, as well as his prose (*A Kind of Order, A Kind of Folly* [1975], and *Next to Last Things: New Poems and Essays* [1985]), the literary kinship between Kunitz and Roethke became clear: both were lost travelers seeking a new world.

Born and raised in Worcester, Massachusetts, the central event in Kunitz's life was the loss of his father, Solomon, who committed suicide by swallowing carbolic acid in a public park when his mother was pregnant with Kunitz.[21] His mother, Yetta, was so devastated by her husband's suicide that she refused to allow his name to be spoken in the house. Forced to support a family of three (two daughters and Stanley) and rescue a bankrupt dressmaking business, she became, in Kunitz's words, "a pioneer businesswoman," who opened a dry goods store and sewed garments in the back room. Unfortunately, her business affairs, which kept her from her family, and her less than passionate nature—Kunitz can't recall ever being kissed by Yetta—made it certain that there would be little warmth from his mother. When Stanley was eight, Yetta married Mark Dine, a gentle and scholarly man Kunitz grew to love; however, he died when Kunitz was fourteen. This tragic childhood became Kunitz's major theme, his "Old Cracked Tune," which is expressed by his speaker, Solomon Levi: "the desert is my home, / my mother's breast was thorny, / and father I had none" (87). Fate, circumstance, and tragedy, as in the Greek dramas, seemed to haunt the Kunitz household, and it was out of these dark autobiographical strands that he sought to transform his life into legend or chaos into myth and achieve "a new ordering of creation."[22]

This insistence that the poet treat his personal experience as myth differentiates Kunitz from Eliot and his followers who insisted that poetry be both mythic and impersonal. "From the beginning," Kunitz declares, "I was a subjective poet in contradiction to the dogma propounded by Eliot and his disciples that objectivity, impersonality, was the goal of art. Furthermore, I despised his politics" (*Next*, 89). Kunitz found it ironic that he would eventually be classified as a late convert to confessional or autobiographical poetry, since from the start his "struggle [had been] to use the life in order to transcend it, to convert it into legend" (89).

There is also a rhetorical mode of subjectivity in Kunitz's poetry that emerges in his quest to find a language and rhythm that not only communicates but, more important, also recreates past emotions and thoughts. It is not the I, the ego, that writes the poem, Kunitz declares, "but my cells, my corpuscles, translating into language the chemistry of a passion" (29). Thus, "the wisdom of the body" occurs when one thinks with one's senses and relies on the primitive, shamanistic, incantatory elements of language; for "poems rise out of the swamps of the hindbrain," (51) and "our best songs are body-songs" (53). "Key images," Kunitz explains, also rise out of the poet's unconscious. These images uniquely mark each poet's work and come from a poet's "childhood and . . . are usually associated with pivotal experiences." This "cluster of key images is the purest concentration of the self, the individuating node, the place where the persona starts" (30). By "revisiting" one's pivotal childhood experiences, "one's state of . . . innocence," the poet hopes "to learn how to live with the child" (30) he once was. As Gregory Orr, poet and former student of Kunitz, points out in his critical study,[23] these images enable the reader to enter Kunitz's world.

The images of the wound in "The Hemorrhage" or the haunted house in "In A Strange House" suggest his lost world of innocence, the absence of father and mother, and his present state of alienation. The image of the journey, in "The Layers," by contrast, suggests the need to move beyond a crippling nostalgia for the past and to transcend an unrelentingly painful existence. The paradox that "we are living and dying at once" is captured in these key images, and it is Kunitz's goal "to report the dialogue" (*Next*, 30).

This contrapuntal music of "nostalgia and desire" is recorded in the subjective "body-language" of the poet. Kunitz's belief in the physiological nature of poetry and his stress on the poet's breath links him to poets like Charles Olson and Robert Creeley. And like Robert Bly and James Wright, Kunitz draws his key images from the deep recesses of his mind, if not from the world of dreams itself. His poetry is not only autobiographical but also expressionistic and, at times, surrealistic. Like the abstract expressionist painters, or action painters, Kline, deKooning and like the poet Roethke, with whom he was friends, he views his work as a subjective "kind of action . . . every achieved metaphor . . . is a gesture of sorts, the equivalent of the slashing of a stroke on canvas" (107).

Given his very personal approach and early metaphysical style—his difficult syntax, complex metaphors, and numerous literary and historical allusions—it is little wonder that his first two volumes (*Intellectual Things* [1930], *Passport to War* [1940]) were not in fashion in either the thirties, the decade of social reform, or the forties, when W. H. Auden's witty, elegant verse dominated the scene. When the confessional mode of the fifties did come about, few were aware that Kunitz had been writing highly personal poetry for nearly three decades. In an early poem, "For the Word is Flesh," for example, he laments his "O ruined father dead, long sweetly rotten / Under the dial . . ." and bitterly concludes "Let sons learn from their lipless fathers how / Man enters hell without a golden bough" (*Poems*, 190, 91).

By the time Kunitz published *Intellectual Things* (1930) he had earned his B.A., summa cum laude (1926), and his M.A. from Harvard (1927), and he had secured a job with the H. W. Wilson Company, a reference publisher in New York City, after being rejected for a teaching position at Harvard University because he was told by the English faculty that the " 'Anglo-Saxon students would resent being taught English by a Jew' " (*Next*, 100). At Wilson's he began a long and distinguished career as an editor of *Authors Biographical Series* and of such important biographical series as *Living Authors* and *Twentieth Century Authors*. His career was disrupted in 1943 when he was drafted as a conscientious objector, shuttled to various training camps, and eventually assigned to the Air Transport Command at Gravely Point, Washington.

Kunitz has identified *Passport to the War* as his "bleakest book." For his "passport," or draft notice, plunged him into the dark night of history. These lines are from "Night Letter," a poem addressed to his beloved: "I suffer the twentieth century, / . . . The slaughter of the blue-eyed open towns, / And principle disgraced, and art denied." The speaker informs his love that "The bloodied envelope addressed to you, / Is history, that wide and mortal pang" (*Poems*, 161). In "Father and Son," one of his most famous and most analyzed poems, the speaker follows his ghostly father through a symbolic, dreamlike landscape that reeks of decay and death to the pond from which his father has come and to which he will return; here the son hopes to communicate with "the secret master of my blood" whose love "Kept me in chains." He rehearses the sins and failures he wishes to confess to his father and then desperately asks his father to come back to him. Then he pleads: " 'O teach me how to work and keep me kind.' " The father, however, can only turn "The white ignorant hollow of his face" (157, 58) toward his son. There are no instructions, directions, or words from the fathers of history. The son must move beyond his obsession with his lost world represented by his suicidal father.

Selected Poems: 1928–58 received numerous awards and established Kunitz as one of the most important midcentury poets; the volume contains a number of the most moving love poems and visionary poems of the period. They also show Kunitz to be an evolving poet: "I am not done with my changes" (36), he writes later in "The Layers" (1978), and certainly one of his more dramatic changes was the shift in style that took place in his fourth volume, *The Testing-Tree* (1971). Prior to this book, Kunitz's complex imagery, difficult syntax, and formal language created a texture that often proved too dense and tangled for many readers. Beginning with *The Testing-Tree*, however, Kunitz's verse becomes direct, immediate, and accessible as he narrates the particular events of his past and present life using a William Carlos Williams–like mode of diction, syntax, and rhythm. In "Journal for My Daughter," for example, the informal nature of a journal is reflected in short, crisp lines and accessible diction as Kunitz renders in journal entries his experiences with his daughter: "I like the sound of your voice / even when you phone from school / asking for money" (41).

And in "The Testing-Tree," composed in Williams's triadic or three-part line and his distinctly American diction, Kunitz sharply depicts his boyhood rituals in the fields and hills surrounding Worcester. This is his entry into the world of nature as he "followed in the steps / of straight-backed Massassoit" (90). It is here that he ritualistically tested his ability to hit an ancient and "inexhaustible oak" (a symbol of the durability of nature) with three rocks. Each successful throw would gain him a valued prize and accomplish his quest:

> In the haze of afternoon,
> while the air flowed saffron,
> I played my game for keeps—
> for love, for poetry,
> and for eternal life—
> after the trials of summer.
>   (91)

The speaker, nearing death, is still haunted by his past as well as his own "murderous times" but knows his journey must continue. As a poet he recognizes that "It is necessary to go / through dark and deeper dark / and not to turn" (92). So he looks once again for his trail and also seeks again his "testing-tree" and his stones to test once more his ability to achieve love, art, and a vision of eternity.

Although Kunitz acknowledges that his basic rhythm "is essentially dark and grieving—elegiac" (*Next*, 96), there are clear notes of endurance, determination, acceptance, and even celebration that appear in these later poems. He is determined to " 'Live in the layers / not on the litter' " (*Poems*, 36). No longer alienated or homeless, he embraces a world of snakes, worms, raccoons, and gardens as well as a world of human love, social justice, and poetry. Indeed, it can be said of Kunitz that "he loved the earth so much / he wanted to stay forever" (*Next*, 19). In his ninetieth year, Kunitz received the National Book Award for *Passing Through: The Later Poems* (1995). The new poems in this collection range from his crystal-clear memories of his childhood days in Worcester ("My Mother's Pears" and "Haley's Comet") to a very poignant love poem dedicated to his wife, Elise Asher.

For nearly seventy years, Kunitz has struggled to survive the personal and historical tragedies of his time and place. That struggle is recorded in ever-changing but always exquisitely crafted poetic forms. His work is simultaneously personal, representative of an age, and universal in its mythic nature. In addition, his lasting contributions as editor, essayist, translator of Russian poets, and mentor and advocate for younger poets speak to Kunitz's dedication to poetry and his long and distinguished career.

JOHN BERRYMAN (1914–1972) Stanley Kunitz's longevity and his ability to move beyond his deep-seated personal problems contrast sharply with the fate of most of his peers. As voiced in "Dream Song 153" from *The Dream Songs* (1969), John Berryman believed it was "god" who "wrecked this generation. / First he seized Ted [Roethke], then Richard [Blackmur], Randall [Jarrell], and now Delmore [Schwartz]. / In between he gorged on Sylvia Plath."[24] Berryman chose to quarrel with and question a God that would act in this way, for he, too, suffered throughout his life and, finally, committed suicide at the age of 57. He could never fully accept his losses, although he did acknowledge that "We suffer on, a day, a day, a day" (172), searching for a means of survival, a way of avoiding madness and self-destruction. Raised as a Catholic, Berryman had a strong belief in humanity's fall, but, like Kunitz, he also believed in the restorative powers of poetry, and both these beliefs play a central role in his work.

Berryman's life became forever shattered when his father, John Smith, a banker most of his life, shot himself just outside his son's bedroom window. Berryman was twelve years old when this tragic event occurred, and that traumatic scene would appear with variations throughout his poetry. Despite acknowledging that his father's "mad drive wiped out [his] childhood," his capacity for love endured. John's mother quickly remarried, and he assumed his stepfather's surname. Although he was treated kindly and generously during his adolescence, he remained overwhelmed with a "sense of total loss / . . . an absolute disappearance of continuity & love" (118).

In "Dream Song 384," he, like Sylvia Plath, desperately attempts to exorcise the hold his father had over him; also like Plath, he used rage and sardonic wit as his weapons:

> I spit upon this dreadful banker's grave
> who shot his heart out in a Florida dawn
> O ho alas alas
> When will indifference come, I moan & rave
> I'd like to scrabble, till I got right down
> away down under the grass.
>
> (406)

To avoid self-pity, Berryman adopts a personal and self-mocking tone and turns the graveyard visit into a dark, grotesque melodrama as he imagines destroying his father's casket with an ax and then planting that ax in his father's heart.

The task for Berryman is to survive that terrible event and to regain some sense of fulfillment and faith. As the speaker indicates in the sixth of "Eleven Addresses to the Lord," published in *Love and Fame* (1971), he had once "served at Mass six dawns a week from five" but "my father," he laments, "blew-it-all when I was twelve / blew out my most bright candle faith, and look at me."[25] Faithless, Berryman became self-destructive early on; he first attempted suicide in 1931 and suffered numerous mental breakdowns, as well as alcoholic binges that required hospitalization and treatment.

In addition to his psychological difficulties, Berryman, like Roethke, had to scramble for a teaching position; at times his drinking problems complicated his professional life. In 1954, for example, he lost his instructor's position at the Writer's Workshop at the State University of Iowa when he was arrested for drunkenness and disorderly conduct. However, teaching and scholarship were important to his survival. After the completion of a B.A. at Columbia (1936) and two years of additional study at Claire College, Cambridge, England, Berryman, like many of his peers, became a scholar, teacher (Wayne State, Harvard, Princeton, and the University of Minnesota), and writer. Despite the difficulties that he experienced in that role, it provided him with a supportive and protective environment. He especially enjoyed teaching in the humanities, as it forced him to enter realms he would not have encountered had he taught only creative writing courses. His academic career also had a strong impact on his poetry, which although personal, is also philosophic, scholarly, and complex.

At the center of Berryman's vision in *Dream Songs*, his most important work, is the world's weight, the tragic side of existence. Yet he would never sink into mere complaining, passive acceptance, or indifference. Instead, Berryman developed a number of strategies to endure or overcome that reality. Sometimes he presents life as a bad joke—a black comedy; sometimes he mocks it in a rant. Infrequently, he experiences a momentary rise or sense of fulfillment that allows him to catch his breath before the next calamity comes along. Very occasionally, he even experiences satisfaction and pleasure.

The Dream Songs is a twentieth-century *Pilgrim's Progress* or *Odyssey* that records Berryman's perception of the modern world in 385 linked and structured poems. The volume, clearly one of the most important poetic sequences written after World War II, propelled Berryman into the ranks of the major poets of his time. Multiperspective narration, which he initially experiments with in *Homage to Mistress Bradstreet* (1956), becomes his primary technique in *Dream Songs*. He asserts that the volume is about "an imaginary character (not the poet, not me) named Henry, a white American in early middle age sometimes in blackface, who has suffered an irreversible loss and talks about himself sometimes in the first person, sometimes in the third, sometimes even in the second; he has a friend, never named, who addresses him as Mr. Bones and variants thereof" (*Dream Songs,* introductory note).

This distinctive invention creates a complex and original mode of narration: Berryman's persona, Henry, is not Berryman but is closely related to the poet. Within that persona, three voices—the objective and subjective modes of the persona as well as the friend's voice, perhaps Henry's alter ego—can be distinguished. Berryman considered Whitman's *Song of Myself* to be "the greatest poem so far written by an American,"[26] and he was no doubt attracted to the multitudes of voices embedded in Whitman's voice. The "I" is not singular in either poet; however, in Berryman's voice there is much more fragmentation than unity. To use R. D. Laing's psychological terminology, this is a "Divided Self," caught in the turbulence of the modern world and tormented by the tensions between his experiences, his memories, and his wants or desires. The contrast between Whitman's and Berryman's voices provides a compelling and disturbing illustration of how troubled the American vision has become since Whitman's confident pronouncements.

Berryman's inverted syntax, use of personal events and feelings, scholarly allusions, puns, jokes, and even blackface dialect create one of the most distinctive styles of this period: a bold and ambitious style that mirrors the unpredictable, multifaceted, and surreal nature of contemporary life. There are doubts, however, as to its staying power. Some readers object to the use of blackface dialect on the grounds that it is racist. Others find Berryman's style too quirky and opaque, too puzzling, too inaccessible.

Throughout *The Dream Songs* Henry experiences pain and failure, but also a touch of pleasure and success. In the first song, the speaker presents Henry's initial trauma:

> All the world like a woolen lover
> once did seem on Henry's side.
> Then came a departure.
> Thereafter nothing fell out as it might or ought.
> I don't see how Henry, pried
> open for all the world to see, survived.
> (*Dream Songs,* 3)

The particulars of Henry's fall into a cruel and loveless world are not given here. They might include his father's death or his very emergence into this world, his birth, but the sense of a lost world is central to this dark song and the entire dream sequence: "Once in a sycamore I was glad / all at the top, and I sang" (3), but now "Henry sats in de bar . . . at odds wif de world & its god" (7). He is bored with life; he has "no / inner resources" (16) and there is "a thing on Henry's heart / só heavy . . ." (33). Later, the speaker envies bats, for they "have no bankers and they do not drink," and he sardonically comments and puns that "Henry for joining the human race is *bats*" (70). Henry is amazed in song 76 that "Nothin very bad happen to me lately. / How you explain that?" (83). Yet despite all his bleak experiences, there are signs of spring in "Dream Song 77," and although he is "prepared to líve in a world of Fáll," he has "in each hand / one of his own mad books and all, / ancient fires for eyes, his head full / & his heart full, he's making ready to move on" (84). As Charles Thornbury asserts, *The Dream Songs'* basic structure is cyclical, "a series of Henry's departures and returns, his deaths and rebirths" (*Collected Poems,* xxxii). They are a testament to human endurance and the desire to survive in the harshest of worlds, and demonstrate the courage to get up when knocked down, again and again. As Berryman explained, "These Songs are not meant to be understood, you understand. / They are only meant to terrify & comfort" (*Dream Songs,* 388).

Berryman's themes of loss, suffering, and endurance are evident throughout his poems. In "The Ball Poem," which appeared in *The Dispossessed* (1948), a young boy watches helplessly as his ball bounces into the harbor waters. The speaker informs us that the youngster now begins to learn "The epistemology of loss" as well as "how to stand up" to those losses (*Collected Poems,* 11). In *Homage to Mistress Bradstreet,* a narrative poem containing fifty-seven stanzas, Berryman focuses on and identifies with Anne Bradstreet's separation from her homeland, England, when she was married and came to the Massachusetts Bay Colony at the young age of sixteen. Berryman recounts her fall into an alien world, her rebellion against the barrenness of her new environment, as well as the suffering and disappointment she experienced throughout her life. Clearly, Berryman sees a link here to his own sufferings, outrage, and rebellion but is not quite ready to address them more directly.

Berryman received the Pulitzer Prize for *77 Dream Songs* (1964) and a National Book Award and Bollingen Prize in Poetry for *His*

Toy, His Dream, His Rest (1968). Despite this recognition, the admiration of his contemporaries, and his renewed faith in Catholicism, as well as his enthusiasm for his autobiographical novel, *Recovery* (1973), which dealt with his alcoholism and rehabilitation, John Berryman ended his life on January 7, 1972, when he leapt from a Minneapolis bridge. His work sustained his life for a substantial period, but in the end he succumbed to the despair he chronicled with such innovation and style.

· TWO ·

Exploring New Terrain: Self and Community

> that known profound presence, untouched
> the sign
> providing witness,
>> occasion,
>> ritual
> for the continuing act of
> nonviolence, of passionate
> reverence, active love.
> —Denise Levertov, "What It Could Be"

While Kees, Jarrell, Lowell, Bishop, Roethke, Kunitz, and Berryman struggled with their personal problems and sense of cultural isolation, a number of important midcentury writers moved beyond the model of the poet as a tortured, alienated outsider, obsessed by a sense of loss. Although the lost world poets sometimes looked toward a larger world in order to establish a meaningful relationship with it, their work primarily reflected the isolation of singular experiences that did not suggest a means of establishing a new sense of salvation for the community at large. By contrast, the more affirmative work of poets like Muriel Rukeyser, Gwendolyn Brooks, Robert Hayden, Richard Wilbur, Denise Levertov, and Robert Duncan envisioned the poet not as a singular suffering soul but rather as a spokesperson for the creation of a just society. Rather than obsessively exploring the worlds they had lost, they examined the terrain about them, acknowledging both the joys and injustices of *this* world and envisioning the possibility of creating a new, transformed civilization. At times their goals were specific and pragmatic; at other times they were broad and sweeping.

Common to all these poets was a new sense of engagement with the social, political, and economic issues of the day. Muriel Rukeyser was a tireless champion of the exploited and an opponent of repression and injustice. And she always kept alive a sense of "possibility"—the belief that humans possessed the potential to create a just society. Poetry, she believed, had to play a role in such a social transformation if it were to remain alive. Along with Gwendolyn Brooks, she became a strong and determined advocate for women; together they served as significant role models for a younger generation of female poets. Brooks and Robert Hayden extended the work of the Harlem Renaissance and ensured that the African-American heritage would continue to play an important social, cultural, and aesthetic role in the evolution of contemporary American poetry. Although Brooks and Hayden went in different directions in the sixties, they both celebrated the African-American community and confronted the contradictions of a racist society.

The range of these engaged poets is best represented by Richard Wilbur and Denise Levertov. Wilbur is committed to the concept of a "poet citizen" who through his wisdom and poetic skill defends the true ideals of a democratic society; Levertov, on the other hand, is fiercely devoted to a more radical concept of both the poet and poetry; often cast as an outsider, she attempts to awaken her readers and to inspire them to social action. While both insist on the importance of poetic form, their approaches are very different. Wilbur is a traditional formalist, Levertov one of the most fervent advocates and practitioners of organic verse, a kind of poetry that emphasizes process and discovery rather than inherited formal structures.

What unites all of these poets, however, is a belief in and commitment to the things of this world. Unlike the lost world poets, they derive a sense of meaning and identity from the realities of the physical world, from their own humanity, and from a connection to their communities. Out of this meaning comes a sense of responsibility, a belief that the poet must be engaged and do his or her part in revealing the value of nature, the worth of all humans, and the need for a just community. While Americans are now accustomed to seeing and hearing politically engaged poetry, critics often overlooked the presence of such poetry in midcentury America and failed to recognize that the African-American, feminist, and ethnic political poetry of the seventies and eighties has its roots in the work of midcentury poets who began to explore this new terrain.

MURIEL RUKEYSER (1913–1980)   Muriel Rukeyser refused to adopt her contemporaries' pessimistic, ironic view of existence. In her critical study of art and society, *The Life of Poetry* (1949), she exclaims, "I do not believe in any Eden of the past. That garden is the future."[1] Her calling as a poet was "To stand against the idea of the fallen world, a powerful and destructive idea overshadowing Western poetry," and to convince her readers that "the child walled-up in our life can be given his growth" (221). Rukeyser admired Herman Melville and Walt Whitman—Melville for his outrage at life's injustices and Whitman for his belief in possibility. For her, they are the "master-poets" who "in all their work, stand at the doors of conflict, offering both courage and possibility" (86, 87). Rukeyser kept alive, in a hostile time, that romantic strain of modernism that appears in Hart Crane and E. E. Cummings, a strain that would by the 1960s be a major force in contemporary American poetry.

From her first volume of poetry, *Theory of Flight* (1935), which won the Yale Series of Younger Poets Award, Rukeyser confronted the dialectical clash between the outrageous pain and injustice that surrounds humanity and the possibility of joy and ecstasy. For example, a "syphilitic woman"[2] lurks outside the concert hall where Rukeyser had just experienced the beautiful music of Brahms. This clash is also internal. In "Poem out of Childhood" she confesses that at fourteen "I had dreams of suicide" and "if light had not transformed that day, I would have leapt" (10). In "The Theory of Flight," she documents the misuse of technology and the corruption of the modern state, as well as the lynching of Jesus; the political trial and electrocution of Sacco and Vanzetti, two radical Italian immigrants; the imprisonment of labor leader Tom Mooney and the Scottsboro Nine, nine young African-American males falsely accused of raping two white women. However, because the possibility of human and social transformation is always present, as symbolized by the advent of the airplane, she can exhort her readers at the conclusion of "Night Flight: New York" to "use yourselves: be: fly. / Believe that we bloom upon this stalk of time" (45).

Louise Kertesz believes that "Theory of Flight" can be favorably compared with Hart Crane's "The Bridge" in that it creates a twentieth-century Whitmanesque song of unity and possibility while truthfully confronting the gritty particulars of an urban, technological world.[3] The poem documents our present state, but it also celebrates the joys and mysteries of existence, the "unverifiable fact, as in sex, dream, the parts of life in which we dive deep . . . where things are shared and we all recognize the secrets" (*Collected Poems,* v).

In developing her transformative vision, Rukeyser presents individual portraits of men and women who have demonstrated the ability to discover new possibilities. In addition to Melville, Whitman, and Hart Crane, she writes about the painters Albert Pinkerton Ryder, an American, and the German artist Käthe Kollwitz as well as rebels such as Jesus Christ and John Brown; the pantheon also includes inventors such as the Wright Brothers, the nineteenth-century mathematician and physicist Willard Gibbs, and the politician/statesman Wendell Wilkie. Unlike many of the subjects of John Dos Passos's biographical studies in *U.S.A.* (Henry Ford, American industrialist, and Thorstein Veblen, American economist and social critic, for example), these individuals transcend social and historical forces; each plays a role in the attempt to create a new world. Like Emerson's, Rukeyser's humanism pushes against the divided world of science and art and against compartmentalization and specialization.

When Rukeyser's *Collected Poems* was published in 1978, the *New York Times* reviewer commented that to read its nearly 600 pages was to review the major events of the century. Central to Rukeyser's vision of poetry was the concept of witnessing, the insistence that the poet be there when injustice was being perpetrated, when freedom was being repressed. She took it as her task to report and struggle against that repression in her poetry. In 1933, she journeyed to Alabama to witness the Scottsboro trials. And in 1936, she went to Gauley Bridge, West Virginia, to see firsthand the terrible outbreak of silicosis among the miners who were forced to drill for silica without the necessary safety precautions. She was present in Spain when the Civil War broke out, sided with the Republicans, was nearly arrested, and rightly viewed the Spanish Civil War as the start of the armed struggle against fascism. In the late 1930s and early 1940s, she joined forces with German author Thomas Mann and his family in their attempts to have the United States intervene on the behalf of the Jews who were experiencing the horrors of the Holocaust. In the 1950s, she battled McCarthyism and the repressive House Un-American Activities Committee. During the 1960s and 1970s, she was one of the most insistent activists against the Vietnam War; in 1972 she visited North Vietnam with Denise Levertov and Jane Hart, the wife of a Michigan senator; also in that year, she was incarcerated for illegally protesting the war in the Senate wing of the U.S. Capitol

Building. In 1975, as president of *P.E.N.* American Center, she flew to South Korea to protest the imprisonment of the poet Kim Chi-Ha.

This is a remarkable life, and given the restrictions and expectations women faced during Rukeyser's lifetime, it becomes even more remarkable. In incorporating her experiences into her poetry, Rukeyser insisted not only on the "evidence itself, the verifiable fact," but also a sense of moral outrage and a strong woman's point of view. Addressing those who had to flee Spain during Franco's brutal war, she insists that "Your job is: / go tell your countries what you saw in Spain" (*Collected Poems*, 139). In "Letter to the Front" she claims that while men will forget that they are fighting for freedom, "Women and poets believe and resist forever" (235, 236) those who "Worked against labor, women, Jews, / Reds, Negroes" (240). "Daring to live for the impossible" and "suffering to be free," women and poets will go beyond fighting just "To hang on to what is [theirs]" (239–40).

This moral imperative was also a major element in her anti–Vietnam War poetry in both *Speed of Darkness* (1968) and *Breaking Open* (1973), wherein she bears witness to yet another devastating war in this century of wars. "Delta Poems," for example, imaginatively links the death of two young Vietnamese lovers to the poet's loss of Otto Boch, a German athlete killed while fighting for the Loyalists during the Spanish Civil War. In *Breaking Open* she records her participation in the resistance movement to the Vietnam War and an awakened sense of community and commitment that she had not experienced since the thirties. When, for example, "Don Baty," a young draft resister, is arrested, all the resisters take on his identity: "we know, / your arrest is mine" (512). Inspired by the activism of a younger generation, she extends that activism even further by envisioning that "the newborn are with us singing" (512).

And it is as a woman and poet that she insists on a revisioning of our culture. In "welcome from war," for example, she acknowledges the need to welcome the returning Vietnam veterans (in itself a remarkable stance at this time), but she also insists that change and healing must occur, for "War came over our house. / Our bed is not the same. / We will set about beginnings" (513). By this time, Rukeyser is convinced that "the whole thing—waterfront, war, city, / sons, daughters, me—must be re-imagined" (528). She anticipates a central contention of the feminism of the 1970s when she argues that there is no separation between the private and public spheres, that "what is meant by the unconscious is the same / as what is meant by history" (529). To reimagine both ourselves and society becomes her goal as a poet, as it later became the goal of important feminist poets such as Adrienne Rich, Marge Piercy, and Audre Lorde. This is why it is so important to "Open the Gates" for the Korean poet, Kim Chi-Ha; for if the poet remains imprisoned, literally or figuratively, then "How shall we speak to the infant beginning to run? / All those beginning to run?" (573).

She rebelled against the capitalistic values of her father. The destitute world she reimagines in her writing is, in fact, the world her father helped build as co-owner of a cement and construction company. Her leftist stance, her devotion to the arts, and her independent lifestyle early on divided daughter and parents.

Rukeyser's one experience with marriage in 1945 was short-lived: it lasted only two months. In 1947, she decided she wanted to have a child, so she "picked a father for her child apparently more for his genes (he was the son of a prominent California poet) than his personality. In later years she said she was disappointed that this man would not marry her, but it is not clear if it was ever that kind of [committed] relationship.[4] Her parents were appalled at the prospect of their daughter bearing a child without a husband, but Rukeyser decided to have the child anyway and eventually had to undergo a life-threatening but successful caesarian section. In "Nine Poems for the Unborn Child," she creates one of the most moving and unique series of poems dealing with the experiences of pregnancy. Courageously, Rukeyser refused to accept the choice of whether to be a woman or a poet. She insisted, instead, that to suppress one side of her would be denying an essential element of her identity.

In fact, one of the central motifs of the *Collected Poems* is Rukeyser's determination to discover self, to reimagine self, to push back the cultural and historical barriers that confront an American-Jewish woman. In *Beast in View* (1944), she quotes Dryden: "'Tis well an old age is out / And time to begin anew" (206). This search for renewal and self is also at the center of "Ajanta," where she uses the metaphor of exploring the mysterious caves of India as a means of looking within for a new way out of a war-torn world, "For the world considered annihilation, a star" (207). The cave becomes "the cave of dream," and "The space of these walls," Rukeyser asserts, "is the body's living space. . . . The painted space of the breast / The real world where every thing is complete" (210). In this remarkable poem

Rukeyser anticipates Adrienne Rich's "Diving into the Wreck "; both poems are about necessary journeys taken to revise and reconstruct the self and the world at large.

Rukeyser's last three volumes record this journey in considerable detail; the poetry here is more direct, more concrete, more personal, and more open in form than in her previous work. In "The Poem as Mask" she insists that there will be "No more masks! No more mythologies!" The phrase became a rallying cry for feminists throughout the world.

As Alicia Ostriker comments in "The Thieves of Language: Women Poets and Revisionist Mythmaking," the "contemporary woman" poet, Adrienne Rich, for example, often simultaneously deconstructs a prior "myth" or "story" and constructs a new one that includes, instead of excludes, herself .[5] Thus at the end of "The Poem as Mask," Rukeyser "for the first time" experiences oneness—"the fragments join in me." She discovers a new self that includes the divine; she becomes both myth and mythmaker, and hence reclaims or "steals" the myth and the language. There is also an insistence on a direct expression of personal truth: "There is no mountain, there is no God, there is memory / of my torn life" (435).

Her directness can be seen, for instance, in "The Speed of Darkness," where she echoes Walt Whitman's "Song of Myself" in a distinctly feminist way:

> Whoever despises the clitoris despises the penis
> Whoever despises the penis despises the cunt
> Whoever despises the cunt despises the life of the child.
> (484)

Now she is "Listening with the whole body" and "silence is become speech / With the speed of darkness" (484). In "Despisals" she vows she will never again "despise the other . . . despise the *it*," never despise our sexuality, our Jews, our blacks, our homosexuals, or any class or group of individuals seen as "other," for, as Rukeyser puts it, "I am it" (492).

Touching, looking, communicating, searching, and relating become for Rukeyser antidotes to the separation, hatred, divisiveness, and violence of our times. In many ways this later poetry records the culmination of a lifelong journey for Rukeyser:

> Then came I entire to this moment
> process and light
> to discover the country of our waking
> breaking open.
>
> (535)

Rukeyser's presentation of a world at war, of the divided self, and of the lifelong attempt to reenvision that world and self through the wisdom of the body, the soul, and the imagination is one of the impressive accomplishments of twentieth-century poetry. Yet for most of her career Rukeyser received scant and often negative criticism. Randall Jarrell, for example, in *Poetry and the Age* (1953), thought she had "considerable talent for emotional rhetoric" but worked "with rather unfortunate models and standards." To him she was an anachronism, reminiscent of "the girl on last year's calendar."[6] However, formalist aesthetics, primarily devised by males, would eventually give way to many of Rukeyser's highly innovative aesthetic principles. In *The Life of Poetry* (1949) she insisted, for example, that poetry was a neglected medium for change. "Human energy," the basis of poetry, she asserts, "may be defined as consciousness, the capacity to make changes in existing conditions" (*Life*, n.p.). She also anticipates Charles Olson's famous essay on projective verse, insisting that poetry is not tied to traditional forms and rules but instead follows "the laws of organic growth" (28). Both Olson and Rukeyser see the poem as a process rather than an object.

In vision and form Rukeyser would become a model and inspiration for many contemporary women poets. Two of her poems, for example, provided the titles for two early feminist anthologies, *No More Masks: An Anthology of Poetry by Women*, edited by Ellen Bass and Florence Howe (1973), and *The World Split Open: Four Centuries of Women Poets in England and America, 1552–1950*, edited by Louise Bernikow, preface by Muriel Rukeyser (1974). Poets such as Adrienne Rich and Denise Levertov would affirm and carry on the tradition of the poet as witness and visionary. Although Rukeyser's place in the traditional canon is still tenuous, Rich believes her poetry "is unequalled in the twentieth century in its range of reference, its openness and generosity of vision and its energy. . . . She rejected all limits derived from restrictive notions of the 'feminine' and wrote unapologetically as a big woman alive both in body and mind. . . . Secular and deeply spiritual Jew, sexually independent woman, her work never fit into the canon of Modernism and has been largely unexplored by critics."[7]

As her prose and poetic homages to Rukeyser suggest, Denise Levertov would certainly agree with Rich's conclusion that her work is "centered in possibilities unrealized by 'the armored and concluded mind'" (25). In addition, younger women poets such as Alice Walker, Jane Cooper, and Sharon Olds[8] also attest to the inspiration and guidance provided by Rukeyser, whose aim was always to "Nourish beginnings," to "Breathe-in experience, breathe-out poetry" (*Collected Poems*, 3).

GWENDOLYN BROOKS (B. 1917) As a black American woman, Gwendolyn Brooks provides a special and revealing perspective on contemporary urban American life. Supported by her parents, teachers, and other poets, Brooks managed to become the first African-American poet to win the Pulitzer Prize for poetry (for *Annie Allen* [1949]). Among her many other honors, she became in 1969 the poet laureate of Illinois and in 1985 was appointed poetry consultant to the Library of Congress. Her mother, who recognized her daughter's rhyming talents when she was only seven, was convinced that she would become the "*lady* Paul Laurence Dunbar" of her times.[9] Her father, the son of a runaway slave, who is remembered by Brooks in "In Honor of David Anderson Brooks, My Father," provided the love, gaiety, and warmth that enabled Brooks to survive an often lonely and secluded childhood. Both parents had to defer their own dreams and careers when they married. Keziah Brooks, an elementary school teacher, had hoped to pursue her musical studies, and David Brooks had to abandon his medical studies at Fisk University after a year to support his family in Chicago with janitorial work. Although they lived in the midst of a world of broken dreams on the South Side of Chicago, an African-American enclave, they recognized their daughter's gifts and provided the time and space for her talents to flourish.

First published at the age of thirteen, Brooks later met and was encouraged by the Harlem Renaissance poets James Weldon Johnson and Langston Hughes. It was Hughes who became Brooks's model for capturing the urban life of black Americans. For "Mightily did he [Hughes] use the street. He found its multiple heart, its tastes, smells, alarms, formulas, flowers, garbage and convulsions. He brought them all to his table-top" (*Report*, 71). In her poetic homage to "Langston Hughes" she saw her mentor as the "helmsman, hatchet, headlight"[10] for black Americans living in a dark world. In 1939 she married Henry Blakely II. Her first child, Henry Jr., was born in 1940 (Nora, her second child, was born in 1951). In the early 1940s, Brooks managed to develop her writing skills and carry on as a wife and mother in a cramped two-room apartment. Again, she found help. In 1941, Inez Cunningham Stark, a rebellious socialite and reader for *Poetry* magazine, dismayed the black community by offering a poetry workshop in the heart of the South Side of Chicago. Gwendolyn Brooks and her husband joined the group, and it was here that Brooks received her introduction to the modern poets as well as the rigorous criticism she needed to sharpen her poetic skills. Eventually, she gathered together the poems for her first collection, *A Street in Bronzeville* (1945), which won praise from Richard Wright, the leading African-American novelist at that time.

Brooks's commitment to honestly portraying her world in all its complexities and ironies marks her initial stages of writing. The world she knew best was the black urban world where people struggled merely to survive and keep alive a sense of joy and dignity. She learned from Langston Hughes's *Weary Blues* that "writing about the ordinary aspects of black life was important" (*Report*, 170). Later she also praised Robert Frost, a rural Yankee poet. Although he hoed in a very different patch, he, too, as Brooks explains in "Of Robert Frost," showed pride in his roots and embraced his world and its "common" inhabitants.

Although autobiographical material finds its way into her first three works, *A Street in Bronzeville*, *Annie Allen* (1949), and *The Bean Eaters* (1960), Brooks's approach is quite objective as she presents a gallery of characters who inhabit a world that cramps existence and threatens to stifle love and creativity. In *A Street in Bronzeville*, for example, "the old marrieds" depicts a married couple who are so exhausted that they are unable to speak despite the signs of spring and love that are present in their world. In "kitchenette building," those who live in a two-room apartment must put dreams aside in order to complete such mundane tasks as paying the rent or finally getting into a tub of lukewarm water after having bathed five children. In "the murder" an older brother, Brucie, sets fire to his infant brother, Percy.

Both men and women suffer indignities and deprivations in Brooks's world. "Gay Chaps at the Bar," a sonnet sequence based on letters received from World War II veterans, records the racism within the armed services and at home. The sequence employs off or imperfect rhyme because, as Brooks explains, the work presents "an off rhyme situation" (*Report,* 156). And "Negro Hero" is an angry and bitter monologue spoken by Dorie Miller, a decorated navy hero who despite saving his shipmates' lives is still rejected by them because of his black blood.

Particularly striking in this early work is Brooks's depiction of the plight of both young and older black women. In "the ballad of chocolate Mabbie," one of a number of poems that address intraracial themes, Brooks presents a dark young girl who is rejected by Willie Boone, a young, black male who prefers a light skinned or "lemon-hued" girl (*Blacks,* 30). "The Ballad of Pearly May Lee" presents the sardonic and tragic response of Pearl to the lynching of her lover, who was seduced by a white woman who then accused him of raping her. And the speaker in "the mother," still a very provocative poem, is unable to put her abortion behind her.

There are also women "ruined" and abandoned and mothers disgraced by their son's indifferent treatment of young black women ("when Mrs. Martin's Booker T"). And "the battle" depicts a physically abused woman who passively accepts her oppression but also presents a woman, the speaker, who responds with anger and rebellion as she imagines how she would respond to such abuse. Mame in "Queen of the Blues" sings soulfully about the unfaithfulness, disrespect, and meanness of men.

Brooks's focus on women's issues is also at the center of *Annie Allen,* a complex, concentrated, and often ironic work. Annie is raised in an environment that fosters passivity and self-denial. She has no space to grow, no chance to become an independent, self-assured woman, and her only escape is her world of fantasies and fairies. She is the child of a mother who taught her to accept what life offers her and to accept with gratitude the world of love and romance that supposedly awaits her. Later Maxie, her mother, would demand that Annie either rise from her bed and wash the floors or find a husband.

Annie is not totally naive. Although she is a devotee of romantic love, she also knows that a woman needs to be able to say "no" to both her mother and a man. But Annie can only remain silent; she cannot say no to the structures and strictures that will fence her in and stifle her potential. All she can do is smile when commanded and pretend her silence is a means of saying no. In the second section, "The Anniad," a mock heroic epic in seven-line stanzas and trochaic meter, Annie's romantic illusions are parodied as she dreams of the arrival of her shining knight, or "paladin." And when he does arrive, she transforms their "lowly" room of love making into a religious shrine. Reality, however, intrudes, as she loses her faithless lover first to the war effort, then to a mistress, and finally to a fatal disease.

Brooks's voicing of the concerns and feelings of black women is an important contribution to the evolution of contemporary feminist poetry. "The Womanhood," the last section of *Annie Allen*, for example, presents a woman's voice that is realistic, mature, and confident. As Claudia Tate notes, Brooks is especially prescient when her speaker requests that her sisters "Rise" and "Combine" (*Blacks*, 140) and form a sisterhood that will enable them to find a new way of life.[11] In a 1971 interview, Brooks stated that "Womens Lib is not for black women for the time being, because black men *need* their women beside them." However, the need for black women to assert their independence and fulfill their potential has been a consistent theme in her work. As she insisted in that same interview, the definition of "the time being" depended on "how you men treat us." (*Report*, 179).

Women's issues in Brooks's early work are not portrayed at the expense of racial issues. In "I love these little booths at Bevenute's," she once again attacks racial stereotypes; "Beverly Hills, Chicago," captures black America's sense of separation and deprivation. However, in *Bean Eaters* Brooks's anger becomes sharper, a development that led a number of readers and critics to ask if she was becoming too bitter and too polemic. She attacks the violent reaction of whites to the integration of the Little Rock, Arkansas, school system ("The Chicago Defender Sends a Man to Little Rock"), satirizes the white "Ladies from the Ladies' Betterment League" who are repulsed by the realities of ghetto life and hope they can dispense their "loathe-love" in a more pleasant manner ("Lovers of the Poor"). "Bronzeville Woman in a Red Hat" depicts a white employer who is appalled when her child is kissed by her black maid. And in "The Ballad of Rudolph Reed," a black man who has courageously moved his family into a hostile white neighborhood is slain while attempting to defend his home and family.

Racial and sexist themes are fused in "A Bronzeville Mother Loiters in Mississippi . . ." This poem is based on the slaying of Emmett

Till, a fourteen-year-old Chicagoan who was murdered in 1955 for allegedly insulting a white woman while visiting his relatives in Mississippi. The poem adopts the point of view of the wife of one of Emmett Tills's slayers, who in the Romantic myth of the South, is to be defended by her gallant husband—her white knight—from any "Dark Villain" (who in this case, ironically, is a fourteen-year-old child). However, when her husband strikes her own child, the mother/wife experiences a shock of recognition as she realizes that her husband is violent, not protective, and that his violence endangers her own children.

A central element in Brooks's life was her encounter with younger, more politically conscious and radical writers and activists such as LeRoi Jones (Amiri Baraka) who were abandoning the goal of integration and insisting on the need for black artists to write about blacks and to blacks. A pivotal meeting took place at the 1967 Writer's Conference held at Fisk University in Tennessee. Young African Americans in the audience treated Brooks and the other older writers with respect; it was the younger writers, however, especially Baraka, who captured the ardor of the audience. Brooks, as stated in an interview with Mari Evans, was struck by the pride and self-confidence displayed by these young people: "They seemed proud and so committed to their own people. I was fascinated by them."[12] Although Brooks insisted that her poetry was political and certainly spoke to black people, she concluded that she wasn't writing consciously with the idea that blacks *must address* blacks, *must write* about blacks (40). She later commented that this new black aesthetic and sense of pride in blackness brought her to a new consciousness and sense of community, "to a surprised queenhood in the new black sun—am qualified to enter at least the kindergarten of new consciousness now" (*Report*, 86).

Brooks, however, was not willing to endorse the harsh antiwhite rhetoric of a number of the new black writers. Although she agreed that the concept of integration that informed her earlier poems "has wound down to farce, to unsavory and mumbling farce," she insisted that the black emphasis must be, "not *against white*, but FOR black" (*Report*, 45).

In Chicago she initiated and later helped finance a writing workshop for the Blackstone Rangers, a Chicago gang. Here she worked and talked with the younger activists and writers from Wilson Junior College (her alma mater) who eventually took over the project. All of these experiences encouraged Brooks to assess her past and future work. As indicated, she strongly defends the political content of her early poems and sees them as models for the poetry of the sixties; however, she now wanted to reach a large black audience that was not often engaged with her previous work, which she now saw as too indirect and literary. In the early seventies, citing Baraka, she wrote: "My aim, in my next future, is to write poems that will some-how successfully 'call' (see Imamu Baraka's 'SOS') all black people: black people in taverns, black people in alleys. . . ." She insists, how-ever, that she "will not be an imitation of the contemporary young black voice which I so admire, but an extending adaptation of today's G.B. voice" (*Report*, 183).

Brooks's approach up to this point was that of a realist who once defined poetry as "life pushed through a strainer," but now she set her mind to how far too often life's pushing bent the body, psyche, and soul of the black people. *In the Mecca* (1968) is Brooks' darkest depiction of that distortion, and the title poem reflects her anger at the spiritless world inhabited by her brothers and sisters. The "Mecca," a once highly fashionable block-long structure, is not, as its name implies, the heavenly city of Islam; it is a Dantesque inferno overcrowded with isolated, suffering inhabitants who are locked in separate cells where they solipsistically wander within their individual dreams and obsessions. Originally conceived as a novel, the poem centers around Mrs. Sallie Smith's attempt to find, after an exhausting day of labor, her missing daughter, Pepita. In 807 lines of free verse—her longest poem—Brooks presents an amazing array of characters. Some, like Prophet Williams, are based on people from her past, in this case an early employee of Brooks who exploited his people by selling them "love potions" and other magical wares. Others, like Amos, who fantasizes about the impending racial wars, are more fictional than real. All of them seem indifferent to Mrs. Smith's quest for her daughter. Pepita, a symbol of lost innocence and spirituality, is eventually discovered murdered in the apartment of Jamaica Edwards, her body covered with dust and roaches.

"After Mecca," the section that follows the central narrative, presents Brooks's political themes and hopes. Slain civil rights leaders Medgar Evers and Malcolm X, in separate poems, are evoked as heroes who forged new and inspiring modes of political action. "The Wall" celebrates the new cultural pride and unity as represented by the murals painted on the walls of a Chicago ghetto building. Brooks is less the objective realist or the reporter in these poems and more the wise leader and even preacher. In her two "Sermons on the Warpland," she instructs and inspires her readers, especially the young, to realize that they can change history and transform their world.

Brooks also encouraged younger poets and activists such as Don Lee (Haki Madhubuti), who appears in "In the Mecca" as a singular visionary and leader. To match her words with deeds, she left her mainstream publisher, Harper and Row in 1971, two years after first publishing materials with Dudley Randall's Broadside Press. In 1974 she also began publishing with Lee's Third World Press and established her own press in the eighties, The David Company, named in honor of her father. All three presses primarily addressed a non-white, non-Euro-American audience.

Brooks's work in this vein includes *Riot* (Broadside Press, 1969), a depiction of the reaction in Chicago to Dr. Martin Luther King Jr.'s assassination; *Family Pictures* (Broadside Press, 1970), which extended the definition of family to include the black community at large; and *Beckonings* (Broadside Press, 1975). The latter volume includes the "Life of Lincoln West," a young black male who overcomes his assumed ugliness by realizing he is "the real thing," that he is black and beautiful. And in *Primer for Blacks* (The David Company, 1980) Brooks praises her sisters who kept their natural hairstyles, for this was "real" and "right" ("To Those of My Sisters Who Kept Their Naturals," 459–60).

In 1987 Brooks published the first edition of *Blacks* with her own David Company. (It was reissued in 1991 by the Third World Press.) The title of her collection emphatically names the subject of her lifelong work. And to read the nearly 500 pages of poems that cover more than forty years of her writings (including her autobiographical novel, *Maud Martha* [1953]), is to read, as D. H. Melhem points out, a poet deeply committed to the welfare of her black "family." Her work, Melhem states, is characterized by two major elements: "caritas," a deep and abiding sense of caring, and "heroism," in which she "responds to the needs of the Black community for pride, liberty, and leadership."[13]

Brooks's later poetry is more global in its subject matter than the earlier work. Sparked by her visits to Africa in 1971 and 1974 as well as her pride in her African heritage, she began to address the atrocities in South Africa. She honors, for example, Steve Biko, the black activist who was murdered in South Africa "for loving his people"

(*Blacks*, 500). In "Near—Johannesburg Boy," her young speaker is not allowed to live in Johannesburg, then an all-white city, but he vows to overturn the system of apartheid. And "Winnie," is a two-part poem spoken first by Nelson and then Winnie Mandela in which Brooks honors the Africanness, courage, and heroism of Winnie and other South African women (*Gottschalk and the Grande Tarantelle*, 1988).

Brooks's poetry gives voice to the struggles, achievements, and dreams of her African people. Like Langston Hughes and Muriel Rukeyser, and like Walt Whitman before them, she carries on the dream of brotherhood, sisterhood, and justice despite the seemingly overwhelming burden of contemporary history.

ROBERT HAYDEN (1913–1980) Robert Hayden's childhood, unlike that of Gwendolyn Brooks, provided him with little personal or emotional support. His natural parents, Ruth and Asa Sheffey, separated soon after Robert's birth, and Ruth, unable to raise her infant son by herself, left Robert in Detroit with foster parents, William and Sue Hayden. Robert never established a close relationship with his natural father, and although Ruth Sheffey often visited her son and encouraged his ambitions, he remained disturbed by her departure and the inevitable tensions that existed between his natural mother and his foster parents. Although well intentioned, the Haydens were ill-equipped to understand and nurture such an imaginative and sensitive child as Robert. The Hayden home was a stern environment, one in which Robert's foster father could not understand why his son was not as physically active as other boys and why he insisted on reading, on creating imaginative worlds and escaping the harshness of his environment by listening to radio programs and watching films. Robert, who was plagued by very poor eyesight and called "Four Eyes," could not and did not want to become the rough, "macho" son that his coal-truck operator father wanted him to be.

His foster mother, Sue, had experienced a shattering marriage with a white man by the name of Jim Barlow. As narrated in "The Ballad of Sue Ellen Westerfield" (*A Ballad of Remembrance*, 1962), she met Barlow while working on the steamship *Memphis Rose*. After a devastating fire nearly destroyed the ship, the two lovers roamed the countryside trying desperately to find a place where their interracial marriage would be accepted. It was not to be; they were forced to separate and that separation made Sue a very bitter woman, for "Until her dying-bed, / she cursed the circumstance."[14] No doubt owing at least in part to that experience, it was extremely difficult for Sue to show Robert the love and tenderness he needed; in fact, in "The Whipping," Hayden recounts the beating he suffered as his mother is "shouting to the neighborhood / her goodness and his wrongs" (40). The whipping, Robert now realizes, is his foster mother's means of venting her frustrations and avenging "in part . . . lifelong hidings / she has had to bear" (40).

Hayden's Detroit neighborhood, Paradise Valley, with its very ironic place-name, was primarily an African-American enclave, but it did contain a rich ethnic mix, including Jews and Chinese. To Robert, it was often a dark, confusing, and threatening world. In his vivid poetic memoir, "Elegies for Paradise Valley," he recalls that his "shared bedroom's window / opened on alley stench / A junkie died in maggots there" (163). And when the outside world, represented by white police officers, appeared in Paradise Valley, he could see "the hatred for our kind / glistening like tears / in the policeman's eyes" (163). It was a world where, despite parental attempts to shelter youngsters from the constant violence, childhood innocence soon vanished. Paradoxically, it was also a world in which the victims of racism became victimizers: "And we must never play / with Gypsy children: Gypsies / all got lice in their hair" (169).

Hayden escaped Paradise Valley with the help of a social worker who was so impressed by his determination to be a poet that she arranged for him to receive a scholarship to attend Detroit City College (now Wayne State University). Hayden's personal and social background suggests the shaping of a lost world poet, a poet who feels disconnected, alien, who can look only to an ideal past or future for his deliverance. And like Elizabeth Bishop, he turned to art for deliverance. In "Monet's 'Waterlilies,' " for example, he escapes the "news from Selma," Alabama, where racial division and violence run rampant, and news from Saigon, where a war rages that "poisons the air like fallout" (101), by viewing Monet's masterpiece at the Museum of Modern Art in New York City. In the painting "space and time exist in light / the eye like the eye of faith believes" (101). Monet's ability to capture light in his "Waterlilies" convinces Hayden that there exists beyond this world of darkness a world of light, a "world / each of us has lost." Monet's painting becomes a figure or platonic "shadow of its joy" (101). While this poem suggests a more paradisaical preexistence, "Traveling through Fog" suggests that our earthly existence, this time and place, is "phantom territory," that it is as obscure as fog and is a "cloudy dark / ensphering us" (122). This world is "Plato's cave," a shadow of the ideal realm that exists beyond this hellish world.

In addition to his need to discover this ideal realm, Hayden consistently portrays his sense of alienation. "The Tattooed Man," is a symbol for the poet/artist, and Hayden laments that he was "Born alien, / homeless everywhere" (160). "Names" recounts his discovery after four decades that Robert Hayden is not his legal name, that his birth name, Asa Bundy Sheffey, had never been legally changed; he feels "deserted, mocked" (171). His lawyer informs him that "You don't exist—at least / not legally." Like Ralph Ellison's Invisible Man, he wonders if he's a "ghost, double, alter ego . . ." (171). Homeless, and now nameless, he feels as estranged as the speaker in "American Journalism," who is an alien from another planet.

Hayden, however, is not a lost world poet; he is able to overcome his personal and social sense of separation and loss and to derive from the things of this world a sense of meaning, purpose, and even joy. He is, for example, able to go beyond the early bitterness he felt toward his parents and to comprehend, if not totally accept, his foster mother's beatings. "Those Winter Sundays," one of his most famous poems, is illuminated by the son's realization that his foster father *did* care, *did* rise early on Sunday morning to start the fire that splintered and broke the cold so that by the time he was called, the room was warm. Although he, as a child, spoke "indifferently to him, / who had driven out the cold," the poet now realizes how little he knew then "of love's austere and lonely offices" (41). In addition, amidst the squalor of his childhood, there were vital, engaging people. In the ancient *ubi sunt* ("where are they now") tradition of poetry, he recalls in a striking Dickensian style the colorful cast of characters who roamed the streets of Paradise Valley.

Hayden has a mystical bent as well. Celestial bodies, the stars, the moon, the sun are emblems of divine light that literally and figuratively illuminate the darkness. And as John Hatcher shows throughout his biographical study, they are the dominant symbols in Hayden's work.[15] In "Stars," for example, the African-American abolitionist and feminist Sojourner Truth not only follows the stars as she leads escaped slaves along the underground railroad, but she also becomes a star, a guiding light, herself; and there is a "Nine-

Pointed Star" that "lights mind and / spirit, signals future light" (138). Hayden also named his daughter after the star Maia, a symbol of future light and progress. Flowers are also natural facts that reveal spiritual truths. Zinnias that hold onto their rich colors speak of a "bravura / persistence" or a "hardy elan," a symbol of our wish for "More More More" (182). In "The Night Blooming Cereus," the title poem of his 1972 volume, Hayden views this exotic flower that blooms only once a year on a moonlit night as a symbol of ancient divinities. He and his wife are awed by the "archaic mysteries" of the natural and the supernatural.

In contrast to the lost world poets, Hayden believed that his pain and alienation were part of life's progressive evolution, that his plight, like that of other African Americans, was a microcosm of the human condition at this point in its history. Throughout his work we witness a racist society isolate and persecute those outside of its so-called mainstream. "Ballad of Remembrance," recalls a 1946 trip to New Orleans, that "down-South arcane city," that "schizoid city" (28), where an African American was not allowed to break bread or take drink with whites. Whether living in Tennessee, where he taught at Fisk University, or traveling through the South, Hayden encountered a world divided by racial hatred. In "Night, Death, Mississippi," an especially grim poem, he constructs a scene wherein three generations of a white southern family celebrate the ritualistic castration and murder of an African American. After the "successful" hunt, the returning son tells his father, his wife, and his children:

> Christ, it was better
> Than hunting bear
> which didn't know why
> you want him dead.
> (16)

Hayden's suffering is a shared historical experience. Just as he is a victim of racism, so, too, was Phyllis Wheatley, an eighteenth-century African-American poet and slave whom Hayden writes about. In his "Letter from Phyllis Wheatley" she tells how she is victimized when visiting England in 1773 with her Boston master. Like Hayden, she "dined apart," and although embraced by the Countess of Huntington as the "Sable Muse," other "foppish would-be Wits" attacked "The Yankee Pedlar / and his Cannibal Mockingbird" (147, 148). Racism, as this poem and his strong historical poem "Middle Passages" illustrate, is an evil that separates, excludes, denigrates, and is ever present in America, Europe, and across the globe. As Phyllis Wheatley puts it in Hayden's epistolary poem, "there is / no Eden without its Serpent" (147).

Just as Hayden's individual suffering is experienced by many African Americans, so too is persecution by other ethnic peoples. One finds in his work an abhorrence of racism and injustice wherever it appears—in Nazi concentration camps, in Johannesburg, South Africa, or in Seoul, Korea, for: "Their struggles are all horizons. / Their deaths encircle me" (46). In "Words in the Mourning Time" (1970) he mourns the tragic deaths of Martin Luther King Jr. and Robert Kennedy; both "destroyed by those they could not save" (90). He condemns the irrationality of the Vietnam War—of "Killing people to save, to free them?" (91)—and its racist underpinnings and violence—"Clean-Cut Boys / From Decent American Homes / are slashing off enemy ears for keepsakes" (98). To Hayden, racist concepts block our humanistic possibilities: these "monsters of abstraction / police and threaten us" (98). He refuses to accept this evil and tries to inspire his readers to

> . . . renew the vision of
> a human world where godliness
> is possible and man
> is neither gook nigger honkey wop nor kike
>
> but man
>
>   permitted to be man.
>   (98)

Hayden's humanistic approach to poetry, as well as his belief in the unity of humankind, caused him to turn away from violence as a solution to problems, whether it be Euro-American violence or the counterviolence of such figures as Nat Turner, John Brown, and 1960s African-American radical H. Rap Brown, who in Hayden's eyes advocated separation and violence (95). Hayden's faith was rooted in the Bahai religion, which emphasizes the need to see humanity as a single entity that can be saved only by love, unity, and adherence to the teachings of the latest of the divine prophets, Baha u'llah, who appeared in the nineteenth century. He is the "Dawnbreaker," "the fire that / will save" (8), for the "auroral darkness which is God" is "made flesh again / in Him" (47). He rejects the "religion" of science and technology, wherein weapons of great destruction and rockets are named after the Gods: "Nike, Zeus, Apollo, Hercules and Zeus" (81). In Hayden's eyes the "Astronauts" become "heroic antiheroes" as they probe the physical surface of the moon but not its spiritual essence. They are adrift in a secular, lifeless moonscape, and we do not know what it is "we wish them / to find for us" (191).

As Hayden recognized, his Bahai faith and platonic outlook give his poetry a neoromantic aura. In contrast to Brooks, for example, he is less grounded in the everyday affairs of African-American life. Instead, he is the "diver" who explores his inner darkness and dangerously listens to the enticing sirens who try to persuade him to be "done with self and / every dinning / vain complexity" (4). Yet he rises from the waters of forgetfulness and reenters his troubled world. In addition to this descent into despair, Hayden also envisions an ascent through art to a transcendental realm. In "For A Young Artist," which is based on a surreal tale, "A Very Old Man with Enormous Wings" by Gabriel Garcia Marquez (*Hatcher*, 199), the artist, like the Greek mythological figure Daedalus, has fallen to the earth, and in this poem lands in a pigsty. A humane but "hostile and afraid" community houses him with the chickens. With his strange wings the poet becomes an object of curiosity and reverence, something between an "actual angel" and "carny freak," who, rather than despairing, continues his attempts to fly beyond his alienated state, and eventually "the angle of ascent / [is] achieved" (133). Like Rukeyser, Hayden acknowledges the possibilities of flight, of ascendance.

Hayden's ascent as a poet was not easy. While at Fisk University, his poetic talents were not recognized and he had to endure the indignities of living in a segregated society. When he finally did achieve his deserved recognition, winning a number of awards, including the Grand Prize for Poetry at the First World Festival of Negro Arts, as well as securing a teaching position at the University of Michigan, he was attacked by younger, more radical African Americans for being too conservative, and refusing to preach separatism and black nationalism. Often ridiculed for, his proper dress and demeanor, and his refusal to join the movement, he was attacked at conferences and in print.

Hayden held his ground. He remained apart from the black aesthetic movement and continued to deal with the African-American experience and poetry in his own fashion. After the heat of the sixties and seventies cooled, Hayden's deeply humanistic sensibilities reached the audience they had always deserved.

RICHARD WILBUR (B. 1921)   Although Richard Wilbur did not dwell on the destruction and chaos of World War II, he did experience them on both the Italian and German fronts, and this had a profound effect on his worldview. Given the horrors of the war, what was needed, Wilbur concluded, echoing Robert Frost, was a form of poetry to act for the moment as a counterpoint to the disorder, disunity, and confusion of contemporary life. His poems, he admits, "may at moments have taken refuge from events in language itself— in word play, in the coverage of new words, in a certain preciosity."[16] He would also turn to nature for his values. As suggested by his figure of the "Juggler," the poet's task was to defy gravity, to overcome "for once . . . the world's weight"[17] but yet not reject the "things of this world," for it is in that realm that humans discover the joys of reality. Edgar Allan Poe, in rejecting the earthy for the ideal, Wilbur claims, took the wrong path because "A World Without Objects Is a Sensible Emptiness" (283).

Wilbur, like Wallace Stevens, examines the dialectic between reality and the imagination, trying to discover the proper balance between the "here and now" and the power of the imagination to discover, arrest, and enhance, through art, the world about us. Wilbur sees beauty and dignity in the common objects of nature, even a potato. Although the world changes and "The Beautiful Changes," they both change in "kind ways, / Wishing ever to sunder / Things and things' selves for a second finding . . ." (392). Like the poetry of Marianne Moore and Elizabeth Bishop, Wilbur's has both a factual and an instructive quality, in which various trees, insects, as well as flowers and birds provide the poet and the reader with a sense of meaning and order. "October Maples, Portland," for example, argues that the brilliant "light of maples . . . will go / But not before it washes eye and brain" (198).

Wilbur, however, is not always celebrative; there are times when a sardonic tone emerges, as in "A Dubious Night," where "one star's synecdochic smirk" reveals to the speaker "that nothing's odd / And firm as ever is the masterwork." Not able to claim that status for himself and humanity, he exclaims, "I weary of the confidence of God" (372). Wilbur is also keenly aware of the limitations of life—as well as the unknowable nature of existence: "Kick at the rock, Sam Johnson, break your bones: / But cloudy, cloudy is the stuff of stones" (288).

One of Wilbur's most celebrated poems, "Love Calls Us to the Things of This World," fuses the physical and the spiritual by means of commitment to the objects and trials of everyday life. For although "The soul shrinks / From all that it is about to remember, / From the punctual rape of every blessed day . . . ," the sun acknowledges "With a warm look the world's hunks and colors" and ". . . descends once more in bitter love / To accept the waking body" (233). It is out of this union that the world is renewed and enlivened, if only to be undone once again. This love, based on Saint Augustine's vision, the source of the poem's title, is what establishes that "difficult balance" between our "pure floating" and "dark habits" (234).

Wilbur, in fact, celebrates the things of this world even more warmly as he perceives the danger of those "vampires" (in "The Undead") who prefer "their dreams . . . To the world with all its breakable toys." In their Poe-like pursuit of the imperishable, the vampires are to be pitied:

> Think how sad it must be
> To thirst always for a scorned elixir,
> The salt quotidian blood.
> Which, if mistrusted, has no savor;
> To prey on life forever and not possess it.
> (197)

Wilbur also rejects the belief that the self is at the center of existence, that all of creation is to be seen and transformed by a mediating individual. To Wilbur, this position is illusionary and solipsistic. In "On The Marginal Way," he illustrates how a too subsuming self can transform seashore rocks into emblems of nude women or the bodies of "Auschwitz' final kill" (121). We must, he insists, take "cover in the facts" of nature, the rocks, the sea, the sky; for even though "On someone's porch, spread wings of newsprint flap / The tidings of some dirty war," the day is still perfect. "And like a breaking thought / Joy for a moment floods into the mind" (122).

Unlike Sylvia Plath—a very subjective and expressionistic poet who in 1963 committed suicide—Wilbur insists on seeing the world as autonomous, not a source for symbols that convey the pained psyche of the poet. More than a decade after Plath's death, Wilbur recalls in "Cottage Street, 1953" how he and Edna Ward attempted to convince Sylvia, then a student at Smith College, not to wish to die. He presents himself as a "half-ashamed," "impotent," and "stupid lifeguard" who cannot save "a girl . . . immensely drowned." Their "genteel chat" proves useless as Plath, for another decade after their meeting, studies and continues to express "her brilliant negative." The resultant poems may be free, but to Wilbur they are "helpless and unjust" (68). They are unjust because they are not true to the facts of this world and because rather than providing a momentary stay against chaos and despair, they darken and confuse perception, thereby cultivating the poet's self-destructive tendencies.

Although Wilbur focuses on the joys of language and the pleasures of the factual world as an answer to disorder, he also asserts the role of the poet to be that of the informed citizen who chastises our political leaders when necessary and upholds the ideals of America. In "Speech for the Repeal of the McCarron Act," Wilbur, arguing for free speech and thought, attacks a law that was passed during the reign of Senator Joseph McCarthy and became the leading weapon of the battles waged against free speech. In "Advice to a Prophet" Wilbur tells the prophet, whose task it is to save us from nuclear destruction, that he will not be successful if he speaks only of cold, abstract statistics, "the long numbers that rocket the mind," for we are "Unable to fear what is too strange." Instead the prophet must "Speak of the world's own change," the loss of natural objects, "the deer," "the lark," "the jack-pine," "the dolphins' arc," "the dove's return" for "What should we be without . . . / These things in which we have seen ourselves and spoken?" (182, 183). If we lose this world, "Our hearts shall fail us . . ." (183).

Wilbur's public poetry, as exemplified in "For the Student Strikers," is always moderate, rational, and "civil." It strikes some readers as being too tepid and cool. There is an emotional restraint and an insistence on rationality that separates Wilbur's more genteel, urbane voice from what he calls "the conventional romantic defiance" (*Responses*, 115). He remains within the establishment as a "citizen poet," who reminds us of our flaws and our failure to live up to our stated ideals. In "On Freedom's Ground," written to mark our nation's bicentennial celebration, he asks us to grieve for

> The tribes pushed west, and the treaties broken,
> The image of God on the auction block,

The immigrant scorned, and the striker beaten,
The vote denied to liberty's daughters.

(46)

Wilbur's moderate tone, his insistence on restraint, his avoidance, for the most part, of personal, confessional poetry, his tendency to dwell on the nonhuman rather than the self, as well as his lifelong adherence to traditional forms and craftsmanship have all aroused a good deal of critical controversy. Because Wilbur "agree[s] with Eliot's assertion that poetry 'is not the expression of personality but an escape from personality.' "[18] Some critics, such as Robert Horan, find his work devoid of personal expression. Unlike Lowell, he refuses to move beyond the aesthetic dictates of the classical modernists. Wilbur himself, in an interesting defense of his approach to poetry, confesses that he is inclined "to avoid the direct, dramatic expression of feeling, and to convey it through rhetoric or through hints imbedded in apparently objective description" (20). Although Robert Horan questions the rightness of seeing Wilbur's verse as too elegant and precious, Horan does miss in Wilber's poetry a "passion that grips rather than graces; an engagement that proclaims the person as well as the persona, and the ache, not just the symbol, of the event" (11).

Wilbur's formalist aesthetic, however, has also won him many awards and prizes. *Love Calls Us to the Things of This World* (1956) claimed the Edna St. Vincent Millay Award and the National Book Award, as well as the Pulitzer Prize. In addition, his later poems do often become more direct and personal than the earlier work. In "The Writer," for example, he tenderly contemplates his daughter's initial attempts to become a writer. By 1990, Wilbur had published two volumes of *Collected Poems* (1963 and 1988); the second volume, which includes these more personal poems, received numerous favorable reviews. Wilbur has also been recognized as one of our most accurate and sensitive translators, especially of the French neoclassicists; he wrote the musical lyrics for the stage version of Voltaire's *Candide,* a play that proved to be both a popular and critical success, and his 1963 translation of Moliére's *Tartuffe* received the Bollingen Poetry Translation Prize. In addition, his critical works, collected in *Responses, Prose Pieces: 1953–1976* (1976), established Wilbur as an engaging and judicious critic. In "Poetry's Debt to Poetry," for example, he examines the debt of such poets as Hart

Crane and Ezra Pound to Whitman but warns that "Literary historians in their taxonomic fury, often talk . . . as if writers simply copied each other's productions, and Macy's might match Gimbel's in item and price" (*Responses*, 166).

Most central, however, is Wilbur's insistence on maintaining a classical pitch, a carefully crafted and highly polished line, a quiet, dignified, often witty, and assured voice in his work, a voice that embraces both nature and the joys of language as expressed through conventional structures. His is a voice that is in marked contrast to the agonized cries of the lost world poets or the open form poets, and clearly anticipates the "neoformalism" of the 1980s. In describing the ". . . Etruscan Poets," he may well have described his own poetic goals and concerns:

> Dream fluently, still brothers, who when young
> Took with your mothers' milk the mother tongue,
>
> In which pure matrix, joining world and mind,
> You strove to leave some line of verse behind
>
> Like a fresh track across a field of snow,
> Not reckoning that all could melt and go.
>
> (55)

DENISE LEVERTOV (B. 1923–1997) In 1967 Denise Levertov stated that from her very first poem, written at the age of five, the dominant myth in her poetry has been that "of a journey that would lead one from one state of being to another . . . the sense of *life as a pilgrimage*."[19] Levertov could point to her "illustrious ancestors" as guides for her spiritual journey. Her father's ancestors included the Russian Hasidic mystic Schneour Zaimon (d. 1831); her mother's ancestors included the Welch tailor and mystic Angel Jones of Mold, Wales. Levertov speaks with pride of their mystical gifts and insists that there is "some line still taut between me and them."[20] Her parents, who met while traveling on the Orient Express, were also talented influences. Her father, Jewish by birth, converted to Christianity, left Russia, lived in Europe, and settled in England, where he hoped to unify Judaism and Christianity; he was ordained as an Anglican priest in 1922. Her mother, Beatrice, a writer, was active in finding homes for refugees fleeing from Hitler. She often read fiction to her daughter and arranged tutorials that became the basis for Levertov's unconventional education; most important, she taught her daughter how "to look; / to name the flowers when I was still close to the ground, / my face level with theirs."[21] Levertov's admiration and love for her mother is expressed most movingly in two poems, "The 90th Year" and "Death in Mexico," both composed soon after her mother's death in June 1967. In her essay "Beatrice Levertoff," Levertov exclaims that "I could not ever have been a poet without that vision she imparted."[22]

In two prose works, *The Poet in the World* (1973) and *Light Up the Cave* (1981), Levertov cites other sources for her lifelong pilgrimage. She remembers reading Bunyan's *Pilgrim's Progress,* as well as the many walks through the picturesque countryside of Essex, England. She also remembers her inner journeys, the dreams that would become a lifelong source for her poems, and the outbreak of war and death in Europe. She and her sister, Olga, listening to BBC news reports on the Spanish Civil War, used to "pretend . . . that the heavy Essex clay was the soil of the Pyrenees and we were secretly crossing the borders to join the International Brigade" (10). She also has vivid memories of the Jewish refugees who were forced to flee Europe.

In the midst of this darkness descending on Europe in the 1930s, she encountered the thoughts and poems of the German-Austrian poet Rainer Maria Rilke (1875–1926), who taught her to live life as intensely as possible and to realize that art must grow out of "necessity." Poetry, she learned from Rilke, must transcend irony and cynicism and discover "joy in the visual" (287). Herbert Read (1893–1968), English curator, editor, poet, and critic, also became a mentor and convinced her that " 'the work of art . . . is itself a created reality, an addition to the sum of real objects in the world' " (237).

Levertov's belief in the joys of the physical world and poetry was tested when she served as a student nurse during World War II. She prepared the dead for burial and watched the elderly waste away. The experience taught her that "praising does not mean a disregard of negatives, a kind of Pollyanna insistence on the affirmative. Praise, rather, is rooted in a recognition of fragility, transience, mortality . . ." (98). Poetry, to cite one of her titles, is *The Freeing of the Dust* (1975).

After the war, Levertov married the American author Mitchell Goodman and moved to the United States in 1948. This stage of her journey was instrumental in the shaping of her poetics. Convinced that the conventional forms, late Victorian language, and neoromantic tones of *Double Image* (1946) would not enable her to become an American poet, she turned to William Carlos Williams, who also believed in the careful scrutiny of the things of this world and the possibility of confronting and overcoming despair.

Most important, however, Williams would provide Levertov with a means of understanding how to use the American language. As she explains, he "made available to us the whole range of the language, he showed us the rhythms of speech *as poetry* . . . not only of what we say aloud but of what we say in our thoughts. . . . He cleared ground, he gave us tools" (*Poet*, 254). Levertov also became friends with Robert Duncan and Robert Creeley, two of the leading Black Mountain poets who rejected the closed forms of the past and invented what they called open, or projective, verse forms, a creed articulated in Charles Olson's famous essay on projective verse. In addition, Duncan, whom Levertov fondly remembers as her "mentor,"[23] introduced Levertov to a richer form of romanticism, one based on a "deeper, older tradition, the tradition of magic and prophecy," an "incantatory tradition" (*Light*, 201). This tradition leads Levertov into the exploration of dreams and myth, an exploration that drew her to the work of the modernist American poet, Hilda Dolittle, H.D.

Levertov quickly became one of our strongest and most perceptive critics of contemporary poetry. From the start she would insist that free verse should not tolerate formlessness or "sloppy garbage." Instead, Levertov "long[s] for poems of an inner harmony in utter contrast to the chaos in which they exist" (*Poet*, 3). This "inner harmony" comes about through the "discovery and revelation of form" (29). To Levertov, every poetic experience has its own essence and its own score or structure, and each poem entails a discovery of sound, line, line break, and revelatory language. Levertov champions the principles of a meticulously wrought form of open or organic verse, declaring in "On the Function of the Line" that "there are few poets today whose sensibility naturally expresses itself in the traditional form . . . and that those who do so are somewhat anachronistic. The closed, contained quality of such forms has less relation to the relativistic sense of life which unavoidably prevails in the late twentieth century than modes that are more exploratory, more open-ended" (*Light*, 61).

Her insistence on a Williams-like "contact" with the world, as well as an exploration of the world of dreams and then a recording of her discoveries in an autonomous, organic, poetic form, appears again and again in her poetry of the late fifties and sixties. In "Pleasures" (1959), for example, she writes "I like to find / what's not found / at once, but lies / within something of another nature, / in repose, distinct."[24] "Matins" (morning prayers), proclaims that the "authentic" is present in our dreams. "It thrusts up close. Exactly in dreams."[25] And in a more comic vein, she insists that the authentic can even be discovered while sitting on the toilet seat and listening to the radiator's "rhythmic knockings." Exploring "the known / appearing fully itself, and / more itself than one knew" (59) is Levertov's pleasure and joy.

Levertov also insisted on dealing with her earthly existence as a woman, and she always confronts that experience honestly and directly. "Hypocrite Women" chastises women for refusing to "speak" of their "own doubts" and for frivolously paring and clipping their dreams as if they were "toenails" or the "ends of / split hair" (*Poems: 1940–1960*, 142). And she is frank and honest when she describes "The Ache of Marriage" or the pain of separation and divorce in "A Time Past" and the "Wedding Ring." Levertov does not avoid the private sphere of a contemporary woman, but it never becomes the dominant motif in her work.

In fact, as the specter of the Vietnam War grew more visible and horrific, Levertov dramatically shifted her attention to the public sphere and became, along with Muriel Rukeyser and Robert Bly, one of the poets most active against and outspokenly critical of that war. In *The Sorrow Dance* (1967) her commitment to the human community is more apparent as she recounts the suffocating effects of the Vietnam War: "our lungs are pocked with it, / the mucous membrane of our dreams / coated with it, the imagination / filmed over with the gray filth of it" (*Poems: 1960–1967*, 229). The devastation of the Vietnamese civilian population is shown in "What Were They Like?" and also in "Two Variations," in which a Vietnamese mother who has seen "her five young children / writhe and die" (235) envisions the "human hand" that released the napalm, the "wet fire, the rain that gave / my eyes their vigilance" (236).

Despite these extremely sorrowful and bleak poems, Levertov retains her faith in the ability of human beings to shape their world. Vietnamese children, for example, in "The Altars in the Street," build Buddhist altars in the streets of Saigon and Hue, bring the war traffic to a halt, and transform "the whole city in all its corruption," into "a temple, / fragile, insolent, absolute" (237). While walking the city streets of the United States, Levertov is painfully aware that "the air / bears the dust of decayed hopes" and that the "killings continue," but she also envisions a world within that painful world, "an otherness that was blessèd, that was bliss. / *I saw Paradise in the dust of the street*" (222).

This vision of the sacred and unrealized potential of humanity fuels Levertov's anger, actions, and social poems. In many ways *The Sorrow Dance* is, as one of the poems in it is called, "A Lamentation," a moving recognition of grief. In addition to the war, she grieves for her recently deceased sister, Olga, in a haunting sequence of "Olga Poems." But if the sequence is one of sorrow it is also a recognition that her sister's life, often sad and disorderly, was dedicated to social change, "to change the course of the river!" (205) to bring justice to the poor and suffering, "to shout the world to its senses" (204). If Olga had once been seen as the black sheep of the family, who defied a sense of order and accomplishment, she is now imaged as having "a white / candle in [her] heart" (204). Olga, in fact, in "A Note to Olga," becomes Levertov's model for social action and her spiritual inspiration as the poet demonstrates in Times Square against the Vietnam War.

Levertov's commitment to the antiwar movement is best seen in *To Stay Alive* (1972), in which she brings under one cover materials from *The Sorrow Dance* and *Relearning the Alphabet* (1970), books that center on her growing involvement in the protest movement. This volume, she insists, is not merely "confessional autobiography, but . . . a document of some historical value, a record of one person's inner / outer experience in America during the '60's and the beginning of the '70's, an experience which is shared by so many."[26] *To Stay Alive* depicts the evolution of a radical, committed activist and is indeed of historical value. But it also reveals Levertov's inner conflicts, her need, for example, to find some relief from the often overwhelming calls for social action. She now acknowledges that revolutionary ardor appears "only in flashes" (81) and that her family, husband and child, as well as her poetry constitutes a more continuous form of love. Still, she continues to hold fast to her admiration for those "who do dare / to struggle, dare to reject" (83) and allies herself with the activist priest Dan Berrigan and the African-American poet Etheridge Knight, "who believe life is possible . . ." (84).

Levertov has continued to argue for and compose political poetry. She claims there is no longer a "sharp dividing" line "between 'political' and 'private' content" (*Poet,* 105). Poetry and politics need not, and indeed cannot, be kept apart" (105). And in her essay "The Poet in the World," she insists that the poet "must live in the body as actively as he lives in his head. . . . If he does not struggle against war and oppression, he will negate whatever his words may say, and will soon have no world to say them in" (*Poet,* 106). Poetry, she insists, must not be "divided from the rest of life" (112). Like Pablo Neruda, she believes that both political and private poetry spring from "a profound and generous passion for life" (*Light,* 135).

Levertov also views the poet as a witness to the injustices of the age. She, like Rukeyser, worked for the release of Kim Chi-Ha, who was finally freed in 1981, six years after Rukeyser's vigil in Korea, and she believed that Rukeyser, "more than any other poet I know of . . . consistently fused lyricism and overt social and political concern . . . she blended the engaged and the lyrical, the life of writing and the life of action" (189). Her "In Memory of Muriel Rukeyser" recalls that Rukeyser "didn't despair, / grieved, worked, / moved beyond shame." It is a moving tribute to a poet whose vision Levertov in many ways shares. In Levertov's eyes, "She was a cathedral."[27]

Levertov's political concerns did not lessen after the end of the war. *Candles in Babylon* (1982) envisions the nuclear age as "The Age of Terror" and Levertov insists in "What It Could Be" that we do have "the human power / *not* to kill, to choose / not to kill . . ." (88). *A Door in the Hive* (1989) recounts the bloody deeds of the death squads in El Salvador. In "El Salvador: Requiem and Invocation," for example, she enables Archbishop Romero, who was assassinated in March 1980, and the three nuns and lay person who were raped and executed nine months later, to present their tales.[28] To Levertov, the poet is a barefooted runner racing through our twentieth-century Babylon streets, holding a candle, trying to keep the flame of hope and faith alive as she attempts to awaken the populace in hopes that "the rhyme's promise was true, / that we may return / from this place of terror / home to a calm dawn . . ." (*Candles,* ix).

Levertov's journey toward that calm dawn includes her continual encounter not only with Babylon, the modern state, but also with personal losses. Her poems consistently acknowledge such losses: the breakup of her marriage; the fact that her son, Nikolai, is now on his own; the death of her parents, especially her mother; and the loss of her own youthfulness. She is once again immersed in personal grief and sorrow. But Levertov once again refuses to become the alienated poet: "there is nothing unique in your losses, / your pain is commonplace / and your road ordained" (10). She also realizes there will be a summer—"an ample landscape" (10) if not here then "over the fathomless waters" (15).

Levertov's later poetry, while retaining its political edge, becomes more mystical and religious as she envisions that last journey "over the fathomless waters." She is now the pilgrim on "A Calvary Path" who retains her faith as she and St. Thomas profess their Credo:

> I believe the earth
> exists, and
> in each minim mote
> of its dust the holy
> glow of thy candle.
> (110)

Evening Train (1992) and *Sands of the Well* (1996) trace Levertov's latest "travels." As "Evening Train" suggests, she's very much aware that she is in the latter stages of her journey. This is her "crow spring" time, when death is ever-present. It is an evening world, a world of shadows and grayness. Yet memory, language, and the vibrant world around her continue to make life meaningful. She is ambivalent about what lies ahead and her relationship to her Creator. However, she closes her last collection with a poem entitled "Primary Wonder," which celebrates God's decision to create a wondrous universe. Levertov's poetry records a contemporary pilgrim's progress through and then beyond the joys and tragedies of our time.

ROBERT DUNCAN (1919–1988)   Along with Jack Spicer (b. 1925) and Robin Blazer (b. 1925), fellow students and poets at the University of California at Berkeley, Robert Duncan was instrumental in bringing about one phase of the San Francisco Renaissance in poetry shortly after World War II. Inspired by Kenneth Rexroth and Ernest Kantorowicz, a German history professor, the Berkeley trio stressed medieval and Renaissance history, the arts, occultism, and their homosexual identities. It was, as Michael Davidson stresses, an association based not on region but on shared values.[29]

Duncan viewed his early work as "a recognition of the spiritual roots of modernism."[30] His goal was to revive a particular aspect of the "Romantic spirit," that Blakeian sense of the sacredness and mythic nature of poetry. For "form is Form, a spirit in itself."[31] The poem, Duncan believed, quoting Keats, is a wondrous field where the inspired imagination freely roams within a world of 'uncertainties, mysteries, doubts, without any irritable reaching after fact and reason—' (207). Like Wallace Stevens, whom Duncan felt provided "a route back to the Romantic" (185), Duncan claims that poems are about as close as we come to Platonic or eternal forms and verities.

The modernists and surrealists, Duncan argues, demonstrated "that in . . . art everything was possible, nothing circumscribed the flowering of being into its particular forms."[32] Existence, or "Beingness," includes dreams, visions, childhood memories, sudden epiphanies and literary, historical, artistic, and philosophic associations; all of this was the stuff of poetry. Duncan's mysticism, inclusiveness, and belief in the essential visionary nature of poetry is effectively illustrated in "Often I am Permitted to Return to a Meadow," one of his most anthologized poems. The meadow, in this poem, is "a made place" that the muse or inspiration permits him to enter and then record the experience that occurs there. It is "near to the heart / an internal pasture folded in all thought,"[33] wherein both the poet and the reader experience mystical delight and a sense of eternal or Ideal Form. Here, "the shadows that are forms fall / Wherefrom fall all architectures" (44). This Platonic experience is neither totally realized nor everlasting; however, the poem that is created out of it is the "everlasting omen of what is" (44).

This poem appears in *The Opening of the Field* (1960), a title that not only reiterates the possibilities of entering that mystical field but also affirms Duncan's belief in the principles of Charles Olson's "projective verse" theories, which, Duncan felt, enabled him to compose his "mature" poems of the sixties. In the fifties, Duncan "allied himself with the 'Black Mountain' followers of Williams and Lawrence— Olson, Creeley, [and] Denise Levertov" (Allen and Buttrick, 390), and in the summer of 1956 he taught at Black Mountain College. The concept that art is an open, boundless process, "a field of action," to use Olson's phrase, dovetailed with Duncan's earlier associations with the New York action painters and provided him with a means of expanding his concept of "open field" poetry. Virtually anything and everything that spontaneously entered the mind during the process of composing a poem might find its way into the poem and find as well its appropriate form. Dreams, childhood experiences, allusions, myths, self-reflexive commentary, as well as contemporary events, thoughts, and emotions and associational links leap freely onto the page. In his more open-form poems there would be no boundaries or closures, as there are in the "Meadow" poem. "Structure of Rime" and "Passages," for example, begun in the sixties and continued throughout the eighties, would be ongoing poems that record the life, mind, and workings of the imagination and psyche of a poet at a given time and place.

Duncan claimed that a myth, especially one remembered from childhood, acts "as a primary reality in itself . . . commending the design of the poem, it calls the past into action" and is "the inherited lore of the soul" (18). He admits to being a "derivative poet" (Allen and Buttrick, 390)—that is, a poet who consciously links himself to past poets, tales, and traditions—but he insists that his use of these myths and traditions enables him to perceive "the nature of man [humanity]" (390), for they are the mirrors of the soul. Duncan's openness, inclusiveness, associational approach, mysticism, and frequent allusions not surprisingly create a complex, erudite, and often difficult body of work. In a "Poem Beginning with a Line by Pindar," for example, Duncan associates a line from Pindar's first *Phythian Ode* with Goya's painting of Cupid and Psyche, which in turn is associated with Duncan's childhood reading of Lucius Apulelus's Cupid and Psyche narrative which is not only a fairy tale and a bed-time story but also a "primordial pattern from which the life of the soul—philosophies, and stories and poetics flows . . ." after (*Fictive Certainties*, 18). It is a tale of love lost, then regained and eternalized, and it reflects Duncan's own Romantic quest to rediscover a world of ideal love. Just as Psyche, who has broken her vow to Cupid, must pass her tests to regain his love, so, too, must Duncan journey through the twists and turns of his creative journey. He moves from the Cupid-Psyche tale to the loveless modern world, records the broken speech of William Carlos Williams after he has suffered a stroke, and recounts the spiritless presidents who followed Abraham Lincoln and led the country into an "age of factories of human misery turning out commodities" (*Selected Poems*, 56). After Lincoln, "There is no continuity . . ." (57), and Whitman's dream of an idealized, democratic America has vanished. Duncan then links his quest for love in both the private and public realms to the mythic poetry of Homer, Pound, Rilke, and Olson, as well as to his own family history and childhood memories. At the poem's conclusion he returns to the Cupid-Psyche myth, the line from Pindar's *Ode*, and his own dreams and visionary experience: "In the dawn that is nowhere / I have seen the willful children / counter and counter-clockwise turning" (62).

This is a full menu for any reader and for some an unpalatable type of poetry. James Dickey, although he acknowledges Duncan's originality and "ingenuousness," considers him "one of the most unpityingly pretentious poets I have ever come across" and objects to his "drifting," "dandified," "high and bookish" manner.[34] In defending himself against such charges, Duncan insists he does not wear his learning on his sleeve but rather rediscovers myths he encountered in his childhood, myths that play an integral part in his psychological development (*Fictive Certainties*, 33).

That psychological development is an important part of one of his strongest poems, "My Mother Would Be a Falconress." It is a haunting and moving piece, both personal and mythic, and leaves the reader with a deep sense of mystery. The poem recounts a dream in which Duncan's mother plays the role of falconer and he the role of a falcon who is controlled by his mother's will: "She draws a limit to my flight. / Never beyond my sight she says." He is torn between his desire to be with her and his desire to go beyond "the curb of her will," he is filled with love and hatred, and "would draw blood" from her wrist if he were not cowered by her "terrifying" eye. In his preface to the poem, Duncan comments on his surprise to discover through this dream that he wished to draw blood, that he could be a predator rather than a passive "chicken." But he then sardonically comments that poets *are* like chickens who "tear at each other, bloody not from hunger, but from malice, furious in their pecking order" (51). Whether the "falconress" is a symbol of his natural mother, who died while delivering Robert, his adoptive mother, the feminine principle, or the muse is thankfully unanswered. What is compelling and certain is the falcon's wish to soar "beyond the ringing hills of the world where / the falcons nest" (53), a world beyond mastery, blood, and limitations. That Romantic yearning is rendered in rich and melodic lines.

Duncan also addresses the public issues of his day. This political aspect of his poetry emerges fully in the sixties with the outbreak of the Vietnam War. In the very first sentence of his introduction to *Bending the Bow* (1968), he laments that the nation is entering "again and again the last day of our history."[35] In "The Multiversity Passage" he defends the free speech movement at the University of California at Berkeley and attacks the authoritarian actions of Chancellor Clark Kerr: "they call out their cops, police law, / the club, the gun, the strong arm, / gang law of the state" (71). In "Up Rising Passages 25" he bitterly predicts that President Johnson "would go up to join the great simulacra of men, / Hitler and Stalin, to work his fame / with planes roaring out from Guam over Asia" (81). Duncan insists that the poet must be a witness to the injustices and atrocities of his or her time.

This insistence was somewhat qualified. At first inspired by Denise Levertov's outrage and anguish over the war, Duncan later publicly expressed his growing disillusionment with what he perceived to be her embrace of violence and destruction. In "Santa Cruz Propositions" he depicts Levertov as Kali, the ancient Hindu goddess of destruction, who is "whirling her necklace of skulls," crying "Revolution or Death!"[36] Never completely comfortable with radical activism, Duncan, unlike Levertov, chose to take his stand within his poetics and his occasional public displays of antiwar sentiments. Unfortunately, Levertov and Duncan ended their long and mutually nurturing relationship over this issue.

Duncan also wished to find love in his private life, and to do that he felt he had to publicly acknowledge his homosexuality. In 1944, while in New York, he published "The Homosexual in Society" in Dwight McDonald's monthly journal, *Politics*. In that article Duncan not only announced his homosexuality but also suggested that "remaining in the closet" because of the dominant culture's values was both psychologically unhealthy and unnecessary. This was a bold pronouncement in the forties. In fact, John Crowe Ransom, after the article's appearance, decided not to print a previously accepted poem by Duncan ("An African Elegy") in the *Kenyon Review*.[37] British born poet Thom Gunn believes that Duncan courageously provided "a way of speaking about homosexuality" and that "It is due more to Duncan than to any other single poet that modern American poetry . . . can deal with overtly homosexual poetry" (160). An early poem, "I Am a Most Fleshy Man" (*Selected Poems*, 5–6), for example, clearly indicates Duncan's insistence on openly acknowledging and celebrating both the homoerotic and spiritual elements of homosexual love. These poems and actions clearly foreshadow the gay and lesbian social activism of the seventies and eighties, and they made it possible for many homosexual poets to openly express their sexuality in their work.[38] Duncan joins that company of visionary poets who insist on revisioning art as well as our private and public lives.

· THREE ·

New Maps for Contemporary Poetry

The poem at last is between two persons
instead of two pages. In all modesty I confess that it may be the death of literature
as we know it.
—Frank O'Hara

"Verse now, 1950, if it is to go ahead," wrote Charles Olson, "if it is to
be of essential use, must, I take it, catch up and put into itself certain
laws and possibilities of the breath, of the breathing of the man who
writes as well as of his listenings."[1] In his influential essay on the
state of American poetry at midcentury, Olson called for a poetry
that originated in the body, that brought the very physical being of
the poet into the work. He stressed the act of composition itself as a
central subject for contemporary poets and pointed to the emergence
of a self-reflexive lyric, a kind of poetry that referred to the process of
its own creation. This highly self-conscious poetics became a dominant mode of the emerging poets of the postmodern generation.

As the rector of Black Mountain College, an experimental art
school in North Carolina in the early 1950s, Olson helped define the
new direction American poetry would have to take to get beyond the
opaque, cerebral, and academic turn that modernist verse had taken.
What was needed was a poetry that connected more fully with the
poet's actual experience than with book learning and what Pound
and Eliot had defined as "the tradition." There was to be less emphasis on tradition and more emphasis on individual talent.

The newly emerging poets of the fifties and sixties began to move
poetry in this direction. In 1956, Allen Ginsberg published *Howl and
Other Poems*, a revolutionary work that epitomized the beat generation and has remained in print consecutively in each decade since. In
fact, *Howl* became the best-known and most influential poem of the
contemporary period. The young Adrienne Rich, whose lyrical gifts
were evident in her early collection *A Change of World*, winner of the

Yale Younger Poets prize for 1951, began to write more fully about "experiencing [herself] as a woman,"[2] and her poetry inspired women throughout the world to "break the silence" that kept them from expressing a woman's view of reality as distinctive and separate from the views of their male peers. In 1960, Sylvia Plath's *The Colossus* hinted at the remarkable talent that was to emerge in her extraordinary posthumously published work—work that concentrated her fury in an original and unprecedented avalanche of shocking and powerful images. In 1962, John Ashbery's *The Tennis Court Oath*, published in the usually cautious Wesleyan series, introduced an avant-garde poetics rooted in surrealism and linguistic innovation. Ashbery was to become the most innovative poet of his generation, moving the language in imaginative new directions with each successive book. Ashbery's good friend, Frank O'Hara, whose career was tragically curtailed when he died in an automobile accident in 1966, invented a "seriously whimsical" poetry of the moment, turning the mundane experiences of daily life into the heightened intensity of poetic lines. In the same year that Ashbery published *The Tennis Court Oath*, Robert Creeley's first major collection, *For Love*, appeared, revealing a new kind of linguistically minimalist poetry that deemphasized imagery and metaphor and, following Olson's lead, stressed the primacy of the writing process and the very breath of the poet writing. Both Robert Bly and James Wright, influenced more deeply by Spanish and Latin American writers than most American poets of their generation, began to explore what they called the poetry of the "deep image," which originated in myth and in the mysterious symbolism of the unconscious. And Diane Wakoski began to construct a "biomythography," a poetry that combined mythology and personal experience to create a new blend of poetry from which virtually no human emotional experience could be excluded.

These poets, taken together, drew up a new set of maps for contemporary poetry, maps that would move it still further beyond the impersonal, objectivist confines of modernism that had already been challenged by the socially conscious poets described in chapter 2 and toward a poetry centered in the physical self of the poet who produced it. They participated collectively in the midcentury poetic climate that revolutionized poetry and greatly broadened its possibilities.

New Maps for Contemporary Poetry

ALLEN GINSBERG (1926–1997)   On the back of the dust jacket of Allen Ginsberg's *Collected Poems*, published in 1984, there is a photograph of Ginsberg holding a bundle of small black and white City Lights paperbacks—the individual pocket-sized volumes where most of the collected poems originally appeared.[3] The City Lights bookstore in North Beach, San Francisco is a beat generation landmark, and its owner, Lawrence Ferlinghetti had been Ginsberg's primary publisher for over 25 years. To read these small books in succession, from *Howl and Other Poems* (1956) through *Plutonian Ode* (1982), is to confront chronologically arranged obituary notices from the anguished soul of America during some of its most troubled days. Ginsberg was always an intensely ambitious poet: from early in his career he aimed at offering a quasi-omniscient view of the American spirit and a diagnosis of its ills. He expressed the repressed Dionysian spirit in America, yoking the poles of the romantic sensibility—the luminous visions of Blake with the democratic vistas of Whitman. These ambitions were realized in the poetry he produced in the 1960s and early 1970s, which reached probably as large an audience as serious poetry ever has reached in this country. Ginsberg became a guru to thousands upon thousands of young people who saw in what they perceived as his unrelenting honesty an alternative to the cant and doublespeak of establishment America during the most hypocritical years of Vietnam and Watergate.

News of Ginsberg during these years emanated less from his poetry than from a series of important social, political, and literary events in which he participated: Ginsberg and the *Howl* obscenity trial; Ginsberg on the road with Ken Kesey's merry pranksters; Ginsberg and the antiwar demonstrations; Ginsberg and the trial of the Chicago Seven; Ginsberg and LSD; Ginsberg and gay rights; Ginsberg expressing outrage that Gregory Corso was denied the National Book Award for *Elegiac Feelings American* one year, and then winning it himself for *The Fall of America* another; Ginsberg protesting at a nuclear facility in Colorado. No other contemporary writer has lived so close to the historical edge of his time.

Though Ginsberg's poetic achievement diverged from the impersonality of modernism, he admired Pound—especially Pound's "musical" ear—and he became the embodiment of several of Pound's most cherished conceptions of the role of the artist in the twentieth century. Two of the most important of these are Pound's description of artists as the "antennae of the race" and his insistence that a fundamental role of the poet is "to purify the language of the tribe." This dual role, both prophetic and cathartic, was a part of Ginsberg's strategy from the beginning. Like Frank O'Hara, a writer with whom he is not often associated, he created new possibilities for a younger generation of poets, pushing them beyond the cool ironic stance of modernism toward a heated involvement in the experience of their time and place.

Experience is a key word in thinking about Ginsberg's work, because the Eliot-Pound legacy demanded attention not so much to the physical and human environment of an individual's daily life but rather to "tradition," to the historical record, and to particular details of poetic craft that could be garnered from that record. Pound's often-repeated adage "make it new" required a contemporary American poet to develop a sense of what poets in the English language had achieved up to the present moment. For most of the modernists, working in the forefront of poetic innovation required an ability to subordinate one's individual talent to the dictates of tradition. But Ginsberg, following Whitman, shouted his "barbaric yawp" over the rooftops of the world in *Howl* and began to change that conception and validate the primacy of personal experience for contemporary poets.

It is a mistake, however, to think of Ginsberg's poetry exclusively in experiential terms. In addition to Whitman and Blake, Ginsberg learned much about writing poetry from Christopher Smart, the eighteenth-century British poet whose poem "Jubliate Agno" ("Rejoice in the Lamb") is an important precursor of *Howl*; from the English Romantics, whose rhapsodic visions of nature inspired poems like "Wales Visitation" and others; from John Milton; from Edgar Allan Poe; and, closer to his own generation, from Pound and William Carlos Williams. He drew on his own Jewish heritage for "Kaddish," the poem many regard as his best, and his intensive study of Tibetan Buddhism infused his work with yet another layer of allusiveness. From the perspective of the last decade of the twentieth century, we can now see both the innovative aspects of Ginsberg's work and its traditional base.

Richard Eberhart describes the unique quality of Ginsberg's early poetry[4] as "an aggression upon the unseen to make it seen."[5] The phrase seems particularly apt to describe the seventy-eight stanza sentence beginning with the words "I saw," which ushers the reader into the world of *Howl*. One is struck by the sheer aggressiveness of the poem's language as well as the exotic and esoteric diction through which Ginsberg struggles to make his vision palpable. For how does one "see" a mind destroyed by madness? Ginsberg responds by creating images that give the abstraction solidity. He learned early from Ezra Pound to "go in fear of abstractions" and from William Carlos Williams to "make a start out of particulars." These intentions are realized through the poem's thoroughly original diction—the first important poetic use of the American hip vernacular—which gives the madness described in the poem a peculiar and unprecedented vitality. This effect is intensified by Ginsberg's startling combinations of adjectives and nouns: "unshaven rooms," "ashcan rantings," "hydrogen jukebox," "bop kaballa," "visionary indian angels," "saintly motorcyclists," "wild cooking pederasty," "symbolic ping pong table," "hotrod-Golgotha jail-solitude watch," "naked and endless head," and dozens more.

Ginsberg's style has been so widely imitated in the popular culture—especially by rock music lyricists—that it is hard to recall that the language did not always appear to have this sort of imaginative adaptability. To the several generations whose cultural sensibilities have been shaped by the subversive rhythms of the Beatles and the Rolling Stones and the social criticism of Bob Dylan, *Howl* may even appear conservative, but it is important to recognize that Ginsberg influenced the lyrics of all these cultural forces.

Structurally as well, *Howl* appears more orderly today than it did when it first entered the literary landscape. Its three long sections, each built around a "fixed base" ("who" in section 1, "Moloch" in section 2, and "I'm with you in Rockland" in section 3), successively offer a description of a generation; an indictment of a merciless, postindustrial society that demands that human beings sacrifice their humanity; and a portrait of a single individual (Carl Solomon) driven to madness by that society. Moloch—a Canaanite fire god "whose worship was marked by parents burning their children as propitiatory sacrifice" (Ginsberg, *Collected Poems*, 760)—used symbolically as an emblem for a society that sacrifices its young to what Dwight Eisenhower called "the military-industrial complex" is the poem's most memorable figure.

Though Ginsberg wrote in a variety of styles characterized by various line lengths, repetitive patterns, long Whitmanesque catalogs, and other devices suited to oral delivery, the essentially visionary, prophetic, and cathartic quality of his poetry has not changed a great deal since he made the breakthrough evidenced by *Howl*. He produced a substantial number of memorable poems characterized by an extraordinary openness to the experiences of his life and the sociopolitical events of his time. "A Supermarket in California" has the young poet encountering the spirit of Walt Whitman in the aisles of a contemporary supermarket; "Kaddish" is a remarkable deeply felt tribute to his mother, Naomi, that is structured on an ancient Jewish tradition; "Siesta in Xbalba" is a lengthy meditation on the relationship between an individual and the civilization of his or her time; "Kral Majales" is a satirical examination of both capitalism and communism in favor of Dionysian excess; "Wichita Vortex Sutra" is a powerful indictment of the corruption of language by both government and the media during the Vietnam War; "Wales Visitation," one of Ginsberg's most delicately crafted visionary poems, evokes the English Romantic literary tradition more fully than anything else in his work, expressing the timelessness of nature as he observes the fecundity of the earth close up, involving all his senses in adoration of the earth as the source and sustainer of all life. "Please Master" is an extraordinarily frank and graphic description of a homosexual act that revels in its unapologetically graphic sexuality. And the long "Poem of These States," which recurs sporadically throughout *The Fall of America* (1972), succeeds in its intention "to cover like a collage a lone consciousness travelling through these states during the Vietnam War."[6]

Ginsberg's poetry continued to be both socially engaged and linguistically inventive, although his later work took a somewhat more introspective turn. As might be expected, the poems in *Mind Breaths* (1978) and *White Shroud* (1986) deal more deeply with the realities of aging and portents of death than those written by the fire-breathing author of *Howl*. "Contest of the Bards" and "Father Death" show a darker Ginsberg directly confronting his own mortality. But *Cosmopolitan Greetings, Poems 1986–1992* (1994) shows us a jauntier Ginsberg, explaining why he writes poetry in a remarkable "Improvisation in Beijing," which serves as a preface to the book, and continuing to rail against the inequities he sees everywhere in the contemporary world. One of the many reasons he writes poetry is precisely because of these inequities. Although *Cosmopolitan Greetings* is a highly politicized book, as all of Ginsberg's collections are, it is also playful and self-effacing, as in "Personal Ad" which describes the life of a poet-professor in his autumn years seeking a helpmate to nurture him through his difficult passage into the country of old age. The playful tone is a part as well of "Put Down Your Cigarette Rag (Don't Smoke)," which shows his continuing connection to social issues that dominate the news. Although the repetitive refrain of this poem ("Don't Smoke" in countless variations) looks silly on the pages of a book, it always got a terrific response when Ginsberg read it to large crowds all over the world.

Throughout his career, Ginsberg gave us a poetry whose true power can be felt when it is read aloud. One of his most important contributions to contemporary verse was to take poetry out of the classrooms and into nonacademic settings—coffee houses, jazz clubs, large public auditoriums, even athletic stadiums. Allen Ginsberg's death in the small hours of the morning on April 5, 1997 ended an era in American poetry. Although he is still seen by some as a "beatnik," whose only major work was "Howl," an impartial look at his extraordinary lifelong contribution will show that his devotion to his craft and art transcended the brief lifespan of the Beat Generation. Of all contemporary American poets, his reputation remains most secure because his work embodies the vastness and contradictions of American life in the second half of the twentieth century.

ADRIENNE RICH (B. 1929) For all its attention to contemporary social issues, Ginsberg's poetry obviously does not address one of the most revolutionary social issues of our time—the change in the status of women and the nature of women's roles that has dominated the later half of the twentieth century. No American poet has chronicled this issue more fully than Adrienne Rich. Her work established the importance of gender in shaping a poetic consciousness, and she became a mentor to thousands of women, enabling them to "speak the unspeakable," to authenticate their unique experience of reality.

The deleterious consequences of leaving things unspoken has been an important continuing theme in Rich's poetry, evident even in her earliest poems. She has insisted on the need to expose the indirection and falsity of "civilized" discourse even when her own poetry is saturated by its conventions. In her first book, *A Change of World* (1951), several poems in orderly rhymes, iambic meters, and structured stanzas pose the question of an unarticulated rebellion beneath the genteel surface of civilized life. In "Five O'Clock, Beacon Hill," the narrator sits sipping "auburn sherry" with a young man who is given to allusive literary conversation—high-class name dropping. At the poem's conclusion the narrator remarks, "What rebel breathes beneath his mask, indeed? / Avant-garde in tradition's lineaments!"[7] Looked at in retrospect, these lines seem to prefigure later developments in Rich's work—the rebellion lurking beneath the "dutiful daughter" of the Anglo-American literary tradition. In "Stepping Backward," another poem from *A Change of World*, she asks "How far dare we throw off the daily ruse, / Official treacheries of face and name, / Have out our true identity?" (*Collected*, 32) Even the titles of some of the poems in this early collection reveal a preoccupation with the unspoken: "An Unsaid Word," "Unsounded," "What Ghosts Can Say."

For Rich, the most important of a poet's functions is to find words for that part of human experience that is ordinarily ineffable: the physical or physiological, the intuitive, the nonlinguistic, and intensely private internal states of mind and body. In a well-known passage from "Planetarium" (in *The Will to Change* [1971]), she defines her role as a "translator" of the nonverbal physicality of life:

> I am an instrument in the shape
> of a woman trying to translate pulsations
> into images   for the relief of the body
> and the reconstruction of the mind.
> (*Collected*, 362)

Though written earlier, "The Demon Lover" from *Leaflets* (1969) goes even further; the poet reconstructs not only the mind but the world as well, because "Only where there is language is there world" (*Collected*, 293). Unless inner states of being can be put into words, they have no *public* existence. Their very reality is ignored and denied in the social forum.

Like many of her contemporaries, Rich attempts to blur the distinctions between her poetry and her life, though she is certainly keenly aware of those distinctions. "What happens between us," one lover tells another in "The Burning of Paper Instead of Children,"

> has happened for centuries
> we know it from literature

still it happens

sexual jealousy
outflung hand
beating bed
dryness of mouth
after panting

there are books that describe all this
and they are useless
(*Collected*, 365–66)

Those last two lines identify the paradox at the center of Rich's poetry: a poet committed to the primacy of experience over book learning continues to write books to express the inexpressible. As a poet she must be committed to language, but she recognizes as well that "a language is a map of our failures" ("The Burning of Paper Instead of Children") and that "the mind of the poet is the only poem" ("Images for Godard"). Words can create our realities, but they can also separate us from one another.

This dichotomy is reflected in the arresting beginning of "Cartographies of Silence," one of the poems that define Rich's concept of the poet's calling. Here she calls attention to the irony inherent in the phrase "common language" by revealing the isolation and impotence that lie behind our words:

A conversation begins
with a lie. And each

speaker of the so-called common language feels
the ice-floe split, the drift apart

as if powerless, as if up against
a force of nature[8]

The poem differentiates between the language of poetry and the language of conversation. Spoken words cannot be retracted; they make tracks in the person they are spoken to, and they sometimes even startle the person who speaks them. Spoken words that are lies are self-generating, leading from one lie to the next to a hypocritical and inauthentic existence. The spoken lies in this poem mask what Rich calls the "unspeakable truth," and the unsaid words reflect the historical condition of many women; they create silences of the isolated self, cut off from and unexpressed in the cultural articulation of its time. Rich's notion of the poet makes her a cartographer of silence—a maker of maps that delineate the outer edges of our language for us. The poet can never choose to acquiesce to the silences but must choose instead "these words, these whispers, conversations / from which time after time the truth breaks moist and green" (*Fact*, 236).

A luminous clarity emerges in Rich's later work as her woman's voice seems to embody the language of so many of the women of her generation. "I can never romanticize language again," she writes in "The Images," "never deny its power for disguise and mystification."[9] For Rich it is important to say the word *lesbian* because "to discard it is to collaborate with silence and lying about our very existence; with the closet-game, the creation of the *unspeakable*."[10] This is not to say that her poetry speaks exclusively to or about lesbians; instead it affirms that the particulars of her experience are as equally "universal" as the experiences of her male counterparts.

In *Your Native Land, Your Life* (1986), she probes deeply into the sources of her personal identity—as a woman, daughter, mother, and wife, as a Jew, a lesbian, and feminist—each facet of herself shaped by a connection to a community, a tradition, a way of life, and a philosophy. *"From where does your strength come?"* she asks in the remarkable long poem "Sources," which chronicles her transformation from "The faithful drudging child / . . . whose penmanship, / hard work, style will win her prizes" to "the woman with a mission, not to win prizes / but to change the laws of history."[11] For Rich "Poetry never stood a chance / of standing outside history" (*Native Land*, 33); because it is rooted in the poet's life, it is implicated in the history of its time and place. A poem about the Canadian landscape painter Emily Carr makes an analogy between Carr's choice of subject and Rich's own:

> you found
> yourself facing the one great art
> of your native land, your life
> (*Native Land*, 64)

The long sequence from this 1986 collection, "Contradictions: Tracking Poems," takes the reader deep into a poet's confrontations with the demons that stalk her life and concludes with a sense of her own uncertainties and contradictions. Though the poem seems to speak for and to the suffering of many women, Rich insists that the reader not take her words as gospel but rather turn toward the particulars of her own life:

> You who think I find words for everything
> this is enough for now
> cut it short
>> cut loose from my words
>> (*Native Land*, 111)

Rich continues to review the landscape of her personal life in *Time's Power* (1989). The link between the personal and the political, so characteristic of all of her work, is taken to an even deeper level. She has mastered what Robert Peters satirically calls the "you" poem—a poem addressed to a "you" that the reader may or may not be able to identify.[12] Almost all of Rich's poems in these late collections are so addressed, but the reader's reaction is not so much to be puzzled by who the "you" might be as to recognize the commonality of human experience in relationships between children and parents, husbands and wives, lovers, and friends. The particular "you" is underscored by the use of very specific details, but it grows into a generic "you" because of the interrelatedness of humanity and the constancies of human nature.

In "Solfeggietto" she describes her childhood struggle with her mother over piano lessons, and the dispute between mother and daughter is encapsulated in this musical metaphor:

> The daughter struggles with the strange notations
> —dark chart of music's ocean   flowers and flags
> but would rather learn by ear and heart   The mother
> says she must learn to read by sight   not ear and heart[13]

This conflict, between the received authority of traditional forms and the intuitive and actual realities of experience, summarizes the gist of Rich's development as a poet. As the late Terence Des Pres observed, Rich's work began "in a formal self-regarding mode devoid of politics . . . but . . . has gone on, by virtue of attention to experience, to establish a major voice in forms overtly political."[14] Hers has become the collective voice of contemporary women demanding attention to their presence, to the realities of their experience, to the autonomy of their choices. It is often a harsh, pained, and even anguished voice, but it is also a voice of enormous strength and power, a distinguished and wholly individual voice that reaches beyond itself to incorporate the inner lives of so many of the women of her time.

In *An Atlas of the Difficult World* (1991) Rich's feminist voice incorporates an even larger territory. The long, thirteen part title poem ranges geographically from California's Pacific shores to a small table in Vermont where the narrator muses about her past, as well as the collective past of her gender and her country. More and more in this volume and in *The Dark Fields of the Republic, Poems 1991–1995* (1995) Rich's voice has become a voice of our national public conscience, speaking out against social and economic injustice wherever she finds it. In July, 1997 she declined to accept the prestigious National Medal for the Arts, one of the highest honors an American artist can receive. In a letter to the Clinton administration declining the award, she cited her belief that democracy in America is on the wane because the gap between the powerful and the weak has been widening. Rich sees poetry as a catalyst for social change and she has stood firmly and strongly behind her beliefs, which are essentially the same beliefs all Americans pledge their allegiance to: liberty, justice and equality for all.

SYLVIA PLATH (1932–1963) Another kind of woman's voice altogether emanates from the poetry of Sylvia Plath. Though her work has been in its own way even more influential than Adrienne Rich's, that influence has been much more problematic. The first lines of her first collection, *The Colossus* (1962), announce the theme she never abandoned: "The fountains are dry and the roses over. / Incense of death. Your day approaches."[15] These lines are from a poem called "The Manor Garden," which, like T. S. Eliot's opening lines in *The Waste Land*, reverses the traditional spring and rebirth associations of pastoral poetry, evoking instead a sense of nature's malevolence. The poem's speaker is apparently addressing an unborn child, preparing it for its legacy of danger and impending death. Life in this poem seems tenuous, fragile, and slight as compared with the overwhelming power of death.

Other early poems make Plath's fixation on mortality even more explicit. "Two Views of a Cadaver Room" recounts an experience she had while dating a young Harvard medical student. According to

Edward Butscher, one of Plath's several biographers, she followed her boyfriend and some other medical students into "an operating room where the students were soon busily dissecting a preserved corpse."[16] Both horrified and mesmerized by the experience, the narrator offers "two views" of the cadaver room as alternate possibilities of depicting death in art. The physical view of death as epitomized by the cadaver room is contrasted with a romantic view of death, represented by a detail from a Brueghel painting depicting two lovers, in the midst of a scene of destruction and devastation, entranced by one another and oblivious to the "smoke and slaughter" all around them. For Plath, this second view was clearly untenable. Once you have confronted the literal physicality of death (as the narrator does in the first stanza), ignoring that reality (as the lovers do in the Brueghel painting) seems hopelessly romantic and naive. The only way to relinquish the painful awareness of impending death and nothingness is to relinquish life itself—which is tragically the alternative Plath chose. On February 11, 1963, at the height of her poetic power, Plath committed suicide in her London flat and thereby moved herself and her work into the domain of myth and psychomystical speculation.

Though she was not the only poet of the contemporary period to self-destruct (John Berryman and Anne Sexton also later committed suicide), Plath's suicide frames and alters our perception of her work. As George Stade remarks, "Our knowledge of her suicide comments on the poetry as we read it. The image of the poet that rises out of the poetry as we read it wears the aspect of her fate. Our knowledge of her suicide not only clarifies what she said and what she meant—it also certifies that she meant what she said."[17]

Plath's poetry may be read as a detailed chronicle of self-destruction, although her best poems are redeemed by a startlingly vital language that clashes with the blank walls of nothingness she stares at. Although some readers find her earlier poems (those in *The Colossus* and the pre-*Colossus* poems gathered by her husband, the British poet Ted Hughes, after her death and published in *The Collected Poems* [1981]) to be quiet, carefully crafted technical exercises rather than the death-obsessed lyrics that emerged in *Ariel* (1965) and *Winter Trees* (1971), a closer look at these earlier poems reveals the same suicidal fixations, the same willingness to look death straight in the eyes, the same Stephen Crane-like impressions of the natural and inanimate worlds as indifferent to human concerns. The power of these worlds is immense and their apparent tranquility is seductive. The difference between Plath's earlier and later work is largely a difference in technique, but that difference, as Hugh Kenner wryly observes, may be very large indeed: "As long as she worked in the manner of *The Colossus* she kept safely alive. One prefers one's poets kept alive."[18]

The publication history of Plath's work further complicates our response to it. She published only one collection of poetry (*The Colossus*) during her lifetime. Although she prepared the poems in *Ariel* for publication before her suicide, the volume as it actually appeared was significantly different from the one she intended.[19] The third and fourth collections, *Crossing the Water* and *Winter Trees*, appeared in 1971, but it was not until 1981 that *The Collected Poems*, arranged in chronological order and annotated by Ted Hughes, finally appeared. Because Hughes and Plath were living apart at the time of her death, and because many see her despair over the breakup of her marriage as a primary factor in her suicide, Hughes's control over the release of Plath's posthumous publications has been problematic. Nonetheless, the assembling of *The Collected Poems* "in as true a chronological order as is possible" (*Collected Poems*, 15) gives as complete a sense of Plath's development as a writer as we are likely to have.

Reading her poetry sequentially and tracing that development makes clear that the poet who wrote the close-to-the-bone lyrics of *Ariel* is also the poet who wrote *The Colossus*; there is not a rupture between these two books but rather a shedding of masks and a movement closer to the austerity and purity of her single major subject: her sense of impending death and her desire to move language as close to the experience of death as is humanly possible.

From the perspective of literary criticism, it is tempting to ignore the fact that the writer of the harrowing self-revelatory lyrics of *Ariel* and the later poems took her own life. Judith Kroll, for example, in her stimulating study of Plath's work, argues for the need to approach the work objectively as literature; Kroll believes that "the fact . . . that she killed herself is irrelevant to the consideration of the meaning of her work; as literature, the poems would mean what they do even if she had not attempted suicide."[20] But would they? Reading the poetry as "Chapters in a Mythology," as Kroll does, puts it in a positive, affirmative light and protects us from the self-destructive reality it chronicles. According to Kroll, virtually all of the apparent "death wishes" in her late poems have the ambiguity of a simultaneous wish for rebirth, which can only be achieved through some kind of "death." It is not that life is unacceptable, but rather " 'that life, even when disciplined, is simply not worth it' (as Robert Lowell says in his foreword to *Ariel*), . . . that life lived on the wrong terms, a life lived by the false self, is not life but an intolerable death-in-life which can be overcome only by dying to that life." The late poems are really exploratory attempts to release the true self and to establish an authentic existence (Kroll, 12).

Such a reading of the poetry ignores the fact that the purveyor of these "exploratory attempts" annihilated both the creative and the destructive aspects of her divided life. If the true self is "released" only to destroy itself, one has to question the validity of the search. Plath's most famous lines from "Lady Lazarus," as well as the title and overall impressions of that poem, clearly take on additional resonance when read with the knowledge of her actual suicide. The poem deals with a lifelong flirtation with suicide, and like the Lazarus of the title, its persona miraculously survives each brush with death. The lines "Dying / Is an art, like everything else. / I do it exceptionally well" (*Collected Poems*, 245) are often cited as the center of Plath's obsession, but Plath's actual suicide mocks their efficacy. Dying, of course, is not an art (unless, as Plath says, everything else is an art), though writing well about dying is, and it is the latter, not the former, that Plath did exceptionally well. Her actual suicide attempts were botched and gruesome, and even her final completion of the act was possibly, according to A. Alvarez, a botched attempt to call attention to herself.[21]

It is possible that suicide for Plath was a performance in much the same way that her poetry was a performance, and both performances are costly to attend. "There is a charge," she writes, again in "Lady Lazarus,"

> For the eyeing of my scars, there is a charge
> For the hearing of my heart——
> It really goes
>
> And there is a charge, a very large charge,
> For a word or a touch
> Or a bit of blood
>
> Or a piece of my hair or my clothes.
> (*Collected Poems*, 244)

The charge Plath refers to is the emotional cost some readers pay for dwelling long under the spell of her seductive and hypnotic language. The Lady Lazarus of Plath's poem at the end is reborn, but reborn as a devourer of others. Like the "Lorelei" of *The Colossus*, who seduce sailors to their deaths, her tense poetry drenched with dread sometimes "Bears a burden too weighty / For the whorled ear's listening" (*Collected Poems*, 94).

Despite the fact that many have difficulty reading Plath in large doses, her contribution to the language and imagery of contemporary poetry is substantial. Her innovations include a sense of language in extremis—words on the edge of existence itself. One of her last poems, written just six days before her suicide, is, in fact, called "Edge," and she writes about her impending death with a detached stoicism.

At its best, Plath's work combines a dramatic sense of both aural and visual imagery. Her poems are filled with questions and exclamations, with startling and unexpected evocations of colors, sounds, visual flashes. A few of the memorable lines from her vast repertoire should make her originality clear:

> What a thrill——
> My thumb instead of an onion.
> The top quite gone
> Except, for a sort of hinge
> ("Cut," *Collected Poems*, 235)

> The womb
> Rattles its pod, the moon
> Discharges itself from the tree with nowhere to go.
> ("Childless Woman," *Collected Poems*, 259)

> There's a stake in your fat black heart
> And the villagers never liked you.
> They are dancing and stamping on you.
> They always *knew* it was you.
> Daddy, daddy, you bastard, I'm through.
> ("Daddy," *Collected Poems*, 224)

Those memorable lines about "Daddy" reflect as well the lifelong impact of the early death of her father on Plath's work. A German linguist and beekeeper, he died when she was nine years old and became, in her mind, a colossus; images of his life and work permeate her poetry and surely dominated much of her inner life. Perhaps she never really was quite able to say "I'm through" until her suicide in 1963.

FRANK O'HARA (1926–1966)   When *The Collected Poems of Frank O'Hara* was posthumously published in 1971, five years after his tragic accidental death, most readers and reviewers were taken aback by the sheer bulk of the volume. Here was a book of 586 pages from a poet who died at age 39 having published three slim collections of poems and a handful of broadsides and pamphlets. As John Ashbery notes in the book's introduction, O'Hara was not always driven to get his work into print:

> Dashing off poems at odd moments—in his office at the Museum of Modern Art in New York where he worked as an Associate Curator, in the street at lunchtime or even in a room full of people—he would put them away in drawers and cartons and half forget them. Once when a publisher asked him for a manuscript, he spent weeks and months combing the apartment, enthusiastic and bored at the same time, trying to assemble the poems. Finally he let the project drop, not because he didn't wish his work to appear, but because his thoughts were elsewhere, in the urban world of fantasy where the poems came from.[22]

O'Hara invented a kind of free-form urban poetry that sharply connected to the frenetic rhythms of New York life. It is a poetry of its time and place, rooted in the immediate exigencies of its author's life. Like the work of Ginsberg, Rich, and Plath, it has had a wide and substantial impact on American poetry—giving others the courage and permission to draw directly from the materials of their lives. But it is unlike the work of those poets in the freedom of its smaller scale, its playfulness, its mockery of IMPORTANT ART and poetic ambition. O'Hara's work gave American poetry an absolutely original voice—urban, funny, both casual and serious at the same time. More than any of his peers he was deeply influenced by the world of the visual arts, especially the revolutionary aesthetic developed by "action painting," or abstract expressionism, the dominant art movement of the 1950s.

O'Hara's connection with the New York art scene dates from the early 1950s, when he first worked at the Museum of Modern Art and became acquainted with many of the most innovative painters of the time. O'Hara wrote important art criticism and developed a literary aesthetic that had clear affinities with the paintings being produced by Jackson Pollock, Franz Kline, Mark Rothko, Willem de Kooning, and other painters of the New York School.[23] For example, the "casual insight" that O'Hara finds at the center of Jackson Pollock's achievement is a description as well of his own poetic style. Writing about Pollock, O'Hara finds the mimetic function of art in his work to be limited to an imitation of the artist's immediate sensibility— what he is like at the moment he is painting the picture—not an external or objective scene, and not a representation of universal human values. The achievement of O'Hara and the abstract expressionists demonstrates that transient matters can be dealt with in an enduring way. The art of the moment does not always have to be tied to rapidly changing social issues. When the moment-to-moment reality of the individual becomes the focus, the art becomes made up of the very stuff of life itself. Art has always been preoccupied with the universal, these artists seem to be saying, but life continues to serve up a steady diet of particulars. It is as a careful chronicler of those particulars that O'Hara made his mark on literary history.

O'Hara's best-known and most often anthologized poem, "The Day Lady Died," illustrates how carefully controlled and well-crafted his "casual" art can be, and how what is seemingly a random list of selected moments from a day in the poet's life is actually a tightly structured, artfully contrived series of effects. The poem records the deep impression that the news of Billie Holiday's death made on him. The emotional impact of that moment is heightened by its juxtaposition of trivial and impersonal details with O'Hara's recollection of hearing "Lady Day" sing. The poem begins with facts and figures—impersonal, trivial, and routine. We learn what time it is, what day it is, what year it is, and what the narrator's plans are for the day. Like Jackson Pollock's "Blue Poles," a painting O'Hara considered "one of the great masterpieces of Western art," random activity is here contrasted with luminous and perceptive sensitivity. After having a hamburger and a malted, going to the bank, browsing in a bookstore, and buying some liquor and cigarettes, the narrator in the poem sees "a NEW YORK POST with her face on it" (*Collected Poems*, 325). There is a stanza break recording the shock and stillness of the moment, and the last four lines are virtually a single breath— appropriately so, for their subject is breathlessness:

and I am sweating a lot by now and thinking of
leaning on the john door in the 5 SPOT
while she whispered a song along the keyboard
to Mal Waldron and everyone and I stopped breathing.

(*Collected Poems*, 325)

Many of O'Hara's poems are playful, "casually insightful" celebrations of the aesthetic autonomy of the creative act. The last stanza of
"Autobiographia Literaria" (the serious, Coleridge-inspired title
totally at odds with the spirit of the poem) specifically celebrates the
involvement of the ego with aesthetics:

And here I am, the
center of all beauty!
writing these poems!
Imagine!

(*Collected Poems*, 11)

The wonder here is a mock wonder, aimed at calling our attention to
the "action" of making the poem. Here, as elsewhere in O'Hara's
work, the mock-heroic posturing is only superficially satirical.
Underlying the casual chronicles of everyday events in his work is a
deep commitment to the transformative qualities of poetry—its ability to open our eyes, sharpen our perceptions, and involve us more
totally with the world around us. Though the phrase may appear
contradictory, O'Hara's whimsy is a *serious* whimsy. This tone,
which permeates the work, is O'Hara's response to the grandiose
solemnity of his modernist predecessors, such as Pound and Eliot.

"Memorial Day, 1950," one of his most remarkable poems, chronicles the struggle of the twentieth-century artist to "make it new," in
Pound's famous phrase, to work on the cutting edge of the art of the
time and transform that art by utilizing its elements in unprecedented ways. The artists and writers O'Hara alludes to in the poem
are all innovators who represent the modernist break from traditional forms (except Auden, who "extended" those forms). The question O'Hara seems to be asking in the poem is how does a midcentury artist follow the "destructive-constructive" revolution of the
great modernists? Pablo Picasso is likened to a "crew of creators"
chopping down plane trees outside his windows to make way for a
new building. This image evokes no lament for the destruction of
nature by modern civilization but rather celebrates the urban energy

of modern art, which made both the poet and the world "tough and quick." For O'Hara, there was no contest between the urban world of modernity and its pastoral precursors: "I can't even enjoy a blade of grass," he wrote, "unless I know there's a subway handy, or a record store or some other sign that people do not totally *regret* life" (*Collected Poems*, 197).

Throughout "Memorial Day, 1950," O'Hara aligns his work with that of revolutionary modernists like Picasso and Gertrude Stein (as well as Max Ernst, Paul Klee, and the Dadaists), but playing on the poem's title, he notes that "the war was over," that is, the struggle to create a unique and distinctly twentieth-century art had already been won. By 1950, the radical aesthetics of the early part of the century—the literary theories of Pound, Eliot, and Stein, the cubism of Picasso, the dadaism of Duchamp and Ernst, the Bauhaus innovations of Klee and Kandinsky—all had begun to seem increasingly remote from actual felt experience. The "modern" had survived both the literal and figurative wars of the century, but only as a highly intellectualized "ism," "and even when you're scared," O'Hara writes, "art is no dictionary."

Drawn to both the serious, socially conscious art of Picasso's *Guernica* and the playful, childlike spirit of Klee, the contemporary American artist, circa 1950, struggled to find a new identity able to subsume both. American painters like Robert Motherwell and Jackson Pollock were demonstrating that the untrammeled freedom of "action painting" could be put to both political and psychological uses. And O'Hara (who wrote monographs on both of these artists) was searching for a poetry that could combine the strong sense of physical action present in the canvases of the abstract painters with a liberation from the "cerebral" insistence of modernist poetics. He invented a poetry that spoke squarely and assuredly from the poet's body: "My mother and father asked me and / I told them from my tight blue pants we should / love only the stones, the sea, and heroic figures" (*Collected Poems*, 17).

The disapproval of elders for the life of the body leaves the imagination of a sexually charged poet like O'Hara devastated: "I wasn't surprised when the older people entered / my cheap hotel room and broke my guitar and my can / of blue paint" (*Collected Poems*, 17). This whimsical yet serious allusion to that modernist emblem of the imagination, "The Man with the Blue Guitar" (from Wallace Stevens's poem of that name and Picasso's painting), signals a major departure for contemporary poetry; for the modernists (Pound, Eliot, Stevens), the imagination was linked primarily to the life of the mind; for the generation of poets emerging in the fifties (Ginsberg, O'Hara, Olson, Plath, and others), it belonged to the body as well. Though it is hard to imagine a poet whose work is further from the historical density of Charles Olson's Maximus poems, O'Hara would certainly have agreed with the pivotal Olson statement quoted at the beginning of this chapter: "Verse, now, 1950 . . . must . . . put into itself certain laws and possibilities of the breath, of the breathing of the man who writes as well as of his listenings." "At that time," O'Hara writes, "all of us began to think / with our bare hands" (*Collected Poems*, 17).

"Memorial Day, 1950," attempts to revivify poetry by tying it directly to the poet's personal and physical world. It heralds a poetry of the person, as O'Hara was to put it some years later in his playful essay on "Personism," a poetry that affirms the primacy of human experience and human relationships in a world overly devoted to artifacts and artificiality: "Poetry didn't tell me not to play with toys / but alone I could never have figured out that dolls / meant death" (*Collected Poems*, 17). The lesson of modern art, according to O'Hara, is vitality; it teaches us to "look things / in the belly, not in the eye" (*Collected Poems*, 18).

JOHN ASHBERY (B. 1927)   Unlike the other poets involved in the reshaping of American poetry at midcentury, John Ashbery did not so much seek to bring poetry back into the poet's body as he did to unhinge language from its traditional referents and to create a kind of "metapoetry," of language floating on the swells and ebbs of its meanings. His first books of poems, *Some Trees* (1956), displayed some formal innovation, though Ashbery utilized many traditional forms, usually with a particularly contemporary twist. His sestina "The Painter," for example, shows the influence of abstract expressionism (like O'Hara, Ashbery is a professional art critic and has long associations with contemporary artists) and draws a playful analogy between the way in which a sestina, a poem in fixed stanzas which repeats six words in a different order in each stanza, "composes itself" once the poet has selected the end words, and the way the abstract painting described in the poem "expressed itself without a brush."

But the innovative elements in *Some Trees* are slight compared with the radical linguistic disjunctions of *The Tennis Court Oath*

(1962). Here is a poetry of seemingly "pure" language, words stripped of their traditional associations; its lines lead anywhere but where the reader might expect them to. Yet it is also a poetry of subtle and insistent allusiveness that requires close attention and eluded paraphrase. The poem "Our Youth," for instance, initially seems cryptic and obscure, but gradually reveals itself as a collective portrait of a poet's youth, with allusions to E. E. Cummings, T. S. Eliot, Archibald MacLeish, Wallace Stevens, W. B. Yeats, and others. "Leaving the Atocha Station," one of the most widely discussed poems in the volume because it appears in several anthologies, illustrates the free-association method that characterized Ashbery's work at this point in his career. The poem's images are generated by subconscious associations, limited by the experience being described. This poem about leaving the Atocha Station in Madrid attempts to capture the totality of the experience by including what is going on (both consciously and subconsciously) in the narrator's mind; what is going on around him in the immediate vicinity of the railroad car (fragments of small talk entering and receding from the narrator's consciousness); and what is occurring in the larger, external environment (the landscape flashing by). Seen from this perspective, the poem emerges as an experiential "canvas" recording an individual's consciousness at a selected moment of his life:

> Leaving the Atocha Station steel
> infected bumps the screws
> everywhere   wells
> abolished top ill-lit
> scarecrow falls   Time, progress and good sense
> strike of shopkeepers dark blood
> no forest you can name drunk scrolls
> the completely new Italian hair . . . [24]

This free association has affinities with O'Hara's "chronicle of the moment" poems, but Ashbery's method is clearly more experimental and less accessible.

Many of the poems in *Rivers and Mountains*, Ashbery's 1966 collection, extend this mode and show ways in which the self-referential properties of language can construct their own reality. Deeply influenced by the French surrealist Raymond Roussel (the subject of his master's thesis), Ashbery was struck by the power of language to shape its own world. "These Lacustrine Cities" is a good example of poetry as generative language. The cities in the poem do not exist in the world outside of it.[25] The exotic word *lacustrine* will send many readers to the dictionary, and when they return to the poem armed with the knowledge that it means "near or by a lake," it will not help them to connect the reference to any "real" cities.

> These lacustrine cities grew out of loathing
> Into something forgetful, although angry with history.
> They are the product of an idea: that man is horrible,
>   for instance,
> Though this is only one example.
>
> (*Rivers*, 9)

Ashbery's lines seem to bring the cities into being as he writes about them, and they disappear shortly after they are created as the poem moves on to other things like the "violent sea," "a mountain of something," and a "single monument,"

> Whose wind is desire starching a petal,
> Whose disappointment broke into a rainbow of tears.
>
> (*Rivers*, 9)

The "single monument" may be the poem itself, which has created lakeside cities, oceans, mountains, winds, and even a "rainbow of tears," all made out of words.

But "The Skaters," which also appears in *Rivers and Mountains*, moves Ashbery toward a meditative, philosophical mode that was to become more characteristic of his mature style. "The Skaters" is absorbed by the question of what should go into art: how many of our fleeting moments are worthy of recording? and what about them makes them different from other moments? The act of skating becomes a metaphor for the artist's graceful glide over the flat surface of existence, leaving his or her mark. Ashbery calls the reader's attention to the lines of the poem, analogous to the lines the skaters make in the ice—neither meaningful in the sense of needing further explanation but each recording its own presence as well as the absence of its creator:

> But calling attention
> Isn't the same thing as explaining, and as I said I am not ready
> To line phrases with the costly stuff of explanation, and shall
>   not,

> Will not do so for the moment. Except to say that the
> > carnivorous
> Way of these lines is to devour their own nature, leaving
> Nothing but a bitter impression of absence, which as we know
> > involves presence, but still.
> Nevertheless these are fundamental absences, struggling to
> > get up and be off themselves.[26]

The theme of art recording both the presence of the artist during the creative moment and his or her absence in our present experience of it is one of Ashbery's central concerns. It is more fully developed in *Three Poems* (1972), one of his most innovative and unusual works. A long prose poem in three parts, it experiments with a kind of language beyond cognitive meaning; it is a symphony of sentences rising and falling, building and deconstructing, swelling and imploding. One reads it with the sense of hearing a distant music, catching snatches of lucidity intermittently, but never quite grasping the whole of a particular sequence. The reader experiences the poem as a faint, lingering melody, a remembered performance, vaguely recalled, but insubstantial as a waking dream. Its final lines are a self-reflexive comment on the poem's own achievement: "The performance had ended, the audience streamed out; the applause still echoed in the empty hall. But the idea of the spectacle as something to be acted out and absorbed still hung in the air long after the last spectator had gone home to sleep."[27] *Three Poems* is Ashbery at his most inventive and a work of literary art that is a landmark of its time.

But even the achievement of *Three Poems* did not quite set the stage for the remarkable title poem in *Self-Portrait in a Convex Mirror* (1975), a *tour de force* of Ashbery's style at its apex. The poem is an extended meditation (550 lines) inspired by a small circular painting by Francesco Parmigianino, one of the masters of the high Renaissance. Ashbery sets out to describe the totality of the painting and its place in the world today—its formal structure, the circumstances of its composition, relevant facts about the life of the artist who produced it, its historical importance, its relevance to contemporary experience, and particularly the experience of the poet who is so moved by it that he uses it as a basis for long meditation of the nature of time, art, and human mortality.

The reader begins to see the painting as a synecdoche for all art that passes down through time the souls of its creators. All art, in this sense, is self-portraiture, for what else has any artist to give us but the imaginative life within? Though totally committed to language, Ashbery emphasizes its inadequacy in conveying the internal life:

> That is the tune but there are no words.
> The words are only speculation
> (From the Latin *speculum*, mirror):
> They seek and cannot find the meaning of the music.[28]

The artist desires to reveal his or her "self"—an individual consciousness—in forms that are inherently without consciousness: some paint on canvas, a block of wood, so many words upon a page. Ashbery continually contrasts the physical actuality of the painting with its transcendent "meaning" and tries to resolve the essential paradox between the physical and the transcendent that characterizes art itself. This paradox culminates in the final lines of the poem's breathtaking first section, which describes Parmigianino's gesture as "pure / Affirmation that doesn't affirm anything."

The interaction between the artist and his audience is an important subject of Ashbery's work. The narrator wonders whether the ideals of Renaissance art can survive the turbulent changes of the late twentieth century. A new "wind" appears to be blowing, a cosmic consciousness that makes human effort seem trivial, thus making us more alive to the present moment. Since it is essential for any artist to be sharply attuned to present experience, the contemporary artist faces the dilemma of whether to continue to tie his or her work to the traditions exemplified by the portrait or to embrace the newer consciousness of the contemporary. This dilemma, however, is illusory, since art remains rooted in individual experience and imagination and the compilation of individual expressions creates traditions. But it is certain that

> What is beautiful seems so only in relation to a specific
> Life, experienced or not, channeled into some form
> Steeped in the nostalgia of a collective past.
> (*Selected Poems*, 197)

Although we view the work of the great masters in museums and read about them in anthologies as representatives of various epochs, movements, and styles, they are really harbingers of our own future: their works are what ours shall become,

> even as the public
> Is pushing through the museum now so as to
> Be out by closing time. You can't live there.
> (*Selected Poems,* 199)

Art teaches us that the eternal present is the only place we can live. "Self-Portrait in a Convex Mirror" is Ashbery's masterpiece, a poem that summarizes "where we live now," to use a phrase from a poem called "Saying it to Keep it from Happening," included in *Houseboat Days,* Ashbery's 1977 collection. The "where" in this phrase refers not to a physical place but to the moment of collective consciousness shared by those of us living in the Western world in the latter part of the twentieth century. The idea of a society or civilization inhabiting a particular psychic historical moment, with the individuals alive at that moment participating in a common, contemporaneous consciousness, is another central idea in Ashbery's work. It influences nearly all of his collections since *The Double Dream of Spring* (1970). This theme reinforces the notion that Ashbery is the most Emersonian of contemporary poets, arguing at one and the same time for the primacy of the self and individual experience (as in "Self-Portrait in a Convex Mirror") and for the existence of a collective sensibility—what Emerson called the Oversoul. Ashbery puts it more flatly, but very succinctly: "Finally this is consciousness / And other livers of it get off at the same stop" (*Selected Poems,* 226).

The dimensions of contemporary consciousness are what Ashbery has attempted to measure in his later work. From *Houseboat Days* (1977) through *As We Know* (1979) and *Shadow Train* (1981) to *A Wave* (1984), *April Galleons* (1987), *Flow Chart* (1991), and *Hotel Lautréamont* (1993), this quest seems central. Equally important to his work, however, is his desire to revitalize traditional poetic forms or discover new ones that can embody that consciousness. "Litany," from *As We Know,* is a long poem printed as two columns to be read simultaneously; ( ) *Shadow Train* is an entire volume of sixteen-line poems consisting of four quatrains each; *A Wave* includes thirty-seven haiku, a description of a masque, and an innovative form of prose poem he calls "Haibun."

Ashbery has remained prolific and innovative throughout the 1990's. The long, dense, and difficult *Flow Chart* (1991), a 216 page poem of long, almost prose-like lines, demands a great deal from the reader, but those attentive to Ashbery's work will recognize a kind of summary of his "published city," all the books he had published to this point. *Hotel Lautréamont* (1993) reprises his life-long interest in surrealism, creating a fictional "hotel" named after the pseudonym of the 19th century French poet, Isidore Ducasse, whose bizarre, nightmarish vision in *Les Chants de Maldoror* influenced several generations of French writers. The long title poem of *And the Stars Were Shining* (1995) pays homage to the "stars" of the poetic firmament—those poets whose work has endured and whose style influenced and shaped his own. And the very title of his 1996 collection, *Can You Hear, Bird*, relates poetry to nature's own songmakers as the work strives to make language as lyrical and melodic as a birdsong.

Although those of us who live in the late twentieth century must continually confront what Ashbery refers to as "a universe of pain," his poetic gifts nearly always move toward an unsentimental affirmation of "things as they are." His truest subject is the wonder on the other side of despair:

> To praise this, blame that,
> Leads one subtly away from the beginning, where
> We must stay, in motion. To flash light
> Into the house within, its many chambers,
> Its memories and associations, upon its inscribed
> And pictured walls, argues enough that life is various.
> Life is beautiful. He who reads that
> As in the window of some distant, speeding train
> Knows what he wants, and what will befall.
>
> (*Selected Poems*, 231–32)

ROBERT CREELEY (B. 1926)   Throughout the 1950s, Robert Creeley was associated with the Black Mountain Poets, a group of writers that included Denise Levertov, Ed Dorn, Fielding Dawson, and others who had some connection, however indirect, with Black Mountain College in North Carolina. Creeley edited the *Black Mountain Review* and developed a close and lasting relationship with Charles Olson, who was the rector of the college; the two engaged in a lengthy, intensive correspondence about literary matters.[29] Together they developed the concept of "projective verse," a kind of poetry that abandoned traditional forms in favor of a freely constructed verse that took shape as the process of composing it was under way. Olson called this process "composition by field," and his essay on the subject, "Projective Verse," was as important for the emerging generation of the fifties as T. S. Eliot's "Tradition and the Individual Talent" was to the poets of the previous generation. Olson credits Creeley with formulating one of the basic principles of this new poetry: the idea that "FORM IS NEVER MORE THAN AN EXTENSION OF CONTENT."[30]

Creeley was a leader in the generational shift that veered away from history and tradition as primary poetic sources and gave new prominence to the ongoing experiences of an individual's life. Because of this emphasis, the major events of his life loom large in his literary work: the early death of his father; his upbringing on a small farm in West Acton, Massachusetts; his formative years with the literary crowd at Harvard; his several marriages and divorces; and his association with both the beat generation writers of the fifties and the Black Mountain group.

Though Creeley published poetry and fiction throughout the fifties and even established his own imprint, the Divers Press, in 1952, his work did not receive important national recognition until Scribners published his first major collection, *For Love*, in 1962. This book collected work that he had been issuing in small editions and minor magazines for the previous decade. At this point in his career, his distinctive poetic voice (and with Creeley one uses the word *voice* both literally and figuratively) gathered large numbers of followers and imitators. It was a voice that conveyed, in William Spanos's phrase, "a music from the edge" that epitomized the poetry revolution of the period. Along with Allen Ginsberg, Lawrence Ferlinghetti, Paul Blackburn, Gary Snyder, and other poets of the time who were intent on linking poetry and performance, Creeley awakened a sense of new rhythmical possibilities for the spoken word. The memorable sound of his voice reading poetry typified Olson's famous dictum that poetry needed to put into itself "the breathing of the man who writes." Creeley's mentors were Ezra Pound, William Carlos Williams, Louis Zukofsky, and Olson, and the odd, off-center sound of his voice as he reads his work seems an amalgam of these influences. "Williams showed me early on," he writes in *A Sense of Measure* (1972), "that rhythm was a very subtle experience, and that words might share equivalent duration even though 'formally' they seemed in no way to do so. Pound said, 'LISTEN to the sound that it makes,' and Olson . . . made it evident that we could only go 'By ear.'

Finally, there was and is the fact of, what it was one had to say—in Louis Zukofsky's sense, 'Out of deep need . . .' "[31]

The very first poem in *For Love*, "Hart Crane," with its unortho- dox, Williams-like line breaks, its nearly hidden internal rhymes, its subtle assonance and sibilance, announces the Creeley style:

> He had been stuttering, by the edge
> of the street, one foot still
> on the sidewalk, and the other
> in the gutter . . .
>
> like a bird, say, wired to flight, the
> wings, pinned to their motion, stuffed.[32]

That style is defined by an intense concentration on the sounds and rhythms of language as well as the placement of the words on the page. This intensity produced a kind of minimal poetry that extracted the bare linguistic bones from ongoing life experiences. In his "Introduction to New Writing in the USA," written in 1965, Cree- ley cites approvingly Herman Melville's definition of "visible truth"—" 'the apprehension of the absolute condition of present things' "—and supplements it with William Burroughs's famous statement from *Naked Lunch* about the writer's task: "There is only one thing a writer can write about: *what is in front of his sense at the moment of writing* . . . I am a recording instrument . . . I do not pre- sume to impose 'story' 'plot' 'continuity.' "[33]

Applying Burroughs's assertion to poetry meant not imposing on his work lyricism, metaphor, paradox, irony, closure, or any of the other conventional elements of poetry. Creeley's most memorable early poems nearly always adopted this antipoetic stance toward both language and experience. They avoid poetic devices in favor of a keen attentiveness to experience and to the ways in which a writer struggles to articulate consciousness. Characteristically, the reader is plunged into the middle of an ongoing occurrence by means of a snatch of conversation or, more usually, an internal monologue that recreates the feeling of a fleeting moment, a sudden awareness, or a traumatic event. The poems are built around Creeley's perception of the event and the "visible truth" he garners from it. That is, he seems to be searching constantly for an absolute truth in a fleeting moment. This pattern is true of almost all of the most often anthologized poems, such as "I Know a Man," "The Whip," "The Warning," and "A Wicker Basket."

Creeley sharpened and developed this style throughout the sixties and seventies in a series of books that seemed designed to exemplify the principles of projective verse and the ideas about poetry he proposed in a number of critical essays and talks. For Creeley, without the words that emanate from experience, life seems "a dull space of hanging actions," as he puts it in a poem called "Waiting" from his 1965 collection, *Words*. He *uses* poetry to takes stock of the world around him and his own state of being at any particular moment.

In *Pieces, A Day Book, Thirty Things* and *Hello*, four books published from 1969 through 1976, Creeley attempts to break down the concept of a "single poem" by offering his readers sequential, associated fragments of poems with indeterminate beginnings and endings. The 1976 book, *Hello*, deals with the last days of Creeley's relationship with his second wife, Bobbie Louise Hawkins. That marriage ended in divorce in 1976, the same year Creeley met Penelope Highton, his third wife, on a trip to New Zealand. There is a sense of deja vu about this book, and it can be described in the same terms that Sherman Paul describes *For Love*: "Poems of two marriages, the breakup of one, the beginning of another."[34] For all of Creeley's experimentation, he has always been an exceedingly domestic poet; his mother, children, wives, and close friends are the subjects of his very best work.

It is not until Creeley's next major collection, *Later* (1979), that the poetry shifts into a new phase, characterized by a greater emphasis on memory, a new sense of life's discrete phases, and an intense preoccupation with aging. He seems pained by the inability of men and women to find happiness together in the world, yet still seeks that elusive grail. These poignant lines from "Myself" capture the exasperating futility as well as the deep humanity that characterizes Creeley's later work:

> I want, if older,
> still to know
> why, human, men
> and women are
>
> so torn, so lost
> why hopes cannot
> find better world
> than this.[35]

While Creeley's earlier work is characterized by an acceptance of things as they are, his later work is tempered by a nostalgia for things as they were. Sometimes in these poems the present seems less something to express wonderment about than a great decline. In "Place," he writes:

> I need the oldtime density,
> the dirt, the cold,
> the noise through the floor—
> my love in company.
> *(Later*, 13)

In *Mirrors* (1984) the poet deepens his commitment to identifying and reconstructing those moments from the past that have most shaped his life. The collection is introduced by an epigram from Francis Bacon:

> In Mirrours, there is the like
> Angle of Incidence, from the Object
> to the Glasse, and from the Glasse
> to the Eye.[36]

Creeley seems to see poetry as such a mirror: it reflects the memory of past experience into our present awareness. Creeley reaches into early childhood in a poem called "Memory, 1930," to illuminate the moment he learned of his father's death at a time when he was obviously too young to comprehend the impact it would have on his entire life. He creates a picture of himself as a child, witnessing what appears as a surreal scene:

> I sit, intent, fat
>
> the youngest of the suddenly
> disjunct family, whose father is
>
> being then driven in an ambulance
> across the lawn, in the snow, to die.
> *(Mirrors*, 4)

Although he had written about the death of his father more obliquely in earlier work, he now brings that momentous event clearly into focus, observing the impact it had on his young self, who sits intently observing its occurrence. The older Creeley watches the young Creeley watching his father being driven away in an ambulance to die.

In poem after poem there are echoes of Ezra Pound's *"dove sta memora,"* that major theme of lost memories in *The Pisan Cantos,* a poem Pound wrote at age sixty, determined to perpetuate the things that meant the most to him. Creeley concludes a poem called "Song" with sentiments strikingly similar to the famous "Pull down thy vanity" passage in Pound's poem:

> . . . All vanity, all mind flies
> but love remains, love, nor dies
> even without me. Never dies.
>
> (*Mirrors,* 6)

The volume on nostalgia gets turned up even higher in *Echoes* (1994) where all of life seems merely a memory of one's past. Echoes are everywhere; the word recurs again and again in the book, including as the title of seven different poems. But love prevails as well, in poems about his wife, friends, and children, the people around him who provide solace against the bleak rush of time.

Love, and its devoted bedfellow, pain, have been constant elements in Creeley's work, and his late poetry continues to express both with a sensitivity and exactness that avoids the sometimes maudlin excesses of "confessional" verse. Throughout his career, he has remained committed to the poetic task of getting things exactly right.

ROBERT BLY (B. 1926) Born in the same year as Robert Creeley, Allen Ginsberg, and Frank O'Hara, and a classmate of John Ashbery at Harvard in the 1940s, Robert Bly offers a sharp contrast to his urban sophisticate peers. More than any other poet of his generation, Bly believes that American poetry took a wrong turn when it abandoned the inner life for William Carlos Williams's focus on the external world of physical reality or Pound and Eliot's cultural world of literary tradition. Bly's mentors and models were South American and European poets, especially Spanish writers like Antonio Machado, Federico García Lorca, and Juan Ramon Jimenez. With James Wright, Bly translated Jimenez and made his work accessible to American readers. For Bly, poetry becomes intensified as it reaches and expresses the deepest regions of the collective psyche. In his magazine, originally called *The Fifties* (then *The Sixties* and *The Seventies* as time passed), he developed an alternative poetic to what he regarded as the debilitating "outwardness" of modernism, which feared the instinctive life and power of spontaneity and wildness, qualities Bly believes nourish the very roots of poetry. A poem is not a small machine made of words, as Williams believed, but rather an expression of the human soul and its longing to be at home in the world. The premeditated, mechanistic aspects of Williams's work were anathema to Bly as he began charting a different mythic and internal course for his own poetry and those writers he published in his magazine. In the eleven issues of the magazine published between 1958 and 1972, Bly railed against what he called "old-fashioned poetry" in America and sought a poetry of revitalized language built around the primacy of the image. The early issues of the magazine were particularly brash and youthful and reflected the spirit of the times: "We have grave doubts about the intelligence of most, if not all, the older men in this country" wrote Bly.[37] Included among the poets Bly published and wrote about in his magazine are Louis Simpson, Robert Creeley, Donald Hall, W. S. Merwin, John Logan, Gary Snyder, James Dickey, David Ignatow, and James Wright. Perhaps prefiguring Bly's later involvement with men's issues, the only woman poet included in all eleven issues is Denise Levertov. Bly's magazine established an alternative to both neoformal traditional poetry and avant garde extensions of modernism. The map that he projected for contemporary poetry was shaped by attention to the deep images of the psyche.

One of the unique features of Bly's *Selected Poems* (1986) is a series of prose introductions, written by Bly, to the various phases of his development as a poet. The book, divided into nine sections of poetry plus a prose section called "Afterthoughts," introduces a number of Bly's critical ideas as they occur specifically in his work. Each of the poetry sections, tied to the sequence of his unpublished and published books, is prefaced by a retrospective summary of Bly's poetic "stance" at the time he wrote the poems that follow. The collection uniquely offers its readers a sense of the education of this particular poet and the course that his poetic career took.

Bly began as a writer of traditional English language poetry, and his earliest attraction to poetry was to its music. His first unpublished book, "The Lute of Three Loudnesses," was written on what he calls the poetic "instrument of the English poets constructed over

centuries," largely the resonant iambic or "accentual-syllabic" line.
These early poems were metrical and musical, but, as he puts it, "the
'I' in them had no weight."[38] It was not long, however, before Bly's
unique personal style began to emerge. An early landmark poem, "A
Man Writes to a Part of Himself," began to define that style. Here Bly
creates a deep internal image of the unacknowledged inner life:

> What cave are you in, hiding, rained on?
> Like a wife, starving, without care,
> Water dripping from your head, bent
> Over ground corn . . .
>
> *(Selected Poems, 17)*

It is a distinctly male poem, addressing the feminine aspect of the
inner male, and asking how men have become so separated from
their feelings. This prosaic summary does not suggest the mythic
dimensions of Bly's poem, but it does point to a larger direction that
his work began to take in the late 1970s and the 1980s. During that
time, Bly became a leader in what has come to be known as the
"mythopoeic" wing of the men's movement, a collective of male
experience that recognizes the terrible psychic costs men have paid
for being so out of touch with their inner lives. In this role Bly
brought poetry to a huge audience of men and underscored the relationship between poetry, life experience, and the deeper regions of a
collective consciousness.

Bly's poetry has also always had a political edge to it. During the
Vietnam War he became particularly activist, organizing a number of
poetry readings against the war and speaking out against what he
regarded as American expansionism, often comparing the United
States to the Roman Empire in its declining phase. His well-known
essay "Leaping Up into Political Poetry" describes the life of a nation
as existing beyond the accumulation of individual lives within it. A
poet with a strong sense of an inner life can "leap up" into the larger
psyche of the nation and give us insights about the national consciousness.

In his fiery speech at the National Book Award ceremony in
March 1968, Bly attacked the publishing industry, the Catholic
Church, and the Metropolitan Museum of Art for their complacency
about the government's actions in Vietnam. David Ignatow
describes the scene: "[F]or me the moment meant a complete and
overwhelming affirmation and vindication of all that Robert stood

for as a crusading, visionary figure in the literary world and in the politics of our nation. . . . It was Robert's finest hour and we who were attached to him through admiration, faith and common goals were affirmed through him and made to feel our significance before the world."[39]

The idea of a "leap" in poetry is not only applicable to Bly's political poems but is central to his poetic values. Bly believes that poets need to leap in and out of their unconscious to move a poem beyond the mundane realities of daily life. "A great work of art," he writes in "Looking for Dragon Smoke," "often has at its center a long floating leap, around which the work of art in ancient times used to gather itself like steel shavings around the magnet."[40] For Bly, this leaping associative quality of poetry is not merely a technique but an element of poetic content. Poems that make this leap are the ones we return to again and again for "News of the Universe."

The anthology Bly published under that title for the Sierra Club in 1980 offers excellent examples of what he calls "poems of twofold consciousness" that link the transitory with the eternal, the individual with the universal, the conscious with the unconscious, the story with the myth. Organized into six sections, the book reflects Bly's views on shifts of human consciousness that have occurred in the modern world. He describes what he calls "the old position," the Descartean, rationalistic universe in which humanity and human rationality is the measure of all things. Romanticism, especially in its German manifestation, mounted an attack on that position throughout the nineteenth century and prepared the way for the twofold consciousness that emerged at the beginning of the twentieth century and continued to develop in Bly's generation. This twofold consciousness conveys both the inner and the outer world simultaneously and constitutes, for Bly, the poetry of our time that will have enduring value.

Some mention must be made also of Bly's remarkable achievement as a translator of world poetry. Throughout his career he has sought out poetry of the inner landscape in many of the world's languages. He has produced English-language versions of the near-Eastern mystics Rumi and Kabir and definitive versions of Rilke, Machado, Neruda, Vallejo, Lorca, and many others. His little book *The Eight Stages of Translation* (1983) is one of the few practical, clearly written guides to the translation process taking us from a literal version of the translated poem to a final, much revised version that takes into account the meaning, sounds, tone, and mood of the original while at the same time being aware of the contemporary idiom. Since the fifties, Bly's major contribution to our poetry may be the great enrichment he brought it through his tireless and energetic translations.

As for his own poetry, it is hard not to agree with Richard Jones and Kate Daniels, who observe, "What we most appreciate about Robert Bly is his constant attempt to reintegrate poetry with life—daily life, the life of the body, political life, moral life" (Jones and Daniels, v). Formally, it occupies a place between the experimental, generative language of Ashbery and the experiential, orally based language of Ginsberg. In "Form that is Neither In nor Out" Bly argues for an intermediate form between the rigidly mechanical and totally open, drawn primarily from the economy of nature. The more "living form" a poem contains, "the closer it comes to a wild animal" (Jones and Daniels, 26).

Bly's 1997 collection, *Morning Poems*, a sequence of short poems written on successive mornings before he arose from bed, is lucid and highly accessible. The poems are infused with a lifetime of devotion to the poetic craft, while at the same time sounding fresh and even innocent. They remind us that seeing and contemplating the world anew each day is one of poetry's primary agendas.

The overall contribution of Robert Bly to contemporary poetry is very large. From his haven in Moose Lake, Minnesota, he has charted a course that redirected poetic energy from the impersonal, objective tenor of modernism and deepened the connection of poetry to individual lives. He brought strains of European, Latin American, and Near Eastern poetry into the mainstream of American verse, freeing it from the limitations of mechanism and from the nihilistic direction of late modernism. He infused American writing with the universal implications of myth and archetypes and, through his work with tens of thousands of men, showed how poetry illuminates and deepens our experience of life.

JAMES WRIGHT (1927–1980) James Wright was a student of John Crowe Ransom at Kenyon College and of Theodore Roethke at the University of Washington (where he completed a Ph.D., writing a dissertation on Charles Dickens), and he was a protege of Robert Bly, with whom he translated a number of Spanish-language poets into English. He was a much admired poet of his generation, and the outpouring of tributes following his death in 1980 led Donald Hall to speculate whether any other American poet has been the subject of so many elegies. Wright produced eleven books of poems, three of which were published posthumously and all of which are gathered in *Above the River: The Complete Poems* (1991).

A sense of midwestern American bleakness permeates much of Wright's work; it often seems "exhausted by the silence of the prairies," as he says of a locomotive in "A Poem Written Under an Archway in a Discontinued Railroad Station, Fargo." The title of that poem is characteristic of Wright. It seems important for him to locate his poems geographically, from the evocation of middle-American landscapes—in poems like "In Response to a Rumor that the Oldest Whorehouse in Wheeling, West Virginia, Has Been Condemned," "The Poor Washed Up by Chicago Winter," and "Gambling in Stateline, Nevada"—to the more exotic place names of his Italian period— such as "Winter, Basoano del Grappa," "A Small Grove in Torri Del Benaco," and "Above San Ferino." This heightened sense of place seems to express a longing for a kind of terra firma—as if Wright could count on nothing but the physical ground beneath his feet.

Wright suffered from depression for much of his life, and alcoholism took its toll on his creative energies. Like Anne Sexton, a poet he mentored and became intimately involved with early in the 1960s,[41] he wrote surprisingly well despite these difficult conditions. In addition to his own suffering, as Robert Hass notes, "What has always been a remarkable, almost singular, fact about his poetry is the way in which the suffering of other people, particularly the lost and derelict, is actually a part of his own emotional life."[42] In his early work Wright buffered this empathic sensibility by creating a series of personae or by finding refuge in the restraint of traditional poetic forms. But toward the end of his second collection, *Saint Judas* (1959), a poem called "At the Executed Murderer's Grave" signals his impatience with literariness and, as Jane Robinett observes, "is perhaps the most dramatic example of the poet's struggle toward a personal poetic" (Stitt and Graziano, 49). Wright taught himself to speak in his own voice, to "name my name," as W. D. Snodgrass put it, and the direct, startling opening of this poem has absorbed that lesson:

> My name is James A. Wright, and I was born
> Twenty-five miles from this infected grave[43]

The poem chronicles Wright's continuing preoccupation with George Doty, a murderer he had already written about in *The Green Wall* (1957), his first collection, and with whom he clearly identifies. Returning to Martin's Ferry, Ohio, his birthplace (and Doty's), he visits Doty's grave:

> where I might lie buried,
> Had I not run away before my time.
> Ohio caught George Doty.

Wright's connection to his native region is complex. Rarely has a poet written so much about a place he feels so ambivalent about, but it is the ambivalence after all that generates the poetry. Sometimes the ambivalence gives way to pure sarcasm, as in Wright's most famous lines characterizing the area:

> For the river at Wheeling, West Virginia,
> Has only two shores:
> The one in hell, the other
> In Bridgeport, Ohio.
>
> And nobody would commit suicide, only
> To find beyond death
> Bridgeport, Ohio.
> (*Above the River*, 173)

The memorability of Wright's poetry is one of its strongest assets. There may be more memorable and anthologized poems in *The Branch Will Not Break* (1963) than in any other single volume of poetry in recent memory. Together with *Shall We Gather at the River* (1968), the book marks the apex of Wright's achievement, a move into a direct "humanly important" poetry, grounded in life experience, rooted to the particulars of place, yet transcendent and compassionate, permeated by both grief and the possibility of wonder.

Wright raises serious questions about the vocation of poetry in his well-known "As I Step over a Puddle at the End of Winter, I Think of an Ancient Chinese Governor." In 1960, while walking in Minneapolis, the narrator momentarily and inexplicably thinks of the ancient Chinese poet Po Chu-i, who represents for him a worldly, distant culture, far beyond and outside of the narrator's present midwestern environment. He speculates as to whether he, as a poet, can feel connected to a tradition and thus to other poets, including those who wrote in distant times and places, or whether writing poetry is an essentially isolate act, requiring solitude and separation from the cultural productions of humanity: its civilizations. The "city of isolated men" that Po Chu-i is looking for beyond the mountains is a place in posterity with other poets who have also sought "a kindness of fate." Is Po Chu-i—whom Wright addresses as a "balding old politician" rather than a poet—really remembered? By whom? Of what does poetic fame consist? Is it solid and substantial as the "terrible oak tree darkening with winter" in the poem, or is it as fragile as the frayed rope that the poet and his tenuous reputation have been clinging to for a thousand years? (*Above the River*, 119) Of course, Wright provides no answer; the poem is a meditation on his life's work and its usefulness in the world.

One thing is clear: Wright wants to write a poetry that matters, not one that is merely literary decoration or linguistic acrobatics. In "Goodbye to the Poetry of Calcium" (also in *The Branch Will Not Break*) he rejects the old formalism that limited his vision and prevented his poetry from breaking into new territory. But *how* to write a poetry that matters continues to preoccupy him. His most famous poem, "Lying in a Hammock at William Duffy's Farm in Pine Island, Minnesota," has been read variously as a lament for wasted time or as a critique of the "busyness" that prevents us from seeing and experiencing the world fully.[44] The imagery of the poem, which involves all the senses, becomes more and more vivid with each passing line, transforming even fossilized horse manure into "golden stones." Such precise, methodical observation and deeply felt experience is possible only through calmness and serenity. The poet has wasted his life by not spending more time lying in the hammock, experiencing the intensity of the physical world.

There are, in fact, a great many remarkable transformations in Wright's poetry. Things become other things with an astonishing, magical acuity:

> Locusts and Poplars change to unmarried women
> ("Two Hangovers," 132)

> My bones turn to dark emeralds
> ("The Jewel," 122)

> Your hands turn yellow in the ruins of the sun
> ("In Memory of a Spanish Poet," 130)

> Suddenly I realize
> That if I stepped out of my body I would break
> Into blossom
> ("A Blessing," 143)

These few examples merely give some indication of the surrealistic tinge that emanates from Wright's often surprising succession of images, although sometimes that imagery seems contrived and precious, as when Wright describes "small antelopes" who "Fall asleep in the ashes / Of the moon" ("Spring Images" 137), or when he asks what a tall woman is doing hiding in the trees as he hears "rabbits and mourning doves whispering together / In the dark grass" ("Fear is What Quickens Me," 123).

"A Blessing" is widely regarded as one of Wright's best poems. Norman Friedman notes that " 'for sweetness, for joy, for precision, for rhythm, for eroticism, for structure, for surprise—for all of these things, this poem is nearly perfect.' "[45] "A Blessing" is indeed a poem of lyrical transcendence, choreographed like a ballet. Two friends come across two horses behind a barbed-wire fence off the highway. They feel a deep affinity for and connection with the animals. The poem is filled with a sense of fluid motion, nearly "liquefying" the experience, blending the human, animal, and vegetal into one natural world. The twilight is bounding on the grass; the horse's eyes "darken with kindness," while the horses themselves "ripple tensely," unable to "contain their happiness." A beautiful, ballet-like line transforms the horses into dancers: "They bow shyly as wet swans. / They love each other."

This lovely observation is followed by a truly surprising and mysterious line, shifting the mood from evocative grace to a sense of the apartness of the human and animal worlds: "There is no loneliness like theirs." This line, occurring in the dead center of the poem, gathers the surrounding motion around its stillness. It is followed immediately by movement, desire, more physical sensations. The experience of being with the horses is eroticized and leads to the poem's epiphany:

> I would like to hold the slenderer one in my arms,
> For she has walked over to me
> And nuzzled my left hand.

> She is black and white,
> Her mane falls wild on her forehead,
> And the light breeze moves me to caress her long ear
> That is delicate as the skin over a girl's wrist.
> Suddenly I realize
> That if I stepped out of my body I would break
> Into blossom
>
> (*Above the River*, 143)

The final lines flirt with the sorts of excesses that sometimes mar Wright's work, but their sheer exoticism and verve allow us to see them as another of his marvelous transformations, charging an ordinary experience with hints of the miraculous.

In the latter part of his career, Wright moved toward a sparer, less exotic style. "The kind of poetry I want to write," he wrote in "Many of Our Waters," "is / The Poetry of a grown man" (*Above the River*, 212). Ironically, this declaration of mature intentions comes in a poem subtitled "Variations on a Poem by a Black Child," which includes verbatim some words a child in New York whispered to Wright while the two were watching men work on a skyscraper's foundation. The child's words are contrasted with the "mangled figures of speech" Wright associates with young New York poets, and they represent a kind of ingenuousness that Wright desires to achieve in his own poetry. Gaping into the huge construction pit, the boy says

> You know,
> if a blind boy
> ride his bicycle
> down there
> he might fall into that water
> I think it's water
> but I don't know
> they call it acid
> and if that poor boy
> drive his poor blind bicycle
> into that acid
> he drown
> he die
> and then
> they bury him
> up
>
> (*Above the River*, 211)

This "found poetry" gives Wright a model of simplicity, directness, and unflinching confrontation with fear and terror. He follows it with autobiographical information and wonders if he is really writing a poem or just rambling. He invites the reader (or listener) to tune out:

> This is not a poem.
> This is not an apology to the Muse.
> This is the cold-blooded plea of a homesick
> vampire
> To his brother and friend.
> If you do not care one way or another about
> The preceding lines,
> Please do not go on listening
> On any account of mine.
> Please leave the poem.
> Thank you.
>   (*Above the River*, 212)

As the black child whispered to him of his fear, Wright confides his truths and insecurities to the reader, learning from a child how to write the poetry of a grown man, a poetry that speaks from his own body and experience and leaves behind "influences," fashions, literary niceties:

> All this time I've been slicking into my own words
> The beautiful language of my friends.
> I have to use my own now.
> That's why this scattering poem sounds the way it does.
>   (*Above the River*, 216)

This poem ushers Wright into the third phase of his work: an experiential poetry of plain statement and self-revelation, moving beyond the formalism of the early work and the "literariness" of the surrealist-deep image phase toward an unmediated personal voice. The tone is sometimes confessional and confidential: "I am almost afraid to write down / This thing" (*Above the River*, 236), although the revelations in the postconfessional world seem, if not ordinary, certainly not outrageous or overly shocking. For example, the "thing" that Wright is afraid to write down in a poem called "The Old WPA Swimming Pool in Martin's Ferry, Ohio," is a childhood suicide attempt during which an angel appeared to him urging him to choose life instead of death. Following the revelations of Plath, Sexton, Lowell, Berryman, and others, Wright's "openness" about this matter seems circuitous and even guarded.

Wright's later work in a variety of forms is for the most part less successful, less memorable than the poems of the middle period. While the new mode allows a more spontaneous expression, it also produces some careless and forgettable writing, hardly of the bone-deep intensity of *The Branch Will Not Break* and *Shall We Gather at the River*. Though his love affair with Italy and a truer sense of Wright's affinity for nature emerges in *Two Citizens* (1974), *To a Blossoming Pear Tree,* (1978) and *This Journey* (1982), his most memorable poems appear in the earlier books, and it is those poems which most identify our sense of Wright's poetic voice, which seems to speak to us from a cavern of infinite sorrow that somehow embodies "the whole loneliness / Of the Midwest" (*Above the River,* 119).

DIANE WAKOSKI (B. 1937) Between 1962 and 1991, Diane Wakoski published forty books, and although some of these reproduce previously published material, this is a prodigious poetic output. One of the most prolific poets of her time, Wakoski writes poetry that is a mythic chronicle of her life, presenting central images and personae that recur throughout the work. A biographical note appended to several of her books informs the reader simply that "Diane Wakoski was born in California in 1937. The poems in her published books give all the important information about her life."

This desire to bridge the gap between poetry and life characterizes nearly all of Wakoski's work. Like William Carlos Williams, a poet from whom she learned a great deal, Wakoski "makes a start from particulars," and her poetry goes in the directions those particulars take her. She thinks of the body of her poetry as an organic whole, almost as a kind of living organism with interrelated parts. This Whitmanesque sense of poetry permeates all of her work, and the reader finds recurring references to figures from what the poet calls her "personal mythology" in books published many years apart.

For Wakoski, a personal mythology is essential to a poetic vocation. Thematically, the creation of a personal mythology has to do with locating significant figures and images from life experience and transforming them into mythic archetypes that have a universal resonance. For example, in "The Father of My Country," a long lament about her absent father, a military man who rarely stayed at home for long periods, her father metamorphoses into George Washington. Wakoski explains the transformation in an interview: "Like my father . . . the figure of George Washington . . . becomes a symbolized father figure. Because he was the father of our country. I began to think of myself, partly with a pun on the word *cunt*, as country. Again, country is a feminine entity, and therefore what the country relates to is the father, the masculine."[46]

Other figures in her work who operate in this mythic-symbolic dimension include Beethoven (an artistic inspiration), the Motorcycle Mechanic (a lover who betrays her), the Steel Man (a metamorphosis of her husband), the Silver Surfer (beautiful, young California men), and the omnipresent King of Spain, who "becomes the symbolic figure for the eternal lover. That mysterious missing lover who is always there because he is never seen" (*New Poetry*, 229–30).

The male-female dynamic energizes and informs all of Wakoski's work. She believes it is a powerful metaphor for discussing human relationships generally "because of the sexual act, meaning that two separate parts come together, not for the purpose of transforming each other into like parts, but for the pleasure of knowing each other's differences for a while, and that . . . is a vision of wholeness and beauty, and what life should be all about" (*New Poetry*, 275). In a late poem from *Medea the Sorceress* (1991), she puts it even more directly:

> Dare I say it?
> The secret of the universe:
> > civilization comes in two parts,
> > the male and the female. Androgyny a perversion
> > of this truth. The two MUST be separate,
> > yet cleave,
> > both must come together,
> > yet always
> > separate.[47]

And further in the same poem,

> This man flaunts his salamander,
> and this woman flaunts her moon.
> Until they share the power,
> offer it to each other in brief recurring moments of union,

neither will understand
the secret:
    duality,

    equality,

    its power.

                                          (92)

Wakoski's vision of human nature is dualistic, with neither sex viewed as self sufficient.

One of Wakoski's primary themes concerns the feeling that she has never been beautiful enough, a theme manifest in the almost painfully self-effacing "I Have Had to Learn to Live With My Face," a poem that expands on the assertion "that reality is / learning to live with what you're born with."[48] The poem underscores the costs of a women's dependency on physical beauty to achieve self-worth, and although the self-loathing reflected in this poem is paradoxical given the self-confidence it takes to write such a poem, it is precisely this unique combination that characterizes much of Wakoski's work.

Technically, Wakoski's use of personal mythology can be illustrated by the manner in which so many of her poems are constructed. Generally, she finds a resonant image from her past and uses it recurrently throughout the poem, digressing from it in various ways as the image gathers additional meanings. For example, her poem "Smudging" (also the title of one of her collections) refers to the process of lighting fires in orchards to protect the fruit trees from overnight frost. For Wakoski, it evokes memories of her childhood in Orange County, California. The image of smudge pots heating the trees is connected to the narrator's need for continuing warmth in her life. Smudge pots are evocative, she writes,

> of my own unripe sour tight
> globular fruit
> hopefully ripening,
> hopefully not killed off
> by a frost.
> Even now,
> my leaves like toes
> reach out
> for warmth.
>   (*Emerald Ice*, 152)

For Wakoski, it is essential to live a heated, impassioned life.

A strong poem, "The Ice Eagle," extends this need to all of America, a country she finds desperately lacking human warmth and connectedness. Here the central image is an eagle carved of ice, sitting in a punch bowl at a pretentious social affair where men and women wear "masks" and relate to one another falsely and without feeling. The ice eagle becomes an emblem for an America that has lost its identity because it refuses to feel:

> Look, look, look
> I want to say; the eagle is a powerful bird.
> In your fear, all you can do is carve him out of ice.
> And that leaves only one alternative
> in this temperate climate.
> The ice eagle can do nothing
> but melt.
>
> (*Emerald Ice*, 89–90)

In addition to the poems collected in *Emerald Ice*, a 1988 compilation of her most important "biomythic" poems, Wakoski's most substantial achievement may be her long poetic chronicle (published in 1984 as *The Collected Greed, 1–13*), and her innovative 1991 book, *Medea the Sorceress*. Wakoski began *Greed* in 1967 with the intention of writing "a long, preachy, didactic poem, using personal and trivial details, names of people, and even gossipy hearsay. I wanted to pontificate about life, to moralize, and yet somehow to write a poem which would have a nobility to it."[49] While these qualities are not absent in the rest of Wakoski's work, the thematic unity of *Greed* and its sheer length give it a quasi-epic feel and relate it to William Carlos Williams's *Paterson* in its attempt to fashion an American epic from material at the end of one's nose. Wakoski's risky attempt to turn what are usually regarded as weaknesses in poetry (didacticism, banality, triviality, self-indulgence, etc.) into strengths gives *Greed* an adventurous zeal, but it also limits many readers' response to the work because it is hard to see how the poem transcends its openly flaunted flaws. If it does transcend them, it is because of a kind of aesthetics of truth is used to confront the most painful self-revelations with a courageous dignity, no matter how unfashionable the sentiments expressed may be.

Pain.
No man has wanted to spend his life with me.
The pain of sharks eating at my throat.
No man has asked me to share my life with him.
The pain of sharks eating at my lips.
No man has wanted to marry me.
The pain of sharks biting at my cheek.
No man has been willing to take care of me or give me
a home.
The pain of sharks eating at my ridged, aching back.

(*Greed*, 67)

Through *Greed*, Wakoski reveals things about herself (or at least the self of her persona) that few writers would without a substantial amount of distancing. Much of the poem seems to celebrate pettiness, small-mindedness, and vindictiveness. These are obviously basic human character traits that we all attempt to deny but that prevail nonetheless. Most people are willing to attribute these qualities to others, but Wakoski takes them on as her own, despite the self-negation they evoke in her. After exposing her envy and jealousy of other poets, as well as her negative feelings toward married women ("I see every married woman as a living symbol to remind me that I am unmarried and unmarriageable"), she writes in a prose section of *Greed*, "How I hate myself for that. Pettiness is a trait I cannot tolerate. It is the source of evil. Not power, as some people say. Power only augments evil. Pettiness creates it" (77).

One of the strongest sections of *Greed* is "The Water Element Song for Sylvia," a poem that utilizes the Plath legend as a symbol of Wakoski's alter ego. Plath's desertion by Ted Hughes was widely viewed as a prominent reason for her suicide (although she was suicidal long before she met Hughes). The narrator in *Greed* is, in contrast to Sylvia, a survivor of men's betrayals. She can tough it out without a man, even though she feels deeply the pain of desertion:

For a woman
there is only one thing which makes sense:
a man who loves her faithfully & keeps her warm at
night.
If he goes, her life does not go,

but it becomes a book with none of the pages in the
right order.
(110–11)

The Plath poem, Wakoski contends, was written in part to answer "male chauvinist" critics who compared her work with Plath's, even though they share little stylistic congruence—"as if all women of the world who write well must be similar" (108).

More important, this poem provides a particularly good example of using personal mythology to explore universal feelings. In fact, Wakoski writes, "I don't for a moment feel that this poem is in any way personal, tho [*sic*] it is written in the most personal terms. If there is anyone who has not felt these things [i.e., self-destructive urges, intense jealousy, betrayal, loss], he is either dishonest with himself or has so far had such a charmed life that I would be loath to believe it were true" (107).

Wakoski's personal mythology reaches its apex in *Medea the Sorceress*, the first volume in projected series with the overall title of "The Archeology of Movies and Books." The truly innovative structure of this work juxtaposes personal letters, excerpts from a scientific study of quantum physics, commentary on art, poetry, music, movies, and other cultural artifacts to create a uniquely contemporary synthesis. The setting shifts from Los Angeles to Michigan to Las Vegas to Vienna—all important landmarks in Wakoski's life—and this shifting enables her to move back and forth in time, providing a kind of retrospective view of that life.

The strengths of the collection are the strengths of all of Wakoski's work writ large: one has the sense of eavesdropping on an ongoing life, participating in the unfolding drama of a personal self. Wakoski always writes as if the most personal things that happen to her will be of interest to everyone, and because she writes about her subject with confidence, they usually are. But Wakoski's work, though often compelling and original, is sometimes weakened by the utter self-centeredness of her persona, who seems to regard the world outside of her head as some illusionary phenomenon from quantum physics. It is as if she has been talking aloud to herself throughout her life, reiterating certain images, and through their reiteration, willing them into being.

There is a poignant moment in the middle of this volume, in a poem called "Moneylight," when the narrator, dancing alone in her room with her shadow, has a surprising revelation:

This is
The King of Spain, I thought.
(*Medea*, 79)

This realization that the mythic images that occupy the pages of her poetry are projections of herself and have no "reality" in the world outside is reinforced as she goes to bed to sleep next to her real husband, who, unlike the mythic lovers, can offer real comfort:

He
        pulls you closer like a child
to assuage you, to hold you, to love you securely,
                                as no father,
as no lover, even the invisible one,
ever has.
(180)

· FOUR ·

The Poetry of Place

"The earth says have a place, be what that place / requires."
—William Stafford

Although Walt Whitman chanted his way across the continent in his celebrative songs, during his lifetime American poetry was an essentially northeastern venture. By the early twentieth century, however, his vision of a national poetry began to take shape. In the Midwest, the prairie poets flourished, and Chicago, home of *Poetry* magazine, became a new literary center. In Nashville, Tennessee, southern poets associated with Vanderbilt University published *Fugitive*, which became one of the leading poetry journals of the time. In California, Robinson Jeffers established his solitary outpost in Carmel and brought to the nation's readers the first significant poems of the Pacific Coast and its rugged terrain. And in the Northeast, Harlem became a new and important literary center, where African-American writers and artists created the Harlem, or "New Negro," Renaissance.

Now, in the last decade of the century, every region of the United States can validate its claim to be an area where poetry is written, published, and appreciated. With the terse mystical verse of Alaskan poet John Haines, as well as the ecologically minded poetry of W. S. Merwin, set in Hawaii, all fifty states, to varying degrees, now appear on the literary map. The irony here is that while the national audience for poetry remains relatively small, regional centers across the country have established a truly national and democratic form of American poetry, a development Walt Whitman would surely have applauded.

To a significant degree this expansion is a result of the amazing growth of university creative writing centers and programs. While there are certainly drawbacks to tying poetry so closely to the academic world, many of the poets discussed in this volume taught in these programs and played an important role in influencing a new generation of poets who then developed new writing programs at universities and colleges throughout the United States. For example, Richard Hugo, after studying with Theodore Roethke at the University of Washington, established a vibrant writing program at the University of Montana, where James Welch was one of his students. Foremost among these programs is the University of Iowa's Writer's Workshop, which, along with many other master's of fine arts programs and writer's workshops throughout the country, has graduated a significant number of notable contemporary poets, including W. D. Snodgrass and William Stafford.

Less traditional institutions and journals also played a role in the expansive and innovative nature of contemporary American poetry. In addition to Robert Creeley, who edited the influential *Black Mountain Review*, published at the experimental North Carolina College, Robert Bly in Minnesota edited *The Fifties*, which not only introduced readers to the "deep image" poetry of Bly and James Wright but also to the surreal poetry of South American writers. In the 1960s, Carolyn Kizer published *Poetry Northwest*, a journal that exemplified the regional strength of American poetry. Cleveland State University and San Jose State University have established thriving poetry centers, and regional periodicals such as the *Georgia Review, ONTHEBUS* (Los Angeles), *Ploughshares* (Boston), and *Hayden's Ferry Review* (Tempe, Arizona) continue to flourish.

Paradoxically, American poetry has also been made more international by poets such as the British W. H. Auden, Thomas Gunn, and Charles Tomlinson, who reversed the Pound/Eliot expatriate pattern and became either U.S. citizens or long-term U.S. residents. This is also the case with writers such as Nobel Prize winner Derek Walcott, a Caribbean poet who teaches at Boston University; Charles Simic, a Yugoslavian native who teaches at the University of New Hampshire; and Andrei Codrescu, a Romanian who publishes a periodical called *Exquisite Corpse* and teaches at Louisiana State University. Although often associated with particular regions, American poets are usually national and international travelers. Sylvia Plath became established as a poet while living in London; Robert Lowell set his poems in New York City, England, and South America, as well as New England; and Gary Snyder, a poet of the Northwest, has numerous poems set in Japan as well as other international locales. And no American poet is more of a "world citizen" than Allen Ginsberg, who read and published his poems all over the planet. Indeed, one of his collections is called *Planet News*.

The United States, however, as William Carlos Williams insisted, remains the place from which ideas and forms are derived, and most often it is from local or regional settings that universal truths emerge. To poets such as Gwendolyn Brooks, Muriel Rukeyser, David Ignatow, Frank O'Hara, John Ashbery, Kenneth Koch, Allen Ginsberg, and Amiri Baraka, the city remains, as Williams suggested, one of the most important of locales, one of the most telling metaphors for twentieth-century American life. And central to Whitman's dream of a national poetry that could be heard from the Atlantic to the Pacific is the role of San Francisco, a city that played an essential role in linking East and West and by doing so established itself as a major locale of the "New American Poetry."

Perhaps even more persistent than the role of cities in shaping American poetry is the continuing presence of landscape, its persistence often rooted in the Emersonian belief that the land nourishes the soul and is the metaphor that holds the secrets of this world and the world beyond. This theme is seen in the poetic landscapes of every region of the United States. It is present in Thomas McGrath's North Dakota poetry, in both the Kansas and Northwest poetry of William Stafford, the California poetry of William Everson, the North Carolinian and Northeast poetry of A. R. Ammons, as well as the Georgian poetry of James Dickey, the New England poetry of Maxine Kumin, and the Northwest poetry of Gary Snyder. Their poetry, with its unique regional landscapes, records the character and geography of the nation. It also maps the inner world of contemporary America, a spiritual and boundless place that is rediscovered in nature and celebrated in lines that often record the human quest for spiritual unity and social justice.

WILLIAM EVERSON (1912–1994) William Everson, a leading member of the San Francisco Renaissance and one of America's most accomplished hand printers, grew up in the small town of Selma, in the San Joaquin Valley. While attending Fresno State College, he heard in the visionary lines of Robinson Jeffers his own calling as a poet; like Jeffers, he saw within the California landscape what he called "one of the deepest needs of the human soul."[1] This need he further defined as "centeredness, a focus of a coherence and signification which confers meaning on the shapelessness of existence" (195). To Everson, landscape or region is more than a particular place; as with the nineteenth-century transcendentalists, it is the means by which the poet reaches a higher state of being. Landscape is a path, Everson explains, to "the abstract principle beyond . . . a mediation point between the two realities is at the heart of what regionalism really is."[2]

Everson believed that the modernist's allegiance to aesthetics rather than place assured that both poets and readers would become or remain alienated and rootless. To Everson, the true religion of the West is pantheism (155), and that certainly is at the center of the poems he wrote during the thirties when he was a San Joaquin resident and farmer. Although his vision of nature, like that of Jeffers, was often harsh and never sentimental, the divine was inevitably present: "What lies outside the closed and hollow music of this verse / Runs in the earth, in the plunge of the sun on the summer sky."[3]

Everson later concluded that his strong attachment to the San Joaquin Valley and the mystical peaks of the Sierra Nevada, which rise some 14,000 feet sixty miles east of Selma, was a limiting factor: "My identification with that area was so profound that it became in the end a threat to my continued development. Once you identify so fully with the local scene, it takes great resilience of mind somehow to probe through to the universal factor" (*Birth*, 63). Everson was expelled from his garden at the outbreak of World War II. A pacifist, he registered as a conscientious objector and was assigned to a federal work camp at Waldport, Oregon, as an alternative mode of service. His first marriage, to Edwa Poulson, did not withstand the tensions of separation, and after spending some three and one-half years at Waldport, he attempted to put his life together again.

His hostility towards and alienation from a world at war, which also echoes Jeffers's position, is recorded in a number of poems. The most striking example is "The Vow," in which he describes the torpedoing of a freighter at sea and the horrors of the survivors starving to death before they are found. Although Everson confesses that the blood of violent warriors is also in his blood, he rejects a masculine ethos of aggression and violence and vows:

> . . . not to wantonly ever take life;
> Not in pleasure or sport,
> Nor in hate,
> Nor in the careless acts of my strength
> Level beetle or beast.
>
> (*Residual*, 79)

Everson's anarchist, pacifist stance drew him to the San Francisco Bay area where other nonconformists of the period had also drifted. Among them was Kenneth Rexroth, who arrived in the thirties and was the guiding force behind the initial phase of the San Francisco Renaissance. According to Everson, the original members of the Renaissance were: Kenneth Rexroth, Robert Duncan, Phillip Lamantia, Richard Broughton, Thomas Parkinson, and Everson himself.

Everson discovered in the San Francisco area a new source of creative energy, one that promised to generate an endless amount of material. The Bay Area, Everson explains is "a marvelous, beautiful, powerfully compelling place. You can create almost endlessly out of its materials; they are that rich" (*Birth*, 163).

Everson also found a new woman to love; his marriage to poet-artist Mary Fabilli, however, took him down a very unexpected path. A devout Catholic, she was the force behind Everson's conversion to Catholicism in 1948. Because Mary's divorce from her first husband was not sanctioned by Catholic dogma, a church wedding was out of the question and the two eventually agreed to separate (divorced in 1963) in order to receive the sacraments. Everson's quest now was to live a sacred existence. In 1951 he entered the Dominican Order as a lay brother, took the name of Brother Antoninus, and remained within the Order for eighteen and one half years. His poetry during this period, collected in *The Veritable Years: 1949–1966* (1978), records his attempt to move beyond the "earthbound" poetry of his first major collection, *The Residual Years* (1948) and experience the absoluteness of the spiritual realm. Albert Gelpi believes that with the publication of *Veritable Years*, Everson / Brother Antoninus became "the most important religious poet of the second half of the century."[4] These religious poems, infused with Christian theology, religious eroticism, and psychological concepts may not speak to a secular minded audience. There are, however, a number of more universal poems that celebrate the fullness of God's creation. In "A Canticle to the Waterbirds," for example, Everson has seemingly cataloged, described, and praised every type of waterbird that inhabits the San Joaquin and the Sacramento Rivers and the westward coasts of North and South America. Like Saint Frances, the patron saint of San Francisco, he speaks to the birds, and exhorts them to praise their creator:

> Curlews, stilts and scissortails, beachcomber gulls,
> Wave-haunters, shore-keepers, rockhead-holders, all cape-top

vigilantes,
Now give God praise.
Send up the strict articulation of your throats,
And say His name.

(85)

For a number of years, Brother Antoninus did not hold any public readings. However, when the Beat writers from the East, Ginsberg and Kerouac, joined Lawrence Ferlinghetti, Gary Snyder, and other younger poets in the San Francisco area, Everson realized that a new opening had appeared, one in which the Dionysian or the prophetic mode of poetry could emerge. Everson believed that Ginsberg and Kerouac provided the spark that was missing in the earlier phase of the Renaissance. Although Rexroth and other poets associated with the first phase of the Renaissance had abandoned an academic mode of poetry, Brother Antoninus felt that they still upheld what he considered to be the Apollonian or rational aesthetics of Williams and Olson. Brother Antoninus also confronted the role of the flesh and sexuality in God's creation and one's spiritual journey. *River Root*, written in 1957, but not published until 1976, contains a very explicit description and celebration of the sexual union of a husband and wife. And *The Rose of Solitude* (1967) is based on his "intense relationship," starting in 1957, with Rose Moreno Tannlund in the late sixties. A woman once again became a catalyst for what Everson considers the third phase of his life and poetry. When he fell in love with Susanna Rickson, his third wife, he was torn between his desire to remain a lay brother and his desire to wed Susanna.[5] On December 7, 1969, at the University of California at Davis, Everson, in a very dramatic poetry reading, read "Tendril in the Mesh" which was written prior to his decision to leave the monastery (he calls it his "Swan Song").[6] He then took off his habit, fled the room and moved with Susanna and her infant son to Stinson Beach (north of San Francisco), the setting for a number of the poems in *Man-Fate* (1974). The book captures Everson's troubled mind and soul as he tries to reconcile himself to his decision to abandon the monastery and his spiritual quest.

As William Stafford, an admirer and fellow western poet has observed, most of Everson's work centers around "the slow turning of a character under duress"[7]; however, in *Man-Fate* the "duress" is sharper and more painful. It is, as indicated in the title of the third section of the volume, "A Time To Mourn," a time to reflect, to engage in confession and the seeking of absolution. Before the sea's "whisper of silence," he pleads

> Old sea, old mother,
> Grant me surcease!
>
> Lave my wounds
> And lift me home!
> (*Man-Fate*, 49)

Everson now sought to reconcile his previous beliefs in pantheism and spirituality. He reenvisioned his writings as "a life-span trilogy entitled *The Crooked Lines of God*." The third volume *The Integral Years*, a work in progress, "charts the synthesis of God-in-nature."[8] One of the more intriguing ways Everson signals this new turn is his change of costume in "The Scout." After abandoning the monk's habit, he dons a "Yellow buckskin," coat worn by an "Old Western scout." The leather frontier-style jacket, allows the poet to go "instinctively back, / Back beyond the first frontier, beyond the advent / Of agriculture or the civilized dream, / Back to the Stone Age myth and the ethos of blood" (*Man-Fate* 64). Like Snyder, Everson longs to return to the ancient religions and a perceived time when humans were one with nature. However, in "Black Hills," which begins as a dream vision, he is cognizant that this costume also signifies the slaughter and exploitation of the Indians. He pays homage to "all the great chiefs" (68), asks that they return, so "that we who must live / May live in peace!" (69) Later, he acknowledges the beauty of the moment but also "The ghost of what was" (73).

As indicated by the title of a collection of Everson's collected interviews, his is a *Naked Heart* (1992), and in such cases excess is often present. But Everson claims that the very landscape he explores in his poetry—whether it is the San Joaquin Valley and its surrounding mountains, or the pounding Pacific surf, or the rugged, Santa Cruz Mountains—is excessive so he expresses the excesses of those places. To Everson, western writers will never be tame or quiet, for their environment encourages both romanticism and a large and open aesthetic where new forms become modes of rebellion.[9]

Everson is a strong advocate of a regionalism that provides for both a sense of rootedness and of transcendence. He believes that modernists who wander within the corridors of the mind or within the abstractions of aesthetics provide no way out for those intent on moving beyond alienation and ecological disaster. The poet must discover "an inherent harmony" that exists between poetry and earth, between man and his feminine principle. And the fiery, visionary poet, who moves beyond utilitarian ends and reveals the mysteries and sacredness of nature will restore our ties to the earth; for "the ecological awakening will not be complete unless the poetic element presides over its consummation" (*Earth Poetry*, 219). Although rooted in the California landscape, Everson's poems and concept of poetry address our most pressing ecological and spiritual issues.

WILLIAM STAFFORD (1914–1993) William Stafford may have been the least alienated of a generation of poets that included John Berryman and Robert Lowell. This is not to say that Stafford is a wide-eyed optimist blind to the cosmic and social pain that marks twentieth-century life; however, because of his strong ties to his family, midwestern community, and the land, his poetry does not convey the extreme sense of isolation so central to many of the "lost world" poets. His voice is singular as he calmly and thankfully "stumbles" into the secrets of the interior meanings and measures of existence. Stafford feels "at home in the world . . . part of the human family."[10]

Central to Stafford's optimism is the role played by his imaginative and caring father who introduced his son to the mysteries of life. In "Listening" Stafford describes his father's ability to not only hear the slightest sounds of nature such as "a moth in the dark against the screen" but also the sacred sounds, "every far sound" for "more spoke to him from the soft wild night / than came to our porch for us on the wind."[11] The mysterious, spiritual realm, first beckons the father, then the son: "we still stand / inviting the quiet . . . / waiting for a time when something in the night / will touch us too from that other place" (33).

Stafford's father also taught him that his " 'job is to find out what the world is trying to be' " (107), and this assigned quest appears throughout the poetry as he explores the natural world:

> World, I am your slow guest,
> one of the common things

that move in the sun and have
close, reliable friends
in the earth, in the air, in the rock.

(157)

Stafford expresses his appreciation of his father's legacy in his "Elegy" and in "A Thanksgiving for My Father" where he tells his father that "Your life was a miracle / . . .Your restless thought / has made the world haunted" (135). In contrast to Lowell and Plath, Stafford's family portraits are strikingly affirmative. His mother is praised for her literary tastes, her voracious reading habits, her independent ways, and his aunt, uncle, and brother are also limned in appreciative tones.

Stafford also values his midwestern roots. He proudly cites that region's moral nature, its plainness, its friendliness, and especially its ties to the land which always sustain and nurture its inhabitants (30). One of Stafford's most affirmative reconstructions of midwestern life appears in the title poem of *The Rescued Year* (1966), where he remembers a time and place when "we weren't at war; we had / each day a treasured unimportance; / the sky existed, so did our town . . ." (116). Here family, love, community and the joys of the natural world are "rescued" through memory, imagination, and words. Stafford invites city dwellers to move beyond their urban existences, to go west and explore the less settled areas of their nation and minds.

Stafford records his mystical relationship to the midwestern landscape in a number of poems. "Across Kansas," recalls the origins of his mystical ties to this particular place and landscape:

Once you cross a land like that
you own your face more: what the light
struck told a self; every rock
denied all the rest of the world.

(114)

An additional experience that ties Stafford to the Kansas landscape, one he compares to an "Indian vision quest" occurred while he was a student. From a vantage point above the Cimmaron River, he marveled at the expansive Kansas sky and stars, the flowing river and seemingly limitless plains. "That encounter with the size and serenity of the earth and its neighbors in the sky has never left me. The earth was my home. I would never feel lost while it held me."[12]

Throughout his poetry Stafford explores the wild, untamed, west of both the land and the imagination. Whether it be Kansas or the Northwest, an area he moved to in 1948, the "west" of the imagination is his central subject. Like Thoreau, he would rely especially on the sounds of nature to decipher its meanings: "Wherever I stand I hear the trees / petition so. By listening / I know I'm born . . ." (*Stories*, 3).

This ability to translate the sounds of nature into poetry is represented in such titles as "Heard Under a Town Sign at the Beach," and "Whispered into the Ground," in which "The wind keeps telling us something / we want to pass on to the world: / Even far things are real" (25). In "Earth Dweller," Stafford is the humble lover of common things that are "precious" because they are the keys to entering that "far" world, that spiritual world, for "The world speaks everything to us. / It is our only friend" (196). We must develop, he tells his readers in "BiFocal," a Blake-like double vision, because "the world happens twice—once what we see it as; / second it legends itself / deep, the way it is" (48).

Stafford's romanticism is clear and strong. Nature contains a spiritual force that is "fixed, inexorable, / deep as the darkest mine" (48). It also is the Rosetta stone that can unlock the secrets of the spiritual realm. Those secrets cannot be attained through reason and fixed systems of thought. Instead receptivity, patience, intuition, and the imagination are the keys that open the doors to revelation and poetry. One "stumbles" into insight, and chance plays an essential role in discovering the mysteries of existence.

This total embrace of the Midwest and later the Northwest have mislead some critics into believing that his work is *essentially* regional. While he insists that place is at center of one's identity, he also insists that a sense of place is a universal need regardless of one's particular locale. "The earth says have a place, be what that place / requires" (75); it says "where you live wear the kind / of color that your life is" (76). To listen to the earth requires the willingness and ability to accept one's part in a larger whole, to be humble and patient. Writing about one's place is not a matter of boasting about one's region, but rather a means of acquiring wisdom and identity through the exploration of the local landscape.

If this view seems at times too blissful, Stafford acknowledges that his rural world is no utopia. Many people suffer; death, pain, small mindedness, and human indifference temper the ties to the land and community seen in many of his affirmative depictions. It is precisely for these reasons that humans need to be compassionate and discover, through patience and receptivity, the stirrings of a sacred realm beyond the frightening world that we live in. In recognizing the darker side of existence that seems inexorably a part of human existence and the result of human folly, Stafford echoes the disillusionment of the modernists: "no one ever promised for sure / that we would sing. We have decided / to moan" (201). Surprisingly, his favorite poet is Thomas Hardy, who acknowledged humanity's limited power to combat the overwhelming forces that shape our lives. In "Traveling Through the Dark," the speaker envisions a Hardy-like world where we are only given "Hobson's Choices, for even your best moves are compromises and complicated" (*Writing*, 122). The poem depicts a man stopping his car to remove a slain deer from the shoulder of a river road. Usually he would roll the carcass over the edge and into the river so that oncoming cars would not have to "swerve" to avoid hitting the deer and in doing so cause an accident. This particular doe, however, is still carrying a live fawn; the man is tempted to intervene and deliver the fawn, but he hesitates. The car, like the horse in Robert Frost's "Stopping by the Woods on a Snowy Evening," seems to be urging him to move on. It seems to have a mind of its own, "purring" and "aiming ahead." At the same time he is aware that the wilderness has its own particular lure. Caught between the human and the non human, he wrestles with his and humanity's dilemma: "I thought hard for us all—my only swerving—." The narrator obviously believes that to try to deliver the fawn on a dark and narrow canyon road would create a substantial hazard. He concludes reluctantly that endangering human life is unacceptable, even if it means sacrificing an animal, so he "pushes her over the edge into the river" (*Stories*, 61).

Stafford's poetry also contains a strong ethical and didactic tone as he attempts to free us from the distortions of reason, logic, human vanity, and false values. This is in keeping with his own strong sense of ethical behavior. Like Everson, he refused to serve in the armed forces during World War II; registered as a pacifist, and served in the Conscientious Objector Work Camps. His account of this experience is recorded in *Down in My Heart* (1947), initially written for his Creative Master's Thesis at the University of Kansas. His later social-action critiques include poems like "At the Un-National Monument Along the Canadian Border," "Watching the Jet Planes Dive," and

The Poetry of Place

"At the Bomb Testing Site." In the latter poem, often anthologized, an ancient and wise lizard, able to see "something farther off / than people could see," perceives the "flute end of consequences" as he awaits apprehensively the birth of the atomic bomb, the product of the mechanistic, fixed thinking that is so antithetical to the organic processes of nature and art. This dangerous form of mechanistic thinking is also captured in "A City is Guarded by Automatic Rockets" wherein Stafford describes the fixed flight of a ballistic missile:

> . . . the rocket
> staggers on its course; its feelers lock
> a strangle hold ahead; and—rocking—finders
> whispering 'target, target,' back and forth,
> relocating all its meaning in the dark,
> it freezes on the final stage. . . .
>
> (121)

Throughout his writing career, Stafford was eager to comment on the writing process and the teaching of poetry writing on college campuses. His easy going, honest, and informative essays, presentations, and interviews on these subjects are collected in *Writing the Australian Crawl* (1978) and *You Must Revise Your Life* (1986). As he readily admitted, his poetry had not changed dramatically since his first major publication, *West of Your City* (1960), which appeared when he was in his mid-forties. An overview of his work can be found in *The Darkness Around Us is Deep. Selected Poems* (1993), which was edited by his close friend, Robert Bly. Compared to poets like Robert Lowell, Adrienne Rich, or John Ashbery, Stafford's style and vision remained steady throughout his life. Within that recognizable mode there is a unique blend of surety and stability, but also risk-taking. In a world where connections seem forever lost, Stafford, while recognizing the difficulties of the life-journey, charts a trail to a new-found sense of place and belonging.

THOMAS McGRATH (1916–1990) With the publication of *Selected Poems: 1938–1988*, Thomas McGrath finally achieved some measure of national recognition. The volume was highly praised by critics and poets such as Terence Des Pres, Philip Levine, and Amy Clampitt when McGrath was awarded the Lenore Marshall/*Nation* Poetry Prize in 1989.[13] The relative neglect of McGrath's work is partially related to his Marxist politics; in the early fifties, for example, he was fired from his first teaching position at Los Angeles State College for refusing to cooperate with the House Un-American Activities Committee and forced to lead the life of a blacklisted academic and writer. In addition to McGrath's political poetry being out of fashion, his frequent use of an expansive line—often six beats; his unique blend of literary, vulgar, and regional speech; and his exaggerated, sometimes surreal, imagery, did not endear him to mainstream critics. McGrath's North Dakota background, which permeates his work, further distanced him from the urbane world of publishing.

That North Dakota locale, however, as Terence Des Pres points out, nurtured McGrath's political and aesthetic visions. The prairie populist stress on battling the oppressive forces of capitalism and constructing a new social order is the underlying source of McGrath's "unaffiliated far left" inclinations.[14] Populism is also the source of his belief in the common people, the workers, who in their cooperative labor present a lasting model for community.[15]

In an early poem, "Up The Dark Valley," McGrath records his ties to the Dakota landscape as he treks through the hills and into the mysteries of nature:

> Darkness hid in the draws. I was soon surrounded.
> Only the wind sound now. All through the evening,
> Homeward I walk, hearing no human sound.
>
> The birds of darkness sang back every call.[16]

Although sometimes idyllic, North Dakota, as depicted in "The Topography of History," can be a harsh land "where the mind is lost / In the mean acres and the wind comes down for a thousand miles" but it is also the land where "that voice crying for justice be heard" (12). That aspect of the land is reflected in "The Seekers," a poem about the original settlers such as McGrath's Irish grandparents, who, with others, "sought to map Fidelity" (19), to find justice in this challenging landscape, but failed in the quest. What they sought was not wealth and power, but rather a new world of community, brotherhood, and equality. However, when they arrived in the United States they were unable to locate such a world:

> Maybe with maps made going would be faster,
> But the maps made for tourists in their private cars

Have no names for brotherhood or justice, and in any case
We'll have to walk because we're going farther.
(*Selected Poems*, 19)

In "The Dreams of Wild Horses" McGrath's ancestors fail again, this time to acknowledge the sanctity of the land, animals and Indians who were here before them. In a very compressed, haiku-like stanza, with end-stopped lines, McGrath evokes a haunting sense of a tragic past:

Crazy Horse is dead
Parched buffalo bones.
Moonlight weathering in the dry corn.
(131)

That tragedy and the specter of capitalism haunt the present. Something seems to be dying throughout North Dakota; McGrath sees it as a place where "nothing goes forward" (84). He believes the region's decline began when the immigrants seized the land from the Indians and accelerated with the outbreak of World War II. Like Randall Jarrell, McGrath in a number of strong poems envisions that war as a plunge into darkness, a time of "long exile / Which the beggarman mind accepts but cannot reconcile" (29).

Despite North Dakota's succumbing to the lures of land-grabbing and capitalism, it remains in much of his poetry a source of potential renewal. In the back country, he continues his quest for a place he can call home. As he explains in "Beyond the Red River," the tourists will head South once the winter winds begin to howl on the prairies; "but still I do not leave. / I am happy enough here, where Dakota drifts wild in the universe, / Where the prairie is starting to shake in the surf of the winter dark" (128).

With the decline of the political left and the rise of McCarthyism after World War II, McGrath's exile lasted longer than he initially imagined. World War II, as well as the Korean and Vietnam wars are for him tragic examples of a fallen world now at the mercy of destructive technology and state repression. However, darkness and despair, McGrath believes, are temporary states that eventually give way to light and joy. "The dark," he explains, in "Two Songs From 'The Hunted Revolutionaries' "

is in love with forms of light,
Tall as you are and more tall.

> Though the violent darkness claims us all
> An indifferent joy is our secret fate.
> The stars shine clearest in darkest night.
> All bitterness in time grows sweet.
>
> (81)

Throughout his poetry, McGrath seeks a community that meets human needs and shares its gifts whether they be material, spiritual, or aesthetic. That oneness cannot be found in cities where workers are exploited, or in towns where commerce rules all, but it is present in the shared activities and memories of his North Dakota past. In "The Bread of This World; Praises III," McGrath's values are enacted in the Christmas Friday ritual of making bread, of providing, out of love and faith, subsistence for all. The bread itself rises "like a poor man climbing up on a cross / Toward transfiguration"(100). McGrath knows human effort is at work here:

> But we who eat the bread when we come in
> Out of the cold and dark know it is a deeper mystery
> That brings the bread to rise:
>   it is the love and faith
> Of large and lonely women, moving like floury clouds
> In farmhouse kitchens, that rounds the loaves and lives
> Of those around them . . .
>   just as we know it is hunger—
> Our own and others'—that gives all salt and savor to
>   bread.
>
> (100)

As Terence Des Pres explains, McGrath is a poet who curses but also praises. He attacks the injustices of contemporary life with biting invective and satire, but he also celebrates the wonders of existence, of love, sexual union, fatherhood, the beauties and mysteries of nature. Even fruits and vegetables become objects of celebration. As he praises, for example, the "bold strength of the celery," with "its green Hispanic / Shout! its exclamatory confetti" (76).

In addition to the shorter poems that appear in both *Movie at the End of the World: Collected Poems* (1973) and *The Selected Poems* (1988), McGrath has written one of the most ambitious longer poems of the late twentieth century, entitled *Letter to an Imaginary Friend*. Parts I and II were published in 1970, parts III and IV in 1985. In a note on parts I and II he calls this work a "pseudo-autobiography—the characters are structures of my own perceptions and feelings."[17] *Letter* also consists of actual and transformed speeches by real or literary characters which he steals, borrows, or parodies. The work represents McGrath's attempt to write primarily in a six beat line. It is complex, but readable, especially when compared to other long poems of the twentieth-century. McGrath is fond of film-like edits that cut, flash back or forward as the narration moves along. There is also, a deliberate blurring of the towns of Lisbon, Portugal, and Lisbon, North Dakota, as well as the use of medieval occult love rituals and American Indian mythology, especially the Hopi Kachina myths. This fusion of place and time provides a unifying element throughout the poem.[18]

Although the poem is 329 pages long and written over a thirty-year period, McGrath's search for unity once again emerges as the central theme of this work, and once again at the center of that unity is his Dakota experience. Like Charles Olson and William Carlos Williams, he believed that one could locate the universal in the local and the particular. Dakota like Williams's Paterson, New Jersey or Olson's Gloucester, Massachusetts represents the world at large. As McGrath puts it, "Dakota is everywhere."

A few lines from this expansive epic capture McGrath's ability to invoke his childhood in lush, effusive language reminiscent of Dylan Thomas:

> Leaving the ark-tight farm in its blue and mortgaged weather
> To sail the want-all seas of my five dead summers
> Past the dark ammonia-and-horse-piss smelling barn
> And the barnyard dust, adrift in the turkey wind
> Or pocked with the guinea-print and staggering script
> Of the drunken-sailor ducks, a secret language; leaving
> Also my skipping Irish father, land-locked Sinbad,
> With his head in a song-bag and his feet stuck solid
> On the quack-grass-roofed and rusting poop-deck of the north
>   forty,
> In the alien corn: the feathery, bearded, and all-fathering
>   wheat.
>
>   (1, 2)

Letter is an odyssey that begins in pain but envisions the possibility of redemption through the special sense of place that informs the work throughout. For McGrath, language not only describes but recreates the landscape and memories that have given meaning to his life. His links to Walt Whitman are strong, and to read his work is to discover not a doctrinaire political poet, but rather a poet with an expansive mind and imagination that mirrors the vast prairie he loved so much.

JAMES DICKEY (1923–1997)   Although his education and career were delayed by his service in World War II and the Korean War, James Dickey's rise in the world of poetry unlike McGrath's, was swift and sure. His first volume of poems *In the Stone* (1960) appeared when he was thirty-seven, but by the end of the sixties, Dickey was one of the most lauded poets in the United States. He received a National Book Award for *Buckdancer's Choice* (1960), was celebrated in *Life* Magazine, appointed Consultant in Poetry at the Library of Congress (1967–1969), published his first collected poems (*Poems: 1957–1969*), was praised as one of the most electrifying readers of poetry since Dylan Thomas, and by the end of the decade was appointed Professor of English and Writer-in-Residence at the University of South Carolina. With the publication of his best selling novel, *Deliverance* (1970), and the film version of that novel (1972), in which he played a southern sheriff, James Dickey became a nationally known figure and presented the nation with a compelling vision of the American South.

Educated at Vanderbilt University, the institution associated with the Fugitive poets and the *Fugitive* literary magazine, Dickey rejected the witty, ironic poems of John Crowe Ransom and the classical values of Allen Tate; however, he did endorse the anti-industrialist stance of the writers who appeared in *I'll Take My Stand* (1930) and was especially taken by Donald Davidson's defense of regionalism. It, Davidson argued, enabled America to express its multifaceted character through its distinctive regional cultures.[19]

Dickey is certainly a southern poet. He paints vivid images of the Georgia coastal plains in "At Darien Bridge," "Salt Marsh," "The Shark's Parlor," and "Slave Quarters." He captures the Georgia mountains in "In the Mountain Tent" and "Springer Mountain," and renders the industrial and rural areas of Georgia in "Chenille." He records the strange landscape of profuse Georgian flora and fauna amidst an automotive junkyard in "Cherrylog Road," recalls the days of slavery and Jim Crow in "Slave Quarters" and "Buckdancer's Choice," and captures the religious rhythms and conflicts of the South in "May Day Sermon." To hear Dickey perform these poems is to listen to the unique rhythms and dialects of southern speech.

Imbedded in many of the poems is a derivation of southern agrarianism. Dickey lashes out at industrialism and the technological, urban world of the twentieth century. Unlike the agrarians, however, he does not romanticize the supposed cultured and humane world of the agrarian South, but instead seeks, like Mary Oliver and Gary Snyder, to restore his ties to the natural world. Dickey comments:

> I like to think the major theme . . . is continuity between the self and the world, and the various attempts by men to destroy this (wars and so on; heavy industry and finance and the volume turnover system). I try to say something about the individual's way or ways, of protecting this sense of continuity in himself, or of his attempts to restore it. Much of my work deals with rivers, mountains, changes of weather, seas, and the air.[20]

The destructive impact of the industrial system is seen in "Chenille," which is set in Dalton, Georgia, a once rural setting that is now dominated by factories producing chenille spreads. To Dickey, there is nothing "sadder than country boys working in factories." The machine and the mass production of goods—the "volume turnover system," produce an unimaginative, distorted, officially sanctioned product:

> These you can buy anywhere.
> They are made by machine
> From a sanctioned, unholy pattern
> Rigid with industry.
> They hoard the smell of oil.[21]

Contrasted to these "unholy" bedspreads are those crafted by a crazed but highly imaginative grandmother. The woven beasts on her spreads are "unofficial," unsanctioned. They "cannot be thought of / By the wholly sane;" they are "Like the beasts of Heaven" (119–20). Dickey has stopped to sleep in her house; in the coldness of that house he is covered with her spread to save him from freezing. This magical weaver, who is not a part of the industrialized, machine world becomes in some respects Dickey's crone / muse figure who is free of those twentieth-century forces that separate humans from the world of animals. Equally as important to Dickey, her imagination is free; she is not tied to an officially approved vision of reality. In his undergraduate days at Vanderbilt University, Dickey learned from his mentor, Monroe Spears, a critic of eighteenth-century literature, that the poet can lie or imagine profitably and through the powers of the imagination and the process of poetry become one with the beasts and nature.

Many of Dickey's strongest poems capture that sense of union with the primal world that is a persistent theme in American Romantic poetry. In "The Owl King," a fantasy poem, an all seeing owl king teaches a blind child to see and believe everything. In "The Salt Marsh," the speaker initially panics as he is lost in a sea of marsh grass that reaches to the top of his head and blocks his sight. However, once the speaker perceives the weaving motions of the moving, swaying grass, and bends with the grass, he becomes part of this infinite sea of grass.

In poems such as "In the Mountain Tent" and "Springer Mountain," Dickey's vision, like Mary Oliver's, dramatizes our need to escape the confines of the technological world and reestablish our ties to the creation at large. Dickey's vision, however, is much more brutal and bestial than Oliver's. In "The Heaven of Animals," he envisions the hereafter through the eyes of animals as they awaken in paradise. Here, those soulless creatures are completely instinctual as they eternally enact their appointed roles as either predator or prey in the most perfect of hunting grounds. Dickey identifies with both prey and predator; however, as indicated in "Encounter in the Cage Country" he seems most celebrative when he can make contact with and is acknowledged by the predatory beasts, in this case a caged black panther in a London Zoo.

One of Dickey's most controversial poems concerning the desire to become one with the animal world is "The Sheep Child." The poem concerns the southern legend of a stillborn sheep child—the offspring of a Georgia farm boy and a ewe that is pickled in alcohol, stored in a jar, and set on a dusty shelf of an Atlanta museum. This legend functions as a tale to ensure that farm boys would marry their own kind and not violate civilization's taboos. What makes Dickey's rendering of this tale both unique and controversial, is his inclusion of the sheep child's tender rendering of the coupling of his parents, man and ewe, and his haunting mystical self image:

In the summer sun of hillside, with my eyes
Far more than human. I saw for a blazing moment
The great grassy world from both sides,
Man and beast in the round of their need.

(253)

Although he now resides in a dark and dusty corner of the museum, the sheep child insists that he is "most surely living / In the minds of farm boys . . ." (253).

Dickey insists that he "intended no blasphemy or obscenity in writing this poem, but rather wanted to illustrate the "blind and renewing need for contact between any kind of living creature with another kind. This need is much larger than and transcends any kind of man-made, artificial boundaries" (*Self*, 165).

Dickey's world, however, is clearly not the harmonious, innocent, pastoral world of many nature poets. Its tooth and claw nature, its lack of law and boundaries suggest a darker vision, and that vision is central to his novel *Deliverance* in which violence itself becomes a means of redemption and revival for a "soft," suburbanized protagonist who enters the primordial wilderness to become initially the prey but later emerges as the predator.

Dickey's poetry does not always dwell on wilderness themes: it also renders, for example, the harmful effects of southern oppression and repression. In "Slave Quarters," the speaker ponders the impact of the southern slave master who venerates his wife but satisfies his sexual urges in the slave quarters with a defenseless black woman. Dickey, familiar with W. J. Cash's *Mind of the South*, as well as Faulkner's work, admonishes the master's hypocrisy and coldheartedness in refusing to acknowledge his mulatto offspring:[22]

What it is to look once a day
Into an only
Son's brown, waiting, wholly possessed
Amazing eyes, and not
Acknowledge, but own?

(239)

In "May Day Sermon," another of his longer poems with a southern setting, a Baptist woman preacher delivers a farewell sermon to the women of Gilmer County, Georgia. Her text is based on a folk tale about a Georgia hill farmer who strips and brutally beats his daughter for her sexual activities as he shouts Scripture at her. Later that night, she kills her father with an ax and runs an ice pick through one of his eyes. She then frees the barn animals and rides away with her one-eyed lover on his motorcycle. To both the speaker and Dickey, the father's repressive vision fails to acknowledge the natural urges of life and the procreative forces of nature, a distortion that is the result of a warped form of southern Puritanism.

"The Slave Quarters," "The May Day Sermon," as well as "Falling" and "Firebombing" are longer poems that take on mythic and / or historical importance and emerge as works that go beyond the theme of individual transformation. Dickey had always been drawn to the mythic, but these extended works are more experimental in terms of content, narration, and line which is often longer and split by open spaces which Dickey uses to accurately record the mind's movement from one thought or image to the next.

As "Firebombing" illustrates, Dickey's work does not always focus on the rural South. In this poem the speaker, lost in the trivialities of suburban life, fails to feel guilty about his participation in the horrendous firebombings of Japanese cities and civilian populations. In addition, "Falling" imaginatively recreates the actual fall of a twenty-nine year old stewardess who was sucked through an emergency door of an airplane and fell to her death in a Kansas cornfield. However, despite these exceptions, the Georgia countryside, is at the center of his work.

Dickey was one of the most provocative poets of the sixties and early seventies. His poetry measures and dramatizes the costs of living in a disconnected world in which our hearts, minds, and souls are shrunken if not destroyed. His is a poetry rooted in southern soil and heritage, but it speaks to the nation and the world at large. What is unfortunate is that his later poetry did not retain the energy and intensity of his earlier work.

This is due partly to his decision to devote most of his time to the writing of novels. But it may also be attributed to the fact that as he aged he became more aware of the difficulties of transformation and renewal, more aware of the aging process and the corrosive impact of time on personal and family relationships. His later poems become more weary, more suggestive of accommodation than ascendance, even though there is a struggle and even an occasional victory. In addition, the poems are more centered on the history of the South, and less tied to the land and the wilderness.

Dickey seems to be on stronger grounds in *The Strength of the Fields* (1979). In the title poem which he wrote for and read at President Carter's inaugural celebration in 1977, he envisions the President, also from Georgia, alone in the fields, asking the "Lord of all the fields" for guidance. The president links himself to the natural world, to the simple things, as he eventually discovers that "Wild hope can also spring from tended strength / Everything is in that / That and nothing but kindness. / More kindness, dear Lord of the renewing green."[23]

If poems like this reflect a more subdued Dickey, he still draws strength from his southern roots and southern soil. The resulting poems are honest and moving, and their language is precise. These are the very qualities that Dickey bases his own demanding and often harsh critical judgments on. *The Whole Motion: Collected Poems, 1945–1992* (1992) gives us the opportunity to survey the fullness of Dickey's poetic achievement. Taken as a whole, Dickey's poems convey a compelling sense of the South, its landscape and its history.

MAXINE KUMIN (B. 1925) Maxine Kumin's connection to the New England landscape is especially strong:

I cannot imagine myself living, as a writer, outside New England. . . . Clearly the impulse for poems is here for me, in the vivid turns of the seasons, in the dailyness of growing things . . . without religious faith and without the sense of primal certitude that faith brings, I must take my only comfort from the natural order of things."[24]

This statement suggests that Kumin's roots are rural and New England; however, she was born and raised in Germantown, Pennsylvania, a fashionable suburb outside of Philadelphia. She spent her early childhood in a Catholic convent school, an experience that created confusion and ambivalence about her Jewish identity. She graduated from Radcliffe in 1946 with a degree in history and literature; soon after she married Victor Kumin. After receiving her M.A. from Radcliffe in 1948, she began her life as a suburban housewife and mother, giving birth to two daughters and a son.

By the mid 1950s, however, Kumin, constricted by her domestic roles, turned to poetry. It was, she explains, "a way of saving myself because I was so wretchedly discontented, and I felt so guilty about being discontented."[25] Kumin enrolled in John Holmes's Poetry

Workshop at the Boston Center for Adult Education, where she, Anne Sexton, Holmes, and later George Starbuck developed their vision and craft. Bonded by their belief in poetry and their dissatisfaction with domestic life, Kumin and Sexton became close friends, sharing and critiquing each other's works and collaborating on a number of children's books. Kumin was shaken by Sexton's suicide and has written a number of prose pieces and moving poems about their relationship.[26]

Kumin's earliest poems show little evidence that she would later turn to nature. Instead, they focus on her childhood, her family, time, death, and the inevitable separation of family members. "Nightmare," for example, recounts the parting of daughter and mother, the latter lamenting: "This dwelt in me who does not know me now, / . . . the first cell that divided separates us."[27]

These "tribal poems," as Kumin calls them, are where she explores her relationships with her family and ancestors, as in, for example, "My Great-Grandfather: A Message Long Overdue." Her portrait of her father in "The Pawnbroker" is a moving elegy that captures the detail and hardships of her father's life and the unspoken love they shared: "Firsthand I had from my father a love ingrown / tight as an oyster, and returned it / as secretly . . ." (194).

The importance of family, whether it be her great-grandparents or her own grandchild, is constant in Kumin's work. In a 1977 essay entitled "The Tribal Poems," Kumin asserted that the "loss of the parent, relinquishment of the child" were "central to her work" (*Make a Prairie*, 115). When interviewed in 1979, she explained: "I feel I have a strong sense of tribe and ancestor, an ancestor worship, or desire to find out about my roots. I think that if you have Eastern European roots, as I do, and if you're a product of immigrant grandparents or great grandparents who left the Old World behind, you have a chronic sense of unfulfillment" (48).

Kumin is constantly seeking a means of gaining fulfillment in this world. Taking her cue from the poet Louise Bogan, she argues that the poet must confront "the tragic elements in human life. . . . Illness, old age, and death. . . . These are the subjects that the poet must speak of very nearly from the first moment that he began to speak" (*Ground Time*, n.p.). Throughout her poetry, however, she turns to family for fulfillment because there exists an unbroken chain of mothers and daughters, an "Envelope of Almost-Infinity" (65).

Kumin logically and emotionally joins this sense of continuity in the human domain to that continuity present in nature. This shift is the result of her eventual move to Warner, New Hampshire, where, like Frost before her, she became farmer and poet. "January 25th," describes the endurance and constancy of nature in the depths of a New Hampshire winter:

> . . . under twelve knee-deep layers
> of mud in last summer's pond
> the packed hearts of peepers are beating
> barely, barely repeating
> themselves enough to hang on.
>
> (205)

"Continuum: A Love Poem" creates a romantic pastoral where she and her husband, Victor, harvest wild grapes in the September rain, an annual ritual that celebrates the continuum of nature's bounty as well as the couple's love.

Although "Pasture Poems" is a major section in *The Nightmare Factory* (1970), it is in *Up Country* (1972) that she adopts the New Hampshire landscape as her dominant setting and source for rural characters. In "The Hermit Poems," for example, Kumin employs a male persona to represent her own love of nature, doubting an audience would accept the notion of a female hermit. She also introduces her neighbor Henry Manley, another rustic character, who appears in a number of poems. The very title of *Up Country* contrasts sharply with that of *The Nightmare Factory*, where dark dreams of personal harm, war, the Holocaust, and fear of death await the dreamer in the title poem. In *Up Country*, neither the new nor the previously published poems ignore death and tragedy; but the themes of love and nature override these notes. The volume earned Kumin the Pulitzer Prize.

Although her work after *Up Country* is not exclusively pastoral, an empathy for the natural world is a persistent theme. Particularly striking are the Amanda Poems in *House, Bridge, Fountain, Gate* (1975, dedicated to Anne Sexton), in which her life-long love of horses develops into a near mystical relationship with her mare:

> O Amanda, burn out my dark.
> Press the warm suede of your horseflesh

against my cold palm.
Take away all that is human.

(*Ground Time*, 135)

Again and again the natural world suggests renewal and salvation. New life is present "In the Pea Patch" when you snap open a pod and ". . . nine little fetuses / nod their cloned heads" (11) or in the urine of the geldings that "drench the everlasting grass / with the rich nitrogen / that repeats them" (85). It even arises out of the horses' excrement. While Kumin is raking the manure from the stalls in the morning, she observes "how sparrows come to pick / the redelivered grain, how inky-cap / coprinus mushrooms spring up in a downpour" and concludes by stating that "I honor shit for saying: We go on" (72).

However, like Frost, Kumin has a multifaceted view of life and nature. "Custodian," describes dogs who kill, devour, and retch up frogs and children who capture "polliwogs in the sun-flecked hollow / . . . and lovingly squeeze / the life out of them in their small fists."[28] In "Encounter in August," the speaker is watching a bear eat the string beans she is growing, she acknowledges that "This is not Eden, . . . where frost never overtook a patch" (22). The book cover for *Nurture* (1989), which has a Disney-like quality, strikes a false or incomplete note given Kumin's often tough realistic images of a world rooted in struggle, violence, and death: "Nature a catchment of sorrows. / We hug each other. No lesson drawn" (24). Still, humans must become custodians of that world, preserving and nurturing rather than destroying nature (14). From "The Vealers," an earlier poem that depicts the brutal and horrendous treatment of calves raised to satisfy the human appetite, to her more recent poems in *Nurture*, Kumin takes it as her task to expose the causes of our ecological disasters. In *Nurture* she forcefully and angrily records how human greed and folly exploit and threaten the caribou, the manatee, the trumpeter swan, the arctic fox, the Aleutian goose, and other endangered species. As a headnote to her collection, *Our Ground Time Here Will Be Brief* (1982), she quotes Gary Snyder: "The *real* work is to be the warriors that we have to be, to find the heart of the monster and kill it. . . . To check the destruction of the interesting and necessary diversity of life on the planet so that the dance can go on a little better for a little longer" (*Ground Time*, n.p.). Kumin willingly takes on the roles of defender and rescuer of animals and becomes the womanly protector of that world:

... I suffer, the critic proclaims,
from an overabundance of maternal genes.

Bring me your fallen fledgling, your bummer lamb,
lead the abused, the starvelings, into my barn.
Advise the hunted deer to leap into my corn.

(*Nurture*, 3)

In addition to assuming this ecological stance in her poetry, Kumin has, in her own words, "grown bolder, more overtly political, and certainly more despairing" (*Make a Prairie*, 177). She moves from her growing awareness of the evils of the Holocaust in "The Amsterdam Poem" to a more engaged, scathing indictment of her own political and social worlds in "The Summer of the Watergate Hearings," where she compares Amanda's worm-infested horse stools with the human parasites infesting the nation's capital. In "Lines Written in the Library of Congress After the Cleanth Brooks Lecture," she sees her role as "Consultant in Poetry," her pastoral life in New Hampshire, and Brooks's urbane lecture as having no impact whatsoever on the inevitable drift toward nuclear destruction. Agreeing with W. H. Auden that "Poetry / makes nothing happen" (*Ground Time*, 41), she laments its powerlessness.

During her travels through the Mideast, recorded in *The Long Approach* (1985), she confronts the madness of that region of the world when she learns of a censored film clip in which President Assad's Syrian troops are "ordered / to strangle puppies and squeeze out blood / to drink as he reviewed the troops...."[29] Kumin is devastated and bewildered: "How did we get here, / the poet wonders, in the name of God" (36)?

"Going home" is the only means of surviving for Kumin. In her early work, "home" suggests the settled land of the pastoral. In her later poetry, however, she is more at home in the wilderness. Quoting from Thoreau's *Maine Woods*, she now sees nature not as a garden but as an uncultivated realm, "not lawn, nor pasture, nor mead, nor woodland, nor lea, nor arable, nor waste-land. It was the fresh and natural surface of the planet Earth, as it was made forever and ever—to be the dwelling of man" (*Long Approach*, preface, n.p.).

Kumin has never taken comfort from religion. In such poems as "Address to the Angels" and "Heaven as Anus," she can be very angry at a God who, if he exists, allows the brutal treatment of humans and animals to occur. Her comfort is derived from personal love, the natural world, language, and poetry. To Kumin, words and metaphors remain honest and holy in a dishonest and unholy world. "The distillation of everyday life experiences," Kumin declares, "is exactly what I am trying to particularize and order in poetry" (*Make a Prairie*, 35). This focus on everyday life and her often plain diction give her poetry a documentary quality; the source of the imaginative realm in her poetry is clearly her gift for metaphor, which provides a unique contrast with its factual content and unembellished diction.

The most controversial aspect of Kumin's work is her ongoing commitment to traditional forms. Kumin cites W. H. Auden's tetrameter line as one of the most influential factors in her development as a poet and insists that traditional form enhances her work and forces her to a level of diction and metaphor that she could never reach in more open forms. She is one of a group of formalist poets who feels comfortable writing in couplets, and she takes special joy in skillfully employing subtle rhymes. The difficulty here is that her traditional aesthetic values may appear to clash with her ongoing interests in social and political concerns and her embrace of the wilderness. Dana Gioia speculates that her utilitarian language creates moving but not memorable poems. She is a writer, Gioia claims, "who has applied her diligence more to exploring her own life than to the possibilities of her medium." By contrast, Alicia Ostriker praises her rhythms and formalist skills as becoming more "sure—so that her poems become increasingly unforgettable, indispensable."[30]

Both the personal elements of her work and her formalist concerns continue to be a factor in her later poems. This late poetry, like that of Elizabeth Bishop's, focuses on "questions of travel," and draws from a wide variety of landscapes. In *Looking for Luck* (1992) she searches far and wide for a "geographic center"—from Bangkok to Alaska, but returns to the pleasures that sustain her in New Hampshire. And *Connecting the Dots* (1996) links the events of her ongoing family life to the rhythms of rural life and the natural world.

In both content and form Kumin carries on a number of the traditions associated with Robert Frost, who believed that writing free verse was like playing tennis without a net: "Yes," she agrees, "I *am* a regional poet. At least I've *become* one . . . I have been twittered with the epithet 'Roberta Frost' which is not a bad thing" (*Make a Prairie*, 48).

The Poetry of Place

The connection is understandable, yet Kumin's commitments and attachments as daughter, mother, farmer, and ecologist, as well as world citizen, create an expansiveness that is not always apparent in Frost's work. Her work, like that of many of the poets in this chapter, may be centered on the local, but the best of it transcends the scenes and events of a particular place and often speaks of larger social issues. In Kumin's case, as in Thoreau's, the New England landscape becomes a looking glass in which one can view the world. As she puts it, "In a poem one can see the scene of place as an anchor for larger concerns, as a link between narrow details and global realities—location is where we start from" (*In Deep*, 170).

A. R. AMMONS (B. 1926)   A. R. Ammons is a committed and insightful seeker of the secrets of nature and the mysteries of art. His explorations of nature mostly take place in the East—the rural countryside of North Carolina (his birthplace), the New Jersey shoreline, and the woodlands of upstate New York, where he lives and teaches (Cornell University). At times, the poem's locales are very specific: "Corson's Inlet" (New Jersey), "Cascadilla Falls" (New York), "Delaware Water Gap" (New Jersey, Pennsylvania). Most frequently, however, he leaves unnamed the beaches, dunes, woods, lakes, streams, and mountains he observes and contemplates. Nature in these poems remains elemental, autonomous, and mysterious.

The primary purpose of his observations of the physical world is to examine our relationship to it. As in Emerson's work, metaphysical and epistemological questions are framed and reframed as the mind tries to wrestle from nature the secrets of existence. Ammons, as Harold Bloom explains, is "like [Wallace] Stevens, a descendent of the great originals of [the] American Romantic tradition, Emerson and Whitman."[31] Like these predecessors, Ammons seeks the infinite in the finiteness of existence and the forms of language.

The complex and many sided nature of the relationship of the mind to the world can be seen in the very title of Ammons's first publication, *Ommateum* (1955), which means "compound eye" and suggests the multiplicity of vision that marks his work. The evolution of this vision is clearly seen in the chronologically arranged *Selected Poems: Expanded Edition* (1986). The very first poem, "So I Said I Am Ezra," recounts the separation of the speaker, Ezra, from the sea and the wind, elements that speak of a world beyond human existence. The persona, based on one of Ammons's childhood friends who was killed during World War II, also suggests the biblical scribe Ezra as well as the American poet Ezra Pound. The poem records the failure of the prophet/poet to assert his identity with and ties to the physical and spiritual realms. Language fails him; three times, he proclaims "I am Ezra," but there is no echo from sea, wind, or land, and "a word too much repeated / falls out of being." Therefore Ezra "went out into the night / like a drift of sand."³² The scene is a hostile wasteland, a symbolic landscape of "bleached and broken fields" in which the human voice is silenced by the unsympathetic, indifferent elements.

The fear of death, the absence of a validated identity, and the sense of alienation in these poems all attest to the impact of modernism on Ammons's voice. Yet amidst the darkness there is a romantic affirmation. In "Bees Stopped" the speaker discovers "life was everywhere / so I went on sometimes whistling" (2). Ammons's work contains what Bloom calls "an oddly negative exuberance" (*Bloom,* 588). While the poet acknowledges the bleakness of existence and the sense of existential angst that permeates twentieth-century thought, he cannot reduce life to a single negative or positive generalization. To look carefully at nature is to realize its complexities and paradoxes. To experience nature is to experience life.

Ammons's complex vision is evident in his examination of the romantic quest to transcend time and space. Although aware of the limitations of finiteness—death and mutability—he fears that in ascending to the infinite, the "overall," as he calls it, he would enter an abstract realm, an "unseasonal, undifferentiated empty stark" sphere (9). Like Stevens, Ammons believes that "Death is the mother of beauty," and to leave this world is to be deprived of the richness and variety of life. In addition, in the infinite realm, there is no place for the imaginative mind and the language of poetry. So it is not surprising that in "Gravelly Run," Ammons is initially content to stay put within the here and now: "I don't know somehow it seems sufficient / to see and hear whatever coming and going is, / losing the self to the victory / of stones and trees (11). Here he claims "cedar's gothic-clustered / spires could make / green religion in winter bones." Ammons, however, is not about to embrace an easy pantheistic solution. Despite his attempts to find unity within the natural world, each natural object exists singularly. So his poetry is not the place for ecstatic Blakean visions. "I see no / god in the holly. . . ." In addition, he and nature remain separate entities; what appeared to be the possibility of union with nature ends with separation, so he tells himself, "stranger, / hoist your burdens, get on down the road" (11).

Ammons, like Stevens, does find solace in the wondrous workings of the mind, or the imagination, a faculty that enables humans to be of this world and yet go beyond the world of the here and now. In "Guide," for example, the wind can be seen as a symbol of the imagination, for it is an immaterial object that can be recognized only by the effects of its motions. And the wind exists at the margins or peripheries of both the physical and spiritual spheres. In contrast with his "Ezra" poem, the wind here *is* his guide and inspiration. It validates his avoidance of the "overall," explaining, "to be / you have to stop not-being and break / off from *is* to *flowing* . . ." (23). This relationship between wind/imagination and poet is reciprocal, because the wind needs some physical form just as the poet's imagination requires words.

The imagination moves Ammons to explore his special place, an ecological realm where both diversity and unity are at work. He is drawn to the borders of existence where opposites interact, where one can avoid "either/or" concepts and embrace "both/and." Throughout his poetry, the sea suggests changelessness while the land signifies both change and diversity. It is at the intersection of these two elements where the one and the many come into play. For Ammons the quest is not to attain that transcendental state of oneness that effaces diversity; instead, it is "To maintain balance / between one and many by / keeping in operation both one and many" (38).

Ammons in "One: Many" records the diversity of nature and America in a marvelous catalogue of images that celebrates the richness of the physical world and the unique diversity of the American nation. The reader hears place-names, sees a variety of scenes, visits cities, towns, and villages. And we hear of diverse events simultaneously taking place in America, even seemingly banal events such as that of a school teacher in Duquesne, Iowa, buying a Volkswagen. His central point is this: "from variety an over-riding unity, the expression of / variety" (40).

Ammons exemplifies that distinctly American perspective that is inclusive rather than exclusive and relies on process and openness rather than on preconceived ideas and rigid mental structures. He is also democratic; as he writes in "Still": "though I have looked everywhere / I can find nothing lowly / in the universe . . . moss, beggar, weed, tick, pine, self, magnificent / with being!" (42). In "Corsons

The Poetry of Place

Inlet," one of his most famous poems, he skillfully adapts his belief in process and openness to the very act of composing a poem. The poem emerges out of the event itself, a walk along a New Jersey inlet. Because he is active, involved in an event and in motion, he is "released from forms, / from the perpendiculars, / straight lines, blocks, boxes, binds / of thought." Geography and form become one as the verse captures the "swerves of action / . . . dunes of motion, / organizations of grass, white sandy paths of remembrance / in the overall wandering of mirroring mind" (43).

Despite this correspondence between nature and art, he is unable to synthesize or unify the scene: "Overall is beyond me" (44). Since nature itself is in a state of flux, and always an unfolding event, poetry must mirror that process. As John Ashbery points out, Ammons's aesthetic is comparable with that of "action painters" such as Jackson Pollock, who viewed painting as an open-ended act, an event or process not hindered by aesthetic boundaries or predetermined subject matter (*Bloom*, 59).

Although Ammons includes the city in his celebration of a diverse world, he is most at home in the rural world. As indicated in the punning title of one of his most moving praises of nature, "The City Limits," urban life limits us, cuts us off from the events of nature that can sustain us. Employing the second person, Ammons draws the reader into his own discovery that the radiance "pours its abundance without selection into every / nook and cranny not overhung or hidden," that it even "illuminates the glow-blue / bodies and gold-skeined wings of flies swarming the dumped / guts of a natural slaughter or the coil of shit . . ." (89). Here, even "the dark / work of the deepest cells is of a tune with May bushes" (89).

However, Ammons cannot find within the landscape an image or metaphor for human longing, and it is partially because of this absence in nature that Ammons refuses to simplistically value one element over another. The finite, the infinite, nature, the city all have limitations, all are incomplete. Like Stevens, Ammons is never comfortable with a final, unconditional vision of existence. It is, in fact, more pleasurable and profitable to imaginatively explore these complexities within the forms and figures of poetry.

Ammons is indeed a witty poet who focuses on a limited number of philosophic themes, yet he employs an amazing variety of perspectives and voices. He can be as expansive as Whitman, piling up his examples to make a point, or, as his 160 or so *Really Short Poems*

(1990) point out, as succinct as Dickinson as he cuts to the bone. There is ample description in his work, but also enough abstract thinking to satisfy the most philosophic of readers. Ammons's voice is original, but it unobtrusively includes echoes from the literary past. Although he is a philosophical poet, his diction can be casual, off-handed, colloquial, and, because of his study of biology and chemistry while an undergraduate at Wake Forest College, it can be highly technical. Long before it was in general use, for example, he used the word *ecology* and composed lines such as: "honor the chemistries, platelets, hemoglobin kinetics, / the light-sensitive iris, the enzymic intricacies / of control" (21). He is experimental, open to new forms and a believer in process. His *Tape for the Turn of the Year* (1965), a verse journal composed on a single roll of adding-machine tape, its breadth of line and total number of lines determined by the size of the tape. *Sphere: The Form of a Motion* (1974), which won the Bollingen Prize, consists of 155 sections, each consisting of four three-line stanzas; amazingly, the entire volume is one continuous sentence. This radical use of enjambment as well as his frequent use of colons throughout the work suggest the ongoing processes of nature and art. All parts are equal and connected to a larger whole.[33] Ammons also considers the relationship between art and nature in "Essay in Poetics," a lengthy and provocative verse essay.

Unlike McGrath or Snyder, Ammons is quick to dismiss any pragmatic or political functions for poetry. "Poetry," Ammons states, "has never seemed to me to be the best instrument for communication of a practical kind. I don't think a poem that is propaganda or speaks to a specific issue is capable of entertaining the manysidedness of one's assent to and exception from realities" (216, 217).

Although Ammons' work is highly regarded by many critics, Robert Pinsky raises an interesting objection to it. He sometimes finds it "dull and strained" as Ammons wrestles with the problem of imposing words on reality, in a skittish and ambivalent fashion. More critical, however, is Pinsky's observation that there is "a diminishing of poetry's scope" in devoting most of one's work to Romantic epistemology." (*Bloom*, 194). Specific human and social affairs are not emphasized in Ammons's poetic landscape, although it is evident from "One: Many" and such poems as "Easter Sunday" and "Parting" that these matters are not altogether excluded. His 1993 *tour de force, Garbage*, is a 121-page poem in unrhymed couplets dedicated to creatures microscopic and large that feed on the refuge of

The Poetry of Place

civilization. But looking at the literal garbage in our lives so intently
forces us to think about it as a metaphor for waste and decay in the
largest sense, although Ammons constantly avoids *specifying* the
metaphor. He wants us, through the *idea* of garbage, to think about
human existence and what it means, in this time and this place.

MARY OLIVER (B. 1935)   Since the publication of her Pulitzer
Prize–winning volume, *American Primitive*, in 1983, Mary Oliver has
become one of America's most revered nature poets. Prior to that volume, she had published *No Voyage and Other Poems* (1963 and 1965);
The River Styx, Ohio, and Other Poems (1972); *Twelve Moons* (1979); and
two chapbooks, *The Night Traveler* (1978) and *Sleeping in the Forest*
(1978). From 1963 to 1983, her work focused on her relationship with
the rural landscapes of Ohio, where she grew up, New England, and
Cape Cod, Massachusetts, her adoptive home. Her poetry has
evolved into one of the strongest reassertions of our ties to the natural
world in contemporary American poetry. Like Robert Frost, she tills
her soil with delight and wisdom; and like Frost, she was first published in England and is often deceptively clear. But in her insistence
on probing the internal mysteries of nature, the mind, the imagination, and the connections that bind humans to the natural realm, she
is also closely linked to James Wright, Galway Kinnell, Theodore
Roethke, and her neighbor on the Cape, Stanley Kunitz.

She also, like Thoreau, insists on confronting the essentials of
nature before ascending into an unearthly realm beyond a present
reality. The title of *American Primitive* is especially apt; in her connection to the land, the wilderness, she, like Thoreau, is both an American and a primitive. Primitive, that is, in her faith in the redemptive
powers of the natural world. Her diction is taut, precise, penetrating,
and evocative. She is accessible yet also mysterious as she leads her
readers to a rediscovery of their ties to nature.

Oliver's embrace of wilderness values is clear in her earliest work.
"Swans on the River Ayr," for example, is a lament for the once wild
creatures who roamed freely over the waterways of the world and
the imagination. Now tamed, they are domesticated, city birds who
beg bread from the visitors to the banks of the River Ayr (Scotland).
Despite this loss of wilderness, which hampers one's ability to
dream and imagine, there remains, for Oliver, as illustrated in
"Morning in a New Land," the possibility of once again experiencing
an Edenic sense of renewal and celebrating the gift of an unspoiled

natural world. In nature there is always another morning and hence a new land for humans to discover.

Oliver is aware that any such transcendent experience is temporary, subject eventually to the corrosive elements of time and the tragic aspects of human existence. Her depictions of rural Ohio continually evoke the cycles of birth, decay, and death. "The River Styx" in *Ohio and Other Poems* presents a bleak, brown, autumn landscape that mirrors the physical decline of an arthritic grandmother and a dying agrarian economy. The speaker, a child, wishes there were some magical way of freeing humans from the darker, harsher side of life; however, fate, time, and mystery rule. It is this realization that plunges the speaker into the adult world of pain and sorrow.

Some of the poems written in the late seventies also capture the darker elements of Oliver's work. In "Farm Country" there is a grizzly image of a farmer about to butcher a chicken, and in "The Barn" a family desperately attempts to survive the death of a grandfather and the sale of his farm. The speaker in "University Hospital, Boston," from *American Primitive,* visiting a sick person whom she loves dearly, contemplates the wounded and dead who were brought to this hospital during the Civil War as well as the attempts of modern doctors to cure the ill. An empty room she enters on her way out of the hospital reminds her that such attempts, despite modern technology, are not always successful.

Because nature itself in Oliver's work can be brutal and indifferent to human pain and suffering, it is difficult to accept Diane Wakoski's characterization of Oliver's world as one fit for a comfortable urban reader who shops from an L. L. Bean catalogue and "never experiences fear, pain, frustration, being out of control, all the miseries that we urbanized creatures usually feel in the wilderness." Nor is it completely credible to claim, as Wakoski does, that "Oliver's poetry gives each reader the illusion that the natural world is graspable, controllable, beautiful."[34]

Oliver's poetry also confronts a number of social and economic inequities. "Tecumseh" and "Learning About the Indians" record the past and present exploitation of the American Indian. In *House of Light* (1990) she witnesses worldwide social injustice and suffering. The speaker in "Indonesia," for example, contemplates the hopeless situation of the peasant field pickers seen while driving through Indonesian plantations. The poem "Singapore" focuses on a female airport employee washing ashtrays in the toilet bowls of the women's restroom. Both poems speculate on whether deliverance from such an unjust existence is possible as well as on the impact of such situations on the speaker's vision of human worth and existence.

If Oliver's social and more existential modes of poetry are overlooked, it is primarily because she envisions our ability to rise above the miseries of human existence and feel at home with its mysteries of existence and with the creatures that inhabit the wilderness. "Blackleaf Swamp" is a place where one can enter the backwaters of the mind and the imagination and reclaim one's animal identity. In that poem, as in "Winter Sleep," in contrast with Dickey's often violent unions, she finds links to the earth as a nourishing, loving mother, a female force that counters the power of time and death. And death itself, as envisioned in "White Owl Flies Into and Out of the Field," is a passage to the spiritual light of innocence and eternity.

Oliver's affirmation and sense of belonging arises out of her conviction that nature is unending and speaks to us of our own eternalness and our identity with the entire family of living creatures. "The Wild Geese," to cite an example, argues that redemption comes not out of being good or doing penance but out of our ability to acknowledge that the world continues despite our individual tragedies. Nature offers us numerous messages—in this case the honking of the returning wild geese—of its continuity, of its ability to rekindle our imaginations and assure us that we are part of the web of life. Like Thoreau, Oliver celebrates "Spring," the season in which the great, dark, female bear reappears and the love of life is renewed. Her *New and Selected Poems* (1992) received a National Book Award,[35] and *White Pine* (1994) is filled with close observations of hummingbirds, snails, porcupines, wrens, mockingbirds, herons, owls, spiders, a toad and even a dead fox. In the highly technological world of the late twentieth century, Oliver's devotion to the particulars of the natural world is an especially welcomed gesture.

GARY SNYDER (B. 1930) Gary Snyder is the best-known American nature poet of our times. In his fourteen volumes of poetry and prose he has captured the beauty, sacredness, and mysteries of nature in language that is clear, precise, graceful, and powerful. He has also become a leading interpreter and defender of nature, revealing to the world both the destructive consequences of its exploitation of nature and its need to comprehend and celebrate the interconnectedness of all life. For only then, Snyder believes, will we feel "at home" in the universe. Central to Snyder's vision is his sense of awe and humility as he interacts with or contemplates nature:

It will not fulfill our conceptions or assumptions. It will dodge our expectations and theoretical models. There is no single or set "nature" either as the "natural world" or "the nature of things." The greatest respect we can pay to nature is not to trap it, but to acknowledge that it eludes us in that our nature is also fluid, open, and conditional.[36]

This view, a radical departure from the homocentric, Euro-American vision, has informed Snyder's stance as a writer and activist and played a major role in transforming the consciousness of a significant number of Americans over the last three decades.

Many influences shaped Snyder's vision of place and nature. His childhood and adolescent explorations of rural Washington and the Columbia River Basin outside Portland, Oregon, brought him into close contact with the rugged Pacific Northwest terrain. In addition, he was an early student of American-Indian culture; while majoring in anthropology and literature at Reed College, he wrote his senior thesis on a Haida Indian (Northwest) myth that recounts a tale of a lost love within the context of current anthropological theories. The summer after his first year at Reed College, Snyder signed up to go to sea for a short stint; this was the first of many jobs he held that renewed his earlier contacts with the working class and developed his manual and physical skills. During his adult life, he has worked as a seaman, logger, and forest lookout. These work experiences, as Michael Davidson points out, form Snyder's concept of a "self-reliant" proletarian who embodies "the ideal of Buddhist detachment as well as the Marxian idea of a totally productive individual within society."[37]

The most important influence on Snyder's work is his study of Zen Buddhism, which includes long periods of instruction during the fifties and sixties in Kyoto, Japan. Zen Buddhism provided Snyder with a means of entering "the nonhuman, nonverbal world, which is nature as nature is itself; and the world of human nature—the inner world—as it is itself, before language, before custom, before culture." For Snyder there are "no words in that realm. There aren't any rules that we know and that's the area that Buddhism studies."[38]

In addition to its mystical tenants, Buddhism also revealed to Snyder the sacredness and unity of all life. Buddhism, he explains, "holds that the universe and all creatures in it are intrinsically in a state of complete wisdom, love and compassion acting in natural response and mutual interdependence."[39] To enter that realm, Snyder insists one has to give up the western concept of a separate and autonomous self.

All these influences inform Snyder's poetry. And to a greater degree than the work of most poets discussed in this chapter, that poetry takes on a pragmatic purpose that goes far beyond self enlightenment as Snyder attempts to speak for the wilderness and initiate a new revolution based on ecological and tribal values. In *Myths and Texts* (1960), for example, Snyder documents the historical devastation of the land brought about by capitalism and Christianity. He contrasts their destructiveness with the shamanistic rituals of Indian hunting and with the restorative elements of both the natural world and Buddhist myths.

Like D. H. Lawrence, Snyder wants to find a way "to belong to the land." He believes that Euro-Americans are "a still rootless population of non-natives who don't even know the plants or where our water comes from."[40] We must return, Snyder believes, to the myths, practices, and values of ancient cultures: "As poet, I hold the most archaic values on earth. They go back to the upper Paleolithic: the fertility of the soil, the magic of animals, the power-vision in solitude, the terrifying initiation and rebirth, the love and ecstasy of the dance, the common work of the tribe" (*Six Poets*, 52).

Snyder's *Turtle Island* (1974), which won the Pulitzer Prize, contains his sharpest attack on what he calls the "unbalance and ignorance of our times" (52). The Euro-American sense of place, he asserts, denies the unity and vitality of all life forms. In naming our land mass North America or our nation the United States—titles that are geographic or political abstractions—Americans have attached "arbitrary and inaccurate impositions on what is really here." The continent, as seen in the creation myths of the indigenous American Indians, is Turtle Island, which is "sustained by a great turtle or serpent-of-eternity." We must, Snyder argues, "Hark again to those roots, to see our ancient solidarity, and then to the work of being together on Turtle Island."[41]

The poems in this volume "speak of place," and it is this "old/new" vision of place that dominates the style and structure of *Turtle*

Island. A clear programmatic voice unabashedly rails against the ecological blindness of the modern world. At times this voice speaks
in prose ("Plain Talk") or lists ("Facts"), or it is heard in a protest
poem, such as "Mother Earth: Her Whales," where Synder attacks
"Capitalist-Imperialist, Third World, Communist bureaucrats" for
assuming to speak for "the green of the leaf . . . the soil" (48). Here
and elsewhere his voice is as angry and ideological as an incensed
Marxist poet; this revolutionary voice, however, goes beyond the
democratic and Marxist revolts and calls for a third revolution, an
ecological revolution, for "If civilization / is the exploiter, the masses
is nature / and the party / is the poets" (*No Nature*, 183).

Charles Altieri considers these poems to be tied to a prophetic tradition in which didacticism, Jeremiads, and invective enter the literary realm. Altieri also considers them to be the weakest of Snyder's
work. Other critics use the term *prepoetry* to describe their prosaic
nature, and some criticize the dogmatic, self-righteous, and simplistic thinking in these pieces. But the use of invective, directness, and
plain talk is useful in both undermining dominant cultural values
and preparing the way for an alternative vision. To Snyder, the poem
is not a disinterested, autonomous art object but can be a means of
communicating clearly, and forcefully, with the intent of persuading
an audience to adopt a particular course of action. This pragmatic
practice is an honored tradition in both Eastern and Western literature, although it has been out of fashion since the rise of the romantic lyric.

Snyder's tone, diction, and imagery shift significantly when he celebrates the old ways, as in *Turtle Island*'s opening poem, "Anasazi,"
wherein he recreates and celebrates ancient Indians who are

> tucked up in clefts in the cliffs
> growing strict fields of corn and beans
> sinking deeper and deeper in earth
> up to your hips in Gods
> > your head all turned to eagle-down
> > & lightening for knees and elbows
> your eyes full of pollen
> > > (*Turtle Island*, 3)

Both speaker and reader are transported through time and space to
participate in the ways of Turtle Island, to join in the oneness and
sacredness of existence.

The dialectical relationship between ancient and modern cultural visions and our need to return to old ways constitute an important theme in Snyder's work and, together with his Buddhist beliefs, muffle the romantic sense of an ego-dominated poem. The presence of an "I" in a Snyder poem is often absent, because place, concept, and/or a collective "we" or "you" dominates the poem.

Snyder's mystical poems compose the most striking aspect of his work. After carefully depicting the particulars of a natural scene, he moves beyond objective imagery and records that point where the mind "interpenetrates" matter, becomes part of the "original mind," and experiences eternal delight. These poems, a marvelous blend of sensory detail, meditation, and revelation, serve as accessible and moving examples of the Buddhist experience of enlightenment. In "By Frazier Creek Falls," for example, he makes clear the sublime and mysterious character of the natural scene:

> The creek falls to a far valley.
> hills beyond that
> facing, half-forested, dry
> —clear sky
> strong wind in the
> stiff glittering needle clusters
> of the pine—their brown
> round trunk bodies
> straight, still;
> rustling trembling limbs and twigs.
> (*Turtle Island,* 41)

He then instructs his readers to "listen"—a single word isolated on the page that indicates the importance of that act which entices the mind not to think but to move to a deeper level, to the level of the original mind, where the turbulence or flow of the outer world (wind-wave) merges with the flow of the inner mind, where the wilderness within and the wilderness without are joined. A threefold vision occurs, each element or discovery to be realized both singularly and cumulatively:

> This living flowing land
> is all there is, forever
>
> We *are* it
> it sings through us—

We could live on this Earth
without clothes or tools!
(*Turtle Island*, 41)

The "we" here signals Snyder's insistence on composing tribal poems that speak to and for all his readers and serve as models for a community that embodies "all of one swift / empty / dancing mind" (*Turtle Island*, 53).

Axe Handles (1983) reiterates a number of the themes and forms in the earlier works, but becomes even more global in expressing its sense of place. Place here includes Japan, Alaska, Africa, and Stockholm as well as Texas and the Pacific Northwest. Often locales are connected; time and space, as well as political and social divisions dissolve, as the mind transcends such boundaries. In "Soy Sauce," for example, Snyder learns that the wood being used for a window frame on his friend's house comes from a "broken-up, two-thousand-gallon redwood / soy sauce tank."[42] The odors from the barrel staves evoke memories of the Nagano uplands in Japan, shinshu pickles, and especially the joy of resting at a farmhouse after an arduous winter hike across the Japanese Alps with his Japanese companion: "taking a late hot bath in the dark—and eating / a bowl of chill miso radish pickles, / nothing ever so good!" (31). The poem ends with Snyder back in a hot, dusty yard in California, but the interconnective workings of his mind enable him to join East and West, past and present, humans and animals. At the end of the poem, he exclaims: "But I know how it tastes / to lick those window frames / in the dark, / the deer" (31).

Snyder, like Ezra Pound, also acknowledges the importance of tradition, "the tale of the tribe." The title poem, "Axe Handles," succinctly illustrates how the wisdom of the past is brought into the contemporary world. In carving an axe handle for his son, Snyder discovers the pattern for the handle in the very tool he is using to form the new implement. This discovery becomes a model for the transmission of literary and cultural traditions. The poem expresses the cyclical and interdependent nature of culture and illustrates how language and form are cultural tools that enable us to pass on our heritage to future generations. Just as a son learns to make an axe handle by observing the model in his hand, Snyder is indebted to literary ancestors such as Ezra Pound, who first introduced him to the maxim about axe handles, and Lu Ji Wên Fu (probably the source of

Pound's reference), as well as Shih Ching, Snyder's Japanese Zen teacher, who translated a fifth-century B.C. folksong that also contains this adage. This keen sense of tradition and the interdependence of culture and nature are at the center of his long-awaited sequence of poems, *Mountains and Rivers Without End* (1996), which Snyder worked on since the 1950's. The form and title of this poem is inspired by a traditional East Asian hand scroll that Snyder encountered when he was a student at Berkeley. The poem is a summing-up of a wide range of Snyder's thoughts, experiences, and feelings throughout his adult lifetime. Much of that lifetime has been devoted to discovering the links that connect our collective cultures.

This sense of cultural continuity and common identity, Snyder believes, mirrors our ties to the natural world. His ecological view of existence is derived in large part from his belief in the sacredness of nature, which creates a respectful, patient, and humble relationship between human beings and the planet. If there is an apocalyptic ring to many of his poems, there is a greater peal of Whitmanesque possibilities that envision humans at home with their bodies, their minds, their cultures, and, especially, their environments.

· FIVE ·

"A Whole New Poetry Beginning Here":
The Assertion of Gender

> I am an instrument in the shape
> of a woman trying to translate pulsations
> into images   for the relief of the body
> and the reconstruction of the mind.
> —Adrienne Rich

Although many of the central poets of the modernist movement were women, including Amy Lowell, Gertrude Stein, H. D., and Marianne Moore, for many male writers, the idea of a "women's poetry" in the late 1950s and early 1960s still conjured visions of genteel lyricism by what were then called "poetesses," such as Sara Teasdale, Josephine Preston Peabody, or Edna St. Vincent Millay. Some of it was skillfully crafted and memorably expressed, but it did not seem to embody the realities of many women's situation in life. Not until poets like Muriel Rukeyser, Adrienne Rich, Sylvia Plath, Anne Sexton, Audre Lorde, and Marge Piercy and, more recently, emergent writers like Sharon Olds, Olga Broumas, Louise Glück, and Marilyn Hacker became established did the phrase "women's poetry" come to imply resistance to the social limitations placed on women's lives.

Rukeyser, Brooks, Rich, and Plath opened new worlds for a whole generation of women who became empowered to speak what had previously been unspeakable. The dissatisfactions of motherhood, the stifling conformity of suburban housewifery, the dominance of male intellectuality, the dismissal of female perceptions of reality, the objectification of women's bodies, the social tolerance of rape and sexual harassment of all kinds, the politics of abortion, the blatant economic inequality of the sexes, and many other subjects previously ignored or actively repressed began to be dealt with openly and in depth. Ironically, "women's poetry" became in some ways the opposite of what it had previously been. No longer genteel and lyrical, it began to carry a political edge. Much of this poetry was controversial and rejected, especially by male critics, who often viewed it as self-indulgent and artless. But as its body began to gather heft and momentum throughout the sixties, seventies, and eighties, it could no longer be ignored as a dominant force in contemporary poetry.

Women were demonstrating that gender is an important component of poetic value, although many writers, both men and women, continued to resist that idea. Elizabeth Bishop, for example, refused to be anthologized in any women-only poetry anthology because she believed that the art of poetry transcends gender. And although Diane Wakoski clearly writes a "woman-centered" poetry that focuses especially on relationships between men and women, she believes that any gender adjective that precedes the word *poet* diminishes it. But to say that gender is a component of poetic value is not to argue that it is the only component. Writing is related to life experience, and the experiences of men and women in our society are significantly different in many respects: childbearing, childrearing, domestic responsibilities, military experience (until recently), and economic opportunities are just a few differences that create the foundation for a poetry influenced by gender.

Some women take the gender issue a step further and talk about a "female poetics" that informs the women's poetry of note in our time. In her important revisionist history of women's poetry in America, Alicia Suskin Ostriker writes about "an assertive desire for intimacy" that she believes characterizes this poetics: "As the poet refuses to distance herself from her emotion, so she prevents us [as readers] from distancing ourselves."[1] For Ostriker and for other feminist writers like Adrienne Rich, Suzanne Juhasz, and Audre Lorde, a woman-centered poetry has emerged that has as its project the definition of a "female self" unmitigated by the assumptions and cultural priorities of male writers. This poetry intends to transform literary culture as well as the social culture it both grows out of and affects. Consequently, much of the women's poetry of our time is involved in revising traditional myths, whether explicitly, as in Anne Sexton's *Transformations*, or implicitly, as in Marge Piercy's reconstruction of male-female relationships. In addition, Adrienne Rich sees "a passion for survival" as one of the great themes of women's poetry today and finds it ironic "that male critics have focused on our suicidal poets, and on their 'self'-destructiveness rather than their capacity for hard work and for staying alive as long as they did."[2] Combining a desire for intimacy with the shaping of a new female identity based on revising the myths of the past and transforming the realities of the present has produced an intensely personal poetry that is also pointedly political. In fact, the distinctive contribution of contemporary women's poetry is that the personal and political are identified with each other and conjoined.

In addition to the women mentioned above, many other writers have been instrumental in creating this new kind of "woman-centered" poetry that departs from the constricted sensibility often associated (usually by men) with feminine norms. These include Sonia Sanchez, Gloria Anzaldúa, Paula Gunn Allen, Wendy Rose, and others who are creating what Adrienne Rich calls "a whole new poetry beginning here." Those women who also broadened the context of writing in the United States by underscoring their ethnic and cultural heritages will be explored more fully in chapter 7. Here we will look at how the assertion of gender reshaped American poetry in the seventies and eighties.

ANNE SEXTON (1928–1974) During her eighteen years as a working poet, Anne Sexton produced eight books of poetry, as well as plays, children's stories, and several prose works. Given her extraordinarily precarious mental state for most of this period, this is a remarkable output. She began writing without a formal education, as an adult woman with two children, at the suggestion of her psychiatrist, who felt that writing might provide a therapeutic outlet for her raging suicidal urges and distracted behavior. She wrote her first "mature" poem after attending a lecture by Harvard Professor I. A. Richards on the sonnet, and shortly thereafter (in 1957) attended an adult education poetry workshop in Boston conducted by John Holmes, a professor of literature at Tufts. There she met the poet Maxine Kumin, who became a friend, confidant, and collaborator and who remained close to Sexton for the rest of her life. Kumin, in fact, may have been the last person to speak with her before she committed suicide in the fall of 1974.

Sexton's uniqueness as a writer resided in "the talent for making poetry the vehicle of autobiography, of self-analysis."[3] She was in psychoanalysis for nearly all of her writing life, and her poetry provided access to her unconscious. For Sexton the source of a writer's strength was the ability to plumb the depths of the unconscious and articulate the vision discovered there (Middlebrook, 165).

Important influences on her work include W. D. Snodgrass (she studied with him at the Antioch Writer's Conference in 1958 after having read *Heart's Needle*, a book she told him " 'walked out at me and grew like a bone inside of my heart' " [Middlebrook, 78]); Robert Lowell (in 1958 she also attended Lowell's writing seminar at Boston University, where she met Sylvia Plath); James Wright, and George Starbuck, both of whom became her lovers at different periods; Anthony Hecht and C. K. Williams, who offered regular commentary on her poetry; and both Kumin and Plath, one a close friend, the other a rival whose suicidal obsessions equaled her own. When Plath actually did commit suicide in 1963, their literary posterity became irreversibly altered. As Diane Middlebrook notes, "It was as if Sylvia Plath, the savvy rival, had leapfrogged right over Sexton's project of becoming famous, in which the fantasized finale was to be a well-publicized suicide. By this singular move Plath had once and for all reversed their positions as senior and junior in the ranks of poetry" (201).

The term *confessional poetry* has been often applied to the work of many of the poets of this group, but it is easy to agree with Sexton's own assessment that she was the only *truly* confessional poet. As Maxine Kumin writes in the introduction to *The Complete Poems*, "She wrote openly about menstruation, abortion, masturbation, incest, adultery, and drug addiction at a time when the proprieties embraced none of these as proper topics for poetry."[4]

Sexton's early work—in *To Bedlam and Part Way Back* (1960) and *All My Pretty Ones* (1962)—combines a traditional formalist technique with unprecedented personal revelations about these controversial subjects. In "Ringing the Bells," for example, a sing-song nursery rhyme cadence accompanies a description of Tuesday mornings in a mental institution:

> And this is the way they ring
> the bells in Bedlam
> and this is the bell-lady
> who comes each Tuesday morning
> to give us a music lesson

> . . . .
> and this is the small hunched squirrel girl
> on the other side of me
> who picks at the hairs over her lip,
> who picks at the hairs over her lip all day
>   (28)

"The Operation," a poem she wrote while recovering from surgery
to remove a nonmalignant ovarian cyst, almost comically presents
the preparatory details in a dense network of rhymes reinforced by
internal near rhymes and repetition. As the rhymes approach dog-
gerel, the hard incontrovertible facts of human mortality intervene:

> Clean of the body's hair,
> I lie smooth from breast to leg.
> All that was special, all that was rare
> is common here. Fact: death too is in the egg.
> Fact: the body is dumb, the body is meat.
> And tomorrow the O.R. Only the summer is sweet.
>   (57)

Sexton had little use for euphemism or the avoidance of hard truths.
She made much of her private life public because she regarded the
invasion of one's own privacy as a basic human right. "It's very
embarrassing for someone to expose their body to you," she told an
interviewer. "You don't learn anything from it. But if they expose
their soul, you learn something. That's true of great writers" (Middlebrook, 329). When she writes a poem about abortion, for example,
she rebukes herself in the last stanza for softening the event after
having repeated the poem's refrain, "Somebody who should have
been born / is gone," three times:

> Yes, woman, such logic will lead
> to loss without death. Or say what you meant,
> you coward . . . this baby that I bleed.
>   (62)

Her third book, *Live or Die* (1966), attempts to move into more positive psychological and aesthetic space without abandoning the insistent self-revelation that had become her trademark. In an author's
note, Sexton offers apologies to the reader for the fact that her

poems, chronologically organized in the volume, "read like a fever chart for a bad case of melancholy" (94). The book's epigram comes from novelist Saul Bellow and captures Sexton's intent to transcend the suicidal, depressive state that characterizes much of her work: "With one long breath, caught and held in his chest, he fought his sadness over his solitary life. Don't cry, you idiot! Live or die, but don't poison everything . . ." (94).

"Flee on Your Donkey," a long narrative about her recommitment to a mental institution, is an important work that signals a shift in her style. An expansion of two lines from Rimbaud, the poem seems a willful attempt to break through barriers that have restrained or moderated self-expression. Much more loosely structured than the "madness narratives" in the first two volumes, Sexton here appears to be trying to bring her poetry closer to the unconscious sources from which it springs. Though occasional rhymes punctuate the irregular stanzas, the essentially free-verse form dominates and suggests a liberation from the traditional poetic structures that restrained full expression of her internal states of mind. The sporadic rhymes and near rhymes provide some structural grounding, but the feeling of "Flee on Your Donkey" is one of a new artistic freedom that parallels what Sexton hoped would be a new experiential freedom—to move on from the world of mental hospitals and suicidal depressions into a more spontaneous and fulfilling life. For Sexton, the line between poetry and life is thin; as the poetry becomes freer, the life becomes freer. The long, winding narrative chronicles her history of mental illness ("Six years of shuttling in and out of this place!" [99]) and culminates in a deliberate decision to move beyond the fixations of her past into a new, uncharted territory:

> Anne, Anne,
> flee on your donkey,
> flee this sad hotel,
> ride out on some hairy beast,
> gallop backward pressing
> your buttocks to his withers,
> sit to his clumsy gait somehow.
> Ride out
> any old way you please!
> In this place everyone talks to his own mouth.
> That's what it means to be crazy.

> Those I loved best died of it—
> the fool's disease.
>
> (104–5)

But the road to liberation in *Live or Die* is not direct and clear. Poems on suicide, addiction, "Menstruation at Forty" (about her fear that she has become pregnant during an extramarital affair) alternate with celebrations of her two daughters and impressions of Europe (Sexton went to Europe on a writer's grant in 1963). One of her most explicit and often quoted statements on suicide occurs in a poem here called "Wanting to Die":

> But suicides have a special language.
> Like carpenters they want to know *which tools*.
> They never ask *why build*.
>
> (142)

The reader comes to the final poem with a sense of great relief. It is called "Live," and in it Sexton seems to favor embracing what she has rather than railing against it, self-acceptance instead of despair, hope and optimism instead of impending doom. And yet despite the shift in mood and message, the poem sounds unmistakably like Sexton, with its odd, domestic similes and its playful self-assessment:

> Here,
> all along,
> thinking I was a killer,
> anointing myself daily
> with my little poisons.
> But no.
> I'm an empress.
> I wear an apron.
> My typewriter writes.
> It didn't break the way it warned.
> Even crazy, I'm as nice
> as a chocolate bar.
>
> (169)

The final lines of the poem, preceded by references to railroad cars, ovens, Adolf Eichmann, and other Plath-like imagery of the Holocaust, signal an intention not to follow Plath's road—to choose life instead of death.

> So I won't hang around in my hospital shift,
> repeating The Black Mass and all of it.
> I say *Live, Live* because of the sun,
> the dream, the excitable gift.
>
> (170)

By the time her third book had been published, Anne Sexton was one of the most widely read poets in America. Her books appealed to people who did not ordinarily read poetry, partly because of their sensationalism, partly because of their glimpse into the ordinarily shrouded world of the mentally ill, partly because of her shrewd sense of self-promotion. And because of the autobiographical candor of her work, readers felt they knew her, that each poem charted some further development in her life. To become involved with Anne Sexton's poetry was to become involved with her life. This idea of poetry as an ongoing chronicle of a life became an approach to writing that influenced a great many of her peers and writers of the next generation.

Love Poems (1969), although it was published on Valentine's Day, is no ordinary book of love lyrics. In some ways it is Sexton's most candid volume because nearly all the poems deal explicitly with extramarital affairs, and it is "the first of her books produced in the atmosphere of celebrity" (Middlebrook, 293). The poems also position Sexton in a problematic relationship to what was then the newly emerging women's movement. On the one hand, many of the poems seem to reinforce the traditional notion of a woman's dependency on men to achieve her own identity. In "The Breast," for example, she speaks about a solidarity with her sisters and implies a rebirth of a new kind of womanhood, but one which remains dependent upon male desire:

> Now I am your mother, your daughter,
> your brand new thing—a snail, a nest.
> I am alive when your fingers are.
>
> (176)

On the other hand, "In Celebration of My Uterus," probably Sexton's most explicitly feminist poem, celebrates a connection shared by women throughout the world, mentioning men not at all. Its catalogue of female diversity makes "In Celebration of My Uterus" an anthem of its time:

> in celebration of the woman I am
> and of the soul of the woman I am
> and of the central creature and its delight
> I sing for you. I dare to live.
> . . . .
> Many women are singing together of this:
> one is in a shoe factory cursing the machine,
> one is at the aquarium tending a seal,
> one is dull at the wheel of her Ford,
> one is at the toll gate collecting,
> one is tying the cord of a calf in Arizona,
> one is straddling a cello in Russia. . . .
>
> (182)

The poetry here, with its virtually interchangeable lines, seems unlike Sexton at her most precise, but readers were anxious to see it as an extension of the affirmative conclusion of *Live or Die*, and it became one of Sexton's most anthologized poems.

Other significant poems in *Love Poems* include "For My Lover, Returning to His Wife," a bitterly ironic poem that contrasts the temporariness of a love affair with the permanence of marriage. The narrator compares herself with her lover's wife and concludes with six lines that many of Sexton's readers clearly recognized:

> She is so naked and singular.
> She is the sum of yourself and your dream.
> Climb her like a monument, step after step.
> She is solid.
>
> As for me, I am a watercolor.
> I wash off.
>
> (190)

The same theme is echoed in "You All Know the Story of The Other Woman," which ends with the lover abandoning the "Other Woman" by placing her "like a phone, back on the hook" (196). And this is also the theme of the widely reprinted "Ballad of the Lonely Masturbator," which repeats the refrain "At night, alone, I marry the bed" at the end of each of its seven stanzas.

But the strongest poem in *Love Poems* is the long autobiographical narrative sequence that concludes the book called "Eighteen Days Without You," a return to Sexton's more characteristic style of intense self-revelation. In this poem about the separation of lovers, she gets at the power of physical love, the anguish of a lover left, and particularly the situation of a woman in love with a married man. How deftly she handles the latter in a couplet rhyming "scissors" with "His. Hers.":

> and of course we're not married, we are a pair of scissors
> who come together to cut, without towels saying His. Hers.
>
> (214)

Each poem in the sequence is dated consecutively from "December 1st" to "December 18th" and follows the course of a doomed relationship (the absent male lover in this particular sequence was her psychoanalyst, who not only had an affair with her but charged her for the hours they spent together [Middlebrook, 159, 293–95]). This is poetry close to the bone and deep in the bloodstream:

> How you come and take my blood cup
> and link me together and take my brine.
> We are bare. We are stripped to the bone
> and we swim in tandem and go up and up
> the river, the identical river called Mine
> and we enter together. No one's alone.
>
> (214)

Transformations (1971) moved Sexton's work in a totally new direction. The book is a contemporary recasting of popular fairy tales from the brothers Grimm ("Rapunzel," "Cinderella," "Hansel and Gretel," "Little Red Riding Hood," "Rumplestilskin," "Sleeping Beauty," "Twelve Dancing Princesses," and some others). The narrator, "a middle-aged witch," tells the stories with a sarcastic flourish. While these poems do not have the compelling urgency of Sexton's more personal poems, most of the tales she chooses to modernize have some connection to mythic conceptions of femininity, which Sexton is pleased to deflate. For example, Cinderella may live "happily ever after," but Sexton gives a new, ironic meaning to that hackneyed phrase:

> Cinderella and the prince
> lived, they say, happily ever after,
> like two dolls in a museum case
> never bothered by diapers or dust,

> never arguing over the timing of an egg,
> never telling the same story twice,
> never getting a middle-aged spread,
> their darling smiles pasted on for eternity.
> Regular Bobbsey Twins.
>
> (258)

Throughout the seventies and eighties, a great many women writers followed Sexton's lead in "transforming" traditional fairy tales into feminist fables.[5]

There are several memorable poems in *The Book of Folly* (1972). "The Ambition Bird" speaks to Sexton's grandiose ambition, a driven quality that animates nearly all of her work. Here she desires simplicity, but "the ambition bird," whose dark wings flop in her heart, will not let her rest, because her poetry is her "lay-away plan" for immortality. "The Silence" indicates the constancy of Sexton's obsession with death and is a reminder that the power of her poetry comes from this source. "Killing the Spring" goes further and revives the self-destructive tendencies of her earlier work. The long "The Death of the Fathers" is an important autobiographical document that chronicles a remarkable event in Sexton's life. She learned from a family friend that he had had an affair with her mother and that he believed Anne was his daughter. This shocking news unsettled her, particularly because she associated much of her mental instability with traumas inflicted by her alcoholic father. If he was indeed not her father at all, her life might be reenvisioned. But this realization brings with it confusion, doubt, regret:

> Father me not
> for you are not my father.
> Today there is that doubt.
> Today there is that monster between us,
> that monster of doubt.
> Today someone else lurks in the wings
> with your dear lines in his mouth
> and your crown on his head.
> Oh Father, Father-sorrow,
> where has time brought us?
>
> (329)

Finally, the second section of *The Book of Folly* is devoted to a sequence called "The Jesus Papers," which signals a focus on unorthodox religiosity that became a larger and larger part of her work in her last few books. The headnote to *The Death Notebooks* (1974), published the year Sexton took her own life, announces an almost triumphant return to Sexton's "grand theme" in the words of another suicidal writer, Ernest Hemingway: "Look, you con man, make a living out of your death." These poems are literal "flirtations" with death, moving closer and closer to the abyss, in much the same manner of Plath's last poems, but with less of the originality and surprise of Sexton's earlier work. In this volume her morbidity appears to be a mannered technique rather than self-revelation, although her suicide on October 4, 1974, as her posthumously published *The Awful Rowing toward God* (1975) was going to press, assures us that she was serious.

Because of Sylvia Plath and Anne Sexton, our poetry will never be the same. Both deeply troubled, intensely ambitious women, they linked their troubles to their ambitions and directly confronted the demons that drove them to and over the edge. Innovative, vital, imagistically and metrically alive, their poetry gave courage to many other writers, both men and women, "to make a clean breast of it," and although their suicides are a tragic legacy, their poetry is a triumphant one.

AUDRE LORDE (1934–1992) In a talk she delivered at Amherst College in 1980, Audre Lorde described herself as a kind of ultimate outsider in the context of contemporary America: "As a forty-nine year-old black lesbian feminist socialist mother of two, including one boy, and a member of an inter-racial couple, I usually find myself a part of some group defined as other, deviant, inferior, or just plain wrong."[6] It is as an inhabitant of each aspect of this multiple identity that she has made a significant impact on the writing of contemporary women. In *Sister Outsider* (1984), a collection of her speeches and essays, Lorde argues that sexism and racism are deeply rooted in the patriarchal foundations of American life. Lorde believes that for women, particularly, poetry is not a luxury but an absolute necessity that enables them to "give name to the nameless so that it can be thought" (37).

Two important essays, "Uses of the Erotic: The Erotic as Power" and "Poetry Is Not a Luxury" articulate her vision of poetry as a means of waging war against what she calls "the tyrannies of silence." Additionally, for Lorde writing is an erotic act that calls upon the fullness of a writer's being. The erotic, she believes, "lies in a deeply female and spiritual plane, firmly rooted in the power of our [women's] unexpressed or unrecognized feeling" (*Sister*, 53). For a woman to begin to trust and unleash this power is to nurture a deeper knowledge than what she regards as superficial rationality. One of her most controversial positions associates rationality with male patriarchy and emotionality with black womanhood: "The white fathers told us: I think, therefore I am. The Black mother within each of us—the poet—whispers in our dreams: I feel, therefore I can be free" (38).

While this dichotomy appears simplistic and stereotypical—women feel, men think—Lorde expands these distinctions in an interview with Adrienne Rich: "I'm not saying that women don't think or analyze. Or that white does not feel. I'm saying that we must never close our eyes to the terror, to the chaos which is Black which is creative which is female which is dark which is rejected which is messy which is. . . . Sinister, smelly, erotic, confused, upsetting" (*Sister*, 101). The erotic, from this perspective, opens up repressed realms of feeling and experience both for poetry and for political action.

Lorde's poetry is dominated by free-verse monologues of anger and rage that grow out of the racism and sexism she sees everywhere in American life. Although her poetry is not technically innovative, it has a cumulative force that addresses issues often considered off-limits for women, particularly issues of power. For Lorde, anger is a sustaining poetic force, and the articulation of anger gives voice to her deepest self. An early poem, "The Woman Thing," expresses the dimensions of that anger through archetypal images of hunters returning empty-handed from a winter hunt, seeking "young girls for their amusement." The hunters are associated with male rage and injustice because they have come home without completing their mission, unable to feed their children. Women are to be used to fill this emptiness. The poem's final stanza counters the hunters' anger at the world's injustice with women's emerging realization of being used and abused to satisfy male egos:

> Meanwhile
> the woman thing my mother taught me
> bakes off its covering of snow
> like a rising blackening sun.[7]

This complex figure extends traditional female associations to a new kind of oxymoronic liberation. A new sun is rising after a long dormant winter, but it is a "blackening" sun, bringing light through self-discovery and awareness—a particularly apt metaphor for a black woman exploring the roots of her identity.

While Lorde's poetry is clearly political and focuses on social issues and political or economic injustice, she also believes, like many feminist poets, that the personal is political and that to articulate the truth about one's life is a political act. The "I" in nearly all of her poems is a direct expression of the personal self, while at the same time it seems to take on the role of spokesperson for all women, all blacks, all lesbians, all socially oppressed groups at various times in the poetry. She wants others to join in her search to root out the "old ways" of oppression and domination:

> Haunted by poems beginning with I
> seek out those whom I love who are deaf
> to whatever does not destroy
> or curse the old ways that did not serve us
> while history falters and our poets are dying
> choked into silence by icy distinction
> death rattles blind curses
> and I hear even my own voice becoming
> a pale strident whisper
>
> (58)

But the fury in Lorde's work usually rises above a pale whisper, even though her expressions of rage are sometimes aphoristic and paradoxical:

> If you do not learn to hate
> you will never be lonely
> enough
> to love easily
>
> (42–43)

In "Need," a powerful "Choral of Black Women's Voices" that concludes *Chosen Poems*, Lorde attempts to find a voice for all black women who have been victims of violence by men. While the tendency to generalize and move from a particular situation to a sociological observation is a weakness she shares with other politically oriented poets, the sense of moral outrage in this story of two black women who were bludgeoned to death by men energizes and empowers it.

In addition to its sources in urban America, Lorde's poetry draws from a rich heritage of African-American experience and, in her *Black Unicorn* collection (1978), from an ancient tradition of African mythology that she mines for parallels and analogies to contemporary life. As Lynda Koolish observes, "Lorde is a contemporary feminist speaking an American diction that draws from linguistic sources and images that are more often white and urban than black. But she is also an African whose sources are ancient, female, and black."[8]

In *Black Unicorn* the presence of her African identity becomes dominant. The book includes a glossary of African names used in the poems to introduce readers to cultural entities like the Orisha, "divine personifications of the Yoruba peoples of Western Nigeria" that include Orishala, a god who shapes humans in the womb before birth, and Seboulisa, "The Mother of us all." The first section of *Black Unicorn* draws on the mythology associated with Abomey, the capital of the ancient kingdom of Dahomey, located near present-day southwestern Nigeria. In "125th Street and Abomey," Lorde materializes a vision of this heritage on the winter streets of Harlem:

> Head bent, walking through snow
> I see you Seboulisa
> printed inside the back of my head
> like marks of the newly wrapped akai
> that kept my sleep fruitful in Dahomey[9]

Although separated from this heritage both geographically and temporally, Lorde sees her poetry as a way to revive these traditions:

> Half earth and time splits us apart
> like struck rock.
> ·
> Seboulisa mother goddess with one breast
> eaten away by worms of sorrow and loss
> see me now
> your severed daughter
> laughing our name into echo
> all the world shall remember.
>
> (12–13)

Perhaps the most striking image in *Black Unicorn* is neither African nor ancient but clearly contemporary. In "Death Dance for a Poet," Lorde envisions an old woman who

> has come to hate slowly
> her skin of transparent metal
> the sinuous exposure without reprieve
> her eyes of clay
>
> (73)

This tough, metallic but openly "transparent" woman is an emblem for the outsider poet who enables people to see through her (in both senses of that phrase), although she feels threatened and endangered in a world that rejects her vision of truth.

The quest for a full, uncompromised identity that embodies all aspects of herself continues in *Our Dead behind Us* (1986). A poem called "To the Poet Who Happens to be Black and the Black Poet Who Happens to be a Woman" concludes with Lorde's commitment to remain faithful to the essential elements of her self-identity, despite the costs of mainstream rejection:

> I cannot recall the words of my first poem
> but I remember a promise
> I made my pen
> never to leave it
> lying
> in someone else's blood.[10]

Lorde's most fervent political cause is the one she is closest to. The final poem in the volume, "Cell," is a litany for black women who carry on the traditions of their ancestors. As Lorde evokes the names of African goddesses, she also calls the names of heroic twentieth-century black women—Rosa Parks, Fannie Lou Hamer, Assta Shaku, and Yaa Asentewa—as well as her mother and Winnie Mandela, all of whom "are singing / in my throat," as she puts it, having become a part of her poetry.

Lorde's fierce and courageous voice insists on confronting the most difficult and divisive subjects because without this confrontation her experience of the world is rendered mute and invisible. In the introduction to *The Cancer Journals* (1988), a book she wrote after having a mastectomy, she writes, "I do not wish my anger and pain and fear about cancer to fossilize into yet another silence, nor to rob me of whatever strength can lie at the core of this experience, openly acknowledged and examined."[11] The same might be said about nearly all the subjects she examines in her poetry: lesbianism, interracial relationships, violence toward women, racist domination, the usurpation of African culture. Her posthumously published *The Marvelous Arithmetics of Distance* (1993) continues to deal with all of these subjects, but also poignantly confronts her impending death with courage and dignity. Hers is a poetry, like Adrienne Rich's, that insists on naming the nameless, on speaking the unspeakable.

MARGE PIERCY (B. 1936)   Born to a working-class family in Detroit, Marge Piercy now lives on two acres in Wellfleet, Massachusetts, and both her midwestern urban roots and her New England village present are important factors in her poetry. A prolific writer, she has published more than a dozen collections of poetry as well as many works of fiction, including *Woman on the Edge of Time* (1976), an important feminist work that influenced a generation of women and encouraged their involvement in the women's movement. Piercy also edited an anthology of American women's poetry in 1987 called *Early Ripening*, in which she argues that women's poetry in late twentieth-century America is characterized by a fused rather than "dissociated" sensibility—emotion and intellect working together rather than at war with each other. Women's poetry in our time, according to Piercy, tends also to be a poetry of "re-invention" that is often confrontational vis à. vis traditional social institutions and structures. There is in much of the work included in *Early Ripening* "a remaking, a renewing, a renaming, a re-experiencing, and then recasting."[12]

This understanding of contemporary women's poetry permeates nearly all of Piercy's own work. Though that work is diverse and reflects different stages of her life, it is important to her that poetry be *useful*, particularly to other women who will recognize themselves in various aspects of her life journey. Several kinds of poem make up the bulk of Piercy's canon. First there are feminist-oriented poems on topics like rape, abortion, abused women, and working-class women that tend to speak directly to other women with the idea of enrolling them in the "we" of the poem. Second, there are poems of social criticism that deal with issues other than those exclusively concerned with women: automation, technology, war, inhumanity, indifference to suffering, and many others that constitute the "cancers" of modern life that need to be exposed and rooted out. Third, there are poems about Piercy's Detroit working-class childhood, especially family poems about her troubled relationship with her mother and father. Fourth, there are love poems, especially apparent in the later work, either celebrating the renewal of love or lamenting its demise. A persistent theme that crosses the boundaries of several of these subjects is the need for transformation, particularly the transformation of relationships between men and women.

Piercy's best work through 1980 is collected in *Circles on the Water: Selected Poems* (1982). Most of these poems were written in the sixties and seventies phase of the contemporary feminist movement and are predominantly political in orientation and militant in tone, although they also deal with the status of male/female relationships in the period. In "Doing it differently,"[13] Piercy makes a dramatic attempt to alter the status quo. She wants to reconstruct male-female relationships and move them out of the wasteland that many have inhabited. Although the poem is preachy, it is also affecting, and very much a document of its time. The lovers in the poem are "bagged in habit," but the woman feels they have the power to choose their destiny and not simply accept the conventions handed down to them. The woman appears vulnerable as she crawls into the man "as a bee crawls into a lily," but while the woman is always vulnerable, the man is vulnerable only when he is making love. The narrator asks if men and women can ever be free of the roles of dominance and submission. Sounding surprisingly apolitical, Piercy evokes the image of a rose as a symbol of male-female union:

> I am a body beautiful only when fitted with yours.
> Otherwise, it walks, it lifts packages, it spades.
> It is functional or sick, tired or sturdy. It serves.
> Together we are the rose, full, red as the inside
> of the womb and head of the penis,
> blossoming as we encircle, we make that symmetrical
>   fragrant emblem,
> then separate into discrete workday selves.
>
> (111)

Can this rosy picture actually become the norm? Can there be a "new man and woman" committed to this kind of beautiful union? The woman in the poem feels powerless to make it happen because her inferiority is encased in the language, laws, institutions, and traditions of society. To create this kind of equal union, men need to take positive steps toward change:

> We are equal only if you open too on your heavy hinges
> and let your love come freely, freely, where it will never be safe,
> where you can never possess.
>
> *(Circles,* 112)

In the books published since *Circles on the Water,* Piercy's poetry is even less politically programmatic, more complex. *Stone, Paper, Knife* (1983), *My Mother's Body* (1986), and *Available Light* (1988) contain some of her strongest work. The central elements of these books are an insistence on dealing with the specifics of her experience; a willingness to see both men and women as individual, real people rather than as stereotypical role models; an introspective sense of self-discovery; and an attempt to understand the roots of the anger that permeates so much of her life and work. For like Audre Lorde and Adrienne Rich, Piercy values anger as a spur for her muse and almost fears its dissipation. In a poem called "How divine is forgiving?" from *Available Light,* she sees forgiveness as a weakness—a recognition of our imperfections rather than a large, magnanimous gesture:

> We forgive because we too have done
> the same to others easy as a mudslide;
> or because anger is a fire that must be fed
> and we are too tired to rise and haul a log.[14]

My Mother's Body, written shortly after her mother's death, locates the source of that anger very specifically:

> The anger turned inward, the anger
> turned inward, where
> could it go except to make pain?
> It flowed into me with her milk.[15]

Rummaging through her mother's things after her death, she finds artifacts that connect her to her mother's experience. Piercy, a middle-class woman, a successful writer, looks back at her mother's working-class life with a feminist eye, venting what she believes were her mother's repressed feelings of anger. She notices that her mother, like so many women of her generation, used "ugly" things for everyday and kept her beautiful things locked in storage. They were never used because "no day of hers was ever good enough" to use them, and so they become an emblem of the repressed beauty and creativity of the women of her mother's generation.

In the lovely title poem of this collection, mother and daughter become interchangeable:

> My mother is my mirror and I am hers.
> What do we see?
>
> (29)

Looking back from the vantage point of a mature and seasoned life, the narrator realizes that the two women are less mother and daughter than twin sisters who happen to live in different times. Her feelings of youthful rebellion and resentment give way to mature self-recognition as the narrator takes on her mother's anger as her own:

> I will not be the bride you can dress,
> the obedient dutiful daughter you would chew,
> a dog's leather bone to sharpen your teeth.
>
> You strike me sometimes just to hear the sound.
> Loneliness turns your fingers into hooks
> barbed and drawing blood with their caress.
>
> My twin, my sister, my lost love,
> I carry you in me like an embryo
> as once you carried me.
>
> (30)

My Mother's Body is also notable for its sequence of love poems called "Chuppah," after the canopy used in Jewish wedding ceremonies. These poems were written for Piercy's marriage to writer Ira Wood, and she includes two poems by Wood in the sequence.

Available Light continues in this vein of self-discovery and retrospection. More than any of her books it chronicles the transformation of a "bad girl" from the inner city into a successful woman and widely respected writer. The poem "Joy Road and Livernois," though clearly feminist in its depiction of the lot of working-class women, is also a very personal poem about Piercy's Detroit upbringing and the grim fate of some of her girlfriends, dead from accidents or drug overdoses, dying of cancer, or trapped in a mental institution. Offering short biographical sketches of each of these women—Pat, Evie, Peggy, Theresa, Gladys—in the vein of Edgar Lee Masters's *Spoon River Anthology*—Piercy emerges as a survivor of a world nearly impossible to transcend.

In a poem called "I see the sign and tremble," inspired by a "Self Storage" sign glimpsed from the highway advertising a company offering storage lockers, Piercy creates a metaphor for the evolution of her poetry. She thinks of her poems as places where she has stored her various "selves" at different parts of her life. The poem itself is a catalog of Piercy's various identities, from "the gang girl running over the tarred / roofs sticky under her sneakers" through "the New York femme fatale dancing through a maze of mirrors" to "the woman alone / in the Midwest of a rented room sent into exile" (16–17).

Available Light is also a very sensuous book, containing some of Piercy's best love poems, rich in the physicality of an opulent sexuality yet also tempered by the actual ups and downs of a long-term relationship. She chronicled the end of one love affair and the beginning of another in *Stone, Paper, Knife*, and here she writes about both the abundance of a happily married sex life as well as the bumpy road to reconciliation after horrendous arguments:

> Eat, drink, I am your daily bread
> and you are mine made every morning fresh
> In the oven of the bed we rise and bake
> yeasty, dark, full of raisins and seeds[16]
> . . . .
> You have come back from your hike
> up the sandblasted mountains of ego
> and I have crawled out from my squat
> in the wind caves of sulk
>
> (70)

Finally, a poignant poem, "Burial by Salt," is an important landmark in Piercy's work, representing her attempt to let go of her anger about her father's distant silence and lack of personal support. The iciness of the father-daughter relationship is captured in two lines that underscore the tragedy of too many American families:

> To you I made no promises. You asked none.
> Forty-nine years we spoke of nothing real
>
> (97)

Although desperate for her father's love, Piercy never felt it. The two have between them, as Piercy sees it, only "history / not love," and as she scatters his ashes to the wind (as she did with her mother's ashes, recorded in an earlier poem, "What remains"), she tries finally to come to terms with that limitation.

Her poetry published in the 1990's, *Mars and Her Children* (1992) and *What Are Big Girls Made Of?* (1997) carry on her lifetime concerns, showing a growing awareness of the "precarious balance" between the social and natural worlds. A poem like "The ark of consequence," which organizes the sections of the former volume according to the colors of the rainbow, deals with ecological issues (the consequences of an oil spill). The title poem of that book, "For Mars and her children returning in March," laments the threat humanity poses to the humpback whale. Animal rights issues surface as well in the latter book. "Death of a doe on Chequesset Neck" projects the narrator into the pain of a dying animal, and "Crow babies" sees the society of crows as superior to our own.

Piercy's poetry is uneven, often raw and unfiltered by a concern for formalist constraints. One critic even describes her poetry as seeming "for the most part to have been poured out and then cut up into lines."[17] That assessment does capture something of the "I must get all of this down" quality of Piercy's work. Yet despite the unedited feel of many of the poems, they also contain what Marianne Moore called "a place for the genuine."

SHARON OLDS (B. 1942) The primary source of the poetry of Sharon Olds is her traumatic childhood in the home of alcoholic parents, where she suffered violence, indignity, deprivation, and neglect. This childhood produced in her a continuing pain so absolute that she would later in life write a line virtually equating life with pain:

> the pain kept coursing through me like
> life, like the gift of life.[18]

Her most memorable work focuses on what Freud, without a sense of irony, called the "family romance," the implacable tensions between mothers, fathers, and children. Despite the prominence of suffering and traumas of all sorts in her work, hers is not a poetry of anguish and despair. Though she has frequently been compared with Sylvia Plath, there is none of the Plath's torment and angst about death and nothingness in her work. Olds is a poet of *this* world, that is, the familiar dysfunctional and maddening world of human fallibility, shortsightedness, greed, and inhumanity. The moods of her poetry run the gamut from horror and humiliation to celebrative joy. The latter stance occurs mostly in poems about her children and in some erotic love poems. She can write elegies for mice and gerbils with the same unflinching eye that observes the violent unpredictability of a drunken father and a hysterical mother. She finds metaphors everywhere that attach themselves to their subject like a virus clinging to its host cell. Her deeply devotional poems to and about her children do not curtail her randy sexuality. One of the distinctive aspects of her work is a refusal to separate the "mother-woman" from the sexual woman, as many men seem to insist on doing.

Her three books published before 1990, *Satan Says* (1980), *The Dead and the Living* (1984), and *The Gold Cell* (1987), share a similar four-part structure that gathers poems around particular loci in her life: public, political issues (generally her least successful genre); her primary family (mother, father, sister, and brother); her emergence from that world (her "journey" poems); and her created family (husband and two children). *The Father* (1992) abandons that structure and chronicles a single traumatic event: the lingering death of her father and his enormous impact on her life. In *The Wellspring* (1996) she returns to a four-part structure, each of the sections dealing with a separate phase of her life.

Although much of the work in *Satan Says* is apprentice work, the powerful title poem speaks to the liberating power of speech, especially for a woman speaking taboo and previously unexpressed thoughts. The narrator is locked in a cedar box and enticed by Satan to say outrageous things if she wants to get out. These things include "My father is a shit," "My mother is a pimp," "fuck the father," "the father's cock," "the mother's cunt." As she is about to leave the box after this exorcism, she realizes that although she is filled with anger, rage, and torment about her mother and father, she cannot help but love them as well. Satan slips away and locks her in the box declaring that it is her coffin. The implication is that she will remain stifled until she is able to go farther than she has in revealing and condemning the parental abuse she suffered as a child. Like so much of the women's poetry of this period, Olds's work is centered around breaking the silences that have suppressed our knowledge of this kind of abuse in the past.

"A Whole New Poetry Beginning Here": The Assertion of Gender

A remarkable poem from *The Gold Cell*, "I Go Back to May 1937," reminiscent of Delmore Schwartz's equally remarkable short story "In Dreams Begin Responsibilities," summarizes the conflicting emotions that the subject of her childhood brings up for Olds. The narrator envisions her mother and father at college just before they married. She is filled with the urge to stop them from getting together because she knows that pain and cruelty lie ahead for both them and her, but she realizes that if she stops the match at this point, she will never come into being. She resists, saying

> I want to live. I
> take them up like the male and female
> paper dolls and bang them together
> at the hips like chips of flint as if to
> strike sparks from them, I say
> Do what you are going to do, and I will tell about it.
>
> (23)

The memorable mixed image of the narrator striking her parents together and producing sparks from them, as well as the stark directness of the final line bestowing the role of family historian on the speaker, epitomizes the condensed energy of Olds's work. On the pages of her books, the fiery friction of her mother and father is recreated and exposed.

The relationship between father and daughter is particularly complicated in Olds's poetry. Although disgusted by his alcoholism and terrorized by his actual and threatened physical abuse, Olds also reveals a taboo sexual attraction to her father and tends to see the lovers in her life as father surrogates. This relationship is depicted in a number of poems, beginning with "The Sisters of Sexual Treasure" in *Satan Says*, which begins with the startling lines,

> As soon as my sister and I got out of our
> mother's house, all we wanted to
> do was fuck.[19]

This poem not only views sex as a defiance of the mother; it also imagines it as a sublimation of daughter-father attraction:

> The men's bodies
> were like our father's body!
> (24)

Even more shocking in its conveyance of socially unacceptable intimate details is "Reading You," where she speaks of the father in explicitly sexual terms ("his cock that I have loved / beyond the others") and speaks of incest as something *she* desired:

> cock promised and never given
> that I would strip my skin for
>
> (70)

For Olds, poetry means taking the risk of breaking the silence of pretending such sentiments do not exist in the world.

This theme is continued in "The Ideal Father," in which the narrator speaks of her father's beatings, drunkenness, vomiting, and generally obnoxious behavior and contrasts him with the "ideal" father, who, among other things, gets an erection in record time and would protect his daughters by

> laying his perfect
> body over their sleep all night long.[20]

In "Fate" Olds takes on her father's alcoholic vision just as he took it on from his father, and in "The Sign of Saturn" she sees traces of her father in her daughter as well.

The father poems in *The Gold Cell* include "Saturn," which envisions her father as the ancient pagan deity who devoured his children. As he lies on the couch, passed out from too much booze, she sees him as having devoured her brother's life because he served as a model for his son, showing him what a man's life is supposed to be like. "Looking at my Father" describes a girl's fascination with the power of her father's body, despite all she knows about his abusiveness and alcoholism, while "The Chute" includes the startling image of the father holding one of his three children upside down in the laundry chute he built while instructing the child to repair some electric wiring within the shaft. The father seems to enjoy the child's fear and pretends he will let go and drop the child into the chute, but Olds's surprising conclusion assures the reader that the poem is

> a story of love
> and release, the way the father pulls you out of nothing
> and stands there foolishly grinning.
>
> (37)

A particularly poignant father poem is "The Blue Dress," which revolves around a birthday present her father sent on her fourteenth birthday, after he left her mother. It is a blue dress from a fancy department store, and she is very excited to get it and loves to wear it. A year later her mother tells her that her father did not buy the dress but told her to buy something inexpensive for his daughter and never even sent her the money for it. She never wears the dress again in her mother's presence, but wears it all the time at boarding school,

> casually mentioning sometimes it was a gift from my father,
> wanting in those days to appear to have something
> whether it was true or a lie, I didn't care, just to
> have something.
>
> (39)

Despite continuing descriptions of traumas she suffered at the hands of both her parents, there is some attempt in *The Gold Cell* to make peace with them. In "Late Poem to My Father" she recalls knowing that he was abused as a child of an alcoholic and says that she would like to reach him in time to prevent what happens later, knowing, of course, that this is impossible. And in "After 37 Years, My Mother Apologizes for My Childhood," she also forgives her mother for the terrible treatment she received as a child. As if sensing that this forgiveness is a major step in self-redefinition, Olds writes,

> I hardly knew what I
> said or who I would be now that I had forgiven you.
> (43)

Although Olds seems able to come to terms with her mother's cruelty in a single poem, an entire volume, *The Father* (1992), does not quite bring her to reconciliation. These are the most harrowing poems she has written, and to read this volume is to experience the paradoxical and conflicting feelings she experienced at the time of his death. This day-by-day chronicle of the events leading up to and following her father's death is almost excruciating in its unsparing candor, looking head-on at even "The Exact Moment of His Death," as one of the poems is called. The book deals bravely with the fact that our love for our parents often transcends personal abuse, despite the fact that it may not be politically correct to acknowledge this fact.

Olds's "public" poems are less affecting than her harrowing family chronicles, but several of them are memorable. These include "The Death of Marilyn Monroe," a haunting description of Monroe's corpse being carried out of her house by male paramedics. The poem turns into a parable about men's idealizations of the female body and the psychic costs of those idealizations for both men and women:

> These men were never the same. They went out
> afterwards, as they always did,
> for a drink or two, but they could not meet
> each other's eyes.
>
> *(Dead and Living,* 10)

The men confront the reality of an icon, which is that mortality is the great leveler of human life and the things men build their dreams on are illusory. The three men react differently to this experience. One falls into a persistent depression, his sleep tormented by nightmares; another finds life diminished, and even his ideas about death change. But the most important transformation occurs in the third paramedic, who finds himself awake at night looking at the woman beside him

> listening to a
> woman breathing, just an ordinary
> woman
> breathing.
>
> (10)

The last two lines, each a single word allowing for an intake of breath between them, separate the existential reality of life from the imaginary and mythic reality we project on movie stars like Marilyn Monroe.

Also worthy of mention are several vivid poems based on historical photographs. Olds enables her readers to virtually walk into the photograph and inhabit the historical reality it depicts. In one of these, two men, nailed to boards and condemned to death in the China of 1905 give us an anguished image of inhumanity. In another, a young, starving Russian girl in the drought of 1921 leans against a sack while a caption under the photo says she will starve to death that winter along with millions of other Russians. Olds makes us see deeper into the image of the starving girl:

"A Whole New Poetry Beginning Here": The Assertion of Gender

> Deep in her body
> the ovaries let out her first eggs,
> golden as drops of grain.
>
> (6)

These gold cells of life are startling juxtaposed against the context of hopelessness represented by the photo. In a sense, this juxtaposition is the thematic center of Olds's poetry: a life of suffering and deprivation, but somehow luminous and transcendent at the core. That luminosity radiates throughout *The Wellspring* (1996), a book which depicts a cycle of sexuality, from her own conception and birth through early sexual experiences, to the birth of her own children and her mature adult sexuality. For Olds, sex is indeed life's wellspring, and nearly always the subject of her strongest poems.

OTHER WOMEN POETS   In *Writing Like a Woman* (1984), **Alicia Suskin Ostriker (b. 1937)** notes that in the past the greatest women writers working in English were almost "always constrained by some pinching corset of timidity, some obscuring veil of inhibition."[21] Many of the women writing poetry in the second half of the twentieth century unlaced and removed the corset completely, and through honest self-expression created a poetry built around an aesthetic of truth. While Emily Dickinson's "Tell all the truth / but tell it slant" may have been the motto for women's writing before 1960, since that time, writes Ostriker, "to tell all the truth and tell it straight has become the program of most women poets" (2).

Although more important to women's poetry in our time as a critic than a poet, Ostriker's seven books of poems, which chronicle important passages in her life, include *A Dream of Springtime* (1979), *A Woman under the Surface* (1982), *The Imaginary Lover* (1986), and *Green Age* (1989).

Anne Waldman (b. 1945) grew up on McDougal Street in Greenwich Village during the heyday of the beat generation. Influenced by both the beats and the so-called "New York School of Poetry," Waldman developed a performance-oriented poetry built on cadences and rhythmical chants. Much of her work is collected in *Helping the Dreamer: New and Selected Poems* (1989), which includes her best-known long poem "Fast Talking Woman," a catalogue celebration of the variety of women within her, based on the chants of a Mazatec Indian female shaman.

Another writer whose origins are with the beat generation is **Diane de Prima (b. 1934)**. Her first collection of *Selected Poems: 1956–75* is much thicker than the more judicious selection published in 1990, although sixteen more years of her writing life is contained in the latter. DiPrima's work draws from both H. D. and the poets of the beat generation. Her most memorable work is a long poem called "Loba," begun in 1971 and published as an uncompleted book in 1978. Written in a ritualistic, shamanistic style, the poem offers various descriptions of the Loba, a mythical creature, half wolf, half woman (or a woman with a wolf's head), that DiPrima evokes as an image of female power, endurance, and survival.

Judy Grahn (b. 1940) writes a woman-centered poetry that cracked open some of the silences surrounding lesbian life in America. Included in her 1978 *The Work of a Common Woman* is a long, unusually structured poem, "A Woman is Talking to Death," that brings together many of the strains of oppression and violence that appear in her work. Beginning with a description of an automobile accident witnessed on the Bay Bridge connecting Oakland and San Francisco, the poem spirals outward from that scene to incorporate a dense collage of historical and personal injustices that have been visited on minorities of all sorts. Although Grahn's work is often "antipoetic," she has produced an underground poetry of survival and endurance that broadens in scope and scale as she develops as a writer.

In extreme stylistic opposition to Judy Grahn is **Marilyn Hacker (b. 1942)**, whose verse is highly traditional and meticulously crafted. Her sestinas, villanelles, and especially sonnets bring the forms of another era squarely to bear on late twentieth-century life. Like the work of Sharon Olds, Hacker's poetry chronicles both the traumas and celebrations of her personal life. She has created a "talking" idiom within the traditional form of the sonnet and sonnet sequence that gives her work a continuing narrative thrust from one book to the next, linking formalist precision with confessional self-revelation. From the award-winning *Presentation Piece* (this 1975 volume won both the National Book Award and the Lamont Poetry Prize) to the 1990 *Going Back to the River*, one can trace the sinews and dislocations of the most important relationships in her life, especially those with her mother, daughter, and several of her lovers. She has lived in Paris, London, New York, and San Francisco, and the geocultural landscape of each of these cities figures in her poetry.

Her most memorable book may be *Love, Death, and the Changing of the Seasons* (1986), a lengthy sonnet sequence (interspersed with a few villanelles) that charts the development of a steamy love affair between an older (age forty-two) and younger (age twenty-five) woman, from the moment they pick up the physical attraction between them to the abrupt and painful end of the relationship. Sexual energy connects the two lovers everywhere—shopping at Bloomingdale's, flying on 747s, riding on trains, walking down the street together, lying in bed. The intense sensuality of these poems vibrates against the formal constraints of the sonnet, almost like earth tremors rocking the foundation of a sturdy old house. One might expect the form to simply come apart, but it does not, demonstrating its astonishing adaptability in the hands of a master. Hacker is one of the few truly innovative neoformalist poets of the late twentieth century.

To observe the artistic development of **Louise Glück (b. 1943)** is to see a poet ridding her language of the appearance of artifice and contrivance. Her early poetry, published as *Firstborn* (1968), reveals an edgy sensitivity in an overly precious poetic voice, while the poems in her second collection, *The House on the Marshlands* (1975), announce an almost cocky confidence:

> I am no longer young. What
> of it? Summer approaches, and the long
> decaying days of autumn when I shall begin
> the great poems of my middle period.[22]

Descending Figure (1980) uses hunger as a metaphor for her sensibility, which sees death as a "mere by-product" of her need for perfection, a need that has haunted her throughout her life:

> It begins quietly
> in certain female children:
> the fear of death, taking as its form
> dedication to hunger,

> because a woman's body
> *is* a grave; it will accept
> anything.[23]

Glück's poetry is a poetry of hunger and desire. Stark and sometimes opaque, it moves through surreal dream images, often with religious undertones. Much of it seems driven by the need to understand the processes that make the world what it is. This is a large task, epitomized by a poem called "Elms" from *The Triumph of Achilles* (1985):

> I have been looking
> steadily at these elms
> and seen the process that creates
> the writhing, stationary tree
> is torment, and have understood
> it will make no forms but twisted forms.[24]

But Glück's masterpiece to date is surely *Ararat* (1990), a book of spare, lean personal meditations that make her earlier work seem positively baroque. The flat, unadorned style of the poems here signals a new minimalist confessional tone that moves beyond the more ornate styles of poets like Plath and Sexton:

> I'll tell you something: every day
> people are dying. And that's just the beginning.
> Every day, in funeral homes, new widows are born,
> new orphans. They sit with their hands folded,
> trying to decide about this new life.[25]

A good place to start in getting to know the work of **Olga Broumas (b. 1949)** is "Namaste," a long autobiographical narrative from her 1979 collection *Soie Sauvage*. Here she accumulates personal details surrounding the emergence of her bisexual identity, chronicling especially her relationships with two men and several women. Sex and sexuality are the primary themes of her work, intertwined with religious imagery and many allusions to her Hellenic heritage. Broumas was the first winner of the Yale Younger Poets Award whose native tongue is not English. Born in Greece in 1949, she did not begin to learn English until age eleven, when she visited America for the first time.

Broumas's political ideology as well as her poetic cadences are indebted to Adrienne Rich. She writes as a radical feminist, aiming to transform the world through language:

> I am a woman committed to
> a politics
> of transliteration, the methodology
>
> of a mind
> stunned at the suddenly
> possible shifts of meaning—for which
> like amnesiacs
>
> in a ward on fire, we must
> find words
> or burn.[26]

The unexpected turns of this figure, from bureaucratic words like "politics," "transliteration," and "methodology" through the hissing sibilance of "stunned," "suddenly," and "shifts" to the blazing monosyllabic conclusion, are illustrative of the very shifts of meaning the poem is describing and are characteristic of the artfully diverse diction in Broumas's work. Her passionate poems about sexuality find sexual metaphors everywhere. These appear in a poem called "Eros":

> On Death's face all religion dances
> like pins on the head of a clit[27]
> . . . .
> faith
> like orgasm is problematic in the mind
> (36)
> . . . .
> strategies
> for prolonging pleasures are the faith
> of oxygen fucking the lungs of life
> (37)

Broumas's work moves with jarring rapidity from joy to sorrow, from anger to empathy, from pain to celebration. Hers is a vital poetry of transience and transition, appropriate to an age in which "future shock" has become a rather ordinary state of affairs.

· SIX ·

Turning Inward:
The Poetry of American Men

> What will they do now
> who have gone so long
> without weeping,
> who seem to have lost forever
> the gradual repertoire,
> the harp and the flute,
> the piccolo and pizzicato?
>
> —Michael Blumenthal, "The Hearts of Men"

Unlike the assertion of gender characteristic of much of the poetry of contemporary American women, the poetry of American men rarely takes on a gender-based viewpoint *consciously*. Even a poet like Robert Bly (discussed in chapter 3), who became a prominent figure in the national "men's movement," moved in this direction relatively late in life, after having established a reputation as a poet whose work is grounded in myth and the "deep image." For the most part, male poets have continued to insist that poetry is gender-neutral, that the best poetry written by both men and women is universal, and that innovation and intensity of language are the defining features of poetic value. By contrast with the feminist poetry discussed in the previous chapter, for most men, the "personal" and the "political" are separate realms, and the poetry they write that grows out of personal experience is not ideologically based. Yet when one reads a substantial amount of work by male poets in this postfeminist age, it is hard not to notice a gender orientation, in some cases nearly as striking as that articulated by feminists, except that this orientation has been the dominant mode for so long in literary history that many readers do not think of it as male at all. Many well-known traditional poems of the English language, particularly poems *about* women—from Andrew Marvell's "To His Coy Mistress" and Robert Herrick's

"Delight in Disorder" through Wordsworth's "Lucy" poems and W. B. Yeats's poems about "Crazy Jane" to T. S. Eliot's "The Love Song of J. Alfred Prufrock"—were clearly written from a distinctly male point of view, but many readers continue to feel it is irrelevant to point that out.

From the 1950s to the present, contemporary male poets have made significant departures from the modernist emphasis on literary allusion, impersonality, objectivity, ironic distancing, and imagery rooted in the world of "things" or "ideas." The poetry of many American men turned inward after midcentury, following the lead of poets like Cummings, Kenneth Rexroth, and Roethke rather than the canonical figures of Pound, Eliot, Stevens, and Williams. Of course, the major modernists remained an influence, and aspects of their work continued to permeate the poetry of both men and women. Still, it is clear that a new kind of emotive sensibility began to emerge in the seventies and eighties that moved deeply into the inner psyche and paid more attention to the gradations of feeling it discovered there than to the niceties of language created to express that feeling.

Men also engaged social issues more directly from the grounding of their personal stance. When Allen Ginsberg wrote "I saw the best minds of my generation," his "I" was not a persona, as is the "I" in Eliot's "Let us go, then, you and I." The new personally direct poetry seemed to adhere to the dictum expressed by Cummings: "since feeling is first / who pays any attention / to the syntax of things / will never wholly kiss you."

These poets were determined to connect poetry to life experience and to move it away from the confines of academia. Each developed a unique and differentiated voice: Galway Kinnell moved from the formalism of his early work to a more expressive poetry connecting his inner psyche to the larger world outside of it; W. S. Merwin's work seemed haunted by a sense of absence as he searched for a language to express the ineffable; Philip Levine worked toward the creation of a "populist" poetry that described the lives of working people; Donald Hall found in his family history materials that would give his finely crafted verse additional resonance; Mark Strand, like Merwin, seemed preoccupied by absences, but he crafted a poetry intended to reflect "the continuous life"; and C. K. Williams invented a new kind of long line that would express the fullness of distinct thoughts as he ruminated about the paradoxes and contradictions at the core of much male experience—the contradiction, for example, between toughing it out and expressing pain.

In nearly all of these poets there remained a tension between trying to retain some sense of optimism about life's possibilities and succumbing to what remained of the modernist vision of a fragmented and lost world. But whatever direction any individual poet took, men's poetry of the seventies and eighties clearly became more personal, more rooted in actual life, and less guarded by literary allusion and artifact than the poetry of earlier generations. Whether it is Kinnell describing the birth of his daughter, Merwin or Strand delineating the deep connections they felt toward their fathers, Levine reminiscing about his childhood neighborhood, Hall chronicling daily life on his family farm in New Hampshire, or C. K. Williams trying to protect his daughter from the terrors of the world, this is the poetry of men's inner lives exposed and brought into the commonality of our outer world.

GALWAY KINNELL (B. 1927)   Between 1960 and 1980, Galway Kinnell published seven important collections of poetry that were then gathered and edited for his *Selected Poems* (1982). His early work, like that of many of the poets of his generation, has a formalist inclination, particularly in the books *What a Kingdom It Was* (1960) and *Flower Herding on Mount Monadnock* (1964), although his first book includes one of his most innovative and memorable poems, "The Avenue Bearing the Initial of Christ into the New World." With *Body Rags* (1968) his naturalistic lyricism reached its pinnacle in poems like "The Bear" and "The Porcupine," which became his best-known, most anthologized works. *The Book of Nightmares* (1971) marked an important inward turn occasioned by the birth of his daughter, Maud, who is the subject of a remarkable poem about childbirth called "Under the Maud Moon." *Mortal Acts, Mortal Words* (1980) continued this introspective and domestic direction, including a number of poems about his son, Fergus. Since the *Selected Poems* appeared in 1982, Kinnell has published *The Past* (1985), an elegiac summation of important life changes; *When One Has Lived a Long Time Alone* (1990), a book published just after the breakup of his twenty-year marriage; and *Imperfect Thirst* (1994). In addition to writing his own poetry, Kinnell has translated the work of Francois Villon, Yves Bonnefoy, and other French poets.

Though Kinnell is not an experimental poet, important formal innovations have characterized much of his work. In an early essay, he offers one of the most intelligent and clear-headed critiques on the limitations of traditional form for the contemporary poet. After demonstrating that rhyme and meter in poetry through the nineteenth century were imitations of nature, he shows that for contemporary poets this comforting analogical universe is untenable. Rhyme and meter have become merely "mechanical aids" for writing that force the poet to pay more attention to how he or she is saying something than what is being said. This attention is unnecessarily restrictive and prevents new perceptions and understandings. "If you were walking though the woods in winter, rhyming would be like following those footprints continually appearing ahead of you in the snow. Fixed form tends to bring you to a place where someone has been before. Naturally, in a poem, you wish to reach a new place."[1]

Among the "new places" Kinnell reached early in his career is the remarkable, strikingly titled poem "The Avenue Bearing the Initial of Christ into the New World." This ambitious poem was initially conceived on a trip to Jerusalem, where he visited the site of the fourteen Stations of the Cross. At the time he speculated on what it would be like to transfer the Stations of the Cross to a modern city. Years later, when he lived on Avenue C in New York, he discovered that the avenue was exactly fourteen blocks long, so he linked the Stations of the Cross idea to a poem about suffering and spirituality in New York City. The result is a fourteen-part poem that operates in a tradition shaped by Walt Whitman's "Crossing Brooklyn Ferry" and Hart Crane's *The Bridge*.

All the above poems are set (at least partially) in lower Manhattan and use the rich, multicultural heritage of New York City as a metaphor for the diversity of humanity and its common bond in suffering and mortality. Like both Whitman and Crane, Kinnell uses the physical landscape of New York as well as the urban symphony of sounds and colors to evoke the sense of a teeming presence, a timeless, orchestrated world of people and life in energetic motion. He adopts a "camera-eye" view of New York that creates a sense of the visual and aural cacophony of lower Manhattan. Setting the scene for the beginning of an urban day, Kinnell evokes the sounds of birds overhead, the blast of a tugboat horn, the swish of a street cleaner's broom, a pushcart clacking through the street, delivery trucks leaving and arriving, a woman setting potted plants on a window ledge, a man walking around a corner, and the flight of a single pigeon leaving the building ledges behind and flying into the distance.

Avenue C in this poem becomes an emblem for the commonality of suffering as well as an entrance to a new world of possibility—a new ghetto as well as a new paradise. The poem is permeated by imagery of the Holocaust as expressed through the Jewish inhabitants of the Avenue, many of whom are its survivors. Its final lines embody the Avenue as a physical organism—heart, lungs, brain, blood—and culminate in an expression of wonder, immediately undercut by a woebegone, ancient Jewish lament:

> The heart beats without windows in its night,
> The lungs put out the light of the world as they
> Heave and collapse, the brain turns and rattles
> In its own black axlegrease—
>
>   In the nighttime
> Of the blood they are laughing and saying,
> Our little lane, what a kingdom it was!
>
>   oi weih, oi wieh[2]

Although the external and urban focus of the Avenue C poem makes it unrepresentative of much of Kinnell's work, the poem does reflect the aural and musical quality of much of his poetry, particularly his attention to noises and sounds that he loves to represent onomatopoetically. The sounds of birds, animals, objects, machines, and people permeate all of his work. A small sampling of Kinnell's exotically expressive diction would include words such as clack / tic ai wuh / mugwumps / crunch / croal / haish / yaw / *cigit cigit* / squinched / rasp / cackle / yap / screech / pelf / fenks / gurry / *scritch scritch scritch* / wee wee wee / cawhjoosh / *dee, dee, dees*. Sometimes these words are used whimsically, but more often they are attentive and accurate representation of what the world sounds like.

A similar combination of playful inventiveness and philosophical seriousness characterizes two of Kinnell's most famous poems, both about animals and both meditations on the relationship between humanity and the rest of the natural world. In "The Porcupine," the narrator first describes the creature objectively, then identifies with it, then *becomes* it. In "The Bear," the identification is even more complete and literal. Here the barrier between human and animal is disposed of in shocking lines describing the narrator eating a blood-soaked bear turd.

"The Bear" is a straightforward, coherent narrative that becomes more elusive and mysterious with each reading. The paradoxical final stanza carries oppositional meanings: has the poet become the bear, who is now recalling his previous life as a poet, or has he become a poet once more, recalling the transformative poetic moment of becoming one with an animal? This paradox may be representative of what Charles Molesworth sees as the dualistic nature of nearly all of Kinnell's work, embodying "two actions which may appear contradictory but are in fact complementary: self-discovery and self-destruction, the heuristic and the incendiary actions of poetry."[3] Poetry can only bring us renewal by destroying our conventional ways of seeing and experiencing the world.

The Book of Nightmares (1971) is Kinnell's most memorable and innovative single volume, rich in its imagery, haunting in its rhythms, evocative and almost terrifying in the poet's desire to look his own life square in the face. It insists on a vision of life not only as illusion but as terrifying illusion. It is a mistake to speak of separate poems in this collection; the whole is a single ten-part poem that begins with a dedicatory work on the birth of his daughter ("Under the Maud Moon") and culminates in a poem of absolute finality ("Lastness") that incidentally describes the birth of his son.[4] The precision of the book's imagery as well as its deep sense of felt life is illustrated by Kinnell's remarkable description of childbirth. The hesitations, stops and starts of the verse, cause the scene to materialize before us in terms of sound as well as image:

> Her head
> enters the headhold
> that starts sucking her forth: being itself
> closes down all over her, gives her
> into the shuddering
> grip of departure, the slow,
> agonized clenches making
> the last molds of her life in the dark.
> *(Selected Poems, 99)*

This is Kinnell at his best, re*creating* rather than simply reporting a major life experience.

While a description of a birth may seem incongruous in the opening poem of a collection called *The Book of Nightmares*, Kinnell immediately tempers any celebrative feelings he may have aroused with another precise description, this time imbuing the literal with its nightmarish metaphoric significance. He describes the infant's first movements:

> they hang her up
> by the feet, she sucks
> air, screams
> her first song—and turns rose,
> the slow,
> beating, featherless arms
> already clutching at the emptiness.
> (*Selected Poems*, 100)

Throughout *The Book of Nightmares*, life is clutching at the emptiness, and in the final poem, Kinnell tells once again the oldest story: "Living brings you to death, there is no other road." Despite the underlying terror of this realization—indeed, because of it—there is in Kinnell's work a deep, nearly awesome respect for the living and for the act of creation.

Between 1971 and 1980, Kinnell did not publish any new books of poetry, although his work continued to appear in literary journals; he also reissued some of his early work and published a book of translations and a prose collection. When his next new collection of poems, *Mortal Acts, Mortal Words*, appeared in 1980, it seemed less innovative and less powerful than his earlier work. However, *The Past* (1985), dedicated to his wife and published in the year of his divorce, showed a renewed poetic energy, embodied in strong and innovative poems like "The Road Between Here and There," "On the Oregon Coast," "The First Day of the Future," and a remarkable sociopolitical poem called "The Fundamental Project of Technology." In the latter poem, Kinnell sees the basis of technology as its desire to "de-animalize" human experience and particularly to purge it of mortality. To eliminate death, technology must first eliminate those who die—a task first attempted at Hiroshima and Nagasaki. Kinnell repeats the words "white flash" in each of the poem's seven stanzas, creating a kind of repetitive, silent explosion, presaging the demise of the human soul that he believes awaits humanity at the end of the technological road.

Kinnell's 1990 collection, *When One Has Lived a Long Time Alone,* is a book of deepening introspection. The title poem is a sequence of eleven curtal (13 rather than 14 lined) sonnets that begin and end with the line "When one has lived a long time alone." These poems, written after the breakup of his marriage, speak of a temporary withdrawal from the human world and an attempt to enter the world of animals and insects:

> and more and more one finds one likes
> any other species better than one's own,
> which has gone amok, making one self-estranged,
> when one has lived a long time alone.[5]

But gradually these quiet meditations move away from the withdrawals of a solitary life toward a rededication to the human world, which for all its flaws and despair remains *our* collective world. The eleventh and final poem in the sequence is a celebration of that collectivity:

> When one has lived a long time alone,
> one wants to live again among men and women,
> to return to that place where one's ties with the human
> broke . . .
>
> (69)

By the end of this volume, ties with the human are restored, and once again there is a sense of deep compassion for all life that is constant in nearly all of Kinnell's work. His 1994 book, *Imperfect Thirst,* examines the sources of poetry in both memory and the physical world. It is among the most sensuous of his collections—"Rapture," and "The Cellist," are unapologetic celebrations of heterosexual male sexuality, and "Holy Shit" takes the adjective that often modifies our excrement quite literally. Once again, Kinnell's sense of reverence toward life comes to the fore—even our waste matter is holy. Four lines from *The Book of Nightmares* characterize that reverence fully:

> on the absolute whiteness of pages
> a poem writes itself out: its title—the dream
> of all poems and the text
> of all loves—"Tenderness toward Existence."[6]

Turning Inward: The Poetry of American Men

W. S. MERWIN (B. 1927)   For W. S. Merwin, human habitats—hotels, houses, train stations, and other places where humanity gathers and dwells—are frail and fragile edifices, surrounded by a vast darkness. Merwin writes about these habitats and about human beings, but in doing so he produces more a negative exposure of our collective existence than a positive photographic print. In his poems we often see what we are not rather than what we are. It is a poetry of things not done, days not lived, places not seen:

> Something I've not done
> is following me
> I haven't done it again and again[7]

This focus on the unsaid, the undone, the unknown creates the impression that external phenomena control life and that these phenomena have a life and vitality of their own—beyond human recognition. As mundane an object as a pencil becomes for this poet a mystical totem because within it are the unwritten words he will write:

> Inside this pencil
> crouch words that have never been written
> never been spoken
> never been taught
>
> they're hiding

> (*Selected Poems*, 203)

Perhaps Merwin's ultimate poem of negation is "Exercise," where the reader is enjoined to practice forgetting what hour it is, then what country he or she lives in, then how to add and subtract, then to forget numbers themselves, then the alphabet, and, finally, to forget fire. As the learned and perceived world falls away, the vacant self remains, but what is that self, emptied of its artifacts?

Commentators and critics of Merwin's work have recognized this portrayal of absence, and the editors of *W. S. Merwin: Essays on the Poetry* speak of a "critical vocabulary collapsing under the strain of describing what is going on in [Merwin's] books of the 1960's and early 1970's."[8] "Enigmatic" is a term commonly used to describe Merwin's work, and it is amplified by Merwin's own distrust of language as descriptive of any tangible reality. As Denis Donogue notes, Merwin's language often strikes readers "as emptied of conventional connotation, speaking its meaning only through its dark tonalities" (Folsom and Nelson, 12). From *A Mask for Janus* (1952) through *The Rain in the Trees* (1988), these dark tonalities have been consistent, although Merwin has shaped and developed the work according to the contours of his life.

In the introduction to Merwin's first volume, W. H. Auden speaks of two sorts of contemporary poetry, confessional and personal on the one hand, and impersonal and mythic on the other. He regards Merwin's early work as an exemplar of the latter style. But although Merwin's work has always retained a mythic and mystical dimension, it has become increasingly personal and self-conscious, tied to particular events in his life: the death of his father, his love life, his travels, particularly his living in Hawaii, and even the death of his dog. So although the poems are permeated by absences, they reflect a lived life as well. In the introduction to his *Selected Poems* (1988), Merwin writes that he has not changed any of the poems he included, "not because I thought they were beyond improvement but because in certain respects I am no longer the person who wrote them" (vii).

The elements of Merwin's style, particularly his elemental diction, have been widely imitated and are easy to parody. He is fond of using a stripped down language of natural elements: words like "dusk," "darkness," "light," "snow," "wind," "rocks," "sea," "mountains," "stones," and so on occur repetitively, juxtaposed against words that suggest personal mental and physical states, such as "blind," "dream," "sleep," "hunger," "death," and "dying." This juxtaposition sometimes creates a sense of preciosity or, as Robert Peters puts it, a feeling that "Poets are supposed to sound like this!"[9] Merwin is particularly drawn to the idea of blindness, which is a pervasive metaphor throughout his work. Blindness, however, is not usually a symbol of infirmity but rather simply an emblem of the human condition. We look out at the universe with vacant eyes. Rocks in their absolute silence are as sure interpreters of the universe as is humanity. For all the pretensions of our language, art and science,

> There is no season
> That requires us
>
> Masters of forgetting

> Threading the eyeless rocks with
> A narrow light
>
> (125)

This Robinson Jeffers-like sense of the *unnecessariness* of humanity
hovers around Merwin's work, sometimes leading to a disintegration of the body that encases the self:

> I dreamed I had no nails
> no hair
> I had lost one of the senses
> not sure which
> the soles peeled from my feet and
> drifted away
> clouds
> It's all one
> feet
> stay mine
> hold the world lightly
>
> (*Selected Poems*, 148)

In fact, the concept of a *self* in Merwin, as expressed through language, is complex and often convoluted. An important poem,
"Finally," sheds some light on the problematic nature of the self as
Merwin conceives it. In the poem a man attempts to confront his true
self, to rid himself of all falsity. According to Charles Altieri, "the
true self calls from the darkness" (Folsom and Nelson, 174). For
Altieri, the poem also indicates a shift in Merwin's style that he sees
as occurring after the publication of *The Drunk in the Furnace* (1960):
"The essence of that style is its negation of the light of ordinary experience" (Folsom and Nelson, 175). The poem may also be seen as a
poet coming to terms with a subject matter born of the inner life
rather than the accoutrements of the outer world. The narrator feels
it is *finally* time to write of the things most important to him—the
things that dominate his psychic life. He invokes the "Self" as a
muse, and although it makes his palms sweat merely to think about
the personal revelations called for in truly honest writing, he steels
himself to plunge ahead:

> My dread, my ignorance, my
> Self, it is time. Your immanence

Prowls the palms of my hand like sweat.
Do not now, if I rise to welcome you,
Make off like roads into the deep night.
The dogs are dead at last, the locks toothless,
The habits out of reach.
I will not be false to you tonight.

(Selected Poems, 90)

All of those things which have prevented honest expression in the past—here symbolized as "dogs," "locks," and "habits" (critics? self-constraint? traditional form?)—are shunted aside as the narrator dares to think the unthinkable and reaches inside himself, hoping to discover the gift of integrity, "something / Which I had lost, which you found on the way." Recovering that integrity requires confronting the darkness of the interior life and writing about it as directly as possible, without the restraints of poetic form or critical fashion. The poem's stunning conclusion finds the narrator putting out the light that symbolizes the comfortable clarity of the "civilized" world, so that he may better see into the darkness:

Come. As a man who hears a sound at the gate
Opens the window and puts out the light
The better to see out into the dark,
Look, I put it out.

(Selected Poems, 90)

Perhaps the most personal poems Merwin has written appear in his 1983 volume, *Opening the Hand*, in which many of the poems deal with the death of his father, a Presbyterian minister who looms as a formidable presence in Merwin's life. In this book Merwin uses a line with a break in the middle of it, as if the event created a fissure in his life:

When my father died I saw   a narrow valley
it looked as though it began   across the river

(Selected Poems, 251)

In addition to dealing with absences and defining the contours of the self, Merwin's poetry has a political dimension. It is not an overtly political poetry, like that of Adrienne Rich or Allen Ginsberg, but its political orientation shows itself most clearly in poems he has written about environmental destruction, as in "For a Coming Extinction," a poem addressed to the gray whale that concerns humanity's devastation of that species, or, more spectacularly, in "The Last One," a poem about the rampant destruction of the American landscape and the arrogance of the European settlers of the New World:

> Well they cut everything because why not.
> Everything was theirs because they thought so.
> *(Selected Poems*, 118)

When the last tree is chopped down and sent crashing into its shadow on the water, the shadow remains and becomes a larger and larger presence, impossible for human beings to eliminate. The shadow of nature—death and nothingness—haunts humanity, and we create cities where people exist "as far as they could" from nature, although "lucky ones" live there with the shadow of nature always present in their life—that is, they remain conscious of our responsibility to preserve and protect it before humanity obliterates it altogether.

This concern becomes paramount in *The Rain in the Trees* (1988), which was shaped by Merwin's experience living in Hawaii, where the encroachments of humanity on nature are starkly visible and nothing short of catastrophic. Here the wind, rain, moon, and stones that are staples of Merwin's poetry are not used as archetypal constructs, as they are in his earlier work, but are imbued with a feeling of our palpable need for them. A connectedness here, rather than merely a series of absences, is tempered by an underlying sense of transitoriness. We are losing even the language to speak about nature:

> I want to tell what the forests
> were like
>
> I will have to speak
> in a forgotten language[10]

This sense of loss, both of nature and the language to describe it, permeates much of this work and is evident in poems like "Losing a Language," "Chord," and "The Lost Originals." For Merwin, the languages of nature are the sounds of insects, birds, animals, the wind, and the trees, not the language of humanity, which has been diverted to commercial and technological uses:

> the children will not repeat
> the phrases their parents speak
>
> somebody has persuaded them
> that it is better to say everything differently
>
> so that they can be admired somewhere
> farther and farther away
>
> (*Rain*, 67)

Another poem, "The Horizon of Rooms," is a reminder of how relatively recent is everything that we call civilization and of how long nature endured before our intrusive arrival. Like much of Merwin's earlier work, it is Jeffers-like in its assertion of both the puniness and illusionary self-importance of humanity. The striking opening line encapsulates that perception:

> There have been rooms for such a short time
> and now we think there is nothing else unless it is raining
>
> (*Rain*, 72)

Merwin's work embodies many of the contrary and conflicting strains in the male poetic tradition of the United States. Paradoxically, his cosmic sense of things is permeated by both Jeffers's sense of humanity's destructiveness and Whitman's sense of the interconnectedness of all life. Some of his poems reflect an anxiety and style reminiscent of T. S. Eliot (see especially "St. Vincents"), while others have a kind of Poundian arrogance (for example, "Gift"). Merwin is like Stevens in his conversion of elements of the real world into a metaphysical, imaginative construct and like Robert Lowell in his use of autobiography. He recorded perhaps the most important thing he learned from another poet in his poem "Berryman," which describes the young Merwin asking the older poet how he can ever be sure if anything he writes is any good. Berryman replies:

> you can't you can never be sure
> you die without knowing

whether anything you wrote was any good
if you have to be sure don't write
(*Selected Poems*, 271)

In addition, Merwin has been deeply influenced by his long history of work on translations. In the foreword to his *Selected Translations: 1968–78*, he speaks of the blurring that has occurred between his own poems and those he has translated:

For several years I tried to maintain illogical barriers between what I trans-lated and "my own" writing, and I think the insistence on the distinction was better than indulging in a view of everything being (presumably inspired) the same. . . . Except in a very few cases it would be hard for me to trace, in subsequent writings of my own, the influence of particular transla-tions that I have made, but I know the influences were and are there.[11]

Among those other influences are the Spanish language writers Jorge Luis Borges, Nicanor Parra, Juan Jose Arreola, and Roberto Juarroz, the Russians Alexander Blok and Osip Mandelstam, and many American Indian and Eskimo poets. This broad grounding in cultures and languages beyond his own gives Merwin's work a receptivity to unfamiliar modes of perception that charges it with a kind of eerie surrealism.

PHILIP LEVINE (B. 1928)   In a reprinted edition of his first collec-tion of poetry, Philip Levine remarks that the original edition was published in a finely set, small print run of 220 copies, although he would have preferred an edition of 50,000, each selling for 99 cents. This populist desire permeates Levine's poetry, which, like Marge Piercy's, is often drawn from his Detroit working-class background. From *On the Edge* (1963) to *What Work Is* (1991), his poetry is peopled with characters who are overworked and underpaid, living from paycheck to paycheck, and who in their own lives have little use for poetry, art, or any sort of culture beyond television and sports. There is something of a dissonance in his work in that he writes about this world with a highly trained poetic sensibility that distances him from it even as he attempts to identify with it. Speaking of a down-and-out black friend who works for the Dodge plant in Detroit, Levine reveals both his empathy with the working class and the cul-tural sensibility that has removed him from it:

He has the brain of a child, and he has a child
named Normandy who lives alone with her son.
In short, his life is as boring as mine.
Meanwhile back in the car there are talismen:

A heater, the splashed entrails of newspapers,
a speedometer that glows and always reads 0.
We have not come here to die. We are workers
and have stopped to relieve ourselves, so we sigh.[12]

The internal rhymes, the striking and exotic imagery, the poetic diction ("talismen," "splashed entrails"), and the symbolic details (a glowing speedometer that registers nothing) all undercut the observation that the poet lives as boring a life as the auto worker. The poet writes interestingly of a boring life, and through that writing, transcends the boredom.

Levine's attitude toward the uses of language in his poetry is paradoxical. On the one hand he insists that language is not the main attraction in his work, that he hopes instead to recreate situations and people that the reader can experience as real: "I'm not much interested in language. In my ideal poem, no words are noticed. You look through them into a vision . . . just see the people, the place. . . ."[13] On the other hand, he sees language as essential to a clear and accurate perception of the world and understands its inherently political nature. "Nothing is more obvious than what our politicians are doing to our language, so that if poets insist on the truth, or on an accurate rendition, or on a faithful use of language, if they for instance insist on an accurate depiction of people's lives as they are actually lived—this is a political act" (*Don't Ask*, 13). Levine seems to echo Adrienne Rich when he argues that poetry, simply as a clear and undistorted record of the way people live, is inevitably political and even revolutionary.

But unlike Rich's poetry, Levine's is not *overtly* political. His themes, in addition to an evocation of urban Detroit working-class life, are the depth and inescapability (for better or worse) of family connections; the importance of work, beyond its economic necessity; and the sense that America's hope and promise has largely been lost. Many of his poems are small moments of personal epiphanies occurring around one another of these themes.

Although his early work is more traditional and formal than the later, his most characteristic form is a page-and-a-half personal narrative in which a pivotal event triggers a memory that is made palpable and resonant. His major influences are Walt Whitman, E. E. Cummings, Kenneth Rexroth, Dylan Thomas, Pablo Neruda, Federico García Lorca, and John Keats. His is an urban American romanticism, nourished in rough-hewn cities like Detroit and Fresno.

Levine is essentially an urban poet, but nature is never far away in his work. Like many of the poets of his generation, he laments the distance modern life has traveled from the natural world. *They Feed They Lion* (1972) is an important collection that walks "The Cutting Edge" (as one of the poems is called) between urban and rural life, as well as between humanity and inanimate nature. The narrator is cut by a stone while walking along a riverbank. He tosses the stone away and goes home, but a year later returns to the spot and finds the stone still there. He feels this is something of an omen and considers taking the stone home with him, but instead scales it over his children's heads back into the water. The episode is a symbolic drama about our connection to the inanimate world as well as our distance from it.

But just as the inanimate world has power in Levine's work, so too has the industrial and urban world. The title poem of *They Feed They Lion* is a Dylan Thomas–like chant, but Americanized—that is, transmuted through Whitman and Cummings—to evoke a sense of the power growing out the American language. "Lion" in the poem seems to be used as an adverb or adjective and sometimes as a verb, but never as a noun, and this usage gives the poem an air of strangeness and force that is uniquely Levine's:

> From my five arms and all my hands,
> From all my white sins forgiven, they feed,
> From my car passing under the stars,
> They Lion, from my children inherit,
> From the oak turned to a wall, they Lion,
> From they sack and they belly opened
> And all that was hidden burning on the oil-stained earth
> They feed they Lion and he comes.[14]

The energy of this poem is the energy of romanticism, but a romanticism toughened by the realities of twentieth-century urban life. Levine often revisits childhood experiences from the perspective of a mature man, but he does so less from a nostalgic impulse than from a sense of recognizing that the boy he carries within himself needs the reassurance of continuity. He often thinks of himself as a quintessential American wandering among dull industrial cities. In a long poem of self-assessment called "Silent in America" he calls himself "Fresno's / dumb bard" (*N&S Poems*, 24) and takes on the role of a spokesperson for all of those silent, unnamed Americans he has written about. "One for the Rose," another poem that provides the title for one of his collections (1981), finds him returning to a street corner in Detroit where twenty-seven years before he boarded a bus to Akron, Ohio. Nothing looks the same, but the experience triggers the memory of the Akron trip, where he went to a wedding and wound up drunk in a bus terminal late at night, waiting for a bus to take him back to Detroit. The poem becomes an ironic lament and a reminder that writers are limited by the materials of their personal lives:

> What was I doing in Akron, Ohio
> waiting for a bus that groaned slowly
> between the sickened farms of 1951
> and finally entered the smeared air
> of hell on US 24 where the Rouge plant
> destroys the horizon? I could have been
> in Paris at the foot of Gertrude Stein,
> I could have been drifting among
> the reeds of a clear stream
> like the little Moses, to be found
> by a princess and named after a conglomerate
> or a Jewish hero. Instead I was born
> in the wrong year and in the wrong place,
> and I made my way so slowly and badly
> that I remember every single turn,
> and each one smells like an overblown rose,
> yellow, American, beautiful, and true.
> (*N&S Poems*, 233–34)

Incidents like this one seem to rise up out of the mists of memory for Levine, as he reconsiders their significance, framing them in a symbolic or representative way.

Another romantic aspect of Levine's work is his sense of a lifedeath continuum that transcends daily experience. The articulation of that continuum presents itself in his poetry as a kind of workingclass mysticism that suffuses ordinary life with profound and mysterious implications. An unseen aura seems to surround our most mundane and isolated moments. A lovely poem with the memorable title "The Poem Circling Hamtramck, Michigan, All Night in Search of You" describes a young man and an older woman sitting separately but near one another in a Michigan bar. Levine strokes evokes the scene sketchily in the poem's first stanza and finds the poetry in it in the second. The world of late-night neighborhood bars is an emblem of the cold world of people existing in isolation from each other, even though they crave connection and warmth. This Edward Hopper–like cityscape is then suffused with poetry. If this man and woman were to transcend their isolation, this time and place would not be what it is. Their mortality and isolation ironically connect them to each other even as they sit in separate spheres.

Levine identifies a kind of collective loneliness in a poem called "Asking," where the narrator recalls a brief contact he had with a young woman who seemed very needy. They talk for a while; he drops her off near her house, saying he will call her but knowing he will not. This moment awakens the realization that

> there must be
> millions of us,
> alone and frightened,
> feeling the sudden chill
> of winter, of time
> gathering and falling
> like a shadow across
> our lives.[15]

"Letters for the Dead" extends this sense of connectedness by exploring the ties between the living and the dead through a long litany of associations the narrator has had with people who have died. The powerful final line undercuts the distancing from death that most of us use as a survival mechanism. As we live longer, "even the dead are growing old" (*N&S Poems,* 53).

Family matters, because they obviously involve human connectedness, are also an important theme in Levine's work. His book *1933* (1974) deals with "the shock that occurs when the world takes the father away" (*1933,* 40). The title poem, "1933," is written to and about his father, who died in 1933, when Levine was five years old. The poem notes many of the changes that have taken place in the world since then, but at its poignant conclusion Levine evokes again the-five-year-old boy shattered by his father's death, walking now "in worn shoes splashing through rain" (*N&S Poems*, 121). The poem takes on additional poignancy when considered alongside a poem from a later volume, "My Son and I" in *The Names of the Lost* (1976), which describes a distant and awkward meeting between Levine and his own son in a New York coffee shop at 3 A.M.

Levine's later work shows some tendency to move beyond the shorter personal narratives that make up the bulk of his poetry. "A Walk With Thomas Jefferson" is a long, meandering poem from the 1989 volume of that title, which is structured by a syllabic meter reminiscent of William Carlos Williams. Once again the poem is occasioned by a visit to the Detroit neighborhood near Tiger Stadium where Levine grew up and later worked in an auto plant. Much of the neighborhood is now devastated and boarded up, but the narrator runs into Tom Jefferson, an old black man who comes originally from Alabama but remembers Joe Louis, who also grew up in this Detroit neighborhood. Levine takes us into Tom Jefferson's life—the backyard garden he plants, the memories of working at the Dodge main plant, the simple biblical faith he sustains. "It's Biblical," a phrase he repeats throughout the poem, refers to the endurance of life amidst the hardships of this Detroit neighborhood. As the narrator walks through the neighborhood with Tom, who pushes a shopping cart, he meditates on his own fate, having come from the same background as Tom, having worked in the same auto plant. The resonant name of the protagonist (ironic in the context of a Detroit ghetto) gives the poem an almost epic sweep, as does the contrast between these two aging men—one black, the other white—walking through the devastated streets of urban America.

Throughout the nineties, Levine's work continued to gain prominence and wide acceptance. He won both the National Book Award and the Pulitzer Prize for his 1991 collection, *What Work Is*, a book that solidified his reputation as a poet of the working class. His memoir, *The Bread of Time: Toward an Autobiography* (1994) gave his readers a biographical context for his life as a working writer. *The Simple Truth* (1994) underscored his increasingly Lowellesque tendency to link his personal life to history in poems like "My Mother with Purse the Summer They Murdered the Spanish Poet," and "My Father with Cigarette Twelve Years Before the Nazis Could Break His Heart."

At its best, Levine's poetry captures the collective heritage of contemporary America—contemporary urban life bound to the history that produced it. And he captures this heritage by writing about his own life experiences rather than by making sweeping pronouncements about American society and history.

DONALD HALL (B. 1928) An eclectic and wide-ranging literary figure, Donald Hall has had a considerable influence on several generations of writers and would-be writers. His freshman composition text, *Writing Well* went through many editions and was for a time the leading title in its field, and as a poet, autobiographer, baseball writer, critic, and editor, he has contributed substantially to the literary dialogue of his time. It is not hard to agree with Donald Davie, who wrote in 1978 that "Hall knows as much about poetry as anyone in America."[16] This knowledge of poetry was particularly useful in his role as general editor of two important critical series published by the University of Michigan Press, which have collected much of the critical prose published by the major contemporary poets of our time as well as critical commentary on their work.[17]

Before the appearance of *Kicking the Leaves* in 1978, Hall's poetry consisted primarily of apprentice work—craftsmanlike poems that demonstrate a mastery of traditional forms and often exude a superior or supercilious tone, sometimes going as far as to reveal contempt for his audience. In "To a Waterfowl," for example, a poem ironically titled after William Cullen Bryant's celebration of nature, Hall is contemptuous of "Women with hats like the rear ends of pink ducks" who come in their limousines to "the Women's Goodness Club" to hear his poems, and he is contemptuous of their husbands and children as well. But the youthful brashness and restrictive formalism on display in the early work is shunted aside in *Kicking the Leaves*, where Hall finds his true subject: the exigencies and realities of his own life and heritage.

In 1975 Hall returned to New Hampshire, after many years as a teacher at the University of Michigan, to live on the family farm that held many fond memories for him, particularly of his grandparents, whose photograph adorns the cover of *Kicking the Leaves*. "I planned long ago I would live here, somebody's grandfather," he wrote in a poem about his grandmother's death, and so he has, for the last several decades, inhabited the actual physical space of his grandparents' lives. *Kicking the Leaves* is an important book for Hall because its title poem gives him an image, as he reminisces about his youth, for a childhood memory—a boy's innocent and helpless anger confronting the first deaths of loved ones. In these poems Hall emphasizes the history of his interior life, a concept central to his notion of what poetry is. "A poem is one man's inside talking to another man's inside. It may *also* be reasonable man talking to reasonable man, but if it is not inside talking to inside, it is not a poem."[18] For Hall, as for many contemporary male poets, the essence of poetry is its ability to express and connect our interior worlds.

One of the more remarkable poems in *Kicking the Leaves* is called "Eating the Pig," in which Hall describes the ritual of roasting, carving, and eating a pig. After five hours of roasting, the pig is devoured in ten minutes by twelve people whom he likens to "an army starving in winter" that is stuffing itself on all the abundance of "a valley of full barns." The skeletal remains of the pig take on a life of their own. The small amount of remaining skin looks "like the map of a defeated country" ravaged by an army. The pig's detached head seems to call to the narrator, and he strokes it and speaks to it as a fellow creature. It becomes an archetypal animal, survivor of the stone age, as the narrator speaks these final words into its ear:

> "Fire, brother and father,
> twelve of us, in our different skins, older and
>   younger,
> opened your skin together
> and tore your body apart, and took it
> into our bodies."[19]

A selection of Hall's best poems written between 1953 and 1958 may be found in *The Day I Was Older* (1989), not quite a selected poems but an introduction to Hall's most important work.[20] The poems here include "My Son, My Executioner," a disturbing poem written in iambic tetrameter quatrains with a traditional abab rhyme scheme. The formal qualities of the poem contrast with a young couple's startling realization that their young son makes them more aware of their own mortality. The selection also includes "The Days," something of a precursor to Hall's later masterpiece, *The One Day* (1988). "The Days" is a strong poem about the accumulation of moments in a life and how they blur, become vague, and dissipate into nothingness:

> Suddenly he has the idea
> that thousands and thousands of his days
> lie stacked into the ground
> like leaves, or like that pressure of green
> which turns into coal in a million years.
>
> (*Older*, 87)

In "The Days," the narrator reminisces about what *may* have happened to a man ten years ago, then realizes that the day he is remembering is not unlike the day he is writing the poem. He imagines being able to travel at will through the various days of his life. A similar episode of time travel occurs in "Maple Syrup" when the narrator discovers a jar of syrup made by his grandfather twenty-five years before. After cleaning off the accumulated dirt, he and his partner open the bottle and taste the syrup, finding within it

> the sweetness preserved, of a dead man
> in the kitchen he left
> when his body slid
> like anyone's into the ground.
>
> (*Older*, 97)

Two of the best poems in this collection are "Merle Bascom's .22" and "The Day I Was Older." The former is a dramatic monologue in which a middle-aged man remembers a gun his father gave him and recalls some major events in his life, realizing that he has less and less use for a gun as he grows older and becoming saddened by the suffering and violence in the world that the gun represents. He hides the weapon, then takes it apart and asks a friend to "hide the firing pin" so that it will be rendered useless. The man rejects the heritage of violence and self-destruction he is heir to, but he cannot reject it completely—cannot destroy or totally get rid of the gun, because, as he concludes, "it was my father's gift" (*Older*, 103). Hall's desire to pay homage to previous generations and his ties to his father are explored as well in "The Day I Was Older," written on the occasion of the poet having lived to an older age than his father did. This poignant and powerful poem observes the pleasures and potential of midlife as well as its anxieties.

Both of these poems appear also in *The Happy Man*, Hall's oddly and ironically titled collection of 1986. The four sections of the book, "Barnyards," "Shrubs Burned Away," "Men Driving Cars," and "Sisters" focus on different aspects of Hall's life as a late twentieth-century male experiencing the traumas of contemporary life while clinging to the more secure verities of a previous age.

The second section especially, "Shrubs Burned Away," contains some of Hall's very best writing, and lays the groundwork for his 1988 masterpiece, *The One Day*, where it is reprinted as the first section of a long three-part poem that summarizes much of Hall's poetic interior life. Hall began the poem in 1971 and worked on it on and off for nine years until he began to shape a vast body of "frequent attacks of language" into "ten line bricks." The poem's original title, "Build a House," extends the construction metaphor, which refers to building a life from the accretion of experiences, heritage, and culture. The three introductory epigrams to the poem embody its central thrust: Montaigne's "Each man bears the entire form of man's estate" speaks to the universality of individual experience (although the language may be called sexist), while Picasso's more embrasive "Every human being is a colony" points to the diversity of voices within the poem. The third quotation, from Abbe Michel de Bourdeille, remarks on the androgynous aspects of the inner life: "There are other voices, within my own skull I daresay. A woman speaks clearly from time to time; I do not know her name. Especially there speaks a man who resembles me overmuch yet is distinctly not me."[21]

The One Day begins with the reminiscence of a middle aged man recalling his mother's bedtime tales, the first of many memories contained in the narrator's psyche; these memories construct the "house of dying" that the narrator has built from his life. Memories of the past and actualities of the present are a part of that house, but significantly missing are hopes for the future. This is largely, especially in the "Shrubs Burnt Away" section, the desolate environment of a hard-drinking, middle-aged man. The middle section, "Four Classics Texts," embodies an individual voice in the collective cultural heritage of various poetic modes. This collective heritage offers a larger context for the despair of the individual, but significantly, the voice of a woman sculptor, introduced in italics in the poem's first section, is missing here. It is as if to underscore how thoroughly male our cultural dialogue has been. Her voice returns, however, in "To Build a House," where it envelops

> the creation, not for what it signifies,
> but for volume and texture thrusting up

> from the touched places. I marry the creation that
> stays
> in place to be worked at, day after day.
>
> (*One Day*, 47)

Although this voice does not dominate the poem, it modifies the male despair to a substantial degree, enough so that the conclusion brings the reader to an eternal present, where the past lives and is reconstructed:

> Under the barn,
> fat and ancient grandfather spider sleeps
> among old spoked wheels: Our breathing shakes his web:
> It is always this time; the time that we live by
> is this time.
>
> (63)

Adding a female component to the dominantly male strands of the narrative brings a balance and harmony that connects past and present, creating a fuller sense of the truth of contemporary life. Like Eliot's *Four Quartets*, Hall's *The One Day* takes us to the "still point" in human history, which is always "now."

MARK STRAND (B. 1934) Mark Strand's *Selected Poems*, published in 1981, gathers the best of his five previously published volumes of work beginning with *Sleeping with One Eye Open* (1964) and continuing through *The Late Hour* (1978). These poems, plus the long prose poem *The Monument* (1978) and Strand's more recent work *The Continuous Life* (1990) and *Dark Harbor* (1993), make up a body of work that has been much imitated and much honored (Strand served a term as the poet laureate of the United States) and that is notable for its consistency of theme and style. That style and theme are evident in the title poem of his first collection, "Sleeping with One Eye Open," which suggests a wariness of and discomfort with engaging the world beyond the self. And yet there is a paradoxical sense of insubstantiality and anxiety about the self as well, a tenuous, besieged construct, impinged upon by the world, assaulted by the vast infinitudes of the cosmos. This stance is similar to that of Weldon Kees, Randall Jarrell, Delmore Schwartz, and other of the lost world poets discussed in chapter 1. In "Violent Storm," the narrator speaks of all of humanity as sitting

                    behind
Closed windows, bolted doors,
Unsure and ill at ease
While the loose, untidy wind,
Making an almost human sound, pours
Through the open chambers of the trees.[22]

That "almost human sound" is not meant to suggest an affinity with
nature but rather an alienation from it, as if it had an eerie unfathomable
presence that renders our humanness trivial and irrelevant. Poets use
nature as a metaphor to heighten our own importance because

The tree we lean against
Was never made to stand
For something else,
Let alone ourselves.
Nor with these fields
And gullies planned
With us in mind.
        (*Selected Poems*, 9)

This stark, deterministic view of the nonhuman landscape permeates nearly all of Strand's work. The sensibility behind that work is
aptly described by David Kirby as "mysticism with both feet on the
ground."[23] The poems are drenched in surrealism but solidly
grounded in this world. They are often drawn from personal experience but are also generic and abstract. Both philosophical and imag-
istic, they are embodiments of mind, landscapes of ideas.

Strand's most famous and most haunting poem, "Keeping Things
Whole," is one of the most fully realized short lyrics of his generation
of poets. It is an excellent example of his work at its very best and
captures a sense of absence more fully and concisely than any other
of his poems. It must be quoted in its entirety because it offers no less
than a transformative view of physical existence, and hence a transformative view of the human presence in nature. The poem recon-
figures our apprehension of a human figure in a landscape by con-
struing the human shape not as a presence but as the absence of
everything else. But paraphrase does not capture the simplicity and
limpidity of the poem:

In a field
I am the absence

of field.
This is
always the case.
Wherever I am
I am what is missing.

When I walk
I part the air
and always
the air moves in
to fill the spaces
where my body's been.

We all have reasons
for moving.
I move
to keep things whole.
        (*Selected Poems,* 10)

The strength of Strand's poetry is also often its weakness. His tendency to create generic figures—"a man," "a woman," "someone," and especially "you"—moves his work toward an archetypal universality, but it also distances it from actual personal experience. Then, too, like W. S. Merwin, Strand makes extensive use of archetypal words, including "cold," "heat," "snow," "fire," "wind," "rain," "sea," and especially "light" and "dark." This tendency appears to have intensified over the years. In fact, if we exclude prose poems, where for some reason he tends toward a more specific diction, the words "light," "dark," or one of their variants appear in virtually *every* poem in Strand's 1990 collection, *The Continuous Life.* The repetitive diction often makes it hard to differentiate one poem from another.

Sometimes, Strand seems haunted by the "you" in his poems, as in "My Life by Somebody Else," where he seeks to confront this alter ego directly, but finds the persona evasive. Who is this poet who has written poems called "My Life" and "My Death" and now feels removed from them? Strand seems to suggest that as a poet he becomes someone other than himself writing about his own life.

But Strand can be personal and direct as well, and when he allows personal revelations to appear in his poetry, it often gathers strength and force. "Elegy for My Father," for example, is one of his most powerful longer poems, because it does not lose the strength of its emotional center in the vague metaphysical air of abstraction. The poem captures the painful intensity of the moment when the poet confronts his father's dead body. It speaks for and to anyone who has had this ineffable life experience—coming into the presence of a body in a funeral home and recognizing the absence of the spirit. The absolute finality of the father's death is driven home by the repetition of the phrase, "But you were not there":

> The hands were yours, the arms were yours,
> But you were not there.
> The eyes were yours, but they were closed and would not open.
> The distant sun was there.
> The moon poised on the hill's white shoulder was there.
> The wind on Bedford Basin was there.
> The pale green light of winter was there.
> Your mouth was there,
> But you were not there.
>
> (*Selected Poems*, 85)

The poem explores the contradictory and difficult relationship between father and son in life, the helplessness of the living in the face of death and dying, the continuing presence of the dead in the lives of the living, the need for mourning but also its futility, and, finally, the assertion of a new life without the presence of the father.

In 1978, Strand published his most ambitious work, a long prose poem called *The Monument*, which he wrote not for the generation of his peers but for posterity. Like Whitman's "Crossing Brooklyn Ferry," which is clearly one of its antecedents, *The Monument* speaks to readers hundreds of years hence. And although it is a mannered, even arrogant book, it has a Whitmanesque sweep and grandeur about it, tempered by a kind of chummy bravado. Strand once remarked that he was less interested in writing "magazine verse or individual poems than in creating a literary spectacle."[24] Certainly in *The Monument* he has succeeded at that, although posterity's view of the poem remains to be seen.

Throughout the 1980s, Strand wrote a number of children's books and additional prose works but continued to write poetry while he taught at the University of Utah and served as poet laureate. The poems he wrote during these years appear in *The Continuous Life*, and the title poem reflects the continuity of the work here with Strand's earliest efforts. It is a brilliant poem, one of Strand's very

best, and reminds us that for all his elusive mannerisms and archetypal distancing, he is capable of eloquent truths:

> Oh parents, confess
> To your little ones the night is a long way off
> And your taste for the mundane grows; tell them
> Your worship of household chores has barely begun;
> Describe the beauty of shovels and rakes, brooms and mops;
> Say there will always be cooking and cleaning to do,
> That one thing leads to another, which leads to another;
> Explain that you live between two great darks, the first
> With an ending, the second without one, that the luckiest
> Thing is having been born, that you live in a blur
> Of hours and days, months and years, and believe
> It has meaning, despite the occasional fear
> You are slipping away with nothing completed, nothing
> To prove you existed.[25]

Like *The Continuous Life, Dark Harbor* (1993), a long, forty-five part
poem written in tercets, extends the confrontation between the
smallness and fragility of an individual life and the sense of immen-
sity that overwhelms us when we think of that life in relation to concepts like infinity and eternity. Life is a brief harbor in the immense
ocean of timelessness, but it is a dark harbor as well, offering us little
solace other than the tenuous immediacies of passing moments.
Reminiscent of W. S. Merwin's portrayal of the emptiness surrounding life, Strand's vision in these poems confronts that emptiness head on and finds in the mundane details of the continuous life
reasons to keep on moving, to keep things whole.

C. K. WILLIAMS (B. 1936)   If one subscribes to T. S. Eliot's belief
that the creation of a new verse form is a major cultural event, then
there is no question that C. K. Williams is an important twentieth-
century poet. As Reginald Gibbons points out, "To invent or renew a
distinct kind of poetic line is not easy in our time, but [Williams] has
done that, as well as shaped a distinct sort of form with his lanky long
lines and dramatic structures."[26] That "lanky long" line evolved over
a period of time. It first appeared in Williams's second book, *I Am the
Bitter Name* (1971), but hit its stride in his third volume, *With Ignorance*
(1977). As the line lengthens for Williams, his poetry becomes more
confidant and revealing, more authentic and less dependent on arti-

fice and predigested forms. Compare the contrivance of an early poem like "To Market" with the straightforward sentiment of the long line that opens a later poem, "The Cave". Here is "To Market":

> here I am still saying I love
> you under the stacks under
> the windows with wires the smoke
> going up I love
> you I love you[27]

The self-conscious line breaks, the clash of industrial language with romantic diction, and the insistent sibilance all contrast with the stark directness of these lines from "The Cave": "I think most people are relieved the first time they actually know someone / who goes crazy" (*Poems*, 155). Unquestionably, this is a prosy line, and Williams's poetry often seems to break into "prose," but that looseness liberates the work from the tyranny of the end-stopped line. For Williams, a line is as long as the thought or image (or both) it contains.

Like Philip Levine, Williams often focuses on working-class men and the contradictions that inform their lives. In "The Sanctity," for example, he contrasts the camaraderie and selflessness of these men with their paradoxical violence toward one another and self-absorption. While visiting a friend's house, the narrator witnesses a strange altercation that leads to a burst of violence:

> I didn't know what it all meant but my friend went wild
>   started breaking
>   things, I went home
> and when I saw him the next morning at breakfast
>   he acted as though nothing had happened.
>
> (*Poems*, 136)

For Williams, these poles of experience—love and violence—often make up the dualism of male life, both tough and easy, both taciturn and filled with free-flowing language and friendship:

> Listen: sometimes when you go to speak about life it's
>   as though your mouth's full of nails
> but other times it's so easy that it's ridiculous
>   to even bother.
>
> (*Poems*, 137)

The image of a life hard as nails occurs as well in one of Williams's best-known short poems, "It is This Way with Men," a poem that captures the distinctive maleness of his work. Williams believes men need to be hard to tough it out in a hostile and often treacherous world. Most men are battered by the world, but they endure:

> They are pounded into the earth
> like nails; move an inch,
> they are driven down again.
>
> (*Poems*, 20)

Williams's work is the poetry of a man trying to make sense of his life while constantly encountering its senselessness. It passes what F. Scott Fitzgerald in his *Notebooks* called "the test of a first rate intellect": the ability to hold two opposed ideas in the mind at the same time and still retain the ability to function—"to realize things are hopeless but be determined to make them otherwise." To say this is merely to say that his poetry is paradoxical and that paradox for Williams is the central life experience. The headnote from Kierkegaard that precedes the title poem of Williams's collection *With Ignorance* captures this sense of paradox exactly: "With ignorance begins a knowledge the first characteristic of which is ignorance" (*Poems*, 165).

Several of Williams's best poems reveal a characteristic sense of urgency. "The Last Deaths" is a deeply touching poem by a father trying to make sense of the world for his daughter. Shortly after a divorce, he is reading a story book to his daughter while the television news is on. An image of a woman screaming appears on the TV. Her husband and children have been killed in a bombing. The narrator's daughter wants to know why the woman is screaming, and he is frustrated—torn between trying to explain the confusion and terrors of the world to his daughter and trying to protect her from them. The narrator anticipates a future separation between himself and his daughter and wonders what it is that keeps love alive between human beings:

> Do we only love because we're weak and murderous?
> Are we commended to each other to alleviate our terror
> of solitude and annihilation and that's all?
>
> (144)

That we love only because of fear is a depressing analysis of human nature, and the narrator moderates it by contrasting his daughter's fears and anxieties with his own lately emergent surprising sense of calm. He seems to have moved into an almost Zen-like acceptance of the whole of the human condition: human suffering in the cosmic scheme of things seems greatly diminished.

But for Williams too often the world is too much with us, and suffering is not so easily distanced. His 1983 volume, *Tar*, is an up-close chronicle of this suffering, which can often be observed by simply looking out the window. "From My Window" is a poem of remarkably precise observation, both reportorial and psychological at the same time. The narrator observes a paraplegic Vietnam veteran and the friend who cares for him walking past his house regularly, often drunk. This particular morning, the wheelchair topples over and both men fall to the street. As neighbors watch, the buddy helps the vet up, but as he does he accidentally "jerks the grimy jeans right off him" revealing the naked indignity of his charge:

> No drawers, shrunken, blotchy thighs: under the thick,
> 　　　　white coils of belly blubber,
> the poor, blunt pud, tiny, terrified, retracted,
> is almost invisible in the sparse genital hair
> 　　　　　　　　　　　　　　　　*(Poems,* 176)

The narrator recalls seeing the friend making figure eights in the snow, late at night, and that image haunts him. The foredoomed quality of all human effort is suggested by the poem's final lines, which transform the view from the window into a parable of the human condition:

> In the morning, nothing: every trace of him effaced,
> 　　all the field pure white,
> its surface glittering, the dawn, glancing from its glaze,
> 　　oblique, relentless, unadorned.
> 　　　　　　　　　　　　　　　　(177)

The indifference of nature to human suffering is a timeless theme, but Williams's bleak and bizarre urban scene gives it a particularly contemporary slant.

"The Color of Time" shows how men become steeled and armored to avoid feeling pain by portraying a boy's sensitivity to the pain of the world and how he learns to numb it. The boy is acutely in touch with the anguish of a neighbor who is regularly brutalized by her alcoholic husband, but because "real men" are not supposed to express their feelings openly, he suppresses his pain as he will again and again later in life. When he becomes filled with anxiety about the neighbor's suffering, he tries to imagine the "warm glow" emanating from his own parent's room, but the darkness stays stubbornly intact, and whatever it is

> shuddering
>   in his chest keeps on
>   I hope I don't cry, he thinks; his thighs lock over his
> fists: he can hold
>   it, he thinks.
>
> (183)

To become a man, he must stop expecting his parents to comfort him, stop crying, and just "hold it." The final "he thinks" has a wonderful resonance: the boy's feelings turn to thoughts—his beliefs supplant his emotional life—and the phrase implies as well that he probably will not be able to "hold it."

This sort of absolute honesty about one's emotional life does not come easy to most men, and Williams's relentlessness around this theme makes his poetry, more than any other body of poetry produced by the men of his generation, a kind of representative voice, a gift that, like Adrienne Rich's poetry in relation to women's verse, "speaks the unspeakable." In a poem called "The Gift" he contrasts his past and present selves. Playing for a moment with a friend's one-year-old daughter, he ignores her pleas for further attention. The fact that he is ignoring the child surprises him, because as a younger man he always paid a lot of attention to children. In fact, he felt it crucial to his self-image to be "unusually gifted" with children. Now older, the narrator sees that his "gift" was self-serving, that it masked other parts of his character because it enabled him to see himself as

> a matrix of innocent warmth instead of
> the sorrowing brute I was
>
> (189)

This sort of self-revelation is a central feature of Williams's work, perhaps best epitomized by "The Gas Station," a poem in which the "let it all hang out" quality surprises even the poet himself. Although the poem describes a common American male adolescent experience, few men write about it with any candor. The narrator and his friends encounter a pimp in Times Square, and he takes them to a dark apartment where a woman, either "his whore, his girl or his wife or his mother," performs fellatio for $2 each. Here is Williams's startling description of the event:

> Did I mention
> that she, the woman, the whore or mother,
> was having her time and all she would deign do was to blow us?
> Did I say that? Deign? Blow?
> What a joy, though, the idea was in those days. Blown! What a
> thing to tell the next day.
> She only deigned, though, no more. She was like a machine. When
> I lift her back to me now,
> there's nothing there but that dark, curly head, working, a
> machine, up and down, and now,
> Freud, Marx, Fathers, tell me, what am I, doing this, telling
> this, on her, on myself,
> hammering it down, cementing it, sealing it in, but a machine,
> too? *Why am I doing this?*
>
> (216)

As if sensing that these extremes need some containment, Williams, in *Flesh and Blood* (1987), refines the long-line form by limiting its expression to two eight-line poems per page, grouped like sonnet sequences, but with a very contemporary feel. The poems read like "takes" on contemporary life, ranging over many topics, from Alzheimer's disease to Bishop Desmond Tutu's 1984 visit to the White House, from observations made on the New York subway to theoretical reconsiderations of history. By limiting his reflections on these (and many more) subjects to eight long lines each, Williams concentrates the detail. Yet while there are some striking single poems in this collection, the sameness and regularity of the form has a dulling effect, and sometimes it just spreads his tendency toward garrulousness over several poems.

But there is power here, as in the concluding long, touching poem in eighteen stanzas of eight lines each, written in memory of his good friend Paul Zweig, who died in 1984. And there are additional startling "unspeakable" subjects that continue to be explored, as in the poem "Normality." The speaker in that poem says that while he is changing his infant son's diapers he gets the urge "to take his little whizzer in my mouth" and asks the reader, "Didn't you ever feel anything like that?" Describing the contemplated act as one of love and affection rather than child abuse, as society would view it, the speaker concludes "Maybe it's you who's fucked up and repressed; I'll bet what I feel for my baby's *normal*."[28] By challenging society's definition of normality in this and other poems, and by insisting on truthful observation of male life throughout his work, Williams has expanded the boundaries of poetry and created an uncompromisingly honest body of work.

OTHER MALE POETS   With the publication of his first collection, *Heart's Needle* (1959), **W. D. Snodgrass (b. 1926)** immediately established his reputation as a frank, "confessional" poet who could speak directly and unflinchingly about his most private personal experiences. A famous line from that collection, "Snodgrass is walking through the universe," illustrates the audacity of naming one's name in a poem, a radical gesture in 1959, although it seems almost quaint today. But the literary climate of the 1990s seems light years away from the restraint and repression that characterized poetic expression in the years before writers like Ginsberg, Plath, Rich, and Snodgrass insisted on using personal experience rather than "tradition" as their poetic sources. Snodgrass was particularly influential in shaping the work of Anne Sexton and Robert Lowell, even though Lowell was nine years his senior.

But despite the critical acclaim Snodgrass received for the courageous personal revelations of his first book (much of it dealing with the pain of "losing" a daughter through divorce), he began, almost immediately, to move away from the personal in his poetry and toward a highly literary formalism, drawing from art, cultural history, music, and other sources that were more objectified and distanced from his personal life. This is exactly the reverse of the direction taken by most male poets of this period. The poems in *After Experience* (1968), a transition volume, blend personal experience with the illuminations of art, particularly in a sequence of interesting poems about paintings that include Matisse's *The Red Studio*, Vuillard's *The Mother and Sister of the Artist*, Monet's *Les Nympheas*, Manet's *The Execution of the Emperor Maximilian*, and Van Gogh's *The Starry Night*. An engaging essay about the genesis of these poems appears in Snodgrass's collection of critical essays, *In Radical Pursuit* (1975).

One of Snodgrass's most ambitious efforts is "The Füehrer Bunker," (1977) a kind of *Spoon River Anthology* for Hitler and his cohorts. The two epigrams to the poem emphasize how impossible it is to remove ourselves from even the deepest evils of which humanity is capable. A quote from Joseph Goebbels tells us that the spirit of Nazism and the Holocaust has "penetrated the hearts of our enemies." It is followed by a startling remark from Mother Theresa, who in response to a question as to when she began her humanitarian work, said, "On the day I discovered I had a Hitler inside me."

All of the poems in this sequence, with the exception of those devoted to Hitler, are written in rigidly formal structures that further distance the material from intense personal revelation. "The Füehrer Bunker" is not an entirely successful sequence, but it is a unique treatment of very difficult material, not often dealt with in such detail by contemporary poets.[29] Criticized by some for humanizing the Nazis in the sequence, Snodgrass responded with a statement that reveals something of his intentions in these poems: "You can't blame *me* for humanizing the Nazis. God did that. They *were* human. If you desire to believe that they were not human, then you are guilty of exactly their worst crime, which is what they tried to do to the Jews, to believe that they were not human.[30]

The untimely death of **James Merrill (1926–1995)** on February 5, 1995, brought forth an outpouring of tributes and reminiscences from throughout the literary community. Among them was W. S. Merwin's review (in the *New York Times Book Review*, March 26, 1995) of Merrill's last book, *A Scattering of Salts* (1995), which lauded him as the "obvious immediate heir of W. H. Auden" (3), a literary precursor with whom he is often compared. Like Auden, Merrill was a consummate literary craftsman, a witty and erudite intellectual who produced a poetry of formal ingenuity and casual elegance. He was a "disciple of perfection," as Merwin has it, and like Auden he created a gallery of finely tuned poetic voices, culminating in his masterwork, *The Changing Light at Sandover* (1982), a swirling, dizzying, 560-page poem that is a unique and monumental contribution to the history of American poetry in the twentieth century.

Merrill began work on that poem in the mid-1970s and in 1976 published *The Book of Ephraim*, a ninety-page display of narrative obsession and literary erudition that became the first part of the larger work. The book tells the story of Merrill's sessions at a Ouija board with his friend and lover David Jackson in the dining room of their home at Stonington, Connecticut. Through this medium, Merrill and Jackson make contact with a "familiar spirit" named Ephraim, who becomes their guide to otherworldly matters and takes them on a grand tour of what the novelist Douglas Adams calls "Life, The Universe, and Everything." Ephraim introduces his communicants to a novel metaphysics: each of us on earth, he tells them, is the representative of a patron who guides our souls in various incarnations through nine stages of being until we ourselves become patrons to guide other living souls. The patrons are forbidden to intervene in our lives except in intervals between incarnations when they renew our spirits to send us to the next life.

A prose summary of the premise behind *The Changing Light at Sandover* may sound like New Age theology, but the experience of reading the poem leaves the reader in awe. Merrill proposes nothing less than a new cosmology, reconciling, at this very late date, science and religion. He sees himself as a vehicle for divine revelation, following in a long line of poets who have served this function from Homer through Yeats. His cast of characters, in addition to Auden, includes the spirits of Gertrude Stein, Wallace Stevens, and Robert Lowell, as well as Jesus, Mohammed, Homer, and Plato. The whole of the physical and metaphysical world is presided over by "God Biology," also called "God B." in the poem. These spirits, speaking through the array of letters and numbers on a Ouija board (representing language and mathematics), unlock for JM and DJ (as Merrill and his friend are identified throughout) the secrets of the universe.

The density and difficulty of Merrill's verse in this volume are a challenge, but so have been all other efforts to create a poetry of epic scope in twentieth-century literature. Merrill's masterpiece belongs on the same shelf as Ezra Pound's *The Cantos*, T. S. Eliot's *The Waste Land*, and Hart Crane's *The Bridge*. Though it bears comparison with these poems in terms of its cosmic sweep and ambition, there is nothing quite like *The Changing Light at Sandover* in all our literature.

The best of the remainder of Merrill's poetry (with the exception of the late poems in *The Inner Room* [1988] and *A Scattering of Salts*) are collected in *Selected Poems: 1946–1985* (1992). This book provides ample evidence of Merrill's consummate lyrical skills and shows his connection to Stevens as well as Auden. Merrill, like Stevens, believed in the transformative power of the imagination and the power of words to shape and alter the physical world. In a touching poem, "Farewell Performance," dedicated to his friend David Kalstone, who died of AIDS, he sees art as a temporary stay against confusion. "Art. It cures affliction," the poem begins, and goes on to describe the scattering of Kalstone's ashes at sea, a finale to that artistic performance which is an individual's life.[31]

All of Merrill's work seems a quest for the perfectly inevitable combination of words suited to any particular topic, and sometimes that quest takes him just to the edge of ineffability. One of his often anthologized poems, "Angel," describes a "patently angelic visitor" that hovers above his desk as he writes, distracting him from the flaws and imperfections of this world:

> Half to tease him, I turn back to my page,
> Its phrases thus far clotted, unconnected.
> The tiny angel shakes his head.
> There is no smile on his round, hairless face.
> He does not want even these few lines written.[32]

Charles Simic (b. 1939) used childhood memories of World War II in his hometown of Belgrade as the backdrop for much of his poetry. Simic came to America in 1954, when he lived in Chicago and worked as a proofreader for a local newspaper. His first poems were published in the *Chicago Review*, and his work seemed immediately distinctive, permeated by an Eastern European surrealism. In Simic's work there is an eerie fascination with common objects and body parts. The reader finds poems on forks, knives, spoons, and shoes, and one on the fingers of the poet's right hand, which he regards, digit by digit, as having specifically defined characteristics—almost "personalities" of their own.

Dismantling the Silence (1971) is filled with terse, involuted, surreal descriptions, which, as the title poem suggests, are an attempt to turn silence into an actual presence, to give it weight in the world. The oddly titled *Return to a Place Lit by a Glass of Milk* (1974) and *White* (1980) parallel this intention by focusing on blankness or absolute whiteness. This focus brings the weight of the void into Simic's work as a palpable presence. Though his is a descriptive poetry, his descriptions really reflect states of mind rather than tangible objects. The objects are essentially artifacts in which one sees oneself. As he puts it in a poem called "Description":

A street which always
somehow resembles me.

Gray day and I
the source of its grayness.

A corner where
a part of myself

keeps an appointment
with another part of myself.

This small world.
This dumb show.[33]

As in the work of Merwin and Strand, there is in Simic "all along the suspicion / that we do not exist" (130). Like theirs, his work is haunting as we read of one absurd, hypothetical situation after another passing by on his surreal merry-go-round: his mother and father work together in a toy factory where a toy firing squad executes a toy prisoner ("Toy Factory," 150); Christopher Columbus, appearing out of nowhere, sings a song from his childhood ("Navigator," 146); a family shrinks in size so they all fit in a suitcase ("A Suitcase Strapped with a Rope," 147). These fabulist events make up the landscape of Simic's world, which exists, as everything else does, between two vast deserts of eternity. This stark vision is best expressed in "Spoons with Realistic Dead Flies on Them" (204), where he conjures "two gusts of nothing and nothing" that one must look at before crossing the street. Those gusts blow up a storm of existential angst that is everywhere in Simic's work.

William Matthews (1942–1997) grew up in Cincinnati and was educated at Yale (B.A., 1965) and the University of North Carolina (M.A., 1966). He has taught at the University of Colorado and worked as an editor at Atlantic Monthly Press. In the 1960s he established the magazine *Lillabularo* while he produced his first volumes of poetry, *Broken Syllables* (1969) and *Ruining the New Road* (1970). The opening poem of the latter volume contrasts a poetry of "technique" and "devices" with a more urgent poetry drawn from the exigencies of his own life. He tells his reader that he doesn't want to "swaddle" his poetry in metaphor and symbolism, but instead says

> *I'm in these poems*
> *because I'm in my life.*[34]

Because his poems are deeply centered in actual life experiences, reading his volumes successively gives you the feeling of traversing the various "seasons" of a man's life, the brashness and romanticism of youth giving way to the darker exigencies of middle age. One of his best poems—and one that traces some of this journey—is "A Happy Childhood," which describes a very mainstream middle American boyhood, with an attentive mother (and even a dog named Spot). But it also includes some ominous foreshadowings. The narrator describes how much he loves to be called into the house for dinner, when the house lights up and the darkness descends outside. The darkness

> leans lightly against the house. Tomorrow
> I'll find the sweatstains it left, little grey
> smudges.[35]

Matthews writes a distinctly male poetry, drawing on his relationships with women, his experience of marriage and divorce, his connection to his sons. It has a free and improvisational feel, like that of the jazz music that inspires him. (Scattered throughout his volumes are poems on Coleman Hawkins, John Coltrane, Bud Powell, Lester Young, and others.) His work of the seventies and eighties—*Sleek for the Long Flight* (1972), *Sticks and Stones* (1975), *Rising and Falling* (1979), *Flood* (1982), *A Happy Childhood, Forseeable Futures* (1984), and *Curiosities* (1989)—is filled with surprising contrasts; one small example occurs in "Spring Snow" (the oxymoron of the title is itself a surprise, linking the regeneration of spring with the finalities of winter.)

A similar juxtaposition occurs in "Moving Again" when he describes moving to a new town with his family. The narrator contrasts a magpie flying onto a pine tree's branches, representing continuities of nature, with the distinctively contemporary human world "of child support and lights" where "people are opening drawers."[36]

Matthews's poetry explores the terrain of both landscapes simultaneously and in so doing creates a third landscape that is uniquely his.

The poetry of **Robert Pinsky (b. 1940)** has absorbed the lessons of his masters. From Frost he learned the importance of traditional forms but also of the need to deviate from rigid forms by saying something in a slightly off-center way. From William Carlos Williams he absorbed the power of exact observation of "things at the end of the nose" and of noticing what's new in the contemporary world that has not yet made its way into poems. Add a sense of imagination creating and shaping reality from Stevens, and an ability to find the universal in the local from Elizabeth Bishop, and you have something of the quality of Pinsky's style. At its best it feels at home in the literary living room of the late twentieth century, but at its weakest it has something of an overwrought quality:

> The devices I arrayed
> Conjured features like mine,
> A familiar shape that I
> Denied—denied as the bane
> Of myself, the multifarious
> Event that pulls my face
> To its own.[37]

Pinsky is a sharp observer of others and of the physical phenomena that surrounds them. In "Poem about People," from his earliest collection, *Sadness and Happiness* (1975), he takes notice of a friend "In his divorced schoolteacher / Apartment" who has hung paintings his wife had kept in the closet. Pinsky observes how deeply human this assertion of self is, creating a particularity that both humanizes us and separates us from one another at the same time. This "Poem about People" becomes archetypal as it ends with "the dark wind crossing / The wide spaces between us" (4).

"Ceremony for Any Beginning," a poem with a similar archetypal quality from the same volume, charts the conflict between a man's soul and the ongoing events of his life, noting how those events sometimes overwhelm and diminish one's sense of self. The weather—nearly always an important element in Pinsky's work—becomes a symbol for the world outside the self that shapes and frames individual identity and leaves it feeling separate from the external world. The long title poem, "Sadness and Happiness," moves around life's moods and events as if with a video camera, having the freedom to point to both the pain and the joy of one's life consecutively—almost simultaneously. The narrator is blessed with a woman who nurtures his work but is also impatient with his tendency toward self-pity and self-destruction. The love that nurtures him and the egotism that undermines him are seamed together in this passage enjambed between two of the poem's sections:

> how happy I would be, or else
> decently sad, with no past: you
> only and no foolish ghosts
> urging me to become some redeeming
>
> Jewish-American Shakespeare
> (or God knows what they expect,
> Longfellow) and so excuse my thorny
> egotism, by hard-ons of self-concern,
>   VII
> melodramas and speeches
> of myself, crazy in love with
> my status as a sad young man
>   (23–24)

This innovative enjambment (which operates throughout the poem) underscores how the narrator (and by extension, most of us) carry our self-conceptions from one phase of life to the next, making "beginnings" and "endings" more illusionary than real.

Virtually all of Pinsky's work, *Sadness and Happiness*; the long *An Explanation of America* (1979), dedicated to his daughter and attempting to explain the contradictory and violent country into which she was born; *History of My Heart* (1984); and *The Want Bone* (1990) as well as twenty-two newer poems are collected in *The Figured Wheel, New and Collected Poems, 1966–1996* (1996). Each successive work published during these thirty years of his development as a poet refines his desire to chronicle both the history of his heart and of his times. Like the poet he most admires, William Carlos Williams, Pinsky is engaged by the intersection between his own life and the socio-political-cultural world around him. He is the contemporary poet as cultural historian and as such was a particularly appropriate choice for poet laureate of the United States, an office he assumed in 1997. He brought to that office a highly refined sensibility, steeped in the poetry of the modernist generation and finely attuned to the political and cultural realities of late twentieth century American life.

Pinsky's predecessor as poet laureate was **Robert Hass (b. 1941).** In three books of poems—*Field Guide* (1973), *Praise* (1979), and *Human Wishes* (1989)—as well as a landmark critical work—*Twentieth-Century Pleasures* (1984)—Hass established himself as an important and innovative figure in late twentieth-century American poetry. The middle-range style of these books—neither extremely political nor apolitical, neither overly formal nor overly spontaneous, neither linguistically conservative nor linguistically radical—made him, like Pinsky, a good selection for the poet laureate post.

The three sections of his first book organize the three primary areas of Hass's poetic temperament: the California landscape, a highly sophisticated sense of literary history and tradition, and his personal life. Called "The Coast," "Pencil," and "In Weather," respectively, these categories become more integrated in Hass's later work, where he is able to create surprising intersections between the physical present, the historical past, and the psychological reality of an inner life.

His widely praised and aptly titled second volume *Praise* illustrates this integration, but it illustrates as well, as Peter Davison has noticed, that "Hass's poetic intelligence is so acute that he keeps, like Hamlet, cerebrating himself into the static condition."[38] The stunning and deftly crafted opening poem, for example, "Heroic Simile," masterfully creates a trope that extends from the Cinemascope screen showing Kurosawa's *Seven Samurai* to the pages of Homer and finally into the lives of a couple waking from the movies "to the house in the silence of separate fidelities." It is those "separate fidelities" the reader wants to hear more about rather than simply admiring the display of literary craft that is displayed in the poem. As if aware of that, the poem's final line flatly states, "There are limits to the imagination."[39] Those limits seem to have to do with excursions away from literariness and into the actual occurrences of life, less self-consciously transformed by artifice. Hass makes these excursions throughout both *Praise* and *Human Wishes*, and the life he describes is an intellectual, literary, and art-oriented middle-class life

in which discussions of Lacan, Käthe Kollwitz, Francis Ponge, Kurosawa, Georgia O'Keefe, and the Sunday *New York Times Book Review*
punctuate meals served with good wine and fresh berries. But it is
also a life permeated by an underlying sadness that waxes and
wanes through the poems, almost crying out to be directly confronted. Occasionally, when it is, Hass's poems reach moments of
exactitude, and these moments almost always have to do with personal epiphanies brought on by a confrontation with the sadness
that forces itself upward through layers of literariness:

> . . . one April, walking into the kitchen,
> I felt like a stranger to my life
> and it scared me, so when the gray doves returned
> to the telephone wires
> and the lemons were yellowing
> and no other task presented itself,
> I finally went into the garden and started
> digging, trying to marry myself
> and my hands to that place.[40]

This from a poem called "Santa Barbara Road," which chronicles the
breakup of a family and captures the difficult and awkward feelings
between parents and children during a time of crisis. Again in "Privilege of Being" a woman reassures her lover that her loneliness cannot be "cured" by his love,

> And the man is not hurt exactly,
> he understands that life has limits, that people
> die young, fail at love,
> fail of their ambitions. He runs beside her, he thinks
> of the sadness they have gasped and crooned their way out of
> coming, clutching each other with old, invented
> forms of grace and clumsy gratitude, ready
> to be alone again, or dissatisfied, or merely
> companionable like the couples on the summer beach
> reading magazine articles about intimacy between the sexes
> to themselves, and to each other,
> and to the immense, illiterate, consoling angels.
>
> (70)

Sadness surfaces again in the final poem in the volume called "On
Squaw Peak" which describes the death of a child and begins:

I don't even know which sadness
it was came up
in me when we were walking down the road to Shirley Lake
(81)

These many sadnesses generate the luminosity of Hass's poetry at its very best.

Frank Bidart (b. 1939) has brought together the best poems of his four collections of poetry as well as some new poems and an engaging interview about his work in *In the Western Night: Collected Poems: 1965–1990* (1990). The volume reveals Bidart to be one of the most original poets of his generation. Like Robert Lowell, with whom he worked closely in the sixties and seventies, deep and traumatic feelings are an essential part of Bidart's work. His narrators, like the boy traumatized by his mother's failures in "Confessional," or the mother's anguish and father's abandonment in "Elegy," all "feel too much." As he puts it in a villanelle that is an envoi to "Elegy": "I feel too much. I can't stand what I feel."[41] The pain embodied in those lines permeates nearly all of Bidart's work, much of which attributes that pain to various personae who serve either as narrators or as actual historical figures who are the subject of Bidart's investigation.

His books are peopled with a gallery of extremists: the great early twentieth-century ballet dancer Vaslav Nijinsky, the anorexic Ellen West, the serial killer Herbert White. These, together with poems about Bidart's own family and traumatic childhood give us a poetry that seems drenched in agony, emblematic of humanity in extremis, a suffering just this side of death. Death, in fact, hovers around all these figures and is Bidart's animating muse. His characters circle it, coax and tease it, pay homage to it, and usually finally succumb to it.

The remarkable "Ellen West," for example, is a "documentary" poem about the case history of an anorexic who commits suicide. Bidart allows us to see this woman from both a clinical perspective—through diagnoses made by physicians during her hospitalization—and from her own perspective within her own psyche. The result is the construction of a woman of nearly pure spirit uncomfortable in the physicality of her body and the material things of this world. Her anorexia is an expression of her longing to return to her natural state, a condition only possible in death.

What is most remarkable about these highly dramatic poems is that Bidart seems to get so fully inside his characters. He does not, for example, view the serial killer and necrophilic Herbert White from a distance; he takes us inside the man's psyche and makes us feel the tingling of his nerve ends. He seems to want to access the darkest parts of the human soul and explore them with a flashlight. He does not allow his readers to experience the criminal and the insane as "other" but rather works toward finding the human links that connect all of us. Speaking of White in the interview, Bidart says he began conceiving the character as a kind of "anti-self" but soon realized that the concept of an anti-self "only has some meaning . . . if he *shares* something fundamental with me; I gave him a family history related to my own" (238). This conception allows Bidart to recognize White's perceptions as his own:

There is a scene in "Herbert White" in which he is looking out the window of his room at home and feels suffocated by the fact that everything is "just *there*, just *there*, doing nothing! / not saying anything!" He wants to see beneath the skin of the street, to see (in Wordsworth's terms) "into the life of things, and cannot. It's of course me feeling that"

(240)

Another unique aspect of Bidart's poetry is his use of typography to underscore meaning. His poetry spreads across the page like a scream, composed of broken irregular lines, words and phrases printed in all caps and italics, dashes, ellipses, and eccentric punctuation. All of these devices work toward producing lines that seem to have a "voice" of their own, that have somehow, as he puts it, " 'fasten[ed] to the page' the voice—and movements of the voice—in my head" (223). Consider how the torment and suffocating closeness of the narrator's relationship with his mother is expressed through the very physical look of the lines in this passage from "Confessional":

she *JUST DIED.*
She wanted them to—;
how can I talk about
the way in which, when I was young,

we seemed to be engaged in an **ENTERPRISE**
together,—

the enterprise of "figuring out the world,"
figuring out her life, my life,—

THE MAKING OF HER SOUL,

which somehow, in our "enterprise"
together, was the making of my soul,—

. . . it's a kind of *CRAZINESS,* which some mothers
drink along with their children
in their *MOTHER'S MILK* . . .

Why are you angry?
THERE WAS NO PLACE IN NATURE WE COULD MEET . . .
—I've never let anyone else
in so deeply . . .

(63)

Bidart is an extremely ambitious poet. For him, the role of the artist involves getting life to *show* itself (240). To achieve this task he takes on subjects many poets might approach only to skirt around the edges. He gets inside the skin of his personae, in a way that is a long distance from the ironic detachment of the modernists. Like the dancer Nijinsky, he can say

I know people's faults
because in my soul
I HAVE COMMITTED THEM
(23)

Although **Raymond Carver (1938–1988)** is known primarily as an innovative writer of short fiction, his contribution to poetry in the late twentieth century is substantial. His premature death from lung cancer in 1988 deprived us of a rare writer who moved across the usual generic limitations of poetry and fiction. As his widow, Tess Gallagher, writes in the introduction to his posthumously published *A New Path to the Waterfall* (1990),

I can imagine that it might be tempting for those who loved Ray's fiction to the exclusion of his poetry to feel he had gone astray in giving so much of his time to poetry in the final years. But this would be to miss the gift of freshness his poems offer in a passionless era. Because judgments about the contribution of poets lag far behind those volunteered toward fiction writers in this country, it will likely be some time before Ray's impact as a poet can be adequately assessed.[42]

Carver's poetic gifts go far beyond "freshness." His work has a clarity and directness that is both accessible and unguarded. The poems are nearly always directly tied to important life experiences. Carver the fiction writer embellishes and elaborates on a situation to create a fictive world. Carver the poet, however, goes right for the essential truth of an experience. In his poems the reader can hear the voice of a man speaking his truth aloud, carefully avoiding any false notes. This carefulness gives the poetry a kind of purity, shorn of everything but the exactness of a particular moment, feeling, or event.

Much of the poetry seems almost antipoetic in that Carver aims for a conversational, off-handed tone that seems deceptively "easy." This produces a highly accessible poetry and one preoccupied, almost obsessed with getting things right. He finds poetry in the most unpromising situations, even just sitting up late at night, eating popcorn, listening to jazz on the radio, and looking out at the sea. He turns these events into a poem called "The Party," which not only makes poetry out of such unlikely material but turns that material into a celebration of life.[43]

Carver's last three collections particularly reveal a mature and developing style that will surely command more attention as the years pass; it rises above clutter and literariness to produce a spare style that is uniquely his. The metaphor of water—especially flowing water—permeates each of these books, and it is, of course, a basic life metaphor as one part of a life flows into and connects with the next. *Where Water Comes Together with Other Water* (1985), *Ultramarine* (1986), and the posthumously published *A New Path to the Waterfall* (1989) all chronicle the traumas and tribulations of Carver's adult life, concerns that are familiar to readers of his fiction as well: alcoholism, divorce, bankruptcy and ongoing financial woes, and fear of death as well as the solace of friends, the gift of love, the blessing of luminous moments. In fact, a number of these poems seem poetic versions of his actual fictions; for example, "The Mail" is a concise version of Carver's story "Elephant," in which a middle-aged man is besieged by financial dependence of his son, daughter, ex-wife, and mother.

Carver often writes about the persistence of memory and the intrusion of feelings from the past that seem to come out of nowhere and become a nearly palpable part of the present. Feelings about his first wife, his alcoholic days, his many jobs, his old girlfriends all remain coiled and ready to spring unannounced into the deceptive calm of a present moment. Memory is a container of emotional intensity, as in the poem "Memory," in which cutting the stems from a quart of strawberries releases a string of memories associated with his wife, a little girl with a dog, the death of a friend's grandmother, and other things that float through the narrator's mind as he engages in this mindless activity. Sometimes, the memory intrudes more forcefully, as it does in "The Projectile." In this poem a polite conversation the narrator is having over tea with someone about the reception of his books in a foreign country is contrasted with his vivid internal memory of himself as a sixteen year old, driving around in a 1950 Dodge and being hit in the head with an ice-packed snowball hurled through a three-inch space made by an open window. Now the memory of that bizarre event is itself a projectile that takes him by surprise in later life.[44]

"The Projectile" and "Memory" are just two of the many Carver poems that trace the operations of the psyche, the restlessness of the mind as it moves from one memory, problem, proposal, fear, anticipation, or activity of any kind to another, hardly stopping to register one before moving on to the next. In "This Morning" he notices how sometimes a walk in nature can quiet the frenetic activity of his mind and keep the most depressing and dispiriting thoughts at bay. Looking out at the beautiful clear blue sky, the gulls dipping and curving against it, the "pure cold light" of nature seems to bring some perspective to the self-generated chaos of the internal life:

> For a minute or two
> it crowded out the usual musings on
> what was right, and what was wrong—duty,
> tender memories, thoughts of death, how I should treat
> my former wife. All the things
> I hoped would go away this morning.
> The stuff I live with every day. What
> I've trampled on in order to stay alive.
>
> (3)

At its best, Carver's poetry chronicles both the demons and angels of his inner life with an exactitude and honesty that is exemplary. He gives us both tenderness and terror, both hope and despair. In a lovely poem called "The Boat" he imagines a boat filled with all the people he loves, doing the things they wish to do, going the places they wish to go, "But nothing dangerous, nothing too serious."[44] This is the world as he would like it to be, the world as it would be if he could shape and direct it as he would on his own boat.

The unforgettable final poems in *A New Path to the Waterfall*, confront his own impending death without diverting his eyes. Two of these poems, "Gravy" and "What the Doctor Said," are the work of a man who loved the things of this world and who could write about them with both eloquence and simplicity. In the latter poem, a doctor has just informed him that he is terminally ill from lung cancer. Here is his response:

> I just looked at him
> for a minute and he looked back it was then
> I jumped up and shook hands with this man who'd just given me
> something no one else on earth had ever given me
> I may even have thanked him habit being so strong
>
> (113)

And in the former poem the word "gravy" becomes a metaphor for all of the life he had lived since he gave up being a drunk and began living, working, and loving attentively and consciously:

> "Don't weep for me,"
> he said to his friends. "I'm a lucky man.
> I've had ten years longer than I or anyone
> expected. Pure gravy. And don't forget it."
>
> (118)

· SEVEN ·

Borderlands:
The Diversity of American Poetry

The Americans of all nations at any time upon the
earth have probably the fullest poetical nature. The
United States themselves are essentially the greatest
poem. . . . Here is not merely a nation but a teeming
nation of nations.
—Walt Whitman

What Whitman envisioned we, the people and the poets of the New
World, embody.
—June Jordan

Despite Whitman's embrace of all his brothers and sisters, whatever
their ethnic origin, race, or economic status, and despite his procla-
mation that the United States was a unique nation of nations, there
was little evidence of this multicultural identity in the literary landscape of the United States up to and during Whitman's lifetime.
Throughout the nineteenth century, American poetry was predominantly an Anglo-American, overwhelmingly male scene. However,
the first half of the twentieth century was to witness a dramatic
remapping of that landscape, extending the borders of American literature beyond its original Anglo-American origins to include European Americans, Jewish Americans, and African Americans. One of
the most notable developments of this period was the Harlem
Renaissance, a movement in which African Americans, in a burst of
creative energy during the 1920s, brought a new vitality and vision
to the literary scene.

The second half of the twentieth century led to an even wider
expansion of the borders of our literary world. As critics and schol-
ars reexamined the canon, some writers previously excluded were
recognized. But, most important, driven by the rebellion against

colonialism in the Third World and the struggle for civil rights in the United States, African Americans, American Indians, Latinos, and Asian Americans began to reexamine their allegiance to an Anglo-European culture and to reassert the value of their own cultures. In many cases, poets were important figures in this rebellion, and they raised ongoing questions about the cultural possibilities of this struggle. Should they, for example, help create a separate nation? should they call for a pluralistic society? should they move toward assimilation?

As might be expected, there were a multitude of responses to these questions during the second half of the century. The result is that there is no one map that accurately draws the boundaries of multicultural literature and poetry. The boundary lines shift as separatist, nationalist, or Third World poets call for a new territory and a new aesthetic, while other poets accept their American heritage and European traditions, blending those traditions with their own ethnic backgrounds. Still others remain somewhere in the borderlands, trying to live outside any cultural or aesthetic definition that creates uncrossable borders, trying to create a world without boundaries. While it is impossible to explore all of these territories in detail, this chapter will attempt to portray the complexity and diversity of the birth of one of the most significant developments in contemporary poetry: the emergence of multiculturalism.

African-American Poetry

The roots of African-American poetry run deep, back to the eighteenth-century poetry of Lucy Terry and Phyllis Wheatley; however, its blossoming, its "Renaissance," as it was called, occurred in Harlem, New York, during the roaring twenties, the jazz age. When Countee Cullen, Jean Toomer, Claude McKay, James Weldon Johnson, and Langston Hughes, among others, added their voices to the diverse strains of modern poetry, they introduced many white readers to a new world, new subjects, images, rhythms, and improvisations. They insisted on and proved that African Americans had a place at the literary table.

Along with Langston Hughes and other Harlem Renaissance poets, Gwendolyn Brooks, Robert Hayden, and Sterling Brown ensured that African-American poetry during the forties and fifties would remain one of the central strains of contemporary poetry. (See chapter 2.) During the sixties, led by Amiri Baraka, some African-American poets embraced a new aesthetic that affirmed and insisted upon a body of poetry that addressed itself to a black audience. In doing so, they created a new black arts movement that further politicized and transformed the nature of African-American poetry. The question of whether African-American poetry should retain a separate identity or remain tied to the larger American tradition mirrored the political debate within the black community about what future direction it should take.

STERLING BROWN (1901–1989) In the decades following the Harlem Renaissance, Sterling Brown taught at Howard University, where future poets such as Amiri Baraka came into contact with a man fully versed in and committed to the teaching of black music, folklore, and poetry. In addition to publishing significant works of criticism, Brown also coedited *The Negro Caravan* (1941), a very influential collection of African-American literature that helped to expand the presence of African-American writers within the accepted canon. As a poet, he is especially known for his use of folk materials and such musical forms as the blues, folk ballads, and work songs. He can be satirical, as in "Slim in Hell," in which the folk character Slim confesses to Peter that he didn't realize that Dixie was Hell, or he can be plaintive, as in his blues poem "Southern Road," the title poem of his volume of poetry published in 1932. Here a member of a chain gang ironically sings out that the white man need not tell him "Damn yo' soul," for

> Chain gang nevah—hunh—
> Let me go;
> Chain gang nevah—hunh—
> Let me go.[1]

Brown's *Collected Poems* (1980) won the National Book Award. In addition, his work has influenced and won praise from such poets as Margaret Walker (b. 1915), who also often works within the folk and oral traditions. However, throughout this century African-American poets such as Jean Toomer, Melvin B. Tolson (1898–1966), Gwendolyn Brooks, Robert Hayden, Amiri Baraka, Michael Harper (b. 1938), and Jay Wright (b. 1935) have in various ways insisted on going beyond African-American folk themes and forms. In their experimentation and incorporation of modernist techniques, they have created a complex and highly imaginative body of work that, while being centered on the African-American experience, goes far beyond the boundaries of folk and vernacular traditions. The blending and, sometimes, the clashing of these two approaches, as well as the emergence of a new black aesthetic, create the richness, diversity, and energy of contemporary African-American poetry.

AMIRI BARAKA (B. 1934)   Amiri Baraka was a major figure in changing the boundaries of African-American and ethnic literature generally in the United States. As William J. Harris, editor of *The Baraka Reader* (1990), notes, "He was the main artist-intellectual responsible for shifting the emphasis of contemporary black literature from an integrationist art conveying a raceless and classless vision to a literature rooted in the black experience."[2] His contributions to the black arts movement of the sixties meant that "no post-Black Arts artist thinks of himself or herself as simply being a human being who happens to be black; blackness is central to his or her experience and art" (xxvi). He influenced older poets such as Gwendolyn Brooks, as well as younger poets such as Haki R. Madhubuti, aka Don Lee (b. 1942), and Nikki Giovanni (b. 1943). Maurice Kenny (b. 1929), an American-Indian (Mohawk) author, critic, and poet, attests to the impact Baraka had on other ethnic writers by means of his insistence on a black aesthetic: "He opened tightly guarded doors for not only Black but poor whites as well and, of course, Native Americans, Latinos, and Asian-Americans. We'd all still be waiting [for] the invitation from the *New Yorker* without him. He taught us all how to claim it and take it" (xxvi).

Baraka covered a lot of territory before he abandoned his integrationist ideology and Anglo-European aesthetics. Born Everett LeRoi Jones in Newark, New Jersey, and raised in an extended middle-class family, he was a brilliant high-school student as well as a devotee of radio shows, comic books, black music, and street language. Language, in fact, became a weapon Jones used early on to "keep people off you."[3] Although he felt pressure to sever his ties to his black urban culture, his love of the blues kept him close to the black experience: "The blues hugged me close to the streets and the people. That was what we breathed" (47). Dizzy Gillespie and Miles Davis were two of his first heroes. While at Rutgers and then

Howard University he was introduced to European and white American writers, but he also discovered at Howard University Sterling Brown, who deepened his knowledge of African-American music and literature. But Jones did not keep up with his studies and flunked out of Howard, an institution he later came to perceive as being dedicated to retaining a hierarchy among black people based on lightness of color and class.

Jones joined the Air Force, experienced racism and anti-Semitism, and began a process of self-education, reading modernist writers such as James Joyce, whom he had not really understood while in college. Eventually, he was discharged as an "undesirable" from the Air Force, on the assumption that his reading of avant-garde literary magazines made him a subversive. He then began to establish himself in Greenwich Village, the center of the beat movement during the 1950s, became part of the Village culture, married Hettie Cohen, a white Jewish woman, and coedited with her the avant-garde literary journal *Yugen* (1958–1963). As he began to write poetry, he fell under the influence of Allen Ginsberg, whose *Howl* presented a world he "could identify with and relate to." Poetry, Jones discovered, "did not have to be about suburban birdbaths and Greek mythology" (150). Jones adopted the vision of the beats and the aesthetics of Charles Olson, the Black Mountain poets Robert Creeley and Robert Duncan, and the New York poets Frank O'Hara and Kenneth Koch. They were all, in Jones's view, "part of a whole antiacademic voice." In "How You Sound," initially published in Donald Allen's *New American Poetry* (1960), his indebtedness to Olson is clear: "There must not be any preconceived notion or *design* for what the poem ought to be. 'Who knows what a poem ought to sound like? Until its thar.' Says Charles Olson . . . & I follow closely with that. I'm not interested in writing sonnets, sestinas or anything . . . only poems" (*Reader*, 16).

The poet must follow "his own voice," but the models Jones mentions are all white—Lorca, Williams, Pound, Eliot, and younger white poets such as Whalen, Snyder, O'Hara, Creeley, and Ginsberg. In addition, Jones saw few connections between poetry, social issues, and politics. Although the poetry rebelled against the "square" culture of the Eisenhower years, it was primarily hip and disengaged, conveying a Bohemian worldview.

The turning point, as Jones indicates in his *Autobiography* (1984), was his trip to Cuba in 1960. Accompanied by the African-American activist Robert Williams, Jones encountered Third World writers who challenged his separation of poetry and politics as well as his willingness to ignore the widespread oppression of people of color in the United States and the Third World. As he witnessed the assassination of President Kennedy and Medgar Evers and the 1963 bombing of a Birmingham Church that resulted in the death of four black girls, he could no longer embrace his early ideas and lifestyle. The most significant literary result of this turmoil and change is manifested in his 1964 play *Dutchman*, which received an Obie award and gained Jones recognition as a leading African-American writer. The play's focus on the themes of ethnic identity and masculinity within a white world clearly reflect Jones's personal struggles at this time in his life.

Jones's return to African-American culture is also seen in his widely acclaimed study *Blues People: Negro Music in White America* (1963) and in the shifting nature of his poetry. In his first book of poetry, *Preface to Twenty Volume Suicide Note* (1961), the poems, although admittedly bluesy and at times focused on black experience, convey, for the most part, a "beat" or "hip" voice that is not speaking from either an obviously black experience or to a black audience. He is certainly not yet attempting to create a black aesthetic. They are poems of alienation and withdrawal from the mainstream culture. Jones laments that "the ground opens up and envelopes me," that "Nobody sings anymore." When the stars do not appear; he can only "count the holes they leave." Even his daughter, Kellie, is left alone, "peeking into / Her own clasped hands" (3). In "Notes for a Speech," Jones sadly stands apart from his African heritage. "African blues / does not know me. Their steps, in sands / of their own / land . . ." Jones can only lament: "Africa / is a foreign place. You are / as any other sad man here / american" (14, 15).

However, in *The Dead Lecturer* (1964), he begins to distance himself from his beat, integrationist lifestyle. "I am inside someone / who hates me" (52). He questions his disengaged aesthetics in poems like "The politics of rich painters" and "Rhythm of Blues (for Robert Williams in Exile)." Jones struggles to become more than a "Dead Lecturer," fearing "that the flame of my sickness / will burn off my face. And leave / the bones, my stewed black skull, / an empty cage of failure" (70). He also struggles with rage: "Come up, black dada / nihilismus. Rape the white girls. Rape / their fathers. Cut the mothers' throats" (72, 73). In "The Liar," a poem that centers on Jones's reshaping of his sense of self and vision of the world, he sees that his old identity is dying, but wonders if his old friends will realize that it is the "Dead Lecturer," the "Liar," who is dying: "When they say, 'It is Roi / who is dead?' I wonder / who will they mean?" (75).

Jones's break with the white world followed the 1965 assassination of Malcolm X, who, Jones asserts, "spoke for me and my friends" (*Autobiography*, 186). He left the Village, his wife, and his children, moved to Harlem, proclaimed he was a black cultural nationalist, began the Black Arts Repertory Theatre, a black nationalist group, and held poetry readings and plays in the streets of Harlem, bringing "black art to black people" (213). In that same year he then published a novel, *The System of Dante's Hell*, and moved back to Newark.

In 1966, he married Sylvia Robinson and published *Home: Social Essays*, which records his return to Newark and his black roots and contains many of his most important essays. The following year he adopted the Muslim name of Imamu Ameer Baraka (later changed to Amiri Baraka), as confirmation of his pride in his blackness (*Reader*, xxv). He was arrested in 1967 during the Newark riots and charged with unlawfully carrying a concealed weapon and resisting arrest; he was found guilty of a misdemeanor and sentenced to one to three years in jail by an obviously biased judge, who read the poem "Black People" as evidence of his guilt, excluding, in his reading, the "obscene" passages, which Baraka shouted out in the courtroom. The sentence was overturned on appeal. His *Autobiography* includes a powerful depiction of his beating by the police, his arrest, and trial.

His publications *Black Music* (1968), music criticism, and *Black Fire* (1968), an important collection of African-American writings, coedited with Larry Neal, a poet and influential critic, as well as *Four Black Revolutionary Plays* (1969) and his startling volume of poems *Black Magic* (1969), attest to the development of his black aesthetic. Prolific and provocative, Baraka became the leading black nationalist writer of his time and a strong catalyst for the tremendous growth of Third World literature in the sixties and seventies. As poet, essayist, novelist, dramatist, critic, editor, and teacher, he emerged as an African-American "man of letters" who called for and helped create a new artistic vision that brought forth a second renaissance in African-American literature.

Baraka's radical, engaged poetry was extremely controversial. Numerous critics objected to its political slogans, its violence, anti-Semitism, racism, sexism, and homophobia; however, as Baraka now tells it, these were phases he had to go through, stages in his process of growth. The cover of *Black Magic*, which "depicts a white, blond-haired, blue-eyed voodoo doll riddled with huge hat pins," as Harris notes, captures "the spirit of the book" (*Reader*, 210). "A Poem Some People Will Have to Understand" articulates Baraka's belief that poetry must become a weapon in the battle to build a black nationalist culture. Tired of waiting for "the coming of a natural phenomenon," he politely asks: "Will the machinegunners please step forward?" (210–11). In "A Poem for Black Hearts" he asks his black brothers, in memory of Malcolm X, to

> look up,
> black man, quit stuttering and shuffling, look up,
> black man, quit whining and stooping, for all of him,
> For Great Malcolm a prince of the earth, let nothing in us rest
> until we avenge ourselves for his death . . .
>
> (218)

Baraka's outrage and anger against whites, his racism, anti-Semitism, and racial pride in blacks is especially evident in "Black Art," in which he redefines black art and poetry. "We want," he writes, " 'poems that kill.' / Assassin poems. . . . / Poems that wrestle cops into alleys / and take their weapons leaving them dead / with tongues pulled out and sent to Ireland." We want, Baraka, insists, "dagger poems in the slimy bellies / of the owner-jews" (219). These lines, openly venomous and bigoted, are meant to destroy any existing connections to the white world so that a separate black world can be constructed. Black pride insists it is black people who "are the lovers and the sons / of lovers and warriors . . . / all the loveliness here in the world." Black pride calls for a separate nation, "a / Black World" (219–220). And in "Ka 'Ba," he proudly asserts, "We are beautiful people / with african imaginations / full of masks and dances and swelling chants" (222). What is the magic spell, he asks, that will enable blacks to destroy the old and create a new nation? "What will be / the sacred words?" (222). In *It's Nation Time* (1970) he declares, it is "time to / get up be come / black genius . . . to be / future of the world" (240).

In his writings, his work at Spirit House—a black arts center and alternative school in Newark, New Jersey—and his political work for Kenneth Gibson, a successful black mayoral candidate in Newark in 1970, Baraka displayed his total commitment to the building of a new African-American nation and culture, one that would be based on its historic and cultural ties to Africa. Eventually, however, Baraka began to question his commitment to African nationalism, noting that it seemed to do little in terms of improving the horrendous living conditions of impoverished black urban dwellers. In his *Autobiography* he confesses that "to the extent that I merely turned white supremacy upside down and created an exclusivist black supremacist doctrine, that was bullshit" (*Autobiography*, 245). Breaking with Ron Karenga's cultural nationalist organization US, he confessed that "the idea that somehow we had to go back to pre-capitalist Africa and extract some 'unchanging' black values . . . and impose them on a 20th-century black proletariat in the most advanced industrial country in the world, was simple idealism and subjectivism" (253).

In 1974 he publicly announced his rejection of black nationalism and his adoption of international socialism. Marx, Lenin, and Mao Tse Tung were his new heroes. A scientific approach, a reliance on organization, analysis, and Third World Marxist models formed the basis for Baraka's new ideological position, which he spells out in the essay "Toward Ideological Clarity," published in *Black World* in 1974.

This Marxist approach is seen in his next collection of poems, *Hard Facts* (1975), which attacks Christianity as an opiate that obstructs revolution: "sing about life, not jesus / sing about revolution, not no jesus" (*Reader,* 253). He also attacks the film industry for its refusal to confront social and economic realities. In Marxist terms, Hollywood's aim is to mystify or delude its audience and thus blunt any meaningful social action: "They can't even show you thinking or demanding the new so- / cialist reality, it's the ultimate / tidal / wave . . ." (255). To Baraka, poetry becomes a means of convincing readers of the benefits of "The Dictatorship of the Proletariat," the horrors of capitalism, for "everywhere / is the death scene. . . ." (260). It becomes "a weapon and a weapon of revolution" (xxviii) to convince the black community to overthrow an oppressive capitalist system and to create a Marxist state.

In the 1980s, Baraka once again seemed to move to a different territory, one in which the focus shifts from didactic Marxism to a broader vision of African-American history and culture. His *Autobiography*, for example, written in a bluesy, jazz-like style, can be seen as one of many African-American personal narratives that capture the spirit of a given writer and his time. His class consciousness is never absent as he reenvisions and narrates his life, but it does not overwhelm the texture of that life, which, with its twists and turns, its abrupt changes and transformations, echoes the improvisations of jazz, a form of music that also sounds the African-American belief in protest and revolution. In "AM/TRAK," the music of Coltrane, Davis, Charlie Parker, and Thelonious Monk becomes "screams against reality" (270) and agents of change and revolution. And his poem "In the Tradition" fuses cultural history and revolution; jazz and blues heroes merge with cultural heroes like Sterling Brown, Richard Wright, W. E. B. Dubois, and Langston Hughes. It's all "in the tradition," and that tradition "says sing / says fight" (310).

Baraka's ongoing interest in African-American history and culture is also the basis for an evolving long poem, "Why's / Wise" (1990, in *Reader*), written "in the tradition of the Griots" (African singer-poet-historians) and of William Carlos Williams's *Paterson* and Charles Olson's *Maximus* "in that it tries to tell the history / life like an ongoing-off-coming Tale" (480). The poem, which initially included twenty-five to thirty parts written over two years, focuses on the devastating consequences of losing one's culture and voice. It was published as a separate title, *Why's, Wise, Y's* in 1995. Baraka's poetry, often published in chapbooks and magazines with limited distribution, has often been difficult to find. However, several recent collections of both his previously published and later uncollected poems, are remedying this situation. These include the *Reader* cited above as well as *Transbluesency* (1995) and *Funk Lore: New Poems* (1984–1995).

In his life and writings, Baraka has worked to resurrect his native culture and to add his voice to its collective history. In doing so he acknowledges certain misdirections along the way—sexism, racism, anti-Semitism, homophobia, for example[4]—but he accepts these detours as part of the process of becoming. He acknowledges that there is some validity in summing up his changing vision as " 'Beat-Black-Nationalist-Communist,' . . . but, like notations of Monk, it doesn't show the complexity of real life" (*Reader*, xi). It doesn't reveal the steps in between the subtle shifts and the "historical and time / place / condition reference that will always try to explain exactly why I was saying how and for what" (xiv).

The import of what Baraka has written over more than thirty years was recognized in 1989, when he received the American Book

Award's Lifetime Achievement Award as well as the Langston Hughes Award from the City College of New York. Because he drew no boundaries around the ideas, the forms, or the styles in which he wrote, Baraka is one of the central figures responsible for the extension of the frontiers of our literature.

SONIA SANCHEZ (B. 1934)   Don Lee (Haki Madhubuti), in his introduction to Sonia Sanchez's first volume of poetry, *Homecoming* (1969), hit upon the central thrust of her work as a poet, dramatist, fiction writer, activist, and educator. Her poetry, he stated, "is all about, the love of self & people," the love of blackness.[5] Her writings, whether marked by sharp invective, wails of pain and sorrow, shouts of joy and praise, tender words, or revolutionary chants, are always placed in the service of her growth as a black woman and the continuance of her people. She has never wavered in the pursuit of these ends, and for that reason she is one of the strongest and most enduring voices of the black aesthetic movement.

Sanchez did not fall into that role; she had to overcome a number of obstacles. At the age of one, she lost her mother, Lena Driver, and lived with various Driver relatives. At the age of nine, her father, Wilson Driver, moved the family from Alabama to Harlem. She was a shy child, inward looking, and a stutterer. In fact, she turned to poetry because it permitted her to use words without speaking. She graduated from Hunter College in 1955 with a degree in political science and then studied with the poet Louise Bogan at New York University. In the early sixties she became active in the civil rights movement and began her writing career, appearing in a number of African-American publications. Watching the plight of her people and listening to the speeches of Malcolm X encouraged her to return to her roots. As the title of her first volume indicates, she experienced a *Homecoming*, a return to her own people. She now saw her role as moving her people to self-love and survival.

Homecoming directly states her case that all Africans should follow her example and come "home." Sanchez sees Malcolm X as "the sun that tagged / the western sky" (16), the man who had the vision and courage to cut his ties to the white world. She calls to all her brothers to come home to their black women: "brother / this sister knows / and waits" (10) and exhorts her black sisters to love their black men for "there aint / no MAN like a / black man. . . . makes U / turn in /

side out" (22). And to all the "blk / record buyers," she insists, "don't play me no / righteous bros. . . . play blk / songs" (26).

The nationalist, separatist themes here are given in sharp, direct, and mostly idiomatic lines and are meant to move her people to love their blackness. But there is one problem within the community itself: the status of black women within the revolution. Because of the sexist nature of the black community, women are relegated to the role of whores of the "Rev. Pimps." Upset that far too many black women accept that role, Sanchez loudly calls for her "Sisters" to "get ur / blk / asses out of that re / volution / ary's / bed" (31). This insistence on black women's rightful place in the movement is again noted in *We a BaddDDD People* (1970), which is dedicated to her mother, Lena, and a long list of "blk / wooomen: the only queens of this universe."[6] In "blk / wooooomen / chant," she and other women "stand befo u / plain ol blk / woomen" and ask their "blk / men / u gon pro tect us / treat us rite / loooovvVVE us" (45).

There are also poems here that deal with her relationship with Etheridge Knight, whom she first met and fell in love with while he was in prison. Knight's inability to overcome his drug addiction blighted their relationship, Sanchez writes, for "blk / lovers cannot live / in wite powder that removes / them from they blk / selves" (38).

Sanchez would continually call for the just treatment of black women. If African Americans are to be a "BaddDDD People," in the positive sense of being strong, proud, and free, then women, Sanchez insists, will have to be treated with love and respect. She also insists that her people move beyond rhetoric and revolutionary slogans to build a new nation.

In this volume and others Sanchez blends public and private concerns. In addition, the black diction and the oral nature of her published poetry are crucial to its impact. As in blues and jazz, she draws out a word as if it were a musical note by adding additional letters; she also signals stress with capital letters, uses space and slash lines to show movement; when she performs she shouts, screams, and chants the poem in what critics call a return to her West African roots. However, when she becomes more introspective, the poem often quiets down, becomes more subtle, more compressed. In fact, she uses the Japanese haiku and tanka, which consists of seventeen and thirty-one syllables, as short forms that allow her to articulate, yet contain, her emotional crises. This restraint is especially true in *Love Poems* (1973) and the later sections of her collection of new and selected poems, *I've Been a Woman* (1981).

From 1972 to 1975, Sanchez was a member of the Nation of Islam movement, and her commitment to Islam is clear in *A Blues Book for Blue Black Magical Women* (1973), which is dedicated to both her familial father as well as her spiritual FATHER, HONORABLE ELI-JAH MUHAMMAD then the leader the nation of Islam in the United States, "who has labored forty-two years to deliver us up from this western Babylon."[7] The text stresses that "Black / woooomen / the only QUEENS OF THE UNIVERSE" (12) must escape the white world, join their black men, "embrace Blackness as a religion / husband," (12) to help build the Nation of Islam.

In *HOMEGIRLS AND HANDGRENADES* (1984), Sanchez abandoned her Muslim positions, mainly because of the conflicts that arose over the status of women. As indicated by the title of the book, there is a tension here between the redemptive force of love and the need for revolution. Repeatedly, she asks if love is permanent: "will you stay love / now that i am here?"[8] And she recalls in "After the Fifth Day" the rose her lover gave her, which she pressed into one of the anticolonial works of Franz Fanan (a French psychiatrist and radical writer who inspired many of the new black leaders and writers of the sixties, 1925–1961) thus joining love and revolution, an event that she remembers as "my birth" (5).

But the blues are also here, the songs of loss and oppression. There is a prose piece on Norma, a brilliant and promising young black woman who is ignored by her teachers and ends up a junkie (19–22). In a poem entitled "Depression," lovers are either too old or too young for love (25). The junkie reappears in "After Saturday Night Comes Sunday" (29), and a desperate street woman appears in "Bluebirdbluebirdthrumywindow" (39–41). They are victims of an unjust social order that drives them toward self-destruction.

Sanchez combines her expressions of love with revolutionary fervor. She praises Margaret Walker's vision of revolution in "For My People" and expresses her love for Ezekiel Mphahlele and his family, who are returning to South Africa after twenty years of exile. "Reflections After the June 12th March for Disarmament" insists that the history, and experience of black women from "the depths of slavery" to the conservative decade of the eighties, "were not in vain" (65). Although "no people / have been asked to be modern day people / with the history of slavery, and still / we walk, and still we talk, and still we plan, and still we hope, and still we sing" (66). She speaks with the determination of her indomitable ancestors: "I shall not give the / earth up to non-dreamers and earth molesters" (68). In "A Letter to Dr. Martin Luther King" on what would have been his fifty-fourth birthday, she evokes his spirit and speaks to him directly: "Now is the changing of the tides, Martin. . . . Great God, Martin, what a morning it will be!" (70, 71). The volume ends with a remembrance of the oppressed in Atlanta, Georgia, in South Africa, in El Salvador and with a call for her readers to join in the fight for freedom.

This insistence on freedom, of course, continually confronts the reality of twentieth-century history. In *Under a Soprano Sky* (1987) Sanchez confronts such horrors as the police helicopter bombing of the MOVE headquarters in Philadelphia on May 13, 1985, in which eleven African-Americans—six adults and five children—were killed and an entire block destroyed. In her elegy for the victims, she lashes out at the spectators who "hurry on down" to "smell the dreadlocks and blk / skins / roasting in the fire."[9] She demands to know "who anointed the city with napalm? / who giveth this city in holy infanticide?" (13) She also mourns the death of her brother, a victim of AIDS, and the death of James Thornevell, a black Vietnam vet who died during an epileptic fit (16). Death and despair push her toward defeat: "i am going in the bluerain that drowns green crystals / i am going to die" (35).

But once again she is able to draw on her past as a source of strength. She remembers her grandmother, called Mama, who insisted that Sanchez follow her own unique path: "Let her be, . . . She got a right to be different." Sanchez replies, "And I be Mama," and becomes the voice of the community that insists that African Americans have a right to express their cultural differences. To the black boy (who is shut out by the white world) she proclaims, "You are the wind choreographer of our flesh / you are the sacred waters baptizing our tongue."

Sanchez's lifelong quest for racial, social, and sexual justice are once again major themes in *Wounded in the House of a Friend* (1995). Her call for black unity ("Catch the Fire") and celebration of the achievements of black women ("A Love Song for Spelman") are also important themes in this collection. Most striking, however, are the poems directly related to the title, which is taken from the Bible (Zechariah, 13:6). The tragic and paradoxical truth—that one's closest friends, relatives, or even parents can be the ones that hurt maim or kill—is startlingly captured in "Love Song #3." In this poem a loving, but too lenient grandmother takes in her crack-addicted granddaughter only to be beaten to death by her with a hammer. And in "Poem for Some Women," a mother sells her seven-year-old daughter to a child molester for a hit of crack-cocaine. These poems are somewhat balanced by a series of haiku and tonka love poems, but the horror and wretchedness of the darker poems have a greater impact.

Sanchez's purpose is always clear. Often rejecting academic and standard forms of English, her voice is the indomitable spirit of her people insisting on their cultural identity. She retains the essence of the black aesthetic of the 1960s, creating moving and inspiring songs primarily for her people. Sanchez's ability to draw large audiences (blacks and whites) to her readings clearly indicates that aesthetic remains a continuing force in contemporary poetry.

ETHERIDGE KNIGHT (1931–1991) When Etheridge Knight published *Born of a Woman* in 1980, he turned to a passage in Job to signify his vision of human existence. "Man that is born of a woman is of few days, and full of trouble."[10] Life to Knight is short, painful, and full of woes. This certainly was the case in his. Born in rural Mississippi, he grew up in an impoverished family, dropped out of school after eight years, hit the streets, got involved with drugs, joined the army at age sixteen to escape this world, was wounded during the Korean War, and turned to drugs once again to ease his pain. Arrested for armed robbery, he was sentenced to ten to twenty-five years in the Indiana State Prison System. It was in prison that, out of desperation, he turned to poetry as a means of salvation. "I died," Etheridge writes, "in Korea from a shrapnel wound and narcotics resurrected me. I died in 1960 from a prison sentence and poetry brought me back to life."[11] Like Malcolm X and Eldridge Cleaver, Knight's experience in prison became his Harvard; it was where he discovered he could "take / your words and scrape / the sky, shake rain / on the desert . . ." (9).

When he entered prison, Knight was already an acknowledged master of the various forms of street talk, especially the toast, a long rhymed narrative recitation, often about a rogue character who manages to outwit his pursuers; it has to be delivered in a crowd-pleasing fashion and often relies on strong rhyme and aggressive language for effect. But many other factors influenced his verse: he looked to both Langston Hughes's blues poems and the strict form of the haiku for economy; he fused the oral rhythms of African-American speech with the metrical forms of traditional verse. His subject was his life, and in his depiction of that life he represented the lives of other African-American males, as well as the anger, rage, pain, and revolutionary cries of the black power movement. Among his heroes were Elijah Muhammed, Malcolm X, LeRoi Jones (Amiri Baraka), and Don Lee (Haki Madhubuti).

Knight's first two publications, *Poems from Prison* (1968) and *Black Voices from Prison* (1965 in Italy, 1970 in the United States), clearly were written out of the new black consciousness. Encouraged by Gwendolyn Brooks, Sonia Sanchez (his first wife), Don Lee, and Dudley Randall (his editor and publisher at Broadside Press), Knight brought forth in his work a soulful but determined voice that seemed to represent the burden and pain of African Americans who found themselves, whether incarcerated or not, living in a prison. In his preface to *Black Voices from Prison* , Knight endorses Malcolm X's statement "That's what America means: prison"[12] and then goes on to attack the excessive oppression of prison life. Knight, however, also believes that "the soul-killing effect of a racist culture on black inmates has been greatly offset by the phenomenal rise of black consciousness" (9).

His prison poems are a lasting and moving depiction of that oppressive existence. The most anthologized is "Hard Rock Returns to Prison from the Hospital for the Criminally Insane," a narrative poem that is told from the point of view of the prisoners who worship Hard Rock, a rebellious black prisoner who would "take no shit," who was the archetypal "mean nigger," and "had the scars to prove it." Their hero, however, is rendered harmless by a state-ordered lobotomy. The prisoners, hearing the news, "waited and watched, like a herd of sheep, / To see if the WORD was true" (*Essential*, 7). When Hard Rock does not respond to racial insults, the black prisoners know it is true; they bemoan the loss of their "Destroyer, the doer of things" but are too paralyzed with fear to rebel without him, for fear "Had cut deep bloody grooves / Across our backs" (8).

Knight's other characters include "Freckle-faced Gerald," a naive sixteen year old who is "thrown" into prison as if he were " 'pig-meat' / for the buzzards to eat." He is brutally raped, but Knight insists that this was all "plotted years in advance / by wiser and bigger buzzards than those / who now . . . light upon his back" (19). To Knight, those buzzards are the racist oppressors who early in our history enslaved and now imprison black men who in turn prey on other black men. There is also the old timer, who teaches the old ways, who knows "the enemy / he has the secret eyes / he sees through stone" (10–11). And there is Etheridge himself, who through his poetry wants to know "can there anything / good come out of / prison" (9).

Life on the outside, Knight illustrates, is no escape. In one of his wittier poems, "The Warden Said to Me the Other Day," a warden asks why more black prisoners don't try to escape. Knight's speaker replies, " 'I reckon it's 'cause / we ain't got nowheres to run to' " (20). On the outside a black male has to watch his seventeen-year-old sister sell her body, painfully wondering what, if anything, he can do about it:

> should I squat
> In the dust and make strange markings on the ground?
> Shall I chant a spell to drive the demon away?
> (Run sister run—the Bugga man comes!)
>
> (26)

As the poem's title indicates, this is "The Violent Space," and all the speaker can do is numb his pain with heroin. In one of his most moving stanzas, Knight captures the agony of the speaker's impotence and loss of self-esteem: "And what do I do. I boil my tears in a twisted spoon / And dance like an angel on the point of a needle" (27).

Knight honestly acknowledges that poetry or art cannot cast out the demons of racism, and he captures the desperation of a powerless black man who turns to drugs because he is unable to save either his sister or his lover, who are forced into prostitution. "I die as I watch you / disappear in the dark streets / to whistle and smile at the johns" (30).

Whether heroin, reefers, alcohol or pills, drugs become a way out of this world of trouble. But this addiction leads to a new set of troubles, trouble with women like Sonia Sanchez, his first wife, who endured, for a time, marriage to a drug addict. His poems chronicle the ongoing trauma of his life: his lover leaves him ("Upon Your

Leaving"); he cannot support his new family ("Report To the Mother"). He experiences the death of his heroes, Malcolm X ("It Was A Funky Deal") and Martin Luther King Jr., of his friends, and of fellow poets, who commit suicide or are shot down by the police. Life seems to be a matter of "attrition," of loss, pain. Like Elizabeth Bishop, Knight learned early that life is a disaster.

All Knight can do is to try through his poetry to bring some light to this darkness. As it is for Sonny in James Baldwin's short story "Sonny's Blues," art or poetry becomes for Knight a means of creating beauty and order out of death and destruction. As he explains in a haiku: "To write a blues song / is to regiment riots / and pluck gems from graves" (17).

So Knight becomes one of the best of our blues poets, building on the legacy of Langston Hughes as he relates to us the turmoil, or "Quality," of his life: "From the moment / My Father grunted and comed / Until now . . . can be felt / In the one word: DESPERATION" (21). He croons the blues in "Feeling Fucked Up," when his woman leaves him: "Lord she's gone done left me done packed / up and split / . . . everywhere the world is bare . . . / dope death dead dying and jiving drove / her away" (34). He skillfully uses black dialect, blues rhythms, slash marks, and the dash to sing the "Con / Tin / U / Way / Shun Blues" (93). Disagreeing with the view that the blues are essentially songs of oppression, he quotes Mary Helen Washington—"blues are more than cries of oppression"—and insists that a blues song is more than "just a slave song / . . . Cause even when we be free, baby— / Lord knows we still have got to die / lovers will still lie / babies will still cry" (93).

This poem indicates a broadening of Knight's audience. Although he never abandons the black experience or his black audience, he does move in *Belly Song* (1973) and *Born of a Woman* (1980) to a more inclusive vision of purpose and audience. Because poetry originates in the belly, is a "Belly Song" that comes "from the bottom / of the sea / in my belly / . . . / is a song / about FEELINGS,"(88) it is available to all human beings; this is true regardless of a person's color or ethnicity. In *Born of a Woman* Knight even changed what he now considered to be racist and sexist words in two of his earlier poems and insisted that poetry not lie or "perpetuate an evil" (*Born*, xiv). Poetry, he insists, is "about and / or for people."

There is a strong humanistic note in Knight's poems that tries to reach out and include rather than exclude. As early as *Black Voices*, he told of a visit from "A Wasp Woman" who comes to the prison to offer him some comfort. Initially he feels no possible connection can exist, but then discovers their common humanness.

For Knight, love is the bond that unites humanity. At times the love is for his extended family, as in one of his most famous poems, "The Idea of Ancestry." Here he views his family, who are represented in the forty-seven pictures tacked to his cell wall. As the one relief from the "gray stone wall damming my stream" (*Essential*, 13), the pictures remind him of his connection to his family and humanity: "I am all of them, / they are all of me," but Knight laments, "I have no children to float in the space between." As a number of critics have pointed out, the poem is a moving testament to the importance of kinship in African-American culture, but it may also move any reader who seeks family connections.

Although, the dominant note in Knight's work is pain, there is also a vision of a new world based on love and family, and there are memorable poems that celebrate the birth of children. "The Stretching of the Belly" of his pregnant wife becomes a "Reaching / For life / For love" (29), and her stretchmarks are juxtaposed with the scars of males that do not "come from stars / Or the moon" but instead "come from wars" and "are stripes of slavery." By contrast, his woman's belly is "bringing forth / Making / music" (29). When it is time for the birth of Isaac Buthie Blackburn Knight, Knight grimly takes note of the world his son will enter. There is news of the mass suicide in Jonestown, Guyana. In Memphis, Tennessee, the setting of his son's delivery, "cops / act / much worse than thieves" (70). He then imaginatively enters Charlene's womb to help his son come into a world where "the Ku Klux / Klan / march like locusts over / this / land," where black leaders like Martin Luther King Jr., Malcolm X, and Medgar Evers "are / shot down." For three days and nights of labor, Knight's "belly becomes a drum and my blood beseech thee." When Isaac is finally born, Knight remarks that *"You / be a loonngg time coming, boy— / But you're wel / come here"* (71).

Love and birth are the forces that give meaning to Knight's life. And when the poems speaking of these forces are read with his darker blues poems, they become even more celebrative and affirmative, as the poet moves from despair to joy. He tells Sonia Sanchez on her thirty-third birthday that despite the shortness of life, "Our time is the constant blooming / of our love" (28). He considers Mary Ellen McAnnally, his second wife, a white woman, to be "a perfect poem," a "song pulse of love" (53), and in "Belly Song," after lamenting his failure to nourish his relationship with Sanchez—"I fell on her / like a stone"—he is still able to turn to love as a means of escaping a sea of troubles.

Rooted in the soil of the oral tradition cultivated by Sterling Brown, as well as in the sharp wit and blues motifs of Langston Hughes, Knight's poetry emerges as a distinctly male cry from the body, a poetry of intense pain, joy, and rebellion. His ability to articulate the plight and intense feelings of African-American men captured the attention of Robert Bly, an early supporter of Knight and a major force in the growth of the men's movement in the eighties. Reading with Bly and other men, including Haki Madhubuti, Knight discovered a new audience for his "belly songs." Unfortunately, his death in 1991 ended that phase of his poetic career far too soon. But he was alive to see his collection of poems, *The Essential Etheridge Knight*, receive the 1986 American Book Award for poetry.

LUCILLE CLIFTON (B. 1936)   Lucille Clifton has given her readers an amazing range of themes and experiences as well as a very distinctive voice and style. From her first volume of poems, *Good Times* (1969), to her 1996 publication, *The Terrible Stories*, she has demonstrated a striking ability to pack a great deal into some of the most terse and compressed poems of the latter half of the twentieth century. As in the work of Emily Dickinson and Lorine Neidecker, brevity in Clifton's poetry paradoxically signals expansiveness in terms of insight and emotion. In addition, Clifton's voice is unique in its rhythms, intonations, and diction as it blends together the strains of her African-American rural southern ancestry, her Christian background, her northern urban experiences, as well as the sophisticated wit of a very observant and wise woman. We hear the words and rhythms of Georgian fields and the street sounds of Buffalo, New York, as well as strains of gospel music, jazz, and the blues.

Central to Clifton's work is her exploration of her African-American ancestry, which on her father's side goes back to her great-great-grandmother, Caroline Donald Sayle, whose life was full of tragedy and struggle. At the age of eight she was taken from her native land, Dahomey, West Africa, separated from her mother and many of her family members, and forced to march from New Orleans to Virginia to begin her life as a slave on the Donald plantation. Later, she witnessed the hanging of her daughter, Lucy, who shot the white father of Lucy's son, Gene. Caroline told and retold these tales to Lucille's father, Samuel, always insisting that he and the other family members were special because they were descendants of the fiercely independent Dahomey women. As indicated in Clifton's prose memoir, *Generations: A Memoir* (1976), "Caroline Donald Sale [was] born free in Afrika in 1822 / died free in America in 1910."[13]

Throughout her memoir and poems, Clifton sings this theme of prideful independence. Her portraits of her father, who was told by Caroline to "Get what you want, you from Dahomey women" (223), are especially notable. Born in Virginia, he came north during the great migration of African Americans in the first half of this century to secure a brighter future. Hired originally as a strike breaker, he traveled to Depew and then Buffalo, New York, to work in the steel mills. Although nearly illiterate, he eventually managed to purchase his own home and send Lucille to college. He took pride in his own and his ancestors' accomplishments, telling Lucille, "We fooled em, Lue, slavery was terrible, but we fooled them / old people. We come out of it better than they did" (260).

Family, ancestory, and community, as in Etheridge Knight's work, provide the basis for stability, permanence, and pride. In her memoir Clifton writes: "When the colored people came to Depew they came to be a family. Everybody began to be related in thin ways that last and last. The generations of white folks are just people but the generations of colored folks are families" (265). Clifton also places great emphasis on being the mother of six children, whom she envisions as "free sons and daughters of free folk" (275).

This spirit of confidence and realistic optimism is present throughout her work, but especially in *Good Times* (1969) and *Good News about the Earth* (1972). In her first volume she counters the stereotypes often associated with African-American urban life. There is certainly hardship and tragedy: "miss rosie," for example, "used to be the best looking gal in georgia / used to be called the Georgia Rose" (19), but is now a senile street lady, "wrapped up like garbage." However, even in this degraded state, Clifton recognizes the worth of this woman: "i stand up / through your destruction / i stand up" (19). While sociologists may coldly call her world the "inner city of Buffalo," a phrase that makes no room for love and family, Clifton declares "we call it / home" and contrasts that home with what she regards as the sterile white world, "uptown," with its "silent nights / and the houses straight as / dead men" (15).

In the title poem of this initial collection, Clifton, in a somewhat ironic but celebratory voice, gladly recalls what many would see as less than a satisfactory existence. "Good Times" mean the rent and the insurance are paid, the lights are back on, and the family is together, drinking and dancing in the kitchen. There is life and family here, and this, she insists to all her children, is what they must contemplate in their struggles: "oh children think about the / good times" (24).

The rage and pain in Clifton's world emerges in her series of poems on the 1960s Buffalo riots, what she calls the "buffalo wars." These poems recall the periodic explosions that take place when, as Langston Hughes put it, dreams are deferred. However, Clifton's purpose in this volume is not to underscore the violence but to provide the saving news, the good news that is easily forgotten in the day-to-day pain of urban life.

Good Times is reminiscent of Gwendolyn Brooks's *Streets of Bronzeville* in that it depicts the urban black world with sensitivity, sympathy, and pride. But like Brooks, Clifton moved to the more politically conscious aesthetic that emerged in the second half of the 1960s. She dedicates *Good News about the Earth* (1972) to the slain African-American students at Jackson State College in Mississippi and Orangeburg College in South Carolina. In "after kent state" she is appalled by the slaying of four white students at Kent State University in Ohio by National Guardsmen on May 4, 1970. The white man, she exclaims, not only "kills his cities / and his trees" but even "his children." She concludes that "white ways are / the way of death" (57).

In contrast, she repeatedly insists that the black way is the key to life. In "the way it was" she berates herself for trying to look white, for straightening her hair, greasing her legs, being "a nice girl / no touching / trying to be white" (59). She apologizes to the Black Panthers for her "whiteful ways," and thanks her brothers "for these mannish days." She also insists that her children realize that despite all the hardships associated with being black, "we have never hated black, . . . we have always loved each other / children all ways / pass it on" (65).

Good News about Earth presents a gallery of black nationalist heroes: "malcolm [x]," "eldridge [cleaver]," and "bobby seale." In addition, a very imaginative and radical reading of the Bible is rendered in the closing section, entitled "some jesus." Traditionally, African Americans have viewed Bible stories as analogs, as a code for their own struggles against oppression. Here, however, the subtleties and analogies are dropped. In theme and style the narratives are clearly black. Solomon blesses "the black skin of the woman"; "daniel" learns the need to "walk manly / he don't stumble / even in the lion's den" (96). Jonah, remembering the joys of Africa, while enslaved in America, the belly of the whale, warns his brothers, "—Be care full of the ocean—." John the Baptist envisions Jesus as a black liberator. Before his resurrection on Easter, Jesus himself sees "red stars and black stars / pushed out of the sky by white ones" and knows "that he had to come and lift men up" (105).

An Ordinary Woman (1974) and *Two-Headed Woman* (1980), focus on Clifton's identity as a black woman. In "sisters," the opening section of *Ordinary Woman*, a number of poems celebrate her relationship to her sister, Elaine, her woman friends—her larger family of sisters—as well as her heroic female predecessors, such as Harriet Tubman and Sojourner Truth, and those ordinary black women who "work hard / trust the Gods / love my children and / wait" (119). However, she is unable to fully connect with her white sisters, whether they be the ancestors of Puritan women "in Salem," Massachusetts, who live behind their "hedges moral as fire," suspiciously watching two black women (111) or the new feminists associated with *Ms* magazine. Addressing this last group, Clifton cannot forget that black women were never called sister by their white sisters when they were field hands or domestics: "and you never called me sister / then, you never called me sister / and it has only been forever . . ." (122).

Clifton's self-examination is brought on by her recognition of her mortality. She felt the need at this point in her life to move beyond social definitions—cages—and to begin "turning into my own / turning on in / to my own self" (143). Initially, she carries on this exploration by trying to identify "lucy" (herself) and her relationship to her mother—"lucy one-eye / she got her mama's ways" (145)—and by exploring her father's past in Virginia and the Sayles family history. She joyfully discovers her African identity: "my soul got happy / and i stayed all day" (151). She then assesses her life after thirty-eight years and concludes that she is as "plain as bread / round as a cake / an ordinary woman" (158). But she insists on being her own woman as she acknowledges her mortality. If she is turning towards that "shining dark," let it be, she insists, not "out of my mother's life" but "into my own" (159).

Two-Headed Woman takes this assessment of her place in life further as Clifton becomes more affirmative, paying "homage" to whatever is hers, including her hips—"these hips have never been enslaved / . . . these hips are magic hips" (168). She praises her hair, in fact, her entire body as her mirror tells her, "you a wonder. / . . . you got a geography / of your own. / . . . you not a noplace" (169). She also praises her children and moves to reconcile herself to the failings of her parents.

If the earlier volumes are to find the good news about the African-American community, these latter volumes are an attempt to find the good news about her inner self, her doubts and struggles, an examination that has been delayed by the needs of both her family and the community. In middle age she becomes "the sensational / two-headed woman / one face turned outward / one face / swiveling slowly in" (185). To capture this inward spiritual journey, Clifton centers her later poems on the presence of light, the Latin source for her name, Lucille (which means to light or shine), as well as the mysterious presence of voices that mystically link her to St. Joan.

In another set of poems Clifton speaks in Mary's voice, retelling the story of her mysterious impregnation, the birth of Jesus, and the eventual crucifixion of her son. To Clifton, neither she nor Mary chose their fates, their mystical lives, or their losses, sufferings, and creations. This inward journey and its unsettling discoveries shook Clifton's "fondest sureties" but, as "a voice from the non dead past" asserts, " 'you might as well answer the door, my child, / the truth is furiously knocking' " (209). Time and space are effaced, past and present become one as the voices of the living and the dead are mingled. Speaking of her dead but still "living" ancestors, she says joyously: "our ancestors continue. / . . . i have heard / their shimmering voices / singing" (221).

As Denise Levertov indicates in her praise of GOOD WOMAN (1987), "the mythic is realized in the quotidian, the humble and everyday is illuminated by the spiritual."[14] So it is not surprising that Clifton would frame her memoir with quotes from Whitman's *Song of Myself* and would in *Next* (1987) extend even further her poetic vision. In that volume she sings a song for Winnie Mandela[15] and a "sorrow song" that embraces suffering children throughout history. She is also able to speak in a wide variety of voices, from the voice of

Crazy Horse to the voice of a dead woman in a Lebanese camp who has witnessed the murders of twenty-seven family members.

These powerful poems present a woman's connection to the pain of others and her outrage over the worldwide atrocities of the past and present. Clifton, who began by focusing on her particular world of twentieth-century Buffalo, becomes, in these poems, a poet who is global in vision. Her role while living in "white America," she explains, is to remind all of us that "it is late"; she is, "a black cat / in the belfry / hanging / and / ringing" (76).

The Book of Light (1993) and *The Terrible Stories* (1996) continue Clifton's exploration of her private and public experiences. She still, as the title of the first volume indicates, seeks the light but that has become more difficult because of the weight and fragility of life; she has had to deal with the death of her parents, her husband, brother, and her own battle against breast cancer which is discussed in "From the Cadavers," the second section of *The Terrible Stories*. Loneliness, widowhood, cancer treatments, the loss of loved ones are "terrible," personal burdens to bear, and public events only increase the weight of those burdens. She laments the bombing of the children of radical activists in Philadelphia (1985) as well as the children in Baghdad, Iraq (1991). When she spends a term in Memphis, Tennessee, she is nearly overwhelmed by the "terrible stories" of the slave trade and the more recent killings of civil rights leaders and activists—Medgar Evers, (1963), James Chaney, Michael Schwerner, and Andrew Goodman (1964).

However heavy the weight, Clifton continues "climbing" towards the light. As she fights her cancer, for example, she is strengthened by the spiritual presence of her Dahomey ancestral sisters as well as Audre Lorde, a recent victim of breast cancer. Like the fox in the first section of *The Terrible Stories*, she is pursued by hounds and hunters, but also dreams when she and the other foxes can lope through the fields without fear ("a dream of foxes"). These fox stories suggest Aesop as well as African-American folk tales, and they along with Clifton's marvelous use of Greek heroes and heroines and Biblical characters (Sisyphus, Atlas, and Leda , Sarah, Naomi, Cain, David, and Lucifer) as narrators or speakers gives her work universality and expansiveness. She is an American original, and her poetic "quilting" links diverse strains of our private and public lives.

QUINCY TROUPE (B. 1943) Quincy Troupe has played a major role in bringing the African-American experience to a large and diverse audience. After graduating from Grambling College with a degree in history and political science, he settled in Los Angeles, where he taught creative writing for the Watts Writers Movement and edited *Watts Poets* (1968), a collection of writings by African Americans that captures the black aesthetic of the 1960s. In the seventies he edited *Giant Talk: An Anthology of Third World Writing* (1975), one of the first national collections of Third World writers, and founded and edited *American Rag*, a journal that specialized in non-European writers. In 1978, he coauthored with David L. Wolper *The Inside Story of TV's "Roots,"* which sold more than 1 million copies. 1989 was a very productive year for Troupe; he published *Soundings*, a collection of essays; coauthored a compelling biography of Miles Davis, *Miles: The Autobiography*; and edited *James Baldwin: The Legacy*, which includes a preface and interview with Baldwin. With the publication of two volumes of poems in the nineties (*Weather Reports*, 1991 and *Avalanche*, 1996), Troupe emerged as highly inventive and engaging poet as well as a powerful proponent of racial and cultural diversity.

In the early 1990's he established an innovative performance series called "Artists on the Cutting Edge" at the San Diego Museum of Contemporary Art in La Jolla. The series, featuring unique combinations of poets, writers, musicians and other artists performing their work has been widely heralded as a distinctive venue for contemporary artists.[16]

Although Troupe depicts a wide range of African-American life in his poetry, at times the content is personal, focusing on family or love relationships, as in the first section of *Skulls along the River* (1984), where he revisits his early years in St. Louis. The poems here are often bluesy and folk-like, echoing the works of Sterling Brown. In fact, "River Town Packin House Blues," dedicated to Brown, is a modern-day version of "The Ballad of John Henry," wherein Big Tom sweats his life away in a meat packing house where he slaughters animals:

> swingin his hamma called death, 260 workdays,
> twenty years,
> like ol John Henry,
> eye say swingin his hammer named death[17]

"Blues for Delmar Dosie" recounts Troupe's first sexual encounter, which was with a wild, tough, young woman: "dosie, you were the first / to taste this burning / love eye carry deep inside me" (17). But now Dosie is "doing a thirty year to life prison stretch / for armed robbery & assault with intent / to kill," so he "dedicate[s] this blues / to your strong, wet once / pulling thighs" (18). And in "River Rhythm Town" (St. Louis), he again gives voice to a black idiom and rhythm:

> River rhythm town
> under sun / moon laughter.
> river blues town filled
> with blues people
> doin' blues dues thangs.
>   (27)

Throughout this volume death lurks, for there are always "skulls along the river": "& eye remember death / shattering as daybreak" (28). What the eye perceives becomes the I, but it is also Troupe's wish to find beauty and love in a world where suffering, death, and pain always reside. Because the blues can, through the magical powers of art, transform suffering into beauty, he calls on the "mellow prophets of crushed grapes & stomped berries" to "grant me holy syllables of your blues laced tongues / perfect eardrums / O grant me sacred light of your blues" (4).

Troupe's earlier poems, in *Snake-Back Solos* (1979), which won the 1980 American Book Award, and *Embryo* (1971), established him as a poet continuing the traditions of the Harlem Renaissance in terms of dialect, rhythm, and subject matter. There are, however, a number of important differences. Troupe readily acknowledges his indebtedness to poets such as Sterling Brown and Langston Hughes, but he also fell under the influence of Caribbean, African, and Latin American surrealists Aimé Cesairé, Jean Joseph Rabearivelo, and Pablo Neruda. Their influence can be seen in the dreamlike, often nightmarish, quality of his imagery. The rush of words and sounds in Troupe's lines seem to explode onto the page, like notes blown from a frenzied horn. This creates a very distinctive style, one that is most effective when heard. Here, for example, is the first stanza of "Up Sun South of Alaska," in which Troupe composes "A Short African-American History Song" for his son, Brandon. The stanza recounts the coming of slavery:

> slit balls hung in southern / american winds then
> when drumheads were slit made mum by rum

& songs hung way down
around our ankles bleeding up sun south of alaska
swinging silhouettes picked clean to bone
by black crows
caw caw razor scars black-winged crows ripping
sunset flights of slashing razors
crows crows
blue caw caws & moans
& blues caw caws & moans.[18]

The use of sound here, whether in rhyme or repetition, clearly underscores the musical nature of Troupe's poetry. As far back as the sixties he had written, like Michael Harper, a praise poem, "Ode to John Coltrane,"[19] that was later slightly revised and included in *Skulls along the River*. "Trane" is imaged as "Black John the jujuman. . . . Trane Trane John the Baptist," whose music wrestled meaning out of suffering:

Trane Trane John Coltrane, you came and while here
breathed light love upon red cold sky
dripping with blood death and fire
so that Black music love
would not falter and die

(42)

These images of music as a countervailing force against blood, death, and fire capture the importance of music to the African-American community. It is that community's counterpoint to a world that is often far too violent and loveless, a world seen, for example, in "Today's Subway Ride," which, like Hart Crane's subway trip in *The Bridge*, becomes a metaphor for a journey through the inferno: "sardine can tight   packin people / starin off into space pit deep black space . . . & everywhere we go headlines / of bizzare madness starin back at us" (*Snake-Back*, 17).

Avalanche is Troupe's most imaginative and ambitious work. It contains new and previously published poems that have been organized and arranged to fit the unifying concept of the book—the three stages of an avalanche. The interplay of the three parts or stages of this event—the awesome breaking away and plunge downward of snow, ice, and debris; the uneven sound of the materials settling; the quiet and serenity after all is settled—create a moving and pleasurable experience for its audience which like the landscape after the avalanche may be transformed, reshaped. The poems in each of the sections mirror and echo stages of the avalanche. The initial, expansive poems with their long lines and rush of words and sounds seem to hurtle down the page. Whereas a number of poems in the third stage contain only six short lines and seem to be permanently settled on the page. These shorter poems, to cite one of their titles, reflect a time of "Stillness" when the awesome power of language, nature, and God are at rest.

Troupe's quest in *Avalanche* is to create a mode of language and a structure that will transform our literary and cultural landscape. If one's previous perceptions of African-American culture and history failed to see the glories of that realm, one's eyes will be opened after reading Troupe's homages to his father, Malcolm X, Magic Johnson, Michael Jordan, the great African-American jazz and blues musicians, and even to "Three Old Black Ladies Standing on Bus Stop Corners." The title poem "Avalanche" celebrates the healing powers of music and poetry; they are holy and transforming. In "Looking at Both Sides of a Question," dedicated to the Oneida Indian poet, Roberta Hill Whiteman and Miles Dewey Davis, Troupe re-envisions America as a confluence of rivers, a medley of melodies, where black, brown, yellow, red, white Americans enter the unifying flow of humanity and create a new America. Although life an be morbid and painful, Troupe remains convinced that ultimately it is holy and beautiful ("Poem for My Friends").

"Avalanche" suggests the primary quality of Troupe's work. Although the cresendo of imagery and rush of words sometimes seem to overwhelm the reader, he is an accessible poet who can go into the streets, taverns, or schools and capture the glory of Magic Johnson's moves on the basketball court, or the magic of love and music. Whether wailing or singing, he seeks the light: "my poems have holes sewn into them / & they run searching for light at the end" (79).

MICHAEL HARPER (B. 1938) Michael Harper's work and life provide clear evidence that it is very misleading to paint African-American poetry with a single brush stroke, for it contains many styles, textures, and tones. Harper's work is, in some ways, in direct opposition to that of the black arts poets. He argues against separation, against writing only for a black audience; he avoids the slashing diction, the political phrase, the single vision, he might say, of the black arts movement. Instead, from the publication of his first volume, *Dear John, Dear Coltrane* (1970), to his *Healing Song for the Inner Ear* (1985), Harper, following in the footsteps of Robert Hayden, searches for a means of achieving unity in a divisive and fragmented world. He does not accept an either/or approach in his world vision or poetics but insists on "both/and" to reconcile individual, social, aesthetic, and philosophic opposites.

As a poet of cultural "double consciousness," black but also American, Harper's aim is to free both identities. He seeks to destroy the racial myths that separate the races, especially those white myths that distort history and bring pain, suffering, and injustice to the victims of racial prejudice. In "Clark's Way West: Another Version," he reenvisions the celebration of the opening of the west to Euro-American conquest and occupation by presenting an image of an indigenous people and a landscape infected with a venereal disease brought to them by members of the Lewis and Clark's expedition.[20] Harper asserts that American history, as we know it, is a false mythology and sees his task as exposing the truth about our racial past and acknowledging its impact on our present lives.

One of his most striking poems on this theme is "History as Apple Tree," which first appeared as the concluding poem in *Photographs: Negatives: History as Apple Tree* (1972). The poem is based on Harper's discovery that his Narragansett Bay home sits on an ancient Indian burial ground. This discovery triggers his reconstruction of the Puritan experience, the historical figures John Winthrop and Roger Williams, the acquisition of the land from the Indians, and the establishment of Providence Plantation, now the state of Rhode Island. He also remembers that "black men" escaped into Sachem Cononicus's tribe, thus linking blacks and Indians in their struggle for freedom. Harper sees American history on both a collective and individual level as multicultural.

Reinterpreting history and becoming part of that history enable Harper to assert his identity, as a black and as an American, an assertion racist America denies. He declares in "Brother John," "I am; I'm a black man; / I am" (*Dear John*, 4). His racial identity does not, of course, negate his existence, although, as Ralph Ellison illustrates, it often results in invisibility. For exactly that reason, Harper feels it is important to make visible the historical presence of Indians and African Americans and to correct false historical myths. As he explains in "Corrected Review," "Our mode is our jam session / of tradition, / past in this present moment / articulated. . . ."[21]

If we were to view poets as musicians, we might see Harper as an improvisational trumpeter fusing past and present, individual and social notes, in jazz-like expressions that require artistry, endurance, and magic. His homages to John Coltrane, Miles Davis, and other jazz musicians mark his recognition of their ability to do just that with their music. Their supreme love of life and art can, like magic,[22] transform both artist and listener and create a new reality. The title of Harper's second volume of verse, *History Is Your Own Heartbeat* (1971), concisely captures the essence of his poetic vision. It also echoes T. S. Eliot's belief that the past is always a part of one's present existence. For example, in "Blue Ruth: America" Harper turns his mother-in-law's operation for gallstones, which required a general anesthetic, into a metaphor for past and present social diseases as well as historical amnesia:

> I am telling you this:
> the tubes in your nose,
> in the esophagus,
> in the stomach . . .
> is America:
> I am telling you this:
> *history is your own heartbeat.*[23]

Harper, in fact, often uses medical terminology and physical diseases as figures for America's social, spiritual, and psychological wounds. For example, "Debridement," a medical term (and the title for a long poem), is "The cutting away of dead / or contaminated tissue from a wound to prevent infection" (98). Debridement is also often the function of Harper's poetry. He first graphically describes the "wound" and then finds the means of eliminating the "diseased" tissue to make the body whole again. Ultimately it is the discovery of connections that overcomes divisions and restores health. In "24th Avenue: City of Roses: Anesthesia:2," for instance, it is Ruth's grandson, a symbol of continuity and love, "who has pulled [Ruth] back / from death with his own / voice" (159).

Images of Kin (1977), Harper concludes, need to be extended, like a long jazz riff, to all members of the human family if we are to move from what seems, at times, a terminal condition. "High Modes: Vision as Ritual: Confirmation" is a poem that captures this intent.

Past and present, Africa and America, and then humanity are joined by a "mode" or force such as art or jazz that unifies and connects:

> And we go back to the well: Africa,
> the first mode, and man, modally,
> touched the land of the continent,
> modality: we are one; a man is another
> man's face, modality, in continuum,
> from man, to man, *contact-high*, to man,
> *contact-high*, to man, high modes, oneness,
> *contact-high*, man to man, contact high
> (177–78)

As this passage shows, Harper's work is often dense and complex, made so by his improvisational style, his abstract reflections, his insistence on fusing past and present, his belief that "when there is no history / there is no metaphor" (*Images*, 69), his use of personal experience and specialized language, as well as his distinctive use of punctuation, especially colons, and his structuring of the poem or poems to signify relationships and process. For example, a frustrated Paul Breslin, in his review of *Images of Kin*, exclaims: "in a poem addressed to some definite you, I can't for the life of me tell who that person is exactly, or what his or her importance to the poem may be . . . some of these obscurities are not to be dispelled until and unless someone does for Michael Harper what Leon Edel did for Henry James."[24]

Harper represents the more intellectual and experimental end of African-American poetry, especially in the highly allusive, complex, and subjective poems in *Healing Song for the Inner Ear* (1985). Although he consistently acknowledges his debt to older African-American writers—Sterling Brown, Zora Neale Hurston and Gwendolyn Brooks to name three—he seems closer to his contemporary Jay Wright (1935), whose poetry is also allusive and intellectually complex. Like Melvin Tolson, whose *Harlem Gallery* (1965) is a strikingly innovative modernist text, Harper demonstrates the fact that experimentation and innovation continue to play a significant role in the evolution of African-American poetry.

Other Ethnic Poetries

By the late 1960s, inspired by African-American writers, other poets began to affirm their ethnic identities and cultural values in strong and distinct voices. Latino poets Pedro Pietri (b. 1944) and Victor Hernandez Cruz (b. 1949), for example, captured in gritty and original language and images the life of Puerto Ricans living in New York City and other urban centers. They and other Puerto Rican writers created a new strain of poetry in the United States, "Nuyorican" poetry, which often sardonically contrasts the ideals of the American dream with the harsh social and economic realities experienced by Puerto Rican immigrants. Cruz moved to San Francisco in the seventies and developed a highly literary, urbane, and surrealistic mode of poetry. Both poets read at the now famous Nuyorican Poets' Cafe in New York City, and both appear as composers of "Founding Poems" in Miguel Algarén's and Bob Holman's (editors) *Aloud: Voices from the Nuyorican Cafe* (1994), an anthology that honors the vernacular, multiethnic, and democratic principles of poets who have read and participated in the poetry slams held at the cafe. From coast to coast an amazing number of talented poets, often educated in American universities, returned in spirit, if not body, to the values, beliefs, and rituals of their traditional cultures.

American Indian Poetry

One of the richest and most lasting of these multicultural movements is American-Indian poetry, which began to appear in written form and in English in the sixties. Versed in Euro-American poetics and written forms, as well as the oral traditions of their indigenous cultures, American Indian poets (most of them prefer that designation to the more politically correct "Native American") introduced to the dominant culture a unique worldview and aesthetic.

N. SCOTT MOMADAY (B. 1934) N. Scott Momaday draws on his Kiowa ancestry as well as his knowledge of southwestern Indian cultures in all of his work. Momaday spent his childhood and adolescence with his parents, who were artists and teachers, on a number of Indian reservations, including the Navaho reservation in Arizona, New Mexico, and Utah and the Jimez Pueblo in New Mexico, which became the setting for his Pulitzer Prize–winning novel, *House Made of Dawn* (1968). In addition to absorbing his own Kiowa history, its traditional myths and tales, and the Pueblo and Navaho ways, Momaday was also educated in the heritage of the Anglo world. He attended the University of New Mexico, the University of Virginia to briefly study law, and eventually Stanford University, where, under the tutelage of the famous modernist critic and poet Yvor Winters, he earned his M.A. and Ph.D. in literature, specializing in the American Renaissance and the poetry of Frederick Goddard Tuckerman and Emily Dickinson.

This diverse background is reflected in his work as he leaps over genre boundaries and literary conventions. *The Way to Rainy Mountain* (1969), for example, is very difficult to classify. Framed by two poems, it is a history of the migration of the Kiowas from Montana to Oklahoma, a repository of Kiowa myths and oral tales, as well as a personal memoir of Momaday's own journey back to his Kiowa roots and identity, a journey sparked by the death of his grandmother, Aho. Although written in prose, its compactness and lyrical qualities lift the style to that of a moving prose poem. Momaday, in fact, in an interview with Joseph Bruchac, speaks of *Rainy Mountain* as "lyrical prose" or "prose poem," commenting that Indian writers are apt to be more comfortable with the lyric than the novel.[25] *Rainy Mountain* magically fuses past and present as well as the historical and the personal. It is both epic and lyric, and the drawings of his father, Al Momaday, add a visual and traditional texture to the words of the text.

In this remarkable composition, Momaday employs his imagination, his memory, and the power of language to give life to a very threatened existence. By the end of this volume, the Kiowa culture, the soul of his grandmother, and his own breathless identity have been revived. Standing in "Rainy Mountain Cemetery" before his grandmother Aho's grave, he acknowledges the power of death: "The wake of nothing audible he hears / Who listens here and now to hear your name." However, the "mountain burns and shines." And language, the word on the gravestone, the writing of her unspoken name, gives substance to his grandmother's spirit: "the shadow that your name defines."[26] The eternal creative force in nature is mirrored and echoed in the images and words of the imaginative poet.

The themes of nature, tradition, and language and their relation to each other are present throughout Momaday's first two volumes of poems, *Angle of Geese and Other Poems* (1974) and *The Gourd Dancer* (1976). In "Angle of Geese," the death of a friend's young son challenges the poet's ability to speak, for death "More than language means."[27] While hunting, however, the pair come upon a "huge ancestral goose" that speaks of both "the pale angle of time / And eternity" (31), that which perishes and that which is everlasting.

Momaday recognizes the power of this "huge ancestral goose," then perceives, imagines, and names a force outside of "hope and hurt . . . Wide of time" (32), and in doing so finds a means of acknowledging, but also overcoming, death.

At times Momaday's poetry draws heavily on traditional Indian forms and myths. "The Delight Song of Tsoai-talee," although written in English, becomes chant-like as it catalogues the delights of the speaker. Tsoai-talee, or "Rock Tree Boy," is Momaday's Kiowa name. It evokes the Kiowa myth that tells how a giant tree saved seven sisters being pursued by their brother, who had been transformed into a bear. The tree that lifted the sisters into the sky is now called Devil's Tower, and is located near Sundance, Wyoming. The seven sisters are the stars that make up the Big Dipper. As Tsoai-talee sings and defines both his nature and the tribe's, he delights in an existence that is tied to nature, the gods, and beauty:

> You see, I am alive, I am alive
> I stand in good relation to the earth
> I stand in good relation to the gods
> I stand in good relation to all that is beautiful.
>
> (27)

Momaday asserts in his interview with Bruchac that he and other American Indian writers are able to overcome the existentialist themes of alienation, separation, and homelessness because of their traditional ties to the land, their tribe, the gods, and the beautiful. These ties, in fact, are one of the primary characteristics that distinguish American Indian literature, a literature that embraces harmony rather than angst as its dominant ethos.

In "The Gourd Dancer," Momaday imaginatively recreates Mammedaty, his Kiowa grandfather, who was known for his skills as a gourd dancer, who carried on the old ways and danced with an "ancestral air," who was given a beautiful horse to honor his abilities and is now being honored in this poem: ". . . And all of this was for Mammedaty, in his honor, / as even now it is in the telling, and will be, as long as / there are those who imagine him in his name" (*Gourd*, 37).

This four-part poem reflects the stylistic range of Momaday's poetry; it begins with two quatrains and ends with a prose poem narration. He can also be quite formal in his stanzaic patterns and rhymes, as in "Before an Old Painting of the Crucifixion" or "The

Bear," composed in syllabic verse. In "Abstract: Old Woman in a Room," dedicated to the Russian poet Olga Sergeevna Akhmanova, he even sets his praise in heroic couplets. But as his later poems reveal, Momaday is also very adept at writing in more open forms. Momaday's themes, set in the traditions of Kiowa, Navaho, and Pueblo Indian cultures, are universal. He views his writings, whether verse or prose, as a single work that in its repeated use of material creates a sense of continuity, unity, and harmony. To some critics, Momaday's insistence on including older material in a new work signals an inability to discover new themes; to Momaday, it is consistent with the traditions of oral literature, which stress incremental repetition, both repeating and building on a theme, idea, or image.

Because he so often links prose and poetry, it is difficult to accurately identify his poetic works. If one considers his only poetry to be the two volumes of poems, the second book incorporating the poems in the first volume, then his early reputation is based on a very small number of poems. If, however, those boundaries that separate poetry and prose are lifted, one discovers another very significant body of poetry. In his novel, *Ancient Child* (1989), for example, there are a number of both prose and verse passages that add to Momaday's poetic vision, his own *Leaves of Grass*. In his 1992 publication, *In the Presence of the Sun*, Momaday collects his poems written over a thirty-year period as well as a series of brief narratives (shield stories) and a number of drawings. The poems include his previous work, a new arrangement of the Billy the Kid poems that appeared in *Ancient Child*, and a separate collection of new poems. They are, Momaday asserts, disinterested "gifts to the world," a truthful rendering through words of his attempt to transcend death and time. Consciously echoing Dickinson, he calls them his "letter to the world."

Momaday's winning of the Pulitzer Prize in 1969 continues to inspire many younger American-Indian writers. His themes, his experimentation with forms and genres, his insistence on the magic of words, and the power of the American-Indian worldview continue to be a central force in the expansion of the boundaries of poetry in the United States.

JAMES WELCH (B. 1940)   James Welch's reputation as a poet rests on a single volume, *Riding the Earthboy 40* (1971), which was reissued in 1976 with a new arrangement and seven additional poems. Yet, this work is unique enough in its vision and style to earn Welch a place in a number of anthologies, including *The Norton Anthology of Modern Poetry* (second edition, 1988). Welch's uniqueness lies in his fusion of Indian experiences and perspective with such European and American contemporary literary trends as existentialism, black humor, and surrealism, all of which he encountered under the tutelage of Richard Hugo at the University of Montana. Welch's voice is complex and unique, one that, in a magical fashion, ties the Indian traditions of dreams and humor to the modernist world of absurdity, irony, and nightmare.[28]

This vision is linked to Welch's experience as a member of the contemporary Blackfeet and Gros Ventre tribes. Raised in Browning, Montana, the headquarters for the Blackfeet reservation, he attended reservation schools and saw firsthand the devastated condition of the Blackfeet people, who once had a proud and fierce plains culture but became mired in defeatism, poverty, alienation, and alcoholism. Central to this decline was the coercive assimilation policy of the United States in the late nineteenth century and first three decades of the twentieth century. Its aim was to destroy Indian cultures and gain access to valued reservation lands. Under the Dawes Act of 1887, Indian land held in common was allotted to individual Indian families—160 acres per family. Any remaining acreage, after allotment, could be purchased by non-Indians; in addition, Indians could sell their allotted land. The resultant loss of land and of the cultural ties to that land was devastating. As Welch rides, listens, observes, and records life on the Earthboy 40, a forty-acre plot on the Fort Belknap reservation allotted to a neighboring Gros Ventre family, he can only conclude that the "The dirt is dead. Gone to seed" and that "Dirt is where the dream must end."[29] His Indian world has become a modern wasteland, despite the promises of "The Man from Washington" "that life would go on as usual," that "everyone . . . would be inoculated / against a world in which we had no part, / a world of money, promise and disease" (35).[30]

Both speaker and reader are quick to register the sardonic irony in this poem as well as in "Harlem, Montana: Just Off the Reservation," where the speaker first berates the white town's hatred of the Indians—"the wild who bring you money"—and then wonders whether the town will remember "the three young bucks" who forcefully took over a grocery store, "locked themselves in and cried for days, we're / rich, / help us, oh God, we're rich" (31).

In a bitter and sarcastic voice, Welch attacks Harlem, his symbol of American racism, as a town "so bigoted, you forget the latest joke" (30), but also a town that with its "money, promise and disease" continues to entice the Indians from the reservation. The inoculation promised by "The Man From Washington" did not take, and as Welch states in his interview with Joseph Bruchac, his characters, although defiant, engage in a battle that they cannot win because "it's the only alternative for certain young men"(*Survival*, 320).

Images of a diseased culture abound in poems like "Magic Fox," where the dreams of the elders, bewitched by a blonde, are confused and distorted; dreams become chaotic nightmares and even "Truth became a nightmare . . ." (*Earthboy*, 3). But Welch insists on balancing "the sense of modern desolation and desperation and the old ways" (*Survival*, 316). In "Christmas Comes to Moccasin Flat," the possibility of birth and renewal, the promises of Christianity, initially seem overwhelmed by reality: "Outside, a quick 30 / below" (26). However, the family still exists and Medicine Woman is there to tell the stories (26). Whether on the reservation or in town, Welch asserts, "To stay alive this way, it's hard" (46), but his people seem determined to do just that.

European and Latin surrealists, as well as Robert Bly and James Wright, a mentor and friend, provided Welch with a means of capturing the tortured and often absurd existence of the postcolonial Indians. Although Welch's poetic world is particular to American Indians, it speaks to all oppressed peoples of the Third World.

Since *Earthboy*, Welch has written four highly acclaimed novels.[31] He abandoned poetry because he felt his "poems were getting kind of constipated and repeating themselves" (*Survival*, 321). Despite these self-doubts, though, Welch has brought a unique vision and voice to contemporary American poetry.

SIMON ORTIZ (B. 1941)   Simon Ortiz's poetry is centered in his identity as a member of the Acoma Acumeh Pueblo people of New Mexico—the Aaquumeh hano. In his writings he remembers with pride and affection the songs, traditions, beliefs, and stories passed on to him by his parents and grandparents in the Acoma language. He also remembers and depicts the Acoma lifestyle, the ties to the land, the sense of community, the history of a culture that has existed for some one or two thousand years, and that still exists despite Spanish and Euro-American attempts at forced acculturation.

Ortiz's village, Deetzcyamah, one of two villages tied to the Acoma pueblo, was renamed McCarty's after an American who established a watering facility for the railroad construction workers. With the railroad came the wage system that would entice the Acoma people to enter the American economy. Ortiz's father, for example, worked as a laborer and then a welder for the railroad, but despite the increased pressure to acculturate, Ortiz's family and the Acoma people continued to till the fields, to tell their tales, and sing their songs. Ortiz's father, in fact, one of the elders of the Antelope clan, was responsible for making sure that the culture would continue, that the prayer songs of the many and various religious ceremonies would survive.[32]

Resistance to acculturation is one of Ortiz's central themes and comes from his experiences as an Indian growing up in the late forties and fifties. While attending Catholic schools, he was forced to learn English and the ways of Catholicism. In his seventh year of schooling, he left home to attend St. Catherine's boarding school and then the Albuquerque Indian boarding schools, which, in keeping with coercive assimilation policies, were dedicated to pushing Indian children into the white world. In addition, "termination," the official federal policy in the 1950s, forced Indians to leave their land and communities and move to the cities to be assimilated into mainstream America. "Indians," Ortiz states, "were no longer to be Indians" ("The Language," *I Tell You Now* 191).

In the sixties, however, Indian resistance stiffened. Inspired by the civil rights movement, Ortiz and others began to fight back, to insist on their cultural identity, their legal rights, their land, and their autonomy. Ortiz asserts: "My writing has a natural political-cultural bent simply because I was nurtured intellectually and emotionally within an atmosphere of Indian resistance"(193). Today, the battle continues, and Ortiz, speaking in a collective voice, writes, "we persist and insist in living, believing, hoping, loving, speaking, and writing as Indians" (194).

Central to Indian continuity, Ortiz believes, is the power of language, for it is language "that brought our grandmothers and grandfathers and ourselves into being in order that there be a continuing life" (194). Without language, Ortiz claims, we do not know or understand our past, our culture, or our relations with all living creatures. For it is language, the most basic element of storytelling, that makes life visible and comprehensible. As indicated in his essay

"Song, Poetry and Language—Expression and Perception," Ortiz believes language is not a linguistic mechanism—a set of divisible parts, phonemes, syllables, words, and grammatical units[33]—but "a spiritual energy that is available to all . . . it includes all of us and is not exclusively in the power of humans" (6). Language and song are the sacred means by which "we experience, perceive and then express our relationship to the world about us" (8).

Ortiz's poetry, although written, is meant to carry on the oral traditions of song that have been passed on to him by his parents and grandparents. His first major publication, *Going for the Rain* (1976), is centered on a journey cycle, a quest for the rain needed to ensure his own and his people's continuance. In "My Father's Song," Ortiz records his father's voice retelling a tale of his experience with Simon's grandfather in a cornfield. While plowing the field, his father's father had "unearthed / the burrow nest of a mouse / in the soft moist sand."[34] After the elder Ortiz lets his son touch the mice, both return the mice to the earth. Ortiz's father concludes his song by remembering the earth, the animals, and his "father saying things" (20). And Ortiz by remembering his father's song, remembers his "father saying things," which enables him to express his continuing relationship to both his father and his grandfather, as well as to the earth and animal life. The song, through its language, is the way to oneness, harmony, and continuity. Through song, language, "his home, children, his language, the self that he is . . . [the] people" (*Going*, xii, xiv) can be experienced, perceived, and expressed.

To Ortiz, the song or poem is not an autonomous art object but rather a means of preserving a culture. It is like the 400-year-old Acoma wall maintained by his father, a skilled mason and carver, and the Acoma masons before him. Like the wall described in "A Story of How a Wall Stands," the poem may appear to be casually constructed and unstable, but as his father points out to Simon, "Underneath / what looks like loose stone, / there is stone woven together." The wall, "which supports hundreds of tons of dirt and bones," may look like it is about to fall down, but because it is built both carefully and patiently it "stands a long long time" (110). The song, which conveys traditional beliefs and traditional modes of craftsmanship, functions as a means of preserving the past and ensuring continuity. Not surprisingly, Ortiz calls his major collection of poems, *Woven Stone* (1992), likening his poetry to a mix of stone and mud "worked carefully" that will help make sure that the past of the Acoma people survives.

In fact, when Ortiz leaves his community, he experiences an agonizing sense of dislocation and alienation. But he knows he must experience the world, meet people, acquire knowledge. "Sometimes the traveling is hazardous. . . . sometimes he finds meaning and sometimes he is destitute [but] he must keep on" (xiii). In "Relocation" he speaks of his pain and the pain of all the Indians relocated in urban America:

> . . . I am in the blinding city.
> The lights,
> the cars,
> the deadened glares
> tear my heart
> and close my mind.
>
> (37)

In the city there is no talk, only "Acres and acres / of silence" (38).

Ortiz's journey through "mainstream" America and its nightmarish urban landscape is depicted forcefully in the middle sections of *Going for the Rain* and also in his next volume, *A Good Journey* (1977). These poems depict a soulless world that is totally alien to Ortiz. One of the most compelling is "A San Diego Poem: January–February 1973." The initial section, "the Journey Begins," recounts the prayers and ritual acts of the traveler about to embark on a threatening journey, in this case a trip to San Diego. In the second section, Ortiz shudders as his plane leaves the beloved earth, and he finds little comfort in the company of his fellow travelers ("Passengers' faces are normally bland"[35]) or in the lifeless drone of the engines. Feeling "trapped" he "seek[s] association with the earth" (26) as he views the Arizona landscape beneath him. Even the plane's return to the earth is a "shudder" and "is much like breaking away from it" (26). This poem contains one of the most effective renderings of spiritual dislocation and alienation in recent years. Stumbling into the "innards" of the airport, Ortiz is disheartened by the cold technology, the concrete mazes, the "bland faces," the "emotionless answers." "America," he laments, "has obliterated my sense of comprehension . . ." (27).

In these first two volumes, Ortiz focuses on his own journey; he is like Coyote, the Indian trickster figure, traveling about the county, "just trucking along," (*Journey*, 17) learning as he goes, and always remembering his home, the center where balance and harmony can be found. In his next two books, *Fight Back* (1980) and *From Sand Creek* (1981), Ortiz's approach is less personal, more collective and more political, as he tells the stories of his people and their exploitation. *Fight Back*, written to commemorate the three-hundredth anniversary of the famous Pueblo revolt against the Spanish colonists in New Mexico in 1680, attacks the new oppressor, the corporations and their allies, especially the uranium companies, which in their quest for "yellow cake" (uranium) pillage the land and wreak havoc on the health of those who labor in the mines. Ortiz, after high school graduation, worked briefly in the mines and is familiar with the hardships suffered by the miners.

His resistance is most effective when he uses biting irony to make his point. "It Was that Indian," for example, tells of Martinez, the Indian who discovered uranium in the Grants, New Mexico, area in the forties and is responsible for the subsequent uranium "boom." Initially, Martinez is celebrated and photographed, a park is even named after him, and the Indians who are in the local jail and at war with the authorities are conveniently forgotten for the moment. Some of the townspeople, however, object to the idea of erecting a statue of Martinez, for that would be "going too far for just an Indian."[36] But when the damage to the environment became visible, and when the death toll began to rise from automobile and mining accidents, when a lack of sufficient affordable housing developed, and when the cancer rate rose, the Grants Chamber of Commerce was quick to point out "that it was Martinez / that Navaho Indian . . . / who discovered uranium / . . . it was that Indian who started the boom" (3).

In his poems and prose accounts of the struggles of his family and his community, Ortiz always insists on the proper relationship between the land and the people:

> Working for the land
> and the people—it means life
> and its continuity. Working not just for the people
> but for the land too
>
>   (35, 36)

This Acoma ethic is pitted against the "capitalist vested interests in collusion with U.S. policy makers . . ." (72). It is this "economic and political oppression" that must be fought and defeated for the sake of the land and its people.

A good deal of *Fight Back* is direct political statement, interspersed with Ortiz's personal narratives and poems of struggle and victory. *From Sand Creek*, which won the 1982 Pushcart Prize for a volume published by a small press, is based on Ortiz's 1974–75 stay at the Fort Lyons, Colorado, VA Hospital. The book's title alludes to the massacre of some 105 women and children and 28 men, all members of the Southern Cheyenne and Arapaho tribes, on November 29, 1864, at Sand Creek in eastern Colorado. The assault was led by Colonel John W. Chivington, head of the Colorado Volunteers, who attacked the camp even though Chief Black Kettle had declared that the tribes were at peace. A flag, given to Black Kettle by President Lincoln to guarantee the people's protection, was flying over Black Kettle's Lodge the day of the attack. The massacre, to Ortiz, vividly illustrates a national sickness.

The book consists of a series of short prose statements, often biting and sardonic, each of which is placed on one of two facing pages, with a poem on the opposite page. The prose pieces and poems work well together, juxtaposing a quick, hard-hitting thematic statement with a more involved, contemplative, and intimate poem on the same subject. Ortiz indicates in his preface that the book explores his identity as both an American and an Indian, both his national and his spiritual human identities. For his Indian readers, he wishes to present "a study of that process which they have experienced as victim, subject, and expendable resource." For European Americans it is to be seen as a study of "their own victimization" (n.p.). It is meant to remind Indians and whites that "We are all with and within each other."[37]

European Americans, Ortiz points out, have seen themselves as an innocent and glorious people who were chosen by God to tame a wild land and its savage inhabitants. In doing so, they repress their historical memories, blotting out such events as the Sand Creek Massacre: "In fifty years / nobody knew / what happened" (15). Ironically, Ortiz explains, European Americans fall prey to self-victimization as they unwittingly refuse to see an alternative way of relating to the natural world and instead blindly embrace their false mythology. Rather than listening to the wind, pioneers, for example, fought the wind and "kept adding rooms. / Built fences." They taught their children to obey and to plan and separated them from pain, beauty, and life. Ortiz sadly concludes that "Warriors could have passed / into their young blood" (35).

After and Before the Lightning (1994) records, in prose and verse, Ortiz's winter-long stay on the Rosebud Lakota Sioux reservation in South Dakota. The bitter, harsh prairie winter—the season without lightning and replenishing rains—is both a reality and a metaphor. Ortiz is forced to face the most brutal elements of the natural world, but also the cold and icy terrain of his own heart and soul. Burdened by the history of his people and his own suffering, he struggles to survive. However, that struggle leads to both strength and wisdom as he marvels at the ability of the Lakota people not only to endure, but also to revere the sacredness and beauty of this harsh landscape. In the concluding poems, the lightning and rains return, and both the landscape and Ortiz's soul are enlivened. This has been a perilous journey, but ultimately one of renewal.

Ortiz is certainly one of the most passionate and moving speakers for the Indian people. His depiction of alienation within a technological nightmare, his insistence on defending the land and the people, and his ecological/communal stance—as well as his questioning of our national myths in *Sand Creek*—are all ingredients that mark Ortiz as an important American writer.

LESLIE MARMON SILKO (B. 1948)   Leslie Marmon Silko, a Laguna Pueblo (New Mexico) woman of Indian, Mexican, and European heritage, like Momaday ignores the boundary lines separating prose and poetry as well as the boundary lines based on blood or race. Her first publication, *Laguna Woman* (1974), is a traditional book of poems, but she also creatively incorporates a number of poems into her highly acclaimed novel *Ceremony* (1977). The novel includes her poetic versions of the myths and tales her great-grandmother (Amooh) and great aunt passed on to her, a number of new poems that speak of contemporary events, and the compelling tale of Tayo, a mixed-blood Laguna Indian who returns from World War II spiritually ill and culturally displaced. He desperately seeks a cure for his sickness and alienation, but also a cure for his people and the arid earth.

The prefatory poems to the novel tell readers that the stories are a gift from Spiderwoman, the creator; they are sacred, and they act as ceremonial cures. In a separate poem, "The Storyteller's Escape," Silko insists that stories are a means by which to "escape almost anything," a means of survival.[38]

Perhaps the most striking poem in *Ceremony* is "Long time ago," a narrative that attributes European immigration to America to a contest between witches to see who can present the darkest of "things." The winner, a mysterious witch, wins by telling of the arrival of the European invaders, which occurs as she tells of it. These Europeans, she claims, see only a lifeless world of "objects."[39] The storyteller then says that these "destroyers" will devastate the land, the Indian community, each other, and eventually life itself with their atomic weapons, manufactured from the uranium mined in Silko's homeland. The other witches desperately ask her to retract her tale, but it is too late. Silko's contemporary myth is a moving, terrifying, and succinct account of her vision of the Indian encounter with European Americans. Only a new storyteller, Silko insists, who incorporates the old myths, as well as the reality of post–Euro-American history and its destructive impact, who works in print forms to spread the tales, can restore balance and harmony.

The importance of storytelling is again stressed in *Storyteller* (1981), a multigenre work that includes photographs, poems, short stories, and prose pieces. In "Prayer to the Pacific," the speaker gratefully recognizes the far eastern origins of Indians who came across the Pacific on the backs of turtles and praises the rain clouds for the "gift" that also comes from the Pacific Ocean and that enables Indians to survive (*Storyteller*, 180).

Silko also praises her Indian relatives, especially her great-grandmother, who "still washed her hair with Yucca roots" (34), and her Aunt Susie, as well as her great-grandfather, her father, and her white great-grandfather, who would not enter a hotel that had refused entry to his half-breed sons. Like Momaday's, her family is resurrected through the retelling of the tales and brought into the present by the new storyteller. Stories and poems may be retold and appear again in a new volume, for it is all one story, a continuum of a people's narrative.

Although there are adjustments made as Silko moves from an oral to a written form of literature, *Storyteller* does manage to capture the essence of the oral tradition as the author and other storytellers present their tales. And if they are familiar, that only affords the reader the opportunity to hear a pleasurable and meaningful tale once again. So tales such as "Long time ago," "One time," and "It was summertime," which appeared in *Ceremony*, are retold. Here, separated from Tayo's narrative, they take on a new life because they are linked to other poems and a number of Silko's most successful short stories, as well as to a collection of photographs taken by her grandfather and father. Like Simon Ortiz, whom she considers "a wonderful poet" and friend, Silko sees the tale as a means of cultural survival. It is the way "to go on" (170).

Also like Ortiz, Momaday, and Welch, Silko has not concentrated only on poetry. After *Storyteller* she published *The Delicacy and Strength of Lace*, a collection of correspondence with the poet James Wright, edited by Anne Wright (1986), and devoted a substantial number of years to the novel *The Almanac of the Dead* (1991). The concept of *poet* in many of these American-Indian writers gives way to the more inclusive term *storyteller*. This in fact becomes one of the more interesting contributions of these writers and suggests, as does performance art, that poetry may become a form within a larger form, and may, as Edmund Wilson predicted in the modernist period, become one with prose. "Words," Silko tells us, endorsing Ortiz's vision of language, "are always with other words, and the other words are almost always in a story of some sort."[40]

WENDY ROSE (B. 1948)   Wendy Rose's poetry is the cry of an anguished and angry "half-breed" woman who is desperately seeking a home, a place that embraces and nourishes her soul. The daughter of a Hopi Indian father and mixed-breed mother (Miwok-Anglo). Rose's childhood and adolescence in Oakland, California filled her adult life with painful memories and psychological scars. She felt rejected by her parents and relatives, and totally out of place in the urban white world. Because of the matrilineal nature of the Hopi people, she could not be formally accepted into that world either. In *Builder Kachina: A Home-Going Cycle* (1979) she describes fleeing California, the white world of her mother, and traveling to the Hopi village of Hotevilla, Arizona, where her father then lived, in hopes of reconciling with her father and entering the Hopi culture.

On that journey, she feels at home in the desert, "where my magic is mapped / in desert pulse: Hopi style / I wrap the wind about my legs / and cuff my wrists in cactus flowers."[41] At Verde Valley, the ancestral home of the Anasazi, she reclaims her past: "I am Anasazi, ancient / cliff-dweller" (n.p.). Here is her true home, not the urban white world, the Bay Area where she grew up, and certainly not Phoenix, where "Alien sounds / on my back pound / and shake the streets" (n.p.). However, she is a half-breed, not a full-blooded Indian, and

> A half-breed goes
> from one half-home to the other;
> strings of half-homes
> all over the world.
>
> (n.p.)

Caught between two worlds, she can only hope her poetry will enable her to gain the acceptance of the Hopi people: "Let me climb, / each word a foothold, into / Kachina Home! Let me find / the Cloud People" (n.p.). Rose, in fact, creates a "Builder Kachina," a spiritual being not recognized by most Hopi. Her Hopi father, however, accepts the Kachina, explaining: "What we can't find" in her matrilineal blood "we'll build but / slowly, / slowly" (n.p.).

The Halfbreed Chronicles and Other Poems (1985), one of her most powerful books, continues to voice her "Halfbreed Cry": As her "people cry ashes, / bleed fire from their eyes," and they and their culture, like "the tree searches its roots / for water," she experiences their pain and desperately seeks to span that "separation / across which I stretch / to almost touch them." She is ready, she explains, to leave "my uselessness behind / for the people to use as they will."[42] But in "If I Am Too Brown Or Too White For You" she still wonders if she, the "garnet woman," will be rejected for a stone, "less clouded, / less mixed" (52, 53). In this case, her friend recognizes that although her blood is not pure, there is a "small light" within her "so pure / it is singing" (53).

As Rose indicates in an interview and in her very moving autobiographical essay, "Neon Scars,"[43] her poetry is often more personal than communal and so has more in common with Anglo-European modernism than with traditional Indian poetry. Her poems echo the plaintive and sometimes angry cries of the lost world poets and Sylvia Plath's sense of abandonment and displacement; they often move beyond specific ethnic concerns and touch the universal themes of alienation and victimization that haunt the pages of twentieth-century literature. An aspect of her work that is especially striking is her powerful indictment of the cruelty and dehumanization found in the modern world. It is impossible to read "The Halfbreed Chronicles" sequence without outrage and deep empathy.

The horrors of the nuclear age, for example, are captured in the chronicle of J. Robert Oppenheimer, the father of the atomic bomb, whose "kids went screaming / from the crotch of the plane / mouth-first onto play yard & roof top / . . . onto hair & flesh" (63). And there is Yuriko, a Japanese woman, who was in her mother's womb when the bomb was dropped on Hiroshima. Her mother died of bone cancer in 1978; Yuriko survived but suffered brain damage. In lines that ring with the passion and outrage of Adrienne Rich, Rose has Yuriko indict the destructive patriarchal order that kills and maims:

> I am the woman of her, papa,
> I am the stone of her singing,
> I am the sound of crackling flesh,
> I was born of your drizzle,
>   her fire.
>
> (65)

Rose objects to being pigeonholed as an Indian poet or as a source for anthropology students. Having trained as an undergraduate and graduate student in anthropology at the University of California at Berkeley, she is especially sensitive to the dehumanization of Indians by white anthropologists. In *Academic Squaw* (1977), a title that expresses her bicultural identity, she angrily lashes out at the transformation of Indian culture into museum artifacts and commodities. In "Three Thousand Dollar Death Song," for example, Rose cites a museum invoice that values "Nineteen American Indian skeletons . . . at three thousand dollars" and then wonders if it is in "cold hard cash" or coins or bills or checks, "paper promises," signed in history but never honored. Like the skeletons, Rose feels "invoiced." "How have you priced us?" she asks. Rejecting the status of specimen, she envisions a resurrection in which the artifacts shake off their labels, "become one, / march out the museum door."[44]

Rose not only attacks the white academic world for turning Indian artifacts into dead objects and museum pieces but also takes on "the White poets who would be Indian," who become "white shamans." To Rose these poets are only transient and exploitative travelers within her culture, engaged "in a temporary tourism / of our souls"(n.p.), who use words to play the Indian for their own ends: "You think of us only when / your voice wants for roots . . ." (n.p.).

Rose in *Going to War with All My Relatives* (1993), conducts a fierce literary attack against the Europeans and Americans who have exploited and destroyed her relatives—defined as indigenous people throughout the world. She is angry, burdened by her studies of history and her experiences as an Indian woman in the twentieth century. Her "relatives" include the Taino people Columbus and his followers enslaved and decimated ("Fifty Thousand Songs"), the California Indians buried beneath the Santa Barbara Mission ("Excavation at Santa Barbara Mission") the Muskagee, one of the Southeastern nations forced—marched to Indian Territory (Oklahoma) along the "Trail of Tears" in the 1830's and 1840's, her blood relatives, the Miwok and Hopi, as well as the victims of U.S. bombing attacks on Hiroshima, Nagasaki (1945) and Baghdad (1991). She also attacks her white relatives—Grandfather Webb for "throwing" her away, forgetting her and great-great-grandmother Margaret Newman, a German immigrant who participated in the California Gold Rush in the mid nineteenth century, an event that eventually led to the extinction of a number of California Indian cultures as well as the desecration of the land. But many of Rose's relatives—expanded in some of her work to include all living creatures—survive and keep their hearts and spirits intact.

Now Poof She Is Gone (1994) is a collection of autobiographical poems, or "me poems" that Rose, up to this point, was too intimidated to publish because she had learned from literary critics that private or personal poetry isn't "true" poetry. Now she wishes to share her sorrows, her childhood and adult experience with her audience. Poem titles such as "Child Held, Child Broken," "Orphan Song," and "No One Is As Lost As This Indian Woman," capture the themes of this volume. The title poem echoes Sylvia Plath's desire to escape from this world, to simply disappear by saying, "Now poof she is gone." And like Plath and other "confessional" poets, the harvest is not in the particulars of her life but in the poetry that comes from that life.

Although at times Rose finds fulfillment, her bicultural identity creates for her a liminal existence of pain and yearning, Her words are exact, cutting, and moving; her rhythms are sure and always in keeping with her subjects; and her voice, is always strong and honest, never flinching, whether angry or joyous. This combination of qualities creates a very moving, honest, and powerful chronicle of our times. Along with Paula Gunn Allen (1939), a poet, novelist, and critic of Laguna, Sioux, and Lebanese ancestry, Wendy Rose has recreated the world of a mixed-blood American-Indian woman.

Chicano/Chicana Poetry

After the Mexican American War and the signing of the Treaty of Guadalupe Hidalgo (1848), Mexico had surrendered two-fifths of its territory to the United States. In 1853, Mexicans sold the American government an additional parcel of land for $10 million dollars. Mexicans who lived in territories that were to become the states of Arizona, California, New Mexico, Utah, Nevada, and parts of Colorado and Texas now became citizens of the United States. Although the treaty guaranteed their constitutional rights, they were soon the victims of numerous land grabs and discrimination. Cut off from both Mexican and Euro-American culture, they were forced into segregated barrios and, at times, physically assaulted, as in the infamous Los Angeles zoot-suit riots of 1943, in which white soldiers attacked Mexican Americans who were wearing zoot-suits and other colorful garb.

It was not until after World War II that Chicanos, much like other oppressed minorities in the United States, began to fight for their civil rights. In the 1960s, in urban barrios, on border and rural towns throughout the United States, Mexican Americans, or Chicanos, began to define their identity as a people they called "La Raza." And they began to confront the Anglo-Europeans who had taken their land and exploited their labor.

RODOLPHO GONZALES (B. 1928)   In 1962, Cesar Chavez, the leader of the United Farm Workers became a national spokesperson and charismatic leader as he struggled to organize farm workers and the following year Reiess Lopez Tijerina began the alliance movement to win back the Spanish and Mexican lands lost through the signing of the Treaty of Guadalupe Hildalgo. Another Chicano activist, Rodolpho "Corky" Gonzales, organized Denver's Crusade for Justice; its aim was to build an urban base for political action and cultural education. In addition to participating in the increasing number of political protests taking place in the second half of the sixties, Gonzales also composed what is commonly accepted to be the first significant literary work of the new Chicano, or La Raza, movement. *I Am Joaquin* (1967), as Gonzales attests in his introduction, is a

Journey back through history, a painful self-evaluation, a wondering search for my people's and, most of all, my own identity. The totality of all social inequities and injustice had to come to the surface. All the while, the truth about our own flaws—the villains and the heroes had to ride together—in order to draw an honest, clear conclusion of who we were, who we are, and where we are going. . . . *I Am Joaquin* was written as a revelation of myself and of all Chicanos who are Joaquin."[45]

The difficulty of living without a clear cultural and personal identity is captured in the first section of the poem, which has become a notable depiction of the Chicano's sense of alienation and confusion:

> I am Joaquin,
> lost in a world of confusion,
> caught up in the whirl of a
> gringo society,
> confused by the rules,
> scorned by attitudes,
> suppressed by manipulation,
> and destroyed by modern society.
>
> (6)

The uninviting choice for Joaquin, and all Chicanos, is to retain his culture and his spiritual identity but suffer "physical hunger" or to accept the "American social neurosis, / sterilization of the soul / and a full stomach" (9). Unable to accept the "monstrous, technical, / industrial giant called / Progress / and Anglo success" (10), he withdraws "to the safety within the / circle of life— / MY OWN PEOPLE" or "MI RAZA" (12, 13). As Juan Bruce-Novoa explains, *I Am Joaquin* is Gonzales's cry to his people, especially to the younger Chicanos, to return to their Mexican roots, to learn their history, "to unite and reclaim the land. Joaquin, the Chicano, Everyman, instructs his children through the poem itself, and it becomes a rallying call for revolution."[46]

In recent years, a substantial number of Chicano poets have added their voices to a newly emerging Chicano literature, whose roots extend back to "1848 and perhaps beyond" (3) but whose growth was especially evident in the 1970s.[47] The themes, techniques, subject matter, and voices of these poets are diverse. Some exemplary directions can be seen in the work of Alurista, Bernice Zamora, and Gloria Anzaldúa.

ALURISTA (B. 1947)   Alurista was born in Mexico City, migrated to California at the age of twelve or thirteen, and graduated from San Diego High School and San Diego State University, where he majored in psychology and later taught creative writing and Chicano thought and culture. During the late sixties, he became a spokesperson for the creation of a "separate reality," a new La Raza for Chicanos. Like Gonzales, Alurista looked to the past for guidance; however, he stressed the Chicano's ties to the indigenous people of Central America, the Nahuatl, the Mayan, and the Aztec cultures. For within this pre-Columbian world, Alurista believes, a harmony existed between humanity, nature, and the divine. Later he would argue this was also true of Indian cultures in North America as well as other Third World cultures. He is, as Juan Bruce-Novoa notes in *Chicano Authors*, "the originator and main exponent of the Amerindian ideology of Aztlan, which synthesizes a Chicano identity, drawing from the Mexican indigenous heritage and the actual realities of barrio living in the United States" (265).

Alurista also plays a central role in the formation of a Chicano aesthetic. Like Gonzales, he sees the role of the poet to be that of the teacher/prophet, leading and inspiring his people to a better life. However, he adopts the role of the Nahuatl prophet who is able, through his poetry, to convey wisdom and truth. The words of the prophetic poem transcend the here and now, and "do not simply reflect reality but create it." As Bruce-Novoa states in *Chicano Poetry*, this can either create a sense of "intuitive revelation" or sound "preachy and arrogant."[48] Alurista tends, especially in his earlier work, to stay within the oral tradition of poetry, employing repetitive sounds, refrains, and musical devices to voice his vision. When read aloud his work is accessible and memorable to almost any audience, no matter what their educational level. When examined on the page, however, it is very complex, as it employs word play and interweaves recurrent sounds, images, and themes throughout a single text.

In his later poetry—*Timespace Huracan* (1976), *A'ngue* (1979), *Spik in Glyph?* (1981), and *Return: Poems Collected and New* (1982)—Alurista begins to shape his poems visually in a style reminiscent of that of the ideographic and concrete poets. His most important distinction, however, is his insistence on writing in a multilingual style that may include some six different languages. Although the dominant languages are Anglo English and Spanish, one can find in any given poem an interlingual mix of "Black English, Anglo English, Mexican Spanish, Chicano Spanish, Nahuatl, and Maya, . . . the full range of colors, the full rainbow" (Bruce-Novoa 1980, 272). Only this rainbow of languages, Alurista asserts, can capture the reality of Chicano existence. As Thomas Ybarra Frausto notes, Alurista's linguistic experimentations have inspired numerous Chicano poets to employ this multilingual approach,[49] as can be seen in "El Louie," a classic depiction of barrio life by José Montoya.

In three volumes of poetry published in the seventies (*Floricanto en Aztlan*, 1971; *Nationchild Plumaroja*, 1972; *Timespace Huracan*, 1976), Alurista employs his words, the accompanying illustrations, his methods of organization, and even his pagination to convince his audience that his messianic poetry can not only bring about their salvation but also present a model of harmony and peace to the world at large. This, Bruce-Novoa explains, is an inclusionary rather than an exclusionary vision:

Alurista evokes the Nahuatl spiritual tradition, not as a closed nationalism, but rather as a basis for a Chicano synthesis of all humane traditions, from Greek mythology to Mexican Revolutionary ideology, from European symphonic music to black jazz to Bob Dylan or the Doors or the Beatles, or to Mexican music of all kinds. He seeks to transform humanity into the Cosmic Race, but only from the starting point of racial equality. (Bruce-Novoa 1980, 18)

Alurista's insistence on forging a separate reality is voiced in the title of his collection *Floricanto in Aztlan*, which comes from the Mexican-Spanish word for the Nahuatl term for poetry; this quickly establishes the links between the Chicano, the Mexican or Mestizo, and the Indian. In the opening poem he begins by asking "Where Raza?" and answers at the end of the poem "now, ahorita define tu mañana hoy,"[50] or "right now define your tomorrow today" (Bruce-Novoa 1982, 73).

Chicanos, Alurista asserts, must resist the temptations of Anglo culture, and, as Don Juan teaches, overcome their fear. If they must play cowboy, Alurista asserts, let them realize that they have their own traditions of the cowboy, a tradition that links the Mexican to the Indian rather than to the instrument of their destruction. Alurista's intent is to lead his people out of the Anglo world and into, at least mentally, a separate reality, so they can proclaim in the last poem, "We're alive Raza!" (100).

This vision of a new Atzlan is spelled out in a prefatory piece to *Nationchild Plumaroja*, entitled "the red spirit of Aztlan: a plan of National Liberation." "[W]e declare," he proclaims, "the independence of our Red Mestizo Nation. [W]e are a Red People with a Red Culture, before the world, before all of northamerickka, before our brothers and sisters in Amerindia, we are a Nation, we are a Union of Free Pueblos, we are Aztlan."[51]

Although there is a great deal of Yankee/gringo bashing throughout Alurista's work, it seems intended as an attack on the *ideology* of the United States, and its spiritless, heartless, self-destructive ways, rather than on the nature of its people. What is needed, Alurista insists, is a new cultural model, a "razaroja" (red people) model. Given his radical ideology and his multilingual approach, it is not surprising that his poetry has not appeared in mainstream anthologies. One can, as Bruce-Novoa does in *Chicano Poetry*, also point to the flaws in his work: the preachiness, the overworked clichés, the overly didactic approach. But it is apparent that Alurista's work speaks forcefully to Chicano and Third World people, and these are his main audiences. One of the challenges for an Anglo audience is to attempt to embrace an aesthetic and ideology that is rooted not in an Anglo-European ideology but that of the Third World.

BERNICE ZAMORA (B. 1938) Unfortunately, Chicana (female) poets could not totally commit to the cry of "La Raza," because it took no notice of the sexism of Mexican culture. To Chicana poets such as Bernice Zamora and Gloria Anzaldúa, borders within the new Aztlan world would have to be redrawn or, better yet, eliminated if Mexican Americans were to participate in a new "Dawn Eye Cosmos." This new culture would have to abandon its macho traditions, its restrictive roles for women—roles that stressed passivity, submissiveness, silence, childbearing, and domesticity.

Bernice Zamora, one of the most influential Chicana poets, grew up in an impoverished family in southern Colorado. Her father was forced to leave farming, work in the coal mines, live in the urban world of Denver, and eventually move to Pueblo, Colorado. Familiar with both the rural and urban worlds, Zamora attended Catholic schools, where the nuns insisted that she learn English. She married early and seemed likely to fall into the traditional roles of wife and mother. However, at the age of twenty-eight, and as the mother of two children, she began her college education, earning her B.A. degree from Southern Colorado University, an M.A. degree from Colorado State, and a Ph.D. from Stanford University.

She composed her first poems at the age of thirty[52] and published some as early as 1970, but it was not until the publication of *Restless Serpent* in 1976 that her work took a discernible shape. The volume contains, in a separate section, the drawings and poems of José Antonio Burago, as well as fifty-eight poems by Zamora, divided into six sections; the last poem in each section is the title poem of that section, and the final poem of the volume, "Restless Serpent," is also the title of the book. The title refers to a folk tale in which a baby is transformed into a snake; a prefatory "Oracle" alludes to the tale: "A serpent intrigued / slithers toward the / foundling."[53]

Zamora, it seems, *is* that restless serpent who has been subjected, as a Chicana child and woman, to exclusion, oppression, violence, and spiritual death. She yearns for inclusion, freedom, and rebirth; she is restless and ready to strike. In "Penitents," Zamora, because she is a woman, is excluded from a traditional Franciscan ritual of self-flagellation and mock crucifixion in memory of Christ's suffering. Although outlawed by both church and state, it remained an important ritual to the rural Chicanos who secretly enacted it. The speaker yearns to join the mysterious, "irresistible ceremony" that "beckoned me many times like crater lakes / and desecrated groves." "I wished," the speaker says, "to swim / arroyos and know their estuaries / where, for one week, all is sacred in the valley"(8).

"Living in Atzlan," however, means that there are sacred and metaphysical boundaries that she and other Chicanas cannot violate. The boundary lines, which ironically exclude life-giving forces, symbolized by images of groves, water, or blood, may be drawn by both Anglo and Chicano males or their indifferent patriarchal God: "We come and we go / But within limits, / Fixed by a law / which is not ours" (17).

Sentenced to a life of oppression and exclusion, a life that denies the "common / . . . experience of love" (17) and sexual union with males, Zamora becomes a "mad Cassandra / . . . straining my eyes / to catch a glimpse of the 'great king, / cold and austere' " (32), who by his own decree separates himself from the life-giving force of the woman. She then becomes that "restless serpent" whose only release is to be found in her poetry, for "Lyrics, / lyrics alone soothe / restless serpents" (74).

She strikes at her male tormentors in "So Not To Be Mottled": "You insult me / When you say I'm / Schizophrenic. / *My* divisions are / Infinite" (52), and in "Pico Blanco" she attacks Robinson Jeffers's pessimistic vision that humanity cannot rise above self-destruction. Rather than adopting Jeffers's "inhumanism," she calls for a new union of males and females, a new community based on equality and love.

This new society would abandon the macho symbols and rituals of violence and adopt the life-giving symbols of the female. For example, in "Sonnet, Freely Adapted," a marvelous parody of Shakespeare's "Sonnet 116," Zamora mocks the male's resistance to mortality and passion. "Masculinity," she mocks, "is not manhood's realm / Which falters when ground passions overwhelm." Instead, it "rides the storm and is never broken" (47). She attacks the sport of boxing, viewing it as an indefensible ritual of violence, insisting to her male audience that "Men sir, are not bell hammers between rounds / Within the rings of bloody gloves and games." Her sharpest parry is delivered with her announcement that she, given the present definition of masculinity, is more comfortable with "gay boys and men"; "Worn, rebuked, and spent" by a machismo culture, she must return "to gentle femininity content" (47).

Restless Serpents skillfully records Zamora's anger and frustration. The poems, often venomous and witty, are tightly coiled, ready to strike out at a culture that negates the sacred union of males and females. They also reflect her interest in modernist techniques as well as Jungian psychology and archetypes. Her stylistically careful attention to the ordering of some fifty-eight poems creates a complex and unified work of art. Add to this the bilingual (Spanish and English) nature of the book's language, and the allusions to modernist authors and techniques, and the result is a challenging collection of contemporary poems. As indicated in "Notes from a Chicano 'Coed,' " which appears in Gloria Anzaldúa's *Making Face, Making Soul* (1990), an anthology of Third World women writers, Zamora can be more direct and accessible. Her *Restless Serpents*, however, continues to shine as a singular accomplishment in Chicana poetry.

GLORIA ANZALDÚA (B. 1946) Gloria Anzaldúa creates yet another territory for the Chicana and possibly other women of color. In *Borderlands: La Frontera* (1987), she, like Alurista, uses a number of languages and dialects, cites Nahuatl history and mythology as well as the more recent history of the exploitation of Chicanos in the Southwest. And, like a number of American-Indian writers, she is comfortable using both prose and poetry as she carves out a moving and mysterious tale of a woman of color, a Chicana, caught between two oppressive cultures—a racist Anglo culture and a sexist Chicano culture.

Alienated from both worlds, she discovers and moves to a new territory, the borderlands, a space between these worlds, where the arbitrary boundaries of race, class, religion, gender, and sexual preference are not present. The borderlands, Anzaldúa envisions, will be the new order, and the "new mestiza" of mixed blood and cultures, a world without borders or dividing lines.

As Anzaldúa explains in her preface, the borderlands is "not a comfortable territory to live in, this place of contradictions. . . . Living on borders and in margins, keeping intact one's shifting and multiple identity and integrity, is like trying to swim in a new element, an 'alien' element."[54] At times, she is the Chicana activist, as committed as Gonzales and Alurista, as she describes the historical and recent injustices inflicted on the Chicanos by racist Anglos. In "We Call Them Greasers," for example, she speaks in the voice of the racist Anglo who drove Chicanos off their land, with the help of exploitative tax laws—"tole'em they owed taxes / had to pay right away or be gone by *mañana*" (134)—and then raped and killed their women in front of their husbands.

As was the case with her own family, Chicanos in the nineteenth and twentieth centuries often had their land taken on the basis of tax laws they could not understand or fight against in court because they did not understand English. Her family, like many Chicano families, became migrant farm workers on the lands they once possessed; in "sus plumas el viento" ("The Wind Feathers"), Anzaldúa captures the feel of the body breaking, the soul wrenching life of migrant farm workers:

> She husks corn, hefts watermelons.
> Bends all the way, digs out strawberries
> half buried in the dirt.
> Twelve hours later
> roped knots cord her back.
>
> (117)

"El sonavabitche" documents the terrible treatment of Mexican families who have been illegally transported to Indiana: "five days packed in the back of a pickup / boarded up tight / . . . no stops / . . . no food they pissed into their shoes" (126). Once there they are forced to live in squalor and labor under oppressive working conditions. "The *sonavabitche* works them / from sunup to dark—15 hours sometimes" (125). This overseer also attempts to deprive the Mexican workers of their wages by calling in immigration officials to round them up when their wages are due and then return the "Wets, free labor, esclavos (slaves)" (126) to Mexico. Infuriated, the Chicana speaker demands their due wages from "the big man" whose "eyes were pin pricks. / Sweat money, Mister, blood money, / not my sweat, but same blood" (128).

The blood ties are acknowledged here and also when she embraces the Alliance position that "The Aztecas del Norte," or Chicanos, will once again claim their homeland. Looking at the barbed-wire fence that separates Tijuana from San Diego, "this Tortilla Curtain" that runs along some 1,950 miles of the Rio Grande River and separates her from her Mexican and Indian ancestors, she declares that "the skin of the earth is seamless. / The sea cannot be fenced, / . . . This land was Mexican once, / was Indian always / and is. / And will be again" (3).

Like Zamora, however, Anzaldúa cannot completely submit to Aztec law and Chicano culture. As a woman and a lesbian, she feels oppressed by a culture she believes is both sexist and homophobic:

The loss of a sense of dignity and respect in the macho breeds a false machismo which leads him to put down women and even to brutalize them. Coexisting with his sexist behavior is a love for the mother which takes precedence over that of all others. Devoted son, macho pig. (83)

Although aware of the origins of this sexism, Anzaldúa can "no longer put up with it" and demands that Chicano males change their ways. To the women, she insists, "It is imperative that mestizas support each other in changing the sexist elements in the Mexican-Indian culture. As long as woman is put down, the Indian and the African American in all of us is put down. The struggle of the mestiza is above all a feminist one" (84).

As an independent lesbian, Anzaldúa violates the cultural definition of womanhood and hence is an alien in her own culture. Rather than submit to a culture in which "nothing would grow in / my small plots except / thistle sage and nettle" (120), she leaves that world to live in the borderlands. As indicated in "Nopalitos," this was a painful decision: "I left and have been gone a long time. / I keep leaving and when I am home / they remember no one but me had ever left" (113).

She draws on the power of "*Cihuacoatl*, Serpent woman, ancient Aztec goddess of the earth, of war and birth, patron of midwives, and antecedent of *la Llorona*," the wailing woman, for support"(35). "Entering Into the Serpent" depicts a poetic journey to the dark side of the psyche where death, but also rebirth, reside, where no cultural borders exist. This journey, although dangerous, painful, and solitary, becomes a means of recapturing an ancient and sustaining sense of self. In contrast to her social poetry, poems such as "The Coatlicue State," "Letting Go," and "I Had to Go Down" are mystical and surreal, at times, frightening, at other times inspirational. They become the record of the journey that allows her to be "Cihuatlyotl, Woman Alone," who has "fought off your hands, *Raza* / father mother church your rage at my desire to be / with myself, alone." The struggle has enabled her to proclaim: ". . . I remain who I am, multiple / and one of the herd, yet not of it" (173). She is "carved / by the hands of the ancients, drenched with / the stench of today's headlines. But my own / hands whittle the final work me" (173).

This new consciousness and independence enables Anzaldúa to break free of any cultural borders and definitions, social or psychological. Living in the borderlands means constantly having to face the social and psychological repercussions of refusing to declare allegiance to a single country or culture or race or gender. "You carry," she writes, "all five races on your back." You are "the forerunner of a new race," even "a new gender." The trick is to survive "the crossfire between camps," the inner conflicts, "the battleground / where enemies are kin to each other." To not just live in, but also "survive the Borderlands / you must live *sin fronteras* [without borders] / be a crossroads" (194–95).

Anzaldúa envisions not a separate cultural reality but a coming together of cultures in which the mestiza, the multicultural woman, free of male imposed borders, becomes the model and forerunner of a new age. To use the metaphor in *This Bridge Called My Back* (1981), a collection of writings by radical women of color, which Anzaldúa coedited with Cherrie Moraga, she is the bridge that "lays down the planks to cross over on to a new place where stooped labor cramped quartered down pressed and caged up combatants can straighten the spine and expand the lungs and make the vision manifest."[55]

In this work and in a second anthology she edited, *Making Face, Making Soul* (1990),[56] Anzaldúa insists on a feminist perspective that does not leave behind the oppressed people of color, female or male; that confronts racist tendencies; that moves beyond, in the case of *Making Face*, a token representation of women of color within the white woman's movement. With these two collections and *Borderlands*, Anzaldúa has become an important spokesperson for both feminism and multiculturalism in the United States. Her views are stated clearly, strongly, imaginatively. Her role as a poet is less clear, as her work up to this point is quite thin and moves between the poles of didactic protest and mysticism; but just as there are no borders between cultures, there are no borders between styles and genres in this new mix of literature. Multicultural poetry, by its very nature, does not take well to borders, whether they be cultural, social, or aesthetic. It insists on changing, in a number of essential ways, not only the content of contemporary poetry in the United States but also the very way the poetic canon is constructed.

Asian-American Poetry

Life has not been easy for many Asian Americans in this country. The Chinese came to the United States after the Civil War to help build the infrastructure of the new industrial, capitalistic order. Along with the Irish, thousands of Chinese immigrants lay the rails for the first transcontinental railroad. When hard times struck in the late 1870's, these immigrants quickly became the targets of angry white unemployed workers. In 1882, Congress passed legislation that forbade Chinese immigration altogether (the Exclusionary Act). At the beginning of the new century, anti-Japanese sentiment also began to grow, and by 1924, Japanese were also excluded from emigrating to the United States. Often the victims of degrading stereotypes in films, cartoons, and newspapers, Asian-Americans struggled to develop positive images of themselves. When the war with Japan started, it fanned the flames of Asian-American prejudice in this country. In 1943, over one hundred thousand Japanese-Americans were interned in "camps," after having their rights suspended and their property confiscated. The next two wars, with Korea and Vietnam, as well as the ongoing Cold War with China only intensified the dominant culture's racist attitudes toward Asians.

Throughout this history, Asian-Americans had great difficulty finding an effective means to give voice to their stories, poems and other artistic expressions. Because much of this art expressed feelings of anger, resentment, and a determination to participate as equals in American society, it was largely suppressed. In the seventies and eighties this repressed cultural heritage began to emerge, as a new generation of writers, inspired by civil rights activists and by the flowering of other ethnic literatures, finally shattered the silence and began to make their literary presence felt.

Lawson Fusao Inada, Jeffrey Paul Chan, Frank Chin, and Shawn Hsu Wong, all young Californians, coedited in 1974 *Aiiieeeee!* an anthology of Asian-American writers who had published their work over the preceding fifty years. In a separate critical essay, the editors declared that the anthology was for all those

Chinese-Americans and Japanese-Americans, Americans born and raised, who got their China and Japan from the radio, off the silver screen, from television, out of comic books, from the pushers of a white American culture that pictured the yellow man as something that when wounded, sad, or angry, or swearing, or wondering whined, shouted, or screamed "aiiieeeee!" Asian America, so long ignored and forcibly excluded from creative participation in American culture, is wounded, sad, angry, swearing, and wondering, and this is its AIIIEEEEE!!! It is more than a whine, shout, or scream. It is fifty years of our whole voice![57]

LAWSON FUSAO INADA (B. 1938)   Born a Sansei, or third-generation Japanese American, Lawson Fusao Inada emerged in the early 1970s as one of a number of energetic, creative, and insistent young poets who attacked the Asian cultural stereotype and demanded that the boundaries of American literature be extended to include Asian American writers.

After the publication of *Aiiieeeee*, he joined with Garrett Kaouri Hongo (1951) and Alan Chong Lau in publishing *The Buddha Bandits Down Highway 99* (1978), a collection of their poems and prose pieces. The volume centers on the memories, experiences, and insights of three Asian-American writers who lived close to California Highway 99 and the valley life of Gardena, Paradise, and Fresno, California. Inada's contributions include a prose memoir, "Right on 99," and "I Told You So," an extended poem that in a hip, bluesy fashion records his return to Fresno and his conflicting emotions as he views a comforting world—"it's peaceful now / you're home"—but also a West Fresno radically changed by "the laws of progress / by the cause of commercial parks."[58] In 1991, Inada and his coeditors issued an expanded version of their *Aiiieeeee!* Titled *The Big Aiiieeeee!* it covered 150 years of Chinese-American and Japanese-American writings.

Inada's role in achieving recognition and critical acceptance for Asian-American writing is clear. His poetic importance, however, rested until the nineties primarily on a single publication, *Before the*

War: Poems as They Happened (1971), which, as Inada notes, is the first poetry book by an Asian American to be published by a major firm (William Morrow).[59] The collection represents his work over the previous ten years. Inada consciously avoids traditional Japanese forms such as the haiku because he believes these forms are "affected" and not true to his American experience. He avoids as well the formal structures of Anglo-European poetry. What he adopts instead are the jazz rhythms of the African-American music that he first heard in the multiracial neighborhoods of West Fresno, California.

The first poem in *Before the War*, "Plucking Out a Rhythm," is a self-portrait of Inada, an accomplished bass player, as a jazz musician with Japanese features: "black pompadour on, . . . sweating, growling / over an imaginary bass— / plucking out a rhythm" (13–14). As in Wallace Stevens's "The Man With the Blue Guitar," music and poetry are imaginatively joined; however, Inada's rhythms, images, and diction are drawn from the particulars of his multiracial influences. As William Saroyan notes (on the back cover of the book), Inada's poetry is "lean, hard, muscular, and yet for all that, it has gentility, humor, and love." The poems move in jazz-like motions and rhythms along a string of intense emotions of anger, irony, pain, and joy, but are never overstated or mired in sentiment.

Elaine H. Kim comments in *Asian-American Literature* that Inada was probably too young to reconstruct clearly from memory the internment experience of Japanese Americans during World War II. Inada and his family, like some 130,000 other Japanese Americans then living in California, were forced to leave their homes and businesses, despite the fact that many were American citizens who supposedly had constitutional protection against such oppression.[60] Many people lost their homes, land, businesses, possessions, and families. Inada is, however, able to recall and recreate that historical and biographical event and provide a contemporary perspective on that central experience of many Japanese Americans. In the poem "From Our Album," he recounts that "Before the War" life was "Fresno, a hedged-in house, / two dogs in the family" (*Before*, 15). During the war and internment it was "Mud in the barracks—/ a muddy room, a chamber pot" (16) or a "desert Japanese garden" (17) decorated with tortoise shells gathered after the guards had smashed the creatures with their rifles.

Two decades later, he published *Legends from Camp* (1992), which contains photos, prose statements, and haunting poems that capture, in Inada's unique tones and rhythms, the centrality of the "camp" experience for the poet and Japanese Americans. He writes: "I've taken matters into my own hands—taken the camp experience in my hands, stood in the sun, and held it up to the light. What did I find? What I expected to find: Aspects of humanity, the human condition."

"Legends from Camp" is a longer poem that begins in fact but soon moves to a depiction of the stories or legends that have taken place many times in Inada's mind over the years. Included among them are those of "Lost Boy," who becomes lost in the bewildering camp when he follows a truck, and "Flying Boy," who inserts a hairpin into an electrical outlet, and Buddy, "the "coyote" or trickster figure who "simply disappeared" (14). There is also the tale of Groucho, a florist, who made everybody laugh, "even on the worst of bad days" (19). Groucho, Inada wryly reports, "died laughing" back home in Sacramento when he heard the news about Hiroshima.[61]

In his "camp" poems, Inada also renders those experiences he can recall from the three camps where he and his family were imprisoned, or "relocated"—Fresno Assembly Center; Jerome Camp, Arkansas; and Amache Camp, Colorado; ironically, Inada notes, Amache Camp was named after an "Indian princess" (18) who was slain in the Sand Creek Massacre. These powerful memories still invade Inada's consciousness. While working at his office at Southern Oregon State College, for example, he is reminded that " 'This is *not* Amache!' " (30). Nor does Inada want his readers to forget their history. In "Concentration Constellation" he asks them to draw, on a map, a connecting line from Manzanar concentration camp to the other eight camps until a configuration that can be compared to a constellation is rendered. Then he asks his readers to acknowledge that this constellation resembles a huge "jagged scar" (28) that disfigures the "massive" American landscape and haunts our minds.

In his early work Inada also finds himself an exile within contemporary America, a dominantly Anglo-European world that he feels is vain, materialistic, violent, and devoid of meaning. In his "Report from the New Country" he is convinced that "popcorn machinery" is "the creator of brains," as he notes that "the kids chant 'Commodity! Commodity!' / on their way to the five-and-ten" (94–95). During a parade, a crazed driver crashes into the procession, killing "five

Shriners and a twitching majorette" (96). This is, he insists, a world to reject. As Elaine Kim notes, the earlier poems that appeared in *The Buddha Bandits* attack Chinese Americans for abandoning Japanese Americans during the war, but also Japanese Americans for their attempts to enter mainstream America (Kim, 225).

To Inada, the "innocence" of America is an illusion; violence is everywhere. In "Bandstand" the mass murderer Richard Speck is dancing, "having a blast" (*Before*, 99) on Dick Clark's famous bandstand television program. In "Countries of War" Inada recounts, in taut diction and rhythms, the casualties of the Vietnam War—or any war fought by a war-abiding country: "Your brothers go: / one by one, canceled. / Your son is torn / open and scattered— / first limbs, an eye . . ." (100). And racism is also always present in America. In "The Inada Report" he asks:

> If there are so many blacks
> slaving in the School Book Depository,
> why are they not getting
> closer than cartons
>
> to books and to schools?
>
> (103)

Because he is alienated from both the Anglo world and his Japanese-American culture, Inada seeks an alternative world. He discovers it in a defiant, self-defining art that moves to the music of Miles Davis and Billie Holiday. In "The Journey" he and Miles and Lady row through the night, row over the troubled waters, as their music fills the air and transports them to happiness:

> our craft so full of music,
> the night so full of stars.
> . . . .
> Never have I been so happy.
> (121)

In his introduction to "Jazz," another section of poems in *Legends from Camp*, Inada explains that he was introduced to jazz by his father, who was " 'enlisted' by the government for work in a munitions factory in Chicago" (*Legends*, 55). He returned to camp with recordings by Fats Waller and Father Hines, which were transported to and played in Fresno when the family returned after the war. Jazz then becomes the music embraced by the various minorities living on the West Side of Fresno. Inada writes that "the music we most loved and played and used was Negro music. It was something we could share in common, like a 'lingua franca' in our 'colored' community" (57). His love of jazz in *Legends* is imaginatively rendered in the various notes and rhythms of his homages to Thelonious Monk, Louis Armstrong, Lester Young, Billie Holiday—whom he met when he was eighteen—Charlie Parker, Bud Powell, and John Coltrane.

Although his work has appeared in periodicals and anthologies and been praised by Denise Levertov, among others, it was, until recent years, largely overlooked. With the publication of *The Big Aiiieeeee!* in 1991 and *Legends from Camp* in 1993, his writings attracted more attention. In 1994, for example, he received an American Book Award; *Drawing the Line*, another volume of poems, was published in 1997. This is a fortunate turn of events for Inada's mix of multicultural themes and notes creates a distinctive form of American poetry.

JANICE MIRIKITANI (B. 1942)   Janice Mirikitani is, as Elaine Kim notes, "One of the most active solicitors of Asian-American literature" (313). She was editor of *Aion*, an Asian-American journal, now defunct, and *Ayumi: A Japanese American Anthology*, which is bilingual and includes poetry and graphics representing four generations of Japanese Americans. She is also very involved with Third World literary movements. She was the editor of *Third-World Woman* (1972), an anthology of poetry and essays by African-American, Chicana, American-Indian, and Asian-American women, and one of two Asian editors of *Time to Greez: Incantations from the Third World* (1975), which includes Asian- and African-American, American-Indian, and La Raza writings.

In "Firepot," the lead poem in *Time to Greez* (or feast), she calls on all Asian Americans to recognize their common experiences and to "experience our connections," to create a "Firepot: a collective soup of many tastes and ingredients," for there is

> the common need to maintain who
> we are, to understand each other though we speak in different
> dialects and

languages though we are born from different roots: Korea Japan
   China
Samoa Philippines Southeast Asia.[62]

Within the Asian-American community itself and within the Third World at large, Mirikitani believes, the need for the "sharing of spirits and a feast of words, music and symbols" (v) is strong; it will only add to the richness of the feast.

Mirikitani's first book, *Awake in the River* (1978), is a collection of poetry and prose. Like Inada, she reconstructs the relocation and internment experience, dwelling especially on the lasting psychological impact of this experience on Japanese Americans. As recounted in "For My Father," her father, a strawberry grower, whips the children for stealing the berries he wished to sell to whites who "ate fresh / strawberries / with cream." Hardened by history and economic need, there was "iron" in his eyes, she explains, "to shield / the pain," for "the desert had dried / his soul."[63] There is also "Crazy Alice," who is driven insane by the horrors of internment and cannot remember names, even her own: "life's so strange / before the war / i had a name" (n.p.) Deprived of their identity and, as indicated in "Lullabye," their ability to speak, there is only denial, an attempt to blot out the truth, to sleep in silence:

> My mother merely shakes
> her head
> when we talk about the war,
> the camps,
> the bombs.
>
> She won't discuss
> the dying/her own
> as she left her self
> with the stored belongings.
>   (n.p.)

Mirikitani's work, like that of the Asian-American prose writer Maxine Hong Kingston, is conscious of breaking out of this silence. Unlike the previous generations, she insists on confronting the traumas of both the past and the present and on "Breaking Tradition," in that she will not be the silent, demure Asian-American woman. In "Japs," for example, she angrily lashes out at the dominant culture:

if you're too dark
they will kill you.
if you're too swift
they will cripple you.
if you're too strong
they will buy you.
if you're too beautiful
they will rape you.

(n.p.)

Because Mirikitani views poetry as a weapon against oppression and injustice, she writes from a global perspective. In "Looking for a Poem" she draws strength from the Chilean poet Pablo Neruda: "Look . . . he is in the streets / 'ready to sing or die' " (*Awake*, n.p.). She also writes out of "A Certain Kind of Madness." She sees in the assassinations of Orlando Letelier of Chile and Steve Biko of South Africa the same form of madness that led to the internment and that is present in all those "who kill free moving things / to stop them from hurting their eyes." Defiant, insistent, Mirikitani exclaims she "will not dwell in a cage / It's my form of madness" (n.p.).

In "Canto a Neruda," she exclaims after the assassination of Chile's Allende that despite the fact that the authorities burn Neruda's words, his "spirit is afire in us. / In our bodies / a terrible thunder / is building its nest" (n.p.). And in "We, the dangerous," she insists that despite all the violence and oppression experienced by Asians—Hiroshima/Vietnam/Tule Lake (the internment camp)— they, Asian Americans, still remain: "We / the dangerous: And yet we were not devoured / And yet we were not humbled / And yet we are not broken" (n.p.).

Mirikitani is also direct when it comes to describing the pleasures or disappointments of love and sex. In "A Song For You—for Cecil," she resists tradition, openly voicing her desire: "I want to / hold / suck / taste your skin" (n.p.). "The Question Is," attacks the racial hang-ups of a white lover who is attracted to "the mysteries of the Orient" in her "slanted eyes" and wants to know "Is / it true / your cunt is slanted too" (n.p.). Her willingness to shatter Asian-American female stereotypes, however, does not mean she is in alliance with white American feminists. In "Ms." she reports that she "got into a thing," or dispute, because she did not address a rich white woman as *Ms.* Her retort to "miss ann / hearst / rockefeller / hughes" is direct and succinct:

And when you quit
killing us
for democracy
and stop calling ME gook.

I will call you
whatever you like.

(n.p.)

Although Mirikitani can be tender and lyrical when writing about her relatives, her daughter, Tianne, or her lover, it is the strong, angry, defiant tones, the incisive words, phrases, and images within the forms of open verse that mark her work. As her editor, George Leong, notes, Mirikitani: "grew / bloomed / fought as a desert flower behind barbed wire. . . . *Awake in the River* screams those memoirs, the lessons and a prophesy as only one from within the case of the American nightmare would know" (*Awake*, Afterword).

The desire to be awake in the river of life, not to sleep and not to remain silent, is the force that gives life to Mirikitani's poetry. This is also the theme of her second volume of poetry and prose, *Shedding Silence* (1987). As the opening poem indicates, to be "Without Tongue" is to be "a dead boat on the bottom of the sea, / a wingless beetle waiting for descending shoe."[64] In "Prisons of Silence," which was performed by the Asian-American Dance Collective in 1983, she calls on those who have been called "Filthy Jap" (3), who could not speak to each other, to "heal our tongues . . . give testimony" and by doing so "soar / from these walls of silence" (9).

Mirikitani wants to escape her mother's fate, "break tradition— unlock this room / where women dress in the dark" (27) and welcome her daughter's "Breaking Tradition." The most moving poem in the volume is "Breaking Silence," where Mirikitani celebrates her mother's willingness, after forty years, to testify about the "experience of Japanese-Americans in World War II concentration camps . . . before the Commission on Wartime Relocation and Internment of Japanese-American Civilians in 1981" (33). The poem weaves together the poet's voice that celebrates this breaking of silence with excerpts from her mother's testimony. To both mother and daughter, "The shedding of silence" is a miracle that leads to a new sense of self. "We must recognize ourselves at last. / We are a rainforest of color / and noise." The people are no longer afraid or silent as they discover "Our language is beautiful" (36).

The centrality of this theme in Asian-American poetry is evidenced in Joseph Bruchac's selection of "Breaking of Silence" as the title poem for his anthology of contemporary Asian-American poets. In his preface to *Breaking Silence* (1983), Bruchac pays tribute to Mirikitani's poem and argues that it "exemplifies what . . . is happening with Asian-American writers in the United States and Canada. They are adding to the literature and life of their nations and the world, breaking both silence and stereotypes with the affirmation of new songs."[65]

· EIGHT ·

Restoring Whitman's Vision: The Anthologies of the Eighties

> This is so much an age of anthologies that it is surprising
> that poets still waste their time on books of verse, instead
> of writing anthologies in the first place.
> —Randall Jarrell, *Poetry and the Age*

Randall Jarrell's pithy observation about the importance of poetry anthologies in the 1950s and 1960s is even more pertinent in the last decades of the century. In fact, one of the surest indexes to the changes that have occurred in American poetry over the past several decades is the proliferation of national poetry anthologies that began in the 1970s and reached its apex in the 1980s. In these anthologies, the conception of American poetry was transformed from what had long been a reductionist, dualistic scheme that usually allowed for two opposing traditions: mainstream or rebellious, academic or anti-academic, traditional or avant-garde, intellectual or antiintellectual, or, in the famous formulation that the *Partisan Review*'s Philip Rahv applied to all of American literature, "paleface" or "redskin." The two major poetry anthologies of the early 1960s, Donald Allen's *The New American Poetry* (1960)[1] and Donald Hall's *Contemporary American Poetry* (this 1961 edition was a revision of the earlier *New Poets of England and America* edited by Hall with Robert Pack and Louis Simpson)[2] embodied this dualism. Allen's book, clearly the more adventurous selection, became the bible of the sixties avant-garde, while Hall's was largely viewed as the canonical guide of the literary establishment. In retrospect, these books together appear to represent a much narrower segment of American writing than they did at the time.

Of the twenty-five poets included in Hall's first edition, twenty-three were white men, nearly half of whom were educated at Ivy League schools. Harvard, Hall's alma mater, was the training ground for six other poets in the collection. There are no African Americans, no unassimilated ethnic minorities, and the two women in the anthology—Denise Levertov and Adrienne Rich—are described as "married to an American" (Levertov) and "married to a Professor at Harvard" (Rich). Of the forty-four poets in Allen's book, five are women and one is African American. The range of cultural background and social class is greater than that represented by Hall, but it is noteworthy that even from a merely geographical standpoint, a good deal of the country is ignored. The division of the poetry into five sections includes one on poets associated with Black Mountain College, one on the poets of the San Francisco Renaissance, one on the beat generation, one on the "New York Poets," and one catchall section on poets from all over, who turn out mostly to be men based in New York, New England, or San Francisco.

Neither Hall nor Allen can be blamed for the narrowness of this vision as it appears from the perspective of the 1990s. This *was* the American poetry of the time—at least the American poetry that could get published. What is surprising is that no one noticed for years what a constricted view of American experience the poetry in these anthologies provided. Four poets—John Ashbery, Robert Duncan, Gary Snyder, and Denise Levertov—appeared in both books and seemed to bridge the dualism a bit, but for most readers of American poetry in the early sixties, poets were either the elite, white, New England, Ivy League men represented by Hall or the radical, white, New York/San Francisco/Black Mountain men in the Allen book. To be sure there were Leroi Jones (who later claimed his African-American heritage as Amiri Baraka), Denise Levertov, Barbara Guest, and a few other women represented by one or two poems, but in no sense does either of these anthologies give us even a glimpse of the diversity of American life as it now appears in our poetry (although a little can be seen in Robert Kelly and Paris Leary's amalgam of the Hall-Allen split, *A Controversy of Poets* [1965]).

It took some prodding. In the introduction to his widely distributed Bantam anthology, *The Black Poets*, published in 1970, Dudley Randall notes that a compilation of black poetry edited by Rosey E. Pool and published in England in 1962 was unable to find a U.S. publisher because "everyone she queried said the book was too special and declined to handle it." By 1970, "after Watts and Detroit, and the Black Arts movement," the situation had changed radically.[3] Randall's anthology by that time was one of a crowd that included

Everett Hoagland's *Black Velvet* (1970), Amiri Baraka and Larry Neal's *Black Fire* (1969), Clarence Major's *The New Black Poetry* (1969), Baird Shuman's *Nine Black Poets* (1968), and Adam Miller's *Dices or Black Bones* (1970). If African Americans could not integrate into the American poetic community, they could certainly establish their separate but unmistakable presence. These anthologies also paved the way for other ethnic and racial groups to identify their own indigenous traditions. In 1975 Duane Niatum edited *Carriers of the Dream Wheel*, an anthology that contained poems by sixteen Native Americans, and in 1987 he edited *Harper's Anthology of Twentieth-Century Native American Poetry*, which represents the work of thirty-six poets, including a newly emerging generation of American-Indian poets.

The dualistic view of American poetry based exclusively on aesthetics took another blow when Florence Howe and Ellen Bass conceived of an anthology of poems by women standing on their own ground and speaking in their own voices of what Adrienne Rich called "the will to change." Their collection was published as *No More Masks: An Anthology of Poems by Women* (1973),[4] and it was the first salvo in a succession of explosions that rearranged the American literary landscape irreversibly. It became no longer possible to think of American poetry simply in terms of mainstream versus avant-garde, formal or antiformal, traditional or rebellious. Women's poetry had a life and tradition of its own, and gender became an inescapable component of poetic identity.

A final shattering of the simplistic dualism of the early sixties came from Jerome Rothenberg and George Quasha, who in 1973 published *America: A Prophecy*,[5] a stunningly revisionary compilation of American verse that extended Rothenberg's work in *Technicians of the Sacred* (1968). In sum, it is a book that defined poetry as pluralistic rather than dualistic. Its subtitle, *A Range of Poetries from Africa, America, Asia, and Oceania*, pointed to the diverse traditions that fed the stream of contemporary American verse—a range that far exceeded the Euro-American orientation of earlier conceptions. In *America: A Prophecy*, modernism and an American-Indian heritage exist side by side on alternate pages, reshaping the possibilities for poetry in our time. Rothenberg introduced the term "ethnopoetics" into the language, and in *Revolution of the Word* (1974) he speaks of the progress of American poetry in terms of its ability to give us "a fundamentally new view of the relationship between consciousness, language & poetic structure" that broadens the possibilities of human awareness and allows us to live more fully conscious of human diversity and its energizing potential.[6]

By the end of the seventies, Edward Field was able to produce *A Geography of Poets* (1979), an anthology that organized poets regionally and moved away from the Northeast/San Francisco orientation of most earlier works. Field notes the antagonism he discovered throughout the country toward the New York literary establishment and chronicles a thriving regional poetry scene, stimulated by the small presses, university presses, and poetry centers scattered throughout the country. The development of several important poetry publishers far from the New York hub of the American publishing scene continued through the eighties. These included Copper Canyon Press, in Port Townsend, Washington; Milkweed and Coffee House Press in Minneapolis; Greenfield Review Press in Greenfield Center, New York; Wampeter Press in Green Harbor, Massachusetts; Bombshelter Press in Los Angeles; as well as the wide range of university presses throughout the country[7] that began or continued to sponsor poetry publications—Illinois, Cleveland State, Pittsburgh, Ohio State, Georgia, Texas Tech, Massachusetts, and Wesleyan, to name just a few.

These four developments—the emergence of African-American and other ethnic poetry as well as women's poetry, a new awareness of ethnopoetics, greater regional diversity, and the concurrent increasing social awareness of American cultural diversity—set the stage for the reconception of American poetry as a force opposing the conservative tenor of American politics in the 1980s. Though literary conservatives were still insisting on the simplistic aesthetic dualism of the sixties (as, for example, in the introduction to Robert Richman's *The Direction of Poetry* [1988], which announces the emergence of a metrical revival after decades of "linguistically flat poetry"[8]), such reductionism was difficult to take seriously. By the eighties, the poetry of the United States had finally begun to resemble the poetry that Whitman had written about so eloquently in the preface to *Leaves of Grass*. In his familiar language:

The Americans of all nations at any time upon the earth have probably the fullest poetical nature. The United States themselves are essentially the greatest poem. . . . Here is not merely a nation but a teeming nation of nations. Here is action untied from strings necessarily blind to particulars and details magnificently moving in vast masses.[9]

Academic debates about the prominence of one poetic school or another seem paltry and petty in this larger context.

In the 1980s the poetry of the United States moved toward a restoration of Whitman's vision. A pluralism based on America's many cultures, not a dualism based exclusively on aesthetic criteria, became the prevalent conception of America's poetic tradition. Apart from the polarized insistence on formal aesthetic criteria as a measure of poetic value—from the neoformalists on the right, from the "language poets"[10] on the left, as well as from what used to be called the "mainstream" in the middle—American poetry flourished in this diversity. But the contention between various groups of poets was a reminder that old ways of seeing are difficult to transcend.

Any summary of the new directions that American poetry took in the 1980s needs to examine both the persistence of academic polarization—a legacy of the modernist revolt—and the emerging pluralism that was the decade's trademark.

The Academic "Mainstream"

The word *mainstream* needs to be put in quotation marks in these last days of the twentieth century because it relegates anything not designated as mainstream to secondary and inferior status. Nonetheless, two anthologies of the eighties tenaciously held to the notion of a moderate center in American poetry. The conservatism of the Reagan era made for what was largely perceived as a climate hostile to experimentation and innovation in poetry, one resistant to the notion of expanding the bounds and limits of what sorts of individuals might be valued as poets in the United States. This viewpoint was reflected in anthologies as diverse as *The Breadloaf Anthology of Contemporary American Poetry* (1985), edited by Robert Pack, Sidney Lea, and Jay Parini, and *The Harvard Book of Contemporary American Poetry* (1985), edited by Helen Vendler.

Neither of these anthologies was a manifesto for neoformalism or aestheic conservatism of any sort, but the very look of the poems on their pages is formal and restrained— iambic lines, rhymed stanzas, quatrains, and even a villanelle or two. Much of the poetry in these two books is beautifully crafted, shaped to a kind of fine inevitability by some of the most accomplished poets of the eighties, but a good deal of it lacks the excitement of an art form undergoing major and fundamental changes. Although these anthologies contain first-rate work by first-rate writers, innovation is lacking. This is not a poetry born of an imperative vision. This is the poetry of *re*vision rather than vision.

This refinement is especially true of *The Breadloaf Anthology*, a book that intends to capture "a moment" in the history of American verse.[11] All of the poems included were written after 1980, and none of them, when selected, had yet been published in individual collections; this is new work by mostly well-established poets. It is difficult to generalize about the work that is included except to say that a lot of these poets seem to inhabit, or at least yearn for, an America unspoiled by the technological and urban encroachments of contemporary life. The anthology reflects the resiliency of nature poetry in the late twentieth century, but, conversely, it seems out of touch with the economic and social realities of contemporary urban life. Apart from a handful of poems, like Galway Kinnell's "The Fundamental Project of Technology," Mark Jarman's "In Hell," Jorie Graham's "Self-Portrait as Both Parties," and Stephen Dobyns's "Spider Web," this work captures nothing essential about American life as it was lived by most Americans in the eighties.

The Harvard Book of Contemporary American Poetry is a more ambitious effort with a weighty canonical look about it. It offers mostly familiar poems by poets that critic Helen Vendler feels have been "elevated to canonical status by the envy and admiration of their fellow poets."[12] The thirty-five poets represent a wide variety of schools and styles, from Allen Ginsberg to James Merrill, from Jorie Graham to Adrienne Rich, from Robert Lowell to Gary Snyder. These poets, by and large, are those taught in contemporary literature classes in universities throughout the country, and it can be argued that they have been elevated to canonical status less by the admiration of their fellow poets than by university professors who write about their work and teach it regularly. Vendler's anthology embodies the current academic "mainstream," and she includes a number of younger poets—Michael Blumenthal, Rita Dove, Jorie Graham, Louise Glück, Robert Pinsky, and Albert Goldbarth. It is too early to tell whether these poets will achieve the stature of most of the others in the anthology, but then, as Vendler graciously points out in her introduction, it is also too early to tell whether *any* of these poets "will belong, hundreds of years from now, to the common music of our century and which ones will survive as major figures" (7).

Language Poetry

Two anthologies of the eighties—Ron Silliman's comprehensive but opaque *In the American Tree* (1986) and Doug Messerli's more modest *Language Poetries: An Anthology* (1987)—mapped the terrain and defined the concepts that illustrate L=A=N=G=U=A=G=E poetry, the movement that often sees itself as the most serious, innovative direction being taken in contemporary poetry. The stylized spelling of the word "language" in all caps with equal signs between each letter is derived from a periodical published in the late seventies that disseminated the poetics of this new poetry.

Among the most prominent poets associated with this movement are Charles Bernstein, Bruce Andrews, Ron Silliman, Lyn Hejinian, Barret Watten, and Clark Coolidge. Most are located in the San Francisco Bay Area or in New York City. While concise and uniform definitions of this movement are difficult to come by, they would all stress the primacy of words as the building blocks of a poem. Language poetry can trace its heritage in the twentieth century to Gertrude Stein, who dismantled and reassembled traditional uses of language in much the same way that the cubist painters reassembled shapes and forms. This deconstruction and resconstruction of language permits words to create a world rather than merely describe one.

Probably nothing characterizes the language poets so well as their sense of high seriousness and purpose. The issues that language poetry deals with "are not to be underestimated. The nature of reality. The nature of the individual. The function of language in the constitution of either realm. The nature of meaning. The substantiality of language. The shape and value of literature itself. The function of method. The relationship between writer and reader."[13] The innovative complexity of language poetry is such that "If nothing in the poem could be taken for granted, then anything might be possible. In turn, the poet must be responsible for everything. A parallel demand is made of the reader" (Silliman, xvi).

Despite the hyperbole of its proponents, language poetry does have some linguistic interest, although it rarely reaches an audience much beyond its practitioners. Doug Messerli blames readers for their failure to understand the nature of language poetry, yet when he searches for an aesthetic that the poets in his anthology have in common, he discovers only three essential qualities that could just as well be applied to a variety of poets *not* affiliated with the language group. All language poets, says Messerli, "foregrounded language itself as the project of their writing."[14] In addition, Messerli argues that they are influenced by both "Olson's process-oriented writing . . . and the disjunctive procedures of the New York School" (3). Marjorie Perloff rightly sees John Ashbery's *The Tennis Court Oath* as a precursor of this sort of writing,[15] but she fails to point out that Ashbery moved on to other things knowing that a poetry that is *essentially* wordplay can never be anything more than a minor art. Charles Olson is a precursor as well, but his idea that writing originates in the body and that the form of a poem will emerge as the poem is composed, influenced a wide range of writers beyond those of the language school.

Neoformalism

The neoformalist parallels to the two language poetry anthologies described above are Philip Dacey and David Jauss's *Strong Measures: Contemporary American Poetry in Traditional Forms* (1986) and Robert Richman's *The Direction of Poetry: An Anthology of Rhymed and Metered Verse Written in the English Language since 1975* (1988). Like the Silliman and Messerli collections, both books appeared within about a year of each other and together constellate several of the informing ideas of the kind of poetry they represent. *Strong Measures* (like *In the American Tree*) is the more comprehensive and less exclusive of the two—it is hard to think of Allen Ginsberg, Gregory Corso, and the late Etheridge Knight as neoformalists, but their wares are happily on display here, while one can hardly imagine them on the pages of *The Direction in Poetry*. Taken together, however, these two anthologies illustrate the persistence of traditional formal structure in a contemporary guise. Poets like X. J. Kennedy, John Frederick Nims, Charles Tomlinson, Donald Justice, and Amy Clampitt, as well as a younger generation including Timothy Steele, Brad Leithauser, Dana Gioia, Mary Jo Salter, and Katha Pollitt, share an enthusiasm for orderly rhythm and rhyme and for the adaptation of conventional poetic forms to twentieth-century language.

But neoformalism is not a movement in the same sense that language poetry is, despite attempts to solidify it as such in books such as Frederick Feirstein's *Expansive Poetry* (1989) and Wyatt Prunty's *Fallen from the Symboled World* (1990). The reason the definition of neoformalism as a movement remains elusive can be garnered from the table of contents of *Strong Measures*, as well as from the sensible foreword (by Richard Wilbur) and introduction (by the editors) to that book. As Wilbur points out:

It does not seem to me that, at the present moment, the assignment of definite meaning or effect to poetic forms can be very persuasive. To be sure, there are people who associate meter and rhyme with order and good sense, or denounce them as affected and reactionary; there are those who regard free verse as sincere and forward-looking, and those who dismiss it as squalidly prosaic. But not much of that blather holds up if we look at what has actually been written in this century, and at what is being written now.[16]

Such moderate and modest views are anathema to Richard Richman, who in the introduction to *The Direction of Poetry* claims that "The free verse orthodoxy that has reigned for the last twenty-five years in the United States and Great Britain has insinuated itself so deeply into our respective poetic cultures that the entire conception of form has been corrupted" (xv). Richman, in fact, castigates the "hybrid" forms of the Dacey-Jauss anthology, "in which the pretense of a traditional form is used without employing any of its technical attributes" (xvi). He argues for a "pure" formalist poetics that makes consistent use of a metrical foot. Of course, nearly all poets at one time or another work in both traditional and nontraditional forms; it is to the credit of *Strong Measures* that it recognizes the value of flexibility, and a weakness of *The Direction of Poetry* that it does not.

The rise of neoformalism is closely related to the proliferation of creative writing programs throughout the country in the 1980s. Formal poetic structures are one aspect of poetry writing that can be taught, and although a great many poets move beyond them once having understood their function, a great many others respond favorably to discipline and become adept at producing well-crafted, carefully measured verse. So it is not surprising or "astonishing," as Andrei Codrescu says it is, that in 1987, "27 years after the Grove book [Donald Allen's *The New American Poetry*], the academics are back in the saddle, and that their influence, through graduate writing programs, continues to spread."[17]

The Poet-Professors

The degree to which contemporary poetry in the United States has been "academized" can be seen clearly in Jack Meyers and Roger Weingarten's *The New American Poets of the 80s* (1984) as well in Dave Smith and David Bottoms's *The Morrow Anthology of Younger American Poets* (1983). Virtually all of the 65 poets in the Meyers-Weingarten collection and nearly all of the 104 poets in the Smith-Bottoms book teach or have taught in universities. Of course, there is nothing wrong with poets making a living as professors, but that these two vocations have become nearly synonymous in our time is a cause for concern. There is no other art form so closely and *exclusively* tied to universities. *Some* musicians, dancers, actors, playwrights, visual artists, sculptors, and so on work at universities, but many do not. This balance keeps the art in question from becoming overly cloistered, overly insulated from social and moral imperatives. The contributors' notes for both of these books read alarmingly alike—directors of MFA programs; grants from Guggenheim, NEA, Ford; teachers of creative writing; often editors of university-based literary magazines. The homogeneous profile of these writers is bound to produce (and is producing) a kind of homogeneous poem—the infamous "workshop" poem, or, as Donald Hall has labeled it, the "McPoem," over which much ink has been spilled and many careers made and broken.

One of the most stimulating and vigorous debates concerning the poetry of the eighties occurred on the pages of the *Associated Writing Programs Chronicle* in response to an essay by Joseph Epstein called "Who Killed Poetry?" that was reprinted there. Epstein argues that "contemporary poetry in the United States flourishes in a vacuum," and he says the primary reason for this vacuum is that poets remain insulated from the "real world":

Today there are more than 250 universities with creative writing programs, and all of these have a poetry component, which means that they not only train aspiring poets but hire men and women who have published poetry to teach them. Many of these men and women go from being students in one writing program to being teachers in another—without, you might say, their feet, metrical or anatomical, having touched the floor.[18]

Responses from the creative writing community to Epstein's remarks filled two issues of the *AWP Chronicle* with impassioned critiques. Significantly, the few commentaries that supported his position came from poets like Dana Gioia and Robert McDowell, who are not affiliated with universities.

Mavericks

Two anthologies, which can't be classified as "mainstream" or language poetry or neoformalism, embody a fourth direction for American poetry in the eighties: Steve Kowit's *The Maverick Poets* (1988) and Andrei Codrescu's *American Poetry since 1970: Up Late* (1987). The assumptions of Kowit and Codrescu are quite different, and only one poet (Kowit) is included in both anthologies. They can be profitably looked at together, though, because in very different ways they extend the idea of an "alternate" American poetry. This "countertradition," was first defined by Donald Allen in 1960 and continues in the antiacademic stances of the present. Kowit's brief introduction proposes that the poets in his collection share "a common resistance to the pervasive style of late 20th century verse, with its debilitating preference of the tepid, mannered and opaque."[19] Whether there *is* a pervasive style of verse in the late twentieth century is a matter open to considerable debate, but Kowit seems to have in mind private and obscure autobiographical narratives, as well as the denser manifestations of both language poetry and neoformalism. Certainly, he does not have in mind much of the poetry in the Codrescu anthology (though Codrescu includes a substantial number of language poets), including anything by Codrescu himself, who has these thoughts about the late twentieth century in one of his own poems, included in *Up Late*:

> So late in the 20th Century
> So late in the 20th Century
> At the end almost of the 20th Century
> I sit in my home
> In my modest and meaningless home
> And worry about my penis
> ABOUT MY PENIS FOR CHRISSAKES!
> (*Up Late*, 82)

This is hardly tepid or opaque verse, and it may be more characteristic of late twentieth-century American poetry than either neoformalism or language poetry. American poetry has always had its
mavericks, from Walt Whitman and Emily Dickinson, through Amy
Lowell and William Carlos Williams, through E. E. Cummings and
Kenneth Rexroth, to Wanda Coleman and Antler, two poets in the
Kowit collection who would be hard to squeeze into any particular
camp outside of their own fertile and inventive imaginations. The
thirty-nine poets in the Kowit anthology share accessibility and
directness, a generally leftist political orientation, and a preference
for the vernacular and informal. *The Maverick Poets* is in a sense the
mirror image of *The Direction of Poetry*.

Codrescu's version of what is vital in contemporary poetry is
broader than Kowit's, partially because he is able to include many
more poets (109 compared to 39) and partially because his conception of energized verse is more eclectic and embracive. Codrescu
would like his collection to be seen as the heir to the Donald Allen
legacy, offering a counter to the academic respectability of anthologies like those of Helen Vendler and the Breadloaf School. For
Codrescu, himself a poet-professor, the influence of the academy on
American poetry in almost any form is pernicious. In addition, he
believes that "Anthologies have not reflected the enormous experimental strength of contemporary poetry" (Codrescu, xxxvi), which
instead resides in literary magazines. He sounds nostalgic when
he refers to "the great mimeos of the late sixties" and says that
university-sponsored quarterlies are of no interest to most contemporary poets. His partiality to the small press publishers is reflected
in his selection of poems, which come primarily from the flourish-
ing underground press scene. Codrescu's eclecticism is invigorat-
ing, but the anthology's sole unifying motif is its devotion to
"experimental poetry," which in the latter decades of the twentieth
century largely eludes definition. It seems to mean, in the context of
Up Late, almost any poetry of the past twenty years that is not written in traditional form. The collection clearly needs more of the
lucidity and incisiveness of the late Ted Berrigan, the poet whose
work opens the volume:

> The heart stops briefly when someone dies,
> a quick pain as you hear the news, & someone passes

from your outside life to inside. Slowly the heart adjusts
to its new weight, & slowly everything continues, sanely.
(*Up Late,* 9)

This is poetry by almost any standard beyond metrical scansion, and it has nothing to do with poetic schools or movements. Unfortunately, there is not enough of this sort of clarity and emotional exactness in most of *Up Late*. Because of his desire to represent "experimental poetry," Codrescu includes too many writers whose words are surely written on the wind.

Although he is included only in Kowit's anthology, the ultimate "outsider" poet is Charles Bukowski (1920–1994), surely one of the most prolific and widely imitated poets of our time. But because Bukowski's writings grate against the sensibilities of most critics of contemporary poetry, his work has been virtually ignored in the academic world. Bukowski writes directly, candidly, and lucidly about drunks, pimps, whores, the homeless, and life on the streets of L.A. The coarseness of his language and his unrelenting and unapologetic obsession with women and alcohol ("Drinking and shacking up with women became my art form," he told an interviewer)[20] have caused many readers to overlook the deep compassion in his work and his empathic understanding of the poor and outcast. He is surely the father of all maverick poets and has stayed up later than any poet in the Codrescu anthology. His prodigious output can be sampled in a series of collections published by Black Sparrow Press, including *Burning in Water Drowning in Flame: Selected Poems, 1955–1973* (1974), *War All the Time: Poems, 1981–1984* (1984), *You Get So Alone at Times that It Just Makes Sense* (1984), *The Roominghouse Madrigals: Early Selected Poems, 1946–1966* (1989), and *Septuagenarian Stew: Stories and Poems* (1990).

The Best American Poetry

One of the most exciting and illuminating developments in the anthologies of the eighties was David Lehman's idea to inaugurate a "Best American Poetry" annual series, with each successive volume edited by an established poet in midcareer. The series debuted in 1988, and the first four volumes—edited respectively by John Ashbery, Donald Hall, Jorie Graham, and Mark Strand—are filled with surprises. Lehman conceives of the series as a publishing experiment "to see whether a single annual volume can accurately reflect the diversity of American poetry . . . and honor excellence regardless of what form it takes, or what idiom it favors, or from what region of the country it comes."[21] When we have ten or so of these volumes on the shelf, they may come closer to representing the American poetry of our time than many of the volumes described above. Because the volume editors have secure reputations and well-established poetic identities, they can afford to be generous and eclectic. Donald Hall writes, "I am afflicted by the desire to *represent* different endeavors; I mean to be eclectic. I hope that a passion for inclusiveness may be as genuine as other people's certainties of exclusion" (xxi–xxii). John Ashbery notes how struck he was by the diversity of the poetry he read, "and by the validity of this diversity, the tremendous power it could have for enriching our lives. . . . Instead of congratulating ourselves on so much diversity we tend, as so often in America, to choose up sides and ignore anyone not on our team."[22] And Jorie Graham concludes that "the diversity of the work is staggering, and reminds one of how truly huge this nation is—how many different kinds of experiences it affords us by its very expanse and variety of landscape."[23]

Taken together, the poems in these collections allow us to "hear America singing" in a way that Whitman would have admired. Here is Yusef Komunyakaa, an African-American Vietnam veteran, haunted by his war experiences; and here is Richard Howard, New York intellectual, grieving the loss of a friend who succumbed to AIDS; here is Donald Hall, from his New Hampshire farm, writing thirty-eight enjambed quintets in "Praise for Death"; here is Phil Levine revisiting his hometown, Detroit, having a long conversation with a black man in a ravaged Detroit neighborhood about Joe Louis, life, and the universe; here is Linda Gregg smelling the sweetness of roses and ruminating about the "dark thing inside the day"; here is Elaine Equi writing a pantoum, a complex, Malayan verse form using recurring lines, in homage to Robbe-Grillet; here is Galway Kinnell describing what it is like for "one who has lived a long time alone"; and here is Rodney Jones bringing dignity to the "bearing of waitresses."

This list, of course, could be greatly extended to make the point that these "best" American poems begin to capture some of the diversity of the United States as Whitman envisioned it. It is beyond the scope of many contemporary anthologies—though some, like Marie Harris and Kathleen Aguero's *An Ear to the Ground* (1989), have taken bold steps in that direction, going well outside the accepted canon to include poetry that reveals something of the ethnic and cultural diversity of American experience. The new breadth of inclusiveness that this and some other poetry anthologies are beginning to demonstrate makes it clear that America has finally begun to recognize that its poetry belongs to no cliquish schools or creeds but rather that, like Whitman, it is large and contains multitudes.

· *Notes* ·

Chapter One

1. Robert Lowell, *Life Studies and For the Union Dead* (New York: Farrar, Straus and Giroux, 1967), 85.

2. James Breslin, *From Modern to Contemporary* (Chicago: University of Chicago Press, 1984). See chapter 1, pp. 1–22.

3. Weldon Kees, *The Collected Poems of Weldon Kees*, rev. ed., ed. Donald Justice (Lincoln: University of Nebraska Press, 1975), ix. Hereafter cited in the text.

4. Leslie Fiedler, "Jarrell's Criticism: A Footnote," in *Randall Jarrell: 1914–1965*, ed. Robert Lowell et al. (New York: Farrar, Straus and Giroux, 1967), 66.

5. Randall Jarrell, *The Complete Poems* (New York: Farrar, Strauss and Giroux, 1969), 145. Further quotations are from this edition.

6. James Dickey, "Randall Jarrell," in Lowell et al., 47–48.

7. Robert Lowell, "Randall Jarrell," in Lowell et al., 103.

8. Robert Lowell, *Lord Weary's Castle and The Mills of the Kavanaughs* (New York: Harcourt, Brace and World, 1961), "Note," n.p. Hereafter cited in the text.

9. Robert Lowell, "On Robert Lowell's 'Skunk Hour,'" in *The Contemporary Poet as Artist and Critic*, ed. Anthony Ostroff (Boston: Little Brown and Co., 1964), 108.

10. See Robert Lowell's "July in Washington" in *Life Studies and For the Union Dead*, second section, 59.

11. Robert Lowell, *History* (New York: Farrar, Straus and Giroux, 1973), "Note," n.p.

12. See for example the title poem in Robert Lowell, *The Dolphin* (New York: Farrar, Straus and Giroux, 1973).

13. Steven G. Axelrod, *Robert Lowell: Life and Art* (Princeton, N.J.: Princeton University Press, 1978), 233–39.

14. Robert Lowell, *Day by Day* (New York: Farrar, Straus and Giroux, 1977), 124.

15. Elizabeth Bishop, *The Complete Poems: 1927–1979* (New York: Farrar, Straus, Giroux, 1983), 178. Hereafter cited in the text.

16. Floyd Schwartz and Sybil Estess, eds., *Elizabeth Bishop and Her Art* (Ann Arbor: University of Michigan Press, 1983), 243.

17. Elizabeth Bishop, *The Collected Prose*, edited by Robert Giroux (New York: Farrar, Straus and Giroux, 1984), 274.

Notes

18. Susan McCabe, *Elizabeth Bishop: Her Poetics of Loss* (University Park, Pa.: Pennsylvania State University Press, 1994). See the introduction and chapter 1 for a review of feminist critiques of Bishop's work.

19. Theodore Roethke, *On the Poet and His Craft*, ed. Ralph J. Mills (Seattle: University of Washington Press, 1965), 8, 9.

20. Theodore Roethke, *The Collected Poems of Theodore Roethke* (Garden City, N.Y.: Anchor Press/Doubleday, 1975), 203. Further quotations are from this edition.

21. See "The Hemorrhage," originally titled "The Man in the Park," in Stanley Kunitz, *The Poems of Stanley Kunitz: 1928–1978* (Boston/Toronto: Atlantic Monthly Press, 1979), 163, 164.

22. Stanley Kunitz, *Next to Last Things: New Poems and Essays* (Boston/New York: Atlantic Monthly Press, 1985), 36.

23. Gregory Orr, *Stanley Kunitz: An Introduction to the Poetry* (New York: Columbia University Press, 1985), 21–41.

24. John Berryman, *The Dream Songs* (New York: Farrar, Straus and Giroux, 1974), 172.

25. John Berryman, *Collected Poems: 1937–1971* (New York: Farrar, Straus and Giroux, 1989), 219.

26. John Berryman, *The Freedom of the Poet* (New York: Farrar, Straus and Giroux, 1976), 330.

Chapter Two

1. Muriel Rukeyser, *The Life of Poetry* (New York: William Morrow, 1974), 203, 204.

2. Muriel Rukeyser, *The Collected Poems* (New York: McGraw–Hill, 1978), 3. Further quotations are from this edition.

3. Louise Kertesz, *The Poetic Vision of Muriel Rukeyser* (Baton Rouge and London: Louisiana State University Press, 1980), 1–44.

4. Commentary by William L. Rukeyser, son of Muriel Rukeyser, in a letter to William Sullivan, June 9, 1996.

5. Alicia Ostriker, "The Thieves of Language: Women Poets and Revisionist Mythmaking," in *Coming to Light*, ed. Diane Wood Middlebrook and Marilyn Yalom (Ann Arbor: University of Michigan Press, 1985), 10–36.

6. Randall Jarrell, *Poetry and the Age* (New York, Vintage Books, 1953), 149.

7. Adrienne Rich, "Muriel Rukeyser, 1913–1978: Poet . . . Woman . . . American . . . ," *Bridges* 1, no. 1 (Spring 1990): 25.

8. See Kate Daniels and Richard Jones, eds., "A Special Issue on Muriel Rukeyser," *Poetry East*, nos. 16/17 (Spring/Summer): 1985.

9. Gwendolyn Brooks, *Report from Part One* (Detroit: Broadside Press, 1972), 56.

10. Gwendolyn Brooks, *Blacks* (Chicago: Third World Press, 1991), 396. First published by the David Company, 1989.

11. Claudia Tate, "Anger So Flat: Gwendolyn Brooks' *Annie Allen*," in *A Life Distilled: Gwendolyn Brooks, Her Poetry and Fiction*, ed. Maria K. Mootry and Gary Smith (Urbana and Chicago: University of Illinois Press, 1987), 15.

12. Claudia Tate, ed., *Black Women Writers at Work* (New York: Continuum, 1983), 40.

13. D. H. Melhem, *Heroism in the New Black Poetry* (Lexington, Ky.: University Press of Kentucky, 1990), 14.

14. Robert Hayden, *Collected Poems*, ed. Frederick Glaysher (New York, London: Liveright Publishing Corp., 1985), 13. Further quotations are from this edition.

15. John Hatcher, *From the Auroral Darkness: The Life and Poetry of Robert Hayden* (Oxford: George Ronald Publisher, 1984).

16. Richard Wilbur, *Responses: Prose Pieces, 1953–1976* (New York and London: Harcourt Brace Jovanovich, 1976), 118.

17. Richard Wilbur, *New and Collected Poems* (San Diego, New York, London: Harcourt Brace Jovanovich, 1988), 297. Further quotations are from this edition.

18. Richard Wilbur, "On Love Calls Us to the Things of This World," in *The Contemporary Poet as Artist and Critic*, ed. Anthony Ostroff (Boston: Little Brown and Co., 1964), 19. See also Richard Eberhart's, Robert Horan's and May Swenson's reactions to this poem, 4–21.

19. Denise Levertov, *The Poet in the World* (New York: New Directions, 1973), 63.

20. Denise Levertov, *The Jacob's Ladder* (New York: New Directions, 1961), 87.

21. Denise Levertov, *Life in the Forest* (New York: New Directions, 1978), 24.

22. Denise Levertov, *Light Up the Cave* (New York: New Directions, 1981), 243.

23. See "To R.D. (Robert Duncan), March 4, 1988," in Denise Levertov, *A Door in the Hive* (New York: New Directions, 1989), 4.

24. Denise Levertov, *Collected Earlier Poems: 1940–1960* (New York: New Directions, 1979), 90.

25. Denise Levertov, *Poems: 1960–1967* (New York: New Directions, 1983), 59.

26. Denise Levertov, *To Stay Alive* (New York: New Directions, 1972), ix.

27. Denise Levertov, *Candles in Babylon* (New York: New Directions, 1982), 91.

28. Denise Levertov, *A Door in the Hive* (New York: New Directions, 1989), 15–39.

29. See Michael Davidson's commentary on the "Berkeley Renaissance" in his study, *The San Francisco Renaissance: Poetics and Com-*

Notes

munity at Mid Century (Cambridge, England: Cambridge University Press, 1989).

30. Donald Allen and George F. Butterick, eds., *The Postmoderns: The New American Poetry Revised* (New York: Grove Press, 1982), 390.

31. Donald Allen and Warren Tallman, eds., *The Poetics of the New American Poetry* (New York: Grove Press, 1973), 186.

32. Robert Duncan, *Fictive Certainties* (New York: New Directions, 1985), 67.

33. Robert Duncan, *Selected Poems*, ed. Robert J. Bertholf (New York: New Directions, 1993), 44.

34. James Dickey, *Babel to Byzantium: Poets and Poetry Now* (New York: Farrar, Straus and Giroux, 1968), 173–74.

35. Robert Duncan, *Bending the Bow* (New York: New Directions, 1968), 1.

36. Robert Duncan, *Ground Work: Before the War* (New York: New Directions, 1984), 45.

37. See Thom Gunn's "Homosexuality in Duncan's Poetry" in *Robert Duncan: Scales of the Marvelous*, ed. Robert J. Bertholf and Ian W. Reid (New York: New Directions, 1979), 143–60, for a full explanation of the incident.

38. See, for example, Karl Moss and Joan Larkin, eds., *Gay and Lesbian Poetry in Our Time: An Anthology* (New York: St. Martin's Press, 1988).

Chapter Three

1. Charles Olson, *Collected Prose* (New York: New Directions, 1966), 15. Olson's essay originally appeared in *Poetry New York* (1950).

2. Barbara and Albert Gelpi, eds., *Adrienne Rich's Poetry* (New York: Norton, 1975), 156.

3. Allen Ginsberg, *Collected Poems* (New York: Harper and Row, 1984). Of course many of Ginsberg's poems first appeared in periodicals rather than the City Lights editions, but the City Lights pocket books represent their first publication in book form.

4. "Early poetry" refers to the poems in *Howl and Other Poems, Kaddish*, and *Reality Sandwiches*. Ginsberg did publish two small volumes of what he calls "raw-sketch practice poems" before these. See *Collected Poems*, xix.

5. Richard Eberhart, *To Eberhart from Ginsberg: A Letter about Howl* (Lincoln, Mass: Penmaen Press, 1976), 8.

6. Michael Andre, "Levertov, Creeley, Wright, Auden, Ginsberg, Corso, Dickey: Essays and Interviews with Contemporary American Poets" (doctoral diss., Columbia University, 1975), 146.

7. Adrienne Rich, *Collected Early Poems, 1950–1970* (New York: W. W. Norton and Co., 1993), 26. Hereafter cited in the text.

8. Adrienne Rich, *The Fact of a Doorframe: Poems Selected and New, 1950–1984* (New York: W. W. Norton and Co., 1984), 232. Hereafter cited in the text.

Notes

9. Adrienne Rich, *A Wild Patience Has Taken Me This Far* (New York: W. W. Norton and Co., 1981), 4.

10. Adrienne Rich, *On Lies, Secrets, and Silence* (New York: W. W. Norton and Co., 1979), 202.

11. Adrienne Rich, *Your Native Land, Your Life* (New York: W. W. Norton and Co., 1986), 23. Hereafter cited in the text.

12. Robert Peters, *Hunting the Snark: A Compendium of New Poetic Terminology* (New York: Paragon House, 1989), 372.

13. Adrienne Rich, *Time's Power* (New York: W. W. Norton and Co., 1989), 4.

14. Terence Des Pres, *Praises and Dispraises* (New York: Viking, 1988), 187.

15. Sylvia Plath, *Collected Poems* (New York: Harper and Row, 1981), 125. Further quotations are from this edition.

16. Edward Butscher, *Sylvia Plath: Method and Madness* (New York: Harper and Row, 1976), 62.

17. George Stade, introduction to Nancy Hunt Steiner, *A Closer Look at Ariel: A Memory of Sylvia Plath* (New York: Vintage Books, 1973), 3.

18. Hugh Kenner, "Sincerity Kills," in *Sylvia Plath: New Views on the Poetry*, ed. Gary Lane (Baltimore: Johns Hopkins University Press, 1979), 41.

19. The editing of Sylvia Plath's poetry for the *Ariel* volume is a matter of some controversy. For a very critical view of Ted Hughes's intentions in this matter, see Marjorie Perloff, "The Two Ariels: The (Re)Making of the Sylvia Plath Canon," *American Poetry Review* 13 (November–December 1984): 10–18.

20. Judith Kroll, *Chapters in a Mythology: The Poetry of Sylvia Plath* (New York: Harper and Row, 1976), 1.

21. A. Alvarez, *The Savage God* (New York: 1973), 36.

22. Donald Allen, ed., *The Collected Poems of Frank O'Hara* (New York: Alfred A. Knopf, 1971), vii.

23. See Dore Ashton, *The New York School: A Cultural Reckoning* (New York: Viking, 1971), for a detailed account of these artists' cultural importance. Frank O'Hara's relation to these artists is also explored in Marjorie Perloff, *Frank O'Hara: Poet among Painters* (Austin: University of Texas Press, 1977).

24. John Ashbery, *The Tennis Court Oath* (Middletown, Conn.: Wesleyan University Press, 1962), 33.

25. See Marjorie Perloff, *The Poetics of Indeterminacy* (Princeton, N.J.: Princeton University Press, 1981), 8–16, for a detailed discussion of this poem.

26. John Ashbery, *Rivers and Mountains* (New York: Holt, Rinehart and Winston), 39.

27. John Ashbery, *Three Poems* (New York: Viking, 1972), 118.

Notes

28. John Ashbery, *Selected Poems* (New York: Viking, 1985), 189. Further quotations are from this edition.

29. See *Charles Olson and Robert Creeley: The Complete Correspondence*, 9 vols., ed. George Butterick (Santa Barbara: Black Sparrow Press, 1980–90).

30. Charles Olson, "Projective Verse," in *The New American Poetry*, ed. Donald Allen (New York: Grove, 1962), 386.

31. Robert Creeley, *A Sense of Measure* (London: Calder and Boyers, 1972), 52.

32. Robert Creeley, *The Collected Poems of Robert Creeley: 1945–1975* (Berkeley: University of California, 1975), 109. Further quotations are from this edition.

33. Quoted in *A Sense of Measure*, 41.

34. Sherman Paul, *The Lost America of Love* (Baton Rouge: Lousiana State University Press, 1981), 22.

35. Robert Creeley, *Later* (New York: New Directions, 1979), 3. Further quotations are from this edition.

36. Robert Creeley, *Mirrors* (New York: New Directions, 1984), title page. Further quotations are from this edition.

37. *The Fifties*, no. 2 (Minneapolis: Fifties Press, 1959), 50.

38. Robert Bly, *Selected Poems* (New York: Harper and Row, 1986), 12. Further quotations are from this edition.

39. Richard Jones and Kate Daniels, eds., *Of Solitude and Silence: Writings on Robert Bly* (Boston: Beacon Press, 1981), 64.

40. Robert Bly, *Leaping Poetry: An Idea with Poems and Translations* (Boston: Beacon Press, 1975), 3–4.

41. Diane Wood Middlebrook, *Anne Sexton: A Biography* (New York: Houghton Mifflin, 1991), 128–34, 148–50.

42. Peter Stitt and Frank Graziano, eds., *James Wright: The Heart of the Light* (Ann Arbor: University of Michigan Press, 1990), 283. Further quotations are from this edition.

43. James Wright, *Above the River: The Complete Poems* (New York: Farrar, Straus and Giroux, 1990), 82. Further quotations are from this edition.

44. See Stitt and Graziano, 162–68, for three distinct and contrary readings of this poem.

45. Quoted in Kevin Stein, *James Wright: The Poetry of a Grown Man* (Athens: Ohio University Press, 1989), 85.

46. Diane Wakoski, *Toward a New Poetry* (Ann Arbor: University of Michigan Press, 1980), 249. Further quotations are from this edition.

47. Diane Wakoski, *Medea the Sorceress* (Santa Rosa, Calif.: Black Sparrow, 1991), 92. Further quotations are from this edition.

48. Diane Wakoski, *Emerald Ice* (Santa Rosa, Calif.: Black Sparrow, 1988), 13. Further quotations are from this edition.

Notes

49. Diane Wakoski. *The Collected Greed 1–13* (Santa Rosa, Calif.: Black Sparrow, 1984), 7. Further quotations are from this edition.

Chapter Four

1. William Everson, *Earth Poetry*, ed. Lee Bartlett (Berkeley, Calif.: Oyez Press, 1980), 195.

2. William Everson, *Birth of a Poet: The Santa Cruz Meditations* (Santa Barbara, Black Sparrow Press, 1982), 161.

3. William Everson, *The Residual Years: Poems, 1934–1948* (New York: New Directions, 1968), 36.

4. Albert Gelpi, afterword to William Everson, *The Veritable Years: 1949–1966* (Santa Barbara, Calif.: Black Sparrow Press, 1975), n.p.

5. See William Everson, "Birth of a Poet," in *Naked Heart* (Albuquerque, N.M.: An American Poetry Book, 1992), 139–40.

6. William Everson, *Man-Fate: The Swan Song of Brother Antoninus* (New York: New Directions, 1973), viii.

7. William Everson, *The Achievement of Brother Antoninus*, edited and with a critical introduction by William Stafford (Glenview, Ill.: Scott, Foresman and Co., 1967), 1.

8. William Everson, "Biographical Note," *The Post Moderns: The New American Poetry Revived*, edited and with a new preface by Donald Allen and George F. Butterick (New York: Grove Press, 1982), 393. See also introduction, *Birth of a Poet*, vii, for an additional description of his life-long trilogy.

9. See William Everson, *Archetype West: The Pacific Coast as a Literary Region* (Berkeley, Calif.: Oyez, 1976), 3–11.

10. William Stafford, *Writing the Australian Crawl: Views on the Writer's Vacation* (Ann Arbor: University of Michigan Press, 1978), 93.

11. William Stafford, *Stories That Could Be True: New and Collected Poems* (New York: Harper and Row, 1977), 33.

12. William Stafford, *You Must Revise Your Life* (Ann Arbor: University of Michigan Press, 1986), 8.

13. See Roger Matuy, ed., *Contemporary Literary Criticism: Yearbook 1989* (Detroit: Gale Research, 1990), 59:173–84.

14. See Terence Des Pres, *Praises and Disparages: Poetry and Politics in the Twentieth Century* (New York: Penguin Group, Viking Penguin, 1988), 151–86.

15. See Philip Levine's tribute, delivered on April 12, 1986, at the Associated Writing Programs annual meeting, reprinted in *Contemporary Literary Criticism,* 59:174.

16. Thomas McGrath, *Selected Poems: 1938–1988*, edited and with an introduction by Sam Hamell (Port Townsend, Wash.: Copper Canyon Press, 1988), 10. Further quotations are from this edition.

Notes

17. Thomas McGrath, *Letter to an Imaginary Friend: Parts I and II* (Chicago: Swallow Press, 1970), "A Note in the Book," n.p.

18. Thomas McGrath, *Letter to an Imaginary Friend: Parts III and IV* (Port Townsend, Wash.: Copper Canyon Press, 1985), "A Note on Parts Three and Four," n.p.

19. See James Dickey, *Self-Interviews* (Garden City, N.Y.: Doubleday and Co., 1977), 33–35.

20. David Ray, "James Dickey," *Contemporary Poets*, Fourth Edition, ed. James Vinson and D. L. Kirkpatrick (London and Chicago: St. James Press, 1985), 195.

21. James Dickey, *Poems: 1957–1967* (Middletown, Conn.: Wesleyan University Press, 1967), 119.

22. See Dickey's discussion of this poem in *Self-Interviews*, 160–62.

23. James Dickey, *The Strength of the Fields* (Garden City, N.Y.: Doubleday and Co., 1979), 17.

24. Maxine Kumin, *In Deep: Country Essays* (New York: Viking, 1987), 158, 159, 162.

25. Maxine Kumin, *To Make a Prairie: Essays on Poets, Poetry, and Country Living* (Ann Arbor: University of Michigan Press, 1979), 32.

26. See *To Make a Prairie*, 78–93.

27. Maxine Kumin, *Our Ground Time Here Will Be Brief* (New York: Penguin Books, 1982), 219.

28. Maxine Kumin, *Nurture* (New York: Viking, 1989), 14, 15.

29. Maxine Kumin, *The Long Approach* (New York: Viking, 1985), 41.

30. See "Maxine Kumin," in *Contemporary Literary Criticism*, ed. Jean C. Stine (Detroit: Gale Research, 1990), 28:225.

31. Harold Bloom, ed., *Modern Critical View: A. R. Ammons* (New York: Chelsea House, 1986), 1.

32. A. R. Ammons, *The Selected Poems: Expanded Edition* (New York: W. W. Norton and Co., 1986), 1.

33. A. R. Ammons, *Sphere: The Form of a Motion* (New York: W. W. Norton and Co., 1974), 62–63.

34. Diane Wakoski, "Mary Oliver," in *Contemporary Poets*, ed. James Vinson and D. L. Kirkpatrick (London and Chicago: St. James Press, 1985), 627, 628.

35. Mary Oliver, *New and Selected Poems* (Boston: Beacon Press, 1992), 252.

36. Gary Snyder, preface to *No Nature: New and Selected Poems* (New York and San Francisco: Pantheon, 1992).

37. Michael Davidson, *The San Francisco Renaissance* (Cambridge, England: Cambridge University Press, 1989), 101.

38. David Kherdian, *Six San Francisco Poets* (Fresno, Calif.: Geligia Press, 1969), 51.

Notes

39. Gary Snyder, "Buddhism and the Coming Revolution," in *The Poetics of the New American Poetry*, ed. Donald Allen and Warren Tallman (New York: Grove Press, 1973), 392.

40. Gary Snyder, *Myths and Texts* (New York: New Directions, 1977), viii.

41. Gary Snyder, introductory note to *Turtle Island* (New York: New Directions, 1974).

42. Gary Snyder, *Axe Handles* (San Francisco: North Point Press, 1983), 30.

Chapter Five

1. Alicia Suskin Ostriker, *Stealing the Language: The Emergence of Women's Poetry in America* (Boston: Beacon Press, 1986), 168.

2. In Judy Grahn, *The Work of a Common Woman* (Trumansberg, N.Y.: Crossing Press, 1978), 18.

3. Diane Wood Middlebrook, *Anne Sexton* (New York: Houghton Mifflin, 1991), 82.

4. Anne Sexton, *The Complete Poems*, with an introduction by Maxine Kumin (New York: Houghton Mifflin, 1981), xxxiv. Further quotations are from this edition.

5. For versions of feminist fairy tales influenced by Sexton's work, see Jay Williams, *The Practical Princess and Other Liberating Fairy Tales* (New York: Parents Magazine Press, 1979), and Tanith Lee, *Red as Blood, or Tales from the Sisters Grimmer* (New York: Daw Books, 1983).

6. Audre Lorde, *Sister Outsider* (Freedom, Calif.: Crossings Press, 1984).

7. Audre Lorde, *Chosen Poems: Old and New* (New York: W. W. Norton and Co., 1982), 15. Further quotations are from this edition.

8. Marie Harris and Kathleen Aguero, eds., *A Gift of Tongues: Critical Challenges in Contemporary American Poetry* (Athens: University of Georgia Press, 1987), 39.

9. Audre Lorde, *Black Unicorn* (New York: W. W. Norton and Co., 1978), 12. Further quotations are from this edition.

10. Audre Lorde, *Our Dead behind Us* (New York: W. W. Norton and Co., 1986), 7.

11. Audre Lorde, *The Cancer Journals* (Argyle, N.Y.: Spinster's Ink, 1980), 9.

12. Marge Piercy, ed., *Early Ripening: American Women's Poetry Now* (London and Boston: Pandora Press, 1987), 1.

13. Marge Piercy, *Circles on the Water: Selected Poems* (New York: Alfred A. Knopf, 1982), 108–13. Further quotations are from this edition.

14. Marge Piercy, *Available Light* (New York: Alfred A. Knopf, 1988), 111. Further quotations are from this edition.

Notes

15. Marge Piercy, *My Mother's Body* (New York: Alfred A. Knopf, 1988), 21. Further quotations are from this edition.

16. Marge Piercy, *Stone Paper Knife* (New York: Alfred A. Knopf, 1983), 68.

17. Anne Stevenson, "Sources of Strength," *Times Literary Supplement*, July 20, 1984, 818.

18. Sharon Olds, *The Gold Cell* (New York: Alfred A. Knopf, 1987), 52. Further quotations are from this edition.

19. Sharon Olds, *Satan Says* (Pittsburgh: University of Pittsburgh Press, 1980), 24. Further quotations are from this edition.

20. Sharon Olds, *The Dead and the Living* (New York: Alfred A. Knopf, 1984), 39. Further quotations are from this edition.

21. Alicia Suskin Ostriker, *Writing Like a Woman* (Ann Arbor: University of Michigan Press, 1984), 1. Further quotations are from this edition.

22. Louise Glück, *The House on the Marshlands* (New York: Ecco Press, 1975), 14.

23. Louise Glück, *Descending Figure* (New York: Ecco Press, 1980), 32.

24. Louise Glück, *The Triumph of Achilles* (New York: Ecco Press, 1985), 50.

25. Louise Glück, *Ararat* (New York: Ecco Press, 1990), 16.

26. Olga Broumas, *Beginning with O* (New Haven, Conn.: Yale University Press, 1977), 24.

27. Olga Broumas, *Perpetua* (Port Townsend, Wash.: Copper Canyon Press, 1989), 34. Further quotations are from this edition.

Chapter Six

1. Galway Kinnell, *The Poetics of the Physical World* (Ft. Collins: Colorado State University Press, 1965), 5.

2. Galway Kinnell, *Selected Poems* (Boston: Houghton Mifflin, 1982), 42.

3. Charles Molesworth, *The Fierce Embrace* (Columbia: University of Missouri Press, 1979), 99.

4. At the 1991 Modern Language Association meeting in San Francisco, Kinnell told Fred Moramarco that when he wrote these birth poems in the late 1960s, he researched the subject to see what had been written about it and could find no poems in English that explicitly described childbirth. From our perspective in the last decade of the twentieth century, it may be astonishing to learn that until very recently accounts of childbirth were a taboo subject for poetry. Kinnell also mentioned that Robert Bly criticized him for writing about birth, which he saw as a woman's mystery and inappropriate for a man to write about.

5. Galway Kinnell, *When One Has Lived a Long Time Alone* (New York: Alfred A. Knopf, 1990), 66.

Notes

6. Galway Kinnell, *The Book of Nightmares* (New York: Houghton Mifflin, 1971), 29.

7. W. S. Merwin, *Selected Poems* (New York: Atheneum, 1988), 194.

8. Ed Folsom and Cary Nelson, eds., *W. S. Merwin: Essays on the Poetry* (Urbana: University of Illinois Press, 1987), 13. Further quotations are from this edition.

9. Robert Peters, *The Great American Poetry Bake-Off* (Metuchen, N.J.: Scarecrow Press, 1979), 265.

10. W. S. Merwin, *The Rain in the Trees* (New York: Atheneum, 1988), 65. Further quotations are from this edition.

11. W. S. Merwin, *Selected Translations: 1968–1978* (New York: Atheneum, 1979), xii.

12. Philip Levine, *Not This Pig* (Middleton, Conn.: Wesleyan University Press, 1968), 13.

13. Philip Levine, *Don't Ask* (Ann Arbor: University of Michigan Press, 1981), 101. Further quotations are from this edition.

14. Philip Levine, *New and Selected Poems* (New York: Atheneum, 1991), 81. Further quotations are from this edition.

15. Philip Levine, *Seven Years from Somewhere* (New York: Atheneum, 1979), 34–35.

16. Donald Davie, "Frost, Eliot, Thomas, Pound," *New York Times Book Review*, February 19, 1978, 15.

17. These are the Poets on Poetry Series (thirty-five titles as of 1991) and the Under Discussion Series (twelve titles as of 1991).

18. *Goatfoot, Milktongue, Twinbird: Interviews, Essays, and Notes on Poetry, 1970–76* (Ann Arbor: University of Michigan Press, 1978), 118.

19. Donald Hall, *Kicking the Leaves* (New York: Harper and Row, 1978), 15.

20. Liam Rector, ed., *The Day I Was Older* (Santa Cruz: Story Line Press, 1989). Further quotations are from this edition.

21. Donald Hall, *The One Day* (New York: Ticknor and Fields, 1988). Further quotations are from this edition.

22. Mark Strand, *Selected Poems* (New York: Atheneum, 1981), 6. Further quotations are from this edition.

23. David Kirby, *Mark Strand and the Poet's Place in Contemporary Culture* (Columbia: University of Missouri Press, 1990), 13.

24. Quoted in Linda Gregerson, "Negative Capability," *Parnassus: Poetry in Review* 9, no. 2 (Fall–Winter 1981): 90–114.

25. Mark Strand, *The Continuous Life* (New York: Alfred A. Knopf, 1990), 21.

26. Reginald Gibbons, "Flesh and Blood," *Triquarterly*, no. 71 (Winter 1988): 224.

27. C. K. Williams, *Poems: 1963–1983* (New York: Farrar, Straus and Giroux, 1988), 15. Further quotations are from this edition.

28. C. K. Williams, *Flesh and Blood* (New York: Farrar, Straus and Giroux, 1987), 43.

29. See Charles Fishman, ed., *Blood to Remember: American Poets on the Holocaust* (Lubbock: Texas Tech University Press, 1991), for a selection of poems on this theme.

30. Paul Garson, *W. D. Snodgrass* (New York: Twayne, 1978), 153.

31. James Merrill, *The Inner Room* (New York: Alfred A. Knopf, 1988), 93.

32. James Merrill, *Selected Poems: 1946–1985* (New York: Knopf, 1992), 78.

33. Charles Simic, *Selected Poems: 1963–1983* (New York: Braziller, 1990), 121. Further quotations are from this edition.

34. William Matthews, *Ruining the New Road* (New York: Random House, 1970), viii.

35. William Matthews, *A Happy Childhood* (Boston: Atlantic Little Brown, 1984), 33.

36. William Matthews, *Rising and Falling* (New York: Atlantic Monthly Press, 1979), 4.

37. Robert Pinsky, *Sadness and Happiness* (Princeton, N.J.: Princeton University Press, 1975), 41.

38. Peter Davison, "The Great Predicament of Poetry," *Atlantic Monthly,* June 1979, 94.

39. Robert Hass, *Praise* (New York: Ecco Press, 1979), 3.

40. Robert Hass, *Human Wishes* (New York: Ecco Press, 1989), 51. Further quotations are from this edition.

41. Frank Bidart, *In the Western Night: Collected Poems, 1965–90* (New York: Farrar Straus Giroux, 1990), 104. Further quotations are from this edition.

42. Raymond Carver, *A New Path to the Waterfall* (New York: Atlantic Monthly Press, 1989), xxx. Further quotations are from this edition.

43. Raymond Carver, *Ultramarine* (New York: Random House, 1986), 11–12. Further quotations are from this edition.

44. Raymond Carver, *Where Water Comes Together with Other Water* (New York: Random House, 1985), 46.

Chapter Seven

1. Sterling A. Brown, *The Collected Poems of Sterling A. Brown,* selected by Michael Harper (New York: Harper and Row, 1980), 53.

2. Amiri Baraka, *The LeRoi Jones/Amiri Baraka Reader,* ed. William J. Harris (New York: Thunder's Mouth Press, 1991), xxvi. Further quotations are from this edition.

Notes

3. Amiri Baraka, *The Autobiography of Leroi Jones/Amiri Baraka* (New York: Freiendlich Books, 1984), 24.

4. See the interview with Baraka in D. H. Melhem, *Heroism in the New Black Poetry* (Lexington: University Press of Kentucky, 1990), 215–63.

5. Sonia Sanchez, introduction to *Home Coming* (Detroit: Broadside Press, 1969), n.p.

6. Sonia Sanchez, *We a BaddDDD People* (Detroit: Broadside Press, 1970), 5.

7. Sonia Sanchez, *A Blues Book for Blue Black Magical Woman* (Detroit: Broadside Press, 1974), dedication page.

8. Sonia Sanchez, *Homegirls and Handgrenades* (New York and Chicago: Thunder's Mouth Press, 1984), 3.

9. Sonia Sanchez, *Under a Soprano Sky* (Trenton, N.J.: Africa World Press, 1987), 12.

10. Etheridge Knight, *Born of a Woman: New and Selected Poems* (Boston: Houghton Mifflin, 1980), n.p.

11. Etheridge Knight, *The Essential Etheridge Knight* (Pittsburgh: University of Pittsburgh Press, 1986), 114. Further quotations are from this edition.

12. Etheridge Knight et al., *Black Voices from Prison* (New York: Pathfinder Press, 1970), 5. Originally published in Italy in 1968.

13. Lucille Clifton, *Good Woman: Poems and a Memoir, 1969–1980* (Brockport, N.Y.: BOA Editions, 1987), 223.

14. See back cover of *Good Woman.*

15. Lucille Clifton, *Next: New Poems* (Brockport, N.Y.: BOA Editions, 1987), 16.

16. For biographical information, see the entry for Quincy Troupe, *Afro-American Poets since 1955,* ed. by Trudier Harris and Thadious M. Davis (Detroit: Gale Research, 1985), 41:334.

17. Quincy Troupe, *Skulls along the River* (New York/Berkeley: Reed Books, 1984), 15.

18. Quincy Troupe, *Snake-Back Solos* (New York: Reed Books, 1978), 9.

19. Quincy Troupe, ed., *Watts Poets: A Book of New Poetry and Essays* (Los Angeles: House of Respect, 1968), 55–59.

20. Michael Harper, *Dear John, Dear Coltrane* (Pittsburgh: University of Pittsburgh Press, 1970), 36.

21. Michael Harper, *Images of Kin: New Poems* (Urbana: University of Illinois Press, 1977), 64.

22. See "Magic: Power: Activation: Transformation," an interview with Michael Harper, in Richard Jackson, *Acts of the Mind* (Tuscaloosa, Ala.: University of Alabama Press, 1983), 183–90.

23. Michael Harper, *History Is Your Own Heartbeat* (Urbana: University of Illinois Press, 1971), 3.

Notes

24. See "Michael S(teven) Harper," *Contemporary Literary Criticism* (Chicago: Gale Research), 22:209.

25. Joseph Bruchac, ed., *Survival This Way: Interviews with American Indian Poets* (Tucson: Sun Tracks and the University of Arizona Press, 1987), 181.

26. N. Scott Momaday, *The Way to Rainy Mountain* (Albuquerque: University of New Mexico Press, 1969), 89.

27. N. Scott Momaday, *The Gourd Dancer* (New York: Harper and Row, 1976), 31. This volume includes the previously published *Angle of Geese*.

28. See Alan R. Velie, "James Welch's Poetry," *American Indian Culture and Research Journal* 3, no. 1 (1979): 19–38, and Peter Wild, *James Welch*, Boise (Idaho) State University Western Writers Series, no. 57, pp. 5–24, for a discussion of Welch's use of these concepts.

29. James Welch, *Riding the Earthboy 40* (New York: Harper and Row, 1976), 32.

30. Wild notes that the word *fabulous* originally preceded *disease* in the last line of the poem. He laments its absence in *Earthboy 40*, as does Welch in his interview with Joseph Bruchac.

31. Welch's novels are *Winter in the Blood* (1974), *The Death of Jim Loney* (1980), *Fools Crow* (1986), and *The Indian Lawyer* (1990).

32. See "The Language We Know," in Brian Swann and Arnold Krupat, eds., *I Tell You Now* (Lincoln: University of Nebraska Press, 1987), 187–94, and "The Story Never Ends," in Joseph Bruchac, ed., *Survival This Way: Interviews with American Indian Poets* (Tucson: Sun Tracks and the University of Arizona Press, 1987), 211–29, for autobiographical information.

33. Simon Ortiz, *Song, Poetry, and Language—Expression and Perception* (Tsaile, Ariz.: Navaho Community College Press, 1977), 4.

34. Simon Ortiz, *Going for the Rain* (New York: Harper and Row, 1976), 20.

35. Simon Ortiz, *A Good Journey* (Tucson: Sun Tracks and the University of Arizona Press, 1977), 25.

36. Simon Ortiz, *Fight Back: For the Sake of the People/For the Sake of the Land* (Albuquerque, N.M.: Institute for Native American Development Literary Journal, vol. 1, no. 1, 1980), 3.

37. Simon Ortiz, *From Sand Creek* (New York: Thunder Mouth Press, 1981), n.p.

38. Leslie Silko, *Storyteller* (New York: Arcade Publishing, Little, Brown and Co., 1981), 247.

39. Leslie Silko, *Ceremony* (New York: Viking Press, 1986), 142.

40. Leslie Silko, "Languages and Literature from a Pueblo Indian Perspective," in *English Literature: Opening Up the Canon*, ed. Leslie A. Fiedler and Houston A. Baker, Jr. (Baltimore: Johns Hopkins University Press, 1981), 55.

Notes

41. Wendy Rose, "Builder Kachina: A Home-Going Cycle," *Blue Cloud Quarterly* (Marvin, S.D.) 25, no. 4 (1979): n.p.

42. Wendy Rose, *The Halfbreed Chronicles* (Los Angeles: West End Press, 1985), 47.

43. Wendy Rose, "Neon Scars," in *I Tell You Now*, ed. Brian Swann and Arnold Krupat (Lincoln: University of Nebraska Press, 1987), 251–63.

44. Wendy Rose, "Academic Squaw: Reports to the World from the Ivory Tower," *Blue Cloud Quarterly* (Marvin, S.D.) 23, no. 4 (1977): n.p.

45. Rodolpho Gonzales, *I Am Joaquin/Yo Soy Joaquin: An Epic Poem* (Toronto, New York, London: Bantam Pathfinder Editions, 1972), 1.

46. Juan Bruce-Novoa, *Chicano Authors: Inquiry by Interview* (Austin: University of Texas Press, 1980), 16.

47. See *Chicano Authors*, pp. 4–9, for titles and publishing chronology of these poets.

48. Juan Bruce-Novoa, *Chicano Poetry: A Response to Chaos* (Austin: University of Texas Press, 1982), 72.

49. Tomas Ybarra-Frausto, "The Chicano Movement and the Emergence of a Chicano Poetic Consciousness," *New Scholar* 6 (1977): 103.

50. Alurista, *Floricanto en Aztlan* (Los Angeles: University of California, Chicano Studies Center, 1971), 1.

51. Alurista, preface to *Nationchild Plumaroja* (San Diego: Toltecas en Aztlan, Centro Cultural de La Raza, 1972), n.p.

52. See *Chicano Authors*, pp. 205–18, for autobiographical information.

53. Bernice Zamora, *Restless Serpents* (Menlo Park, Calif.: Disenos Literarios, 1976), dedication page.

54. Gloria Anzaldúa, preface to *Borderlands/La Frontera: The New Mestiza* (San Francisco: Aunt Lute Books, 1987), n.p.

55. Gloria Anzaldúa and Cherrie Moraga, eds., *This Bridge Called My Back: Writings by Radical Women of Color* (New York: Kitchen Table, Women of Color Press, 1990), vi, vii.

56. Gloria Anzaldúa, ed., *Making Face, Making Soul* (San Francisco: Aunt Lute Foundation Book, 1990).

57. Houston A. Baker, Jr., *Three American Literatures: Essays in Chicano, Native American, and Asian-American Literature for Teachers of American Literature* (New York: Modern Language Association of America, 1982), 197.

58. Garrett Kaoru Hongo, Alan Chong Lau, and Lawson Fusao Inada, *The Buddha Bandits Down Highway 99* (Mountain View, Calif.: Buddhahead Press, 1978), n.p.

59. Lawson Fusao Inada, *Before the War: Poems as They Happened* (New York: William Morrow and Co., 1971), endpage.

60. Elaine H. Kim, *Asian American Literature: An Introduction to the Writings and Their Social Context* (Philadelphia: Temple University Press, 1982), 148.

Notes

61. Lawson Fusao Inada, *Legends from Camp* (Minneapolis: Coffee House Press, 1992), 3.

62. Janice Mirikitani et al., eds., *Time to Greez!: Incantations from the Third World* (San Francisco: Glide Publications, 1975), v.

63. Janice Mirikitani, *Awake in the River* (San Francisco: Isthmus Press, 1978), n.p.

64. Janice Mirikitani, *Shedding Silence* (Berkeley, Calif.: Celestial Arts, 1987), 1.

65. Joseph Bruchac, *Breaking Silence: An Anthology of Contemporary Asian American Poets* (Greenfield Center, N.Y.: Greenfield Review Press, 1983), xiv, xv.

Chapter Eight

1. Donald Allen, ed., *The New American Poetry* (New York: Grove, 1960).

2. Donald Hall, ed., *Contemporary American Poetry* (New York: Collier, 1961).

3. Dudley Randall, ed., *The Black Poets* (New York: Bantam, 1971).

4. Ellen Bass and Florence Howe, eds. *No More Masks: An Anthology of Poems by Women* (Garden City, N.Y.: Anchor, 1973). Though extremely influential in the seventies, *No More Masks* was by no means the first anthology of American women's poetry in America. That distinction belongs to Rufus Griswold's *Gems from American Female Poets*, published in 1844.

5. Jerome Rothenberg and George Quasha, eds., *America: A Prophecy* (New York: Vintage, 1974).

6. Jerome Rothenberg, ed., *Revolution of the Word* (New York: Seabury Press, 1974), xvi.

7. Edward Field, ed., *A Geography of Poets* (New York: Bantam, 1979), xxxviii.

8. Robert Richman, ed., *The Direction in Poetry* (Boston: Houghton Mifflin, 1988), xiii.

9. Walt Whitman, *Poetry and Prose* (New York: Library of America, 1982), 5.

10. See Lynn Emmanuel, "Language Poets, New Formalists, and the Techniquization of Poetry," in *Poetry after Modernism*, ed. Robert McDowell, (Brownsville, Ore.: Story Line Press, 1990), 276–99, for an excellent discussion of the aesthetics behind these two groups.

11. Robert Pack, Sidney Lea, and Jay Parini, eds., *The Breadloaf Anthology of Contemporary American Poetry* (Hanover, N.H.: University Press of New England, 1985), vi.

12. Helen Vendler, ed. *The Harvard Book of Contemporary American Poetry* (Cambridge Mass.: Harvard University Press, 1985), 7.

Notes

13. Ron Silliman, ed., *In the American Tree* (Orono, Me.: National Poetry Foundation, 1986), xix.

14. Doug Messerli, ed., *Language Poetries: An Anthology* (New York: New Directions, 1987), 2.

15. Marjorie Perloff, "Language Poetry," *American Poetry Review*, May–June 1984.

16. Philip Dacey and David Jauss, eds., *Strong Measures: Contemporary American Poetry in Traditional Forms* (New York: Harper and Row, 1986), 14.

17. Andrei Codrescu, ed., *American Poetry since 1970: Up Late* (New York: Four Walls Eight Windows Press, 1987), xxxii.

18. Joseph Epstein, "Who Killed Poetry?" *Associated Writing Chronicle*, May 1989, 2.

19. Steve Kowit, *The Maverick Poets* (San Diego: Gorilla Press, 1988), 2.

20. Robert Wennersten, "Paying for Horses: An Interview with Charles Bukowski," *London Magazine*, December 1974/January 1975, 35–54.

21. Donald Hall, ed., *The Best American Poetry: 1989* (New York: Collier, 1989), ix.

22. John Ashbery, ed., *The Best American Poetry: 1988* (New York: Collier, 1988), xvi–xvii.

23. Jorie Graham, ed., *The Best American Poetry: 1990* (New York: Collier, 1990), xxx.

· *Selected Bibliography* ·

This bibliography includes works on esthetics, multiple authors, movements, themes and other aspects of contemporary American poetry. It does not include works on individual authors or individual books of poems cited in the text.

Aguero, Kathleen and Marie Harris, eds. *A Gift of Tongues: Critical Challenges in Contemporary American Poetry*. Athens: University of Georgia Press, 1987.

Allen, Donald and Warren Tallman, eds. *The Poetics of the New American Poetry*. New York: Grove Press, 1973.

Altieri, Charles. *Enlarging the Temple: New Directions in American Poetry During the Sixties*. Lewisburg, Pa.: Bucknell University Press, 1979.

———. *Painterly Abstraction and Modernist American Poetry: The Contemporaneity of Modernism*. Cambridge: Cambridge University Press, 1989.

———. *Self and Sensibility in Contemporary American Poetry*. Cambridge: Cambridge University Press, 1984.

Barlett, Lee. *The Sun is but a Morning Star: Studies in West Coast Poetry and Poetics*. Albuquerque: University of New Mexico Press, 1989.

———. *Talking Poetry: Conversations in the Workshop with Contemporary Poets*. Albuquerque: University of New Mexico Press, 1987.

Bawer, Bruce. *The Middle Generation: The Lives and Poetry of Delmore Schwartz, Randall Jarell, John Berryman, and Robert Lowell*. Hamden, Conn.: Archon Books, 1986.

Bellamy, Joe David. ed. *American Poetry Observed: Poets on their Work*. Urbana: University of Illinois Press, 1984.

Bennett, Paula. *My Life a Loaded Gun: Female Creativity and Feminist Poetics*. Boston: Beacon Press, 1986.

Berg, Temmer, ed. *Engendering the Word: Feminist Essays in Psychosexual Poetics*. Urbana: University of Illinois Press, 1989.

Berke, Roberta Elzey. *Bounds Out of Bounds: A Compass for Recent American and British Poetry*. New York: Oxford University Press, 1981.

Blasing, Mutlu Konuk. *Politics and Form in Postmodern Poetry: O'Hara, Bishop, Ashbery, and Merrill*. Cambridge, England: Cambridge University Press, 1995.

Bloom, Harold, ed. *American Poetry, 1946–1965*. New York: Chelsea House, 1987.

———. *American Woman Poets*. New York: Chelsea House, 1986.

———. *Contemporary Poets*. New York: Chelsea House, 1986.

Selected Bibliography

Bly, Robert. *American Poetry: Wildness and Domesticity*. New York: Harper & Row, 1990.

Breslin, James E.B. *From Modern to Contemporary: American Poetry, 1945-1965*. Chicago: University of Chicago Press, 1984.

Breslin, Paul. *The Psycho-political Muse: American Poetry Since the Fifties*. Chicago: University of Chicago Press, 1987.

Bruce-Novoa, Juan D. *Chicano Authors: Inquiry by Interview*. Austin: University of Texas Press, 1980.

———. *Chicano Poetry: A Response to Chaos*. Austin: University of Texas Press, 1982.

Bruchac, Joseph, ed. *Survival this Way: Interviews with American Indian Poets*. Tucson: Sun Tracks and the University of Arizona Press, 1987.

Candelaria, Cordelia. *Chicano Poetry: A Critical Introduction*. Westport, Conn.: Greenwood Press, 1986.

Carroll, Paul. *The Poem in Its Skin*. Chicago: Follett Publishing Company, 1968.

Castro, Michael. *Interpreting the Indian: Poets and the Native American*. Albuquerque: University of New Mexico Press, 1983.

Charters, Ann, ed. *The Portable Beat Reader*. New York: Penguin, 1992.

Charters, Samuel. *Some Poems, Poets; Studies in American Underground Poetry Since 1945*. Berkeley: Oyez, 1971.

Cherkovski, Neeli. *Whitman's Wild Children*. Venice, Ca.: Lapis Press, 1988.

Christopher, Nicholas. *Walk on the Wild Side: Urban American Poetry Since 1975*. New York: Collier Books; Toronto: Maxwell Macmillan Canada; New York: Maxwell Macmillan International, 1994.

Clark, Tom. *The Poetry Beat: Reviewing the Eighties*. Ann Arbor: University of Michigan Press, 1990.

Clauson, Jan. *A Movement of Poets: Thoughts on Poetry and Feminism*. Brooklyn: Long Haul Press, 1982.

Conniff, Brian. *The Lyric and Modern Poetry: Olson, Creeley, Bunting*. New York: P. Lang, 1988.

Conte, Joseph ed. *American Poets Since World War II*. Detroit: Gale Research, 1996.

———. *Unending Design: The Forms of Postmodern Poetry*. Ithaca: Cornell University Press, 1991.

Damon, Maria. *The Dark End of the Street: Margins in American Vanguard Poetry*. Minneapolis: University of Minnesota Press, 1993.

Davidson, Michael. *The San Francisco Renaissance*. Cambridge: Cambridge University, 1989.

Davison, Peter. *The Fading Smile: Poets in Boston, 1955–1960, from Robert Frost to Robert Lowell to Sylvia Plath*. New York: Knopf, 1994.

DeShazer, Mary K. *Inspiring Women: Reimagining the Muse*. New York: Pergammon Press, 1986.

Des Pres, Terrence. *Praise and Dispraises: Poetry and Politics in the Twentieth Century.* New York: Viking, 1988.

Dickey, James. *Babel to Byzantium: Poets and Poetry Now.* New York: Ecco Press, 1981.

————. *The Suspect in Poetry.* Madison, Minn.: Sixties Press, 1964.

Dickie, Margaret. *Stein, Bishop, & Rich: Lyrics of Love, War, and Place.* Chapel Hill: University of North Carolina Press, 1997.

Dodd, Wayne. *Toward the End of the Century: Essays into Poetry.* Iowa City: University of Iowa Press, 1992.

Donoghue, Denis. *Connoisseurs of Chaos: Ideas of Order in Modern American Poetry.* New York: Macmillan, 1965.

Duberman, Martin. *Black Mountain: An Exploration in Community.* New York: Dutton,1972.

Elder, John. *Imagining the Earth: Poetry and the Vision of Nature.* Athens: University of Georgia Press, 1996.

Fass, Ekbert, ed. *Towards a New American Poetics: Essays and Interviews.* Santa Barbara: Black Sparrow, 1978.

Feinstein, Fredrick. *Expansive Poetry: Essays on the New Narrative and the New Formalism.* Santa Cruz: Storyline Press, 1989.

Feinstein, Sascha. *Jazz Poetry: From the 1920s to the Present.* Westport, Connecticut: Greenwood Press, 1997.

Finkelstein, Norman. *The Utopian Moment in Contemporary American Poetry.* Lewisburg, Pa.: Bucknell University Press, 1988.

Foster, Edward Halsey. *Understanding the Black Mountain Poets.* Columbia, S.C: University of South Carolina Press, 1995.

Foster, Jeanne. *A Music of Grace: The Sacred in Contemporary American Poetry.* New York: P. Lang, 1995.

Frank, Robert and Henry Sayre, eds. *The Line in Postmodern Poetry.* Urbana: University of Illinois Press, 1988.

Fredman, Stephen. *Poet's Prose: The Crisis in American Verse.* Cambridge: Cambridge University Press, 1990.

French, Warren G. *The San Francisco Poetry Renaissance, 1955–60.* Boston: Twayne, 1991.

Gardner, Thomas. *Discovering Ourselves in Whitman: The Contemporary American Long Poem.* Urbana: University of Illinois Press, 1989.

Gayle, Addison, Jr. *The Black Aesthetic.* Garden City, New York: Doubleday, 1971.

Gery, John. *Nuclear Annihilation and Contemporary American Poetry: Ways of Nothingness.* Gainesville: University Press of Florida, 1996.

Gibson, Donald B. ed. *Modern Black Poets; A Collection of Critical Essays.* Englewood Cliffs, N.J.: Prentice-Hall, 1973.

Gitenstein, R. Barbara. *Apocalyptic Messianism and Contemporary Jewish American Poetry.* Albany: SUNY Press, 1986.

Selected Bibliography

Gotera, Vicente. *Radical Visions: Poetry by Vietnam Veterans.* Athens: University of Georgia Press, 1994.

Gould, Jean. *Modern American Women Poets.* New York: Dodd, Mead, 1984.

Grahn, Judy. *The Highest Apple: Sappho and the Lesbian Poetic Tradition.* San Francisco: Spinster's Ink, 1984.

Gray, Richard J. *American Poetry of the Twentieth Century.* London & New York: Longman, 1990.

Greiner, Donald J., ed. *American Poets Since World War II.* Detroit: Gale Research, 1980.

Hall, Donald., ed. *Claims for Poetry.* Ann Arbor: University of Michigan Press, 1982.

———. *Death to the Death of Poetry: Essays, Reviews, Notes, Interviews.* Ann Arbor: University of Michigan Press, 1994.

Hartley, George. *Textual Politics and the Language Poets.* Bloomington: Indiana University Press, 1989.

Hayman, Ronald. *Arguing with Walt Whitman: An Essay on His Influence on 20th Century American Verse.* London: Convent Garden Press, 1971.

Holden, Jonathan. *The Fate of American Poetry.* Athens: University of Georgia Press, 1991.

———. *The Rhetoric of the Contemporary Lyric.* Bloomington: Indiana University Press, 1980.

———. *Style and Authenticity in Postmodern Poetry.* Columbia: University of Missouri Press, 1986.

Homberger, Eric. *The Art of the Real: Poetry in England and America Since 1939.* London: Dent; Totowa, New Jersey: Rowman and Littlefield, 1977.

Howard, Richard. *Alone in America: Essays on the Art of Poetry in the United States.* New York: Atheneum, 1969.

Ingersoll, Earl G. et al., eds. *The Post-Confessionals: Conversations with American Poets of the Eighties.* Rutherford, N.J.: Fairleigh Dickenson University Press, 1989.

Jackson, Richard. *Acts of Mind: Conversations with Contemporary Poets.* Tuscaloosa: University of Alabama Press, 1983.

———. *The Dismantling of Time in Contemporary Poetry.* Tuscaloosa: University of Alabama Press, 1988.

Johnson, Kent and Craig Paulenich, eds. *Beneath a Single Moon: Buddhism and Contemporary American Poetry.* Boston: Shambhala Press, 1991.

Jones, Richard, ed. *Poetry and Politics: An Anthology of Essays.* New York: Quill, 1985.

Juhasz, Suzanne. *Naked and Fiery Forms: Modern American Poetry by Women: A New Tradition.* New York: Octagon Books, 1976.

Kalaidjian, Walter B. *Languages of Liberation: The Social Text in Contemporary American Poetry.* New York: Columbia University Press, 1989.

Selected Bibliography

Kalstone, David. *Five Temperaments: Elizabeth Bishop, Robert Lowell, James Merrill, Adrienne Rich, John Ashbery*. New York: Oxford University Press, 1977.

Keller, Lynn. *Re-making it New: Contemporary American Poetry and the Modernist Tradition*. Cambridge: Cambridge University Press, 1987.

Kherdian, David. *Six San Francisco Poets*. Fresno: Geligia, 1969.

Kim, Elaine H. *Asian-American Literature: An Introduction to the Writings and Their Social Context*. Philadelphia: Temple University Press, 1982.

Kostelanetz, Richard. *The New Poetries and Some Old*. Carbondale: Southern Illinois University Press, 1991.

Kuusisto, Stephen, Deborah Tall, David Weiss, eds. *The Poet's Notebook: Excerpts from the Notebooks of Contemporary American Poets*. New York: W.W. Norton, 1995.

Lacey, Paul A. *The Inner War: Forms and Themes in Recent American Poetry*. Philadelphia: Fortress Press, 1972.

Lamon, Martin. ed. *Written in Water, Written in Stone: Twenty Years of Poets on Poetry*. Ann Arbor: University of Michigan Press, 1996.

Larrissy, Edward. *Rereading Twentieth Century Poetry: The Language of Gender and Objects*. Oxford & Cambridge, Mass.: Basil Blackwell, 1990.

Lazer, Hank. *Opposing Poetries*. Evanston, Ill.: Northwestern University Press, 1996.

Lehman, David. *The Line Forms Here*. Ann Arbor: University of Michigan Press, 1992.

Leiberman, Lawrence. *Beyond the Muse of Memory: Essays on Contemporary American Poets*. Columbia: University of Missouri Press, 1995.

―――. *Unassigned Frequencies: American Poetry in Review*. Urbana: University of Illinois Press, 1978.

Lensing, George S. *Four Poets and the Emotive Imagination*. Baton Rouge: Louisiana State University Press, 1976.

Libby, Anthony. *Mythologies of Nothing: Mystical Death in American Poetry*. Urbana: University of Illinois Press, 1984.

Limon, Jose Eduardo. *Mexican Ballads, Chicano Poems: History and Influence in Mexican-American Social Poetry*. Berkeley: University of California Press, 1992.

Lyfshin, Lynn. *Lips Unsealed: Confidences from Contemporary Women Writers*. Santa Barbara: Capra Press, 1990.

Madhubuti, Haki R. *Dynamite Voices*. Detroit: Broadside Press, 1971.

Maio, Samuel. *Creating Another Self: Voice in Modern American Personal Poetry*. Kirksville, Missouri: T. Jefferson University Press, 1995.

Malkoff, Karl. *Crowell's Handbook of American Poetry*. New York: Crowell, 1973.

―――. *Escape from the Self: A Study in Contemporary American Poetry and Poetics*. New York: Columbia University Press, 1977.

Selected Bibliography

Martin, Robert K. *The Homosexual Tradition in American Poetry.* Austin: University of Texas Press, 1979.

Matterson, Stephen. *Berryman and Lowell: The Art of Losing.* Basingstoke: Macmillan, 1988.

Mazzaro, Jerome. *Postmodern American Poetry.* Urbana: University of Illinois Press, 1980.

McClatchy, J.D. *White Paper: On Contemporary American Poetry.* New York: Columbia University Press, 1989.

McCorkle, James. *The Still Performance: Writing, Self, and Interconnection in Five Postmodern American Poets.* Charlottesville: University Press of Virginia, 1989.

———— ,ed. *Conversant Essay: Contemporary Poets on Poetry.* Detroit: Wayne State University Press, 1990.

McDowell, Robert, ed. *Poetry After Modernism.* Brownsville, Oregon: Story Line Press, 1990.

Meiners, R.K. *Everything to be Endured: An Essay on Robert Lowell and Modern Poetry.* Columbia: University of Missouri Press, 1970.

Melhem, D.H. *Heroism in the New Black Poetry.* Lexington: University of Kentucky Press, 1990.

Meltzer, David, ed. *The San Francisco Poets.* New York: Ballantine Books, 1971.

Merrin, Jeredith. *An Enabling Humility: Marianne Moore, Elizabeth Bishop and the Uses of Tradition.* New Brunswick: Rutgers University Press, 1990.

Mersman, James. *Out of the Vietnam Vortex: A Study of Poets and Poetry Against the War.* Lawrence: University Press of Kansas, 1974.

Meyers, Jack and David Wojohn, eds. *A Profile of Twentieth Century American Poetry.* Carbondale: Southern Illinois University Press, 1991.

Meyers, Jeffrey. *Manic Power: Robert Lowell and His Circle.* New York: Arbor House, 1987.

Middlebrook, Diane and Marilyn Yalom. *Coming to Light: American Women Poets in the Twentieth Century.* Ann Arbor: University of Michigan Press, 1985.

Miller, Baxter R. ed. *Black American Poets Between Worlds, 1940–1960.* Knoxville: University of Tennessee Press, 1987.

Mills, Ralph J. *Contemporary American Poetry.* New York: Random House, 1965.

————. *Creation's Very Self: On the Personal Element in Recent American Poetry.* Fort Worth, Texas: TCU Press, 1969.

————. *Cry of the Human: Essays on Contemporary American Poetry.* Urbana, Ill.: University of Illinois Press, 1974.

Mole, John. *Passing Judgments: Poetry in the Eighties.* Bedminster, Bristol: Bristol Classical Press, 1989.

Molesworth, Charles. *The Fierce Embrace: A Study of Contemporary American Poetry.* Columbia: University of Missouri Press, 1979.

Montefiore, Jan. *Feminism and Poetry: Language, Experience, Identity in Women's Writing.* London & New York: Pandora, 1987.

Moyers, Bill. *The Language of Life: A Festival of Poets.* New York: Doubleday, 1995.

Murphy, Margueritte S. *A Tradition of Subversion: The Prose Poem in English from Wilde to Ashbery.* Amherst: University of Massachusetts Press, 1992.

Myers, Jack and David Wojahn eds. *A Profile of Twentieth-Century American Poetry.* Carbondale: Southern Illinois University Press, 1991.

Nelson, Cary. *Our Last First Poets: Vision and History in Contemporary American Poetry.* Urbana: University of Illinois Press, 1981.

Nemerov, Howard, ed. *Poets on Poetry.* New York: Basic Books, 1966.

Nielsen, Aldon Lynn. *Black Chant: Languages of African-American Postmodernism.* Cambridge, England: Cambridge University Press, 1997.

———. *Rereading Race: White American Poets and the Racial Discourse in the Twentieth Century.* Athens, Ga.: University of Georgia Press, 1988.

Oberg, Arthur. *Modern American Lyric: Lowell, Berryman, Creeley and Plath.* New Brunswick: Rutgers University Press, 1978.

Ossman, David. *The Sullen Art: Interviews with Modern American Poets.* New York: Corinth Books, 1963.

Ostriker, Alicia. *Stealing the Language.* Boston: Beacon Press, 1986.

Ostroff, Anthony, ed. *The Contemporary Poet as Artist and Critic.* Boston: Little Brown, 1964.

Pacernick, Gary. *Memory and Fire: Ten American Jewish Poets.* New York: P. Lang, 1989.

Pack, Robert and Jay Parini, eds. *Touchstones: American Poets on a Favorite Poem.* Hanover, New Hampshire: University Press of New England, 1996.

Packard, William, ed. *The Craft of Poetry: Interviews from the New York Quarterly.* Garden City, New York: Doubleday, 1974.

Parini, Jay. *The Columbia History of American Poetry.* New York: Columbia University Press, 1993.

Parkinson, Thomas. *Poets, Poems, Movements.* Ann Arbor: UMI Research Press, 1987.

———, ed. *A Casebook on the Beats.* New York: Crowell, 1961.

Paul, Sherman. *Hewing to Experience: Essays and Reviews on Recent American Poetry and Poetics, Nature and Culture.* Iowa City: University of Iowa Press, 1989.

———. *In Search of the Primitive: Rereading David Antin, Jerome Rothenberg and Gary Snyder.* Baton Rouge: Louisiana State University Press, 1986.

Selected Bibliography

————. *The Lost America of Love: Rereading Robert Creeley, Edward Dorn, and Robert Duncan*. Baton Rouge: Louisiana State University Press, 1981.

Perez-Torres, Rafael. *Movements in Chicano Poetry: Against Myths, Against Margins*. New York: Cambridge University Press, 1995.

Perkins, David. *A History of Modern Poetry*. Vol 2: *Modernism and After*. Cambridge: Belnap Press of Harvard University Press, 1987.

Perloff, Marjorie. *The Dance of the Intellect: Studies in the Poetry of the Pound Tradition*. Cambridge & New York: Cambridge University Press, 1985.

————. *Poetic License: Essays on Modernist and Postmodernist Lyric*. Evanston: Northwestern University Press, 1990.

————. *The Poetics of Indeterminacy: Rimbaud to Cage*. Princeton: Princeton University Press, 1981.

————. *Radical Artifice: Writing Poetry in the Age of Media*. Chicago: University of Chicago Press, 1991.

Philips, Robert S. *The Confessional Poets*. Carbondale: Southern Illinois University Press, 1973.

Pinsky, Robert. *Poetry and the World*. New York: Ecco Press, 1988.

————. *The Situation of Poetry: Contemporary Poetry and its Traditions*. Princeton: Princeton University Press, 1976.

Pope Deborah. *A Separate Vision: Isolation and Contemporary Women's Poetry*. Baton Rouge: Louisiana State University Press, 1984.

Prunty, Wyatt. *Fallen from the Symboled World: Precedents for the New Formalism*. New York: Oxford University Press, 1990.

Redmond, Eugene. *Drumvoices: The Mission of Afro-American Poetry, A Critical History*. Garden City, New York: Anchor Press, 1976.

Reinfeld, Linda. *Language Poetry: Writing as Rescue*. Baton Rouge: Louisiana State University Press, 1992.

Rexroth, Kenneth. *American Poetry in the Twentieth Century*. New York: Herder & Herder, 1971.

Rosenthal, M.L. *The New Poets: American and British Poetry Since World War II*. New York: Oxford University Press, 1967.

————. *Our Life In Poetry: Selected Essays and Reviews*. New York: Persea Books, 1991.

Sanchez, Marta Ester. *Contemporary Chicana Poetry: A Critical Approach to an Emerging Literature*. Berkeley: University of California Press, 1985.

Shaw, Robert, ed. *American Poetry Since 1960: Some Critical Perspectives*. 1974.

Shetley, Vernon. *After the Death of Poetry: Poet and Audience in Contemporary America*. Durham, North Carolina: Duke University Press, 1993.

Silliman, Ronald. *The New Sentence*. New York: Roof Press, 1987.

Simpson Louis. *A Revolution in Taste: Studies of Dylan Thomas, Allen Ginsberg, Sylvia Plath and Robert Lowell*. New York: Macmillan, 1978.

Spiegelman, Willard. *The Didactic Muse: Scenes of Instruction in Contemporary American Poetry*. Princeton: Princeton University Press, 1989.

Stein, Kevin. *Private Poets, Worldly Acts: Public and Private History in Contemporary American Poetry.* Athens: Ohio University Press, 1996.

Stephanchev, Stephen. *American Poetry Since 1945.* New York: Harper & Row, 1965.

Sutton, Walter. *American Free Verse: The Modern Revolution in Poetry.* New York: New Directions, 1973.

Swann, Brian, and Arnold Krupat. *I Tell You Now.* Lincoln: University of Nebraska Press, 1987.

Taggart, John. *Songs of Degrees: Essays on Contemporary Poetry and Poetics.* Tuscaloosa: University of Alabama Press, 1994.

Taylor, Henry. *Compulsory Figures: Essays on Recent American Poets.* Baton Rouge: Louisiana State University Press, 1992.

Thurley, Geoffrey. *The American Moment: American Poetry in the Mid-Century.* London: Edward Arnold, 1977.

Tytell, John. *Naked Angels: The Lives and Literature of the Beat Generation.* New York: McGraw-Hill, 1976.

Vendler, Helen. *The Given and the Made: Strategies of Poetic Redefinition.* Cambridge, Mass: Harvard University Press, 1995.

———. *The Music of What Happens: Poems, Poets, Critics.* Cambridge; Harvard University Press, 1988.

———. *Soul Says: On Recent Poetry.* Cambridge, Mass.: Belknap Press of Harvard University Press, 1995.

Von Halberg, Robert. *American Poetry and Culture, 1945-1980.* Cambridge, Mass.: Harvard University Press, 1985.

Walker, Cheryl. *Masks Outrageous and Austere: Culture, Psyche and Persona in Modern Women Poets.* Bloomington: Indiana University Press, 1991.

Ward, Geoff. *Statutes of Liberty: The New York School of Poets.* New York: St. Martin's Press, 1993.

Whitehead, Kim. *The Feminist Poetry Movement.* Jackson, Mississippi: University Press of Mississippi, 1996.

Wiget, Andrew. *Native American Literature.* Boston: Twayne Publishers, 1985.

Williamson, Alan. *Eloquence and Mere Life: Essays on the Art of Poetry.* Ann Arbor, Michigan: University of Michigan Press, 1994.

———. *Introspection and Contemporary Poetry.* Cambridge: Harvard University Press, 1984.

Woods, Gregory. *Articulate Flesh: Male Homoeroticism in Modern Poetry.* New Haven: Yale University Press, 1987.

Yorke, Liz. *Impertinent Voices: Subversive Strategies in Contemporary Women's Poetry.* London & New York: Routledge, 1991.

· Index ·

abstract expressionism, 3, 28, 89, 93
African-American poetry, 246–47
Aguero, Kathleen, 328
Aiiieeeee!, 305
Algarén Miguel, 277
Allen, Donald, *The New American Poetry*, 2, 314, 315, 322, 324
Allen, Paula Gunn, 165, 293
Aloud: Voices from the Nuyorican Cafe, 277
Altieri, Charles, 159, 205
Alurista, **295–98**, 300, 301; *A'ngue*, 296; *Floricanto in Aztlan*, 297; *Nationchild Plumaroja*, 297; *Return: Poems Collected and New*, 296; *Spik in Glyph?*, 296; *Timespace Huracan*, 296, 297
Alvarez, A., 87
America: A Prophecy, 316
American Poetry Since 1970: Up Late, 324, 325–26
Ammons, A. R., 124, **149–54**: "Bees Stopped," 150; "Cascadilla Falls," 149; "City Limits, The," 152; "Corson's Inlet," 149, 151–52; "Delaware Water Gap," 149; *Garbage*, 153; "Gravelly Run," 150; "Guide," 151; *Ommateum*, 149; "One: Many," 151; *Really Short Poems*, 152; *Selected Poems: Expanded Edition*, 149; "So I Said I Am Ezra," 149; *Sphere: The Form of a Motion*, 153; "Still," 151; *Tape for the Turn of the Year*, 153
Andrews, Bruce, 320
anti-Semitism, 252, 254
Antler, 325
Anzaldúa, Gloria, 165, 295, 298, **300–04**; *Borderlands: La Frontera*, 300, 303; "Coatlicue State, The," 303; "Entering Into the Serpent," 302; "I Had to Go Down," 303; "Letting Go," 303; *Making Face, Making Soul*, 300, 303; "Nopalitos," 302; "sonavabitche, El," 301; "sus plumas el viento," 301; *This Bridge Called My Back*, 303; "We Call Them Greasers," 301
Armies of the Night, The, 14
Armstrong, Louis, 309
Arreola, Juan Jose, 209

Asentewa, Yaa, 178
Ashbery, John, 74, 89, **93–99**, 104, 108, 124, 133, 152, 315, 321, 326, 327: *And the Stars Were Shining*, 99; *April Galleons*, 98; *As We Know*, 98; *Can You Hear, Bird*, 99; *Double Dream of Spring, The*, 98; *Flow Chart*, 98; "Haibun," 98; *Hotel Lautréamont*, 98, 99; *Houseboat Days*, 98; "Leaving the Atocha Station," 94; "Litany," 98; "Our Youth," 94; "Painter, The," 93; *Rivers and Mountains*, 94, 95; "Saying it to Keep it from Happening," 98; "Self-Portrait in a Convex Mirror," 96–98; *Self-Portrait in a Convex Mirror*, 96; *Shadow Train*, 98; "Skaters, The," 95; *Some Trees*, 93; *Tennis Court Oath, The*, 74, 93, 321; "These Lacustrine Cities," 94–95; *Three Poems*, 96; *Wave, A*, 98
Asher, Elise, 31
Asian-American Literature, 306
Asian-American poetry, 304–5
Associated Writing Programs Chronicle, 323, 324
Auden, W. H., 1, 6, 29, 91, 123, 147, 148, 204, 230, 231
Axelrod, Stephen, 16

Bacon, Francis, 103
Bahai religion, 56
Baldwin, James, 262
Baraka, Amiri, 49, 50, 124, 247, **248–55**, 260, 315, 316; *Autobiography*, 249, 251, 253; *Baraka Reader, The*, 248; "Black Art: A Poem," 252; *Black Fire*, 251; *Black Magic*, 251, 252; *Black Music*, 251; *Blues People*, 250; *Dead Lecturer, The*, 250; "Dictatorship of the Proletariat, The," 253; *Dutchman*, 250; *Four Black Revolutionary Plays*, 251; *Funklore*, 254; *Hard Facts*, 253; *Home: Social Essays*, 251; "How You Sound," 249; "In the Tradition," 254; *It's Nation Time*, 252; "Ka 'Ba," 252; "Liar, The," 250–51; "Notes for a Speech," 250; "Poem for Black Hearts, A," 252; "Poem Some People Will Have

Index

Baraka, Amiri (*continued*)
to Understand, A," 252; *Preface to a
Twenty Volume Suicide Note*, 250;
"Rhythm of Blues," 250; *System of
Dante's Hell, The*, 251; "Toward
Ideological Clarity," 253;
Transbluesency, 254; "Why's/Wise,"
254; *Why's, Wise, Y's*, 254
Barlow, Jim, 52
Bass, Ellen, 44, 316
beat generation, 79, 127, 191, 315
Beatles, 77
Beethoven, Ludwig van, 116
Bellow, Saul, 168
Bernikow, Louise, 44
Bernstein, Charles, 320
Berrigan, Dan, 66
Berrigan, Ted, 325
Berryman, John, 15, **31–36**, 37, 85, 115,
129; "Ball Poem, The," 35;
Dispossessed, The, 35; *Dream Songs,
The*, 15, 33–36; "Dream Song 77," 35;
"Dream Song 153," 31; "Dream Song
384," 32; "Eleven Addresses to the
Lord," 32; *His Toy, His Dream, His
Rest*, 36; *Homage to Mistress
Bradstreet*, 33, 35; *Love and Fame*, 32;
Recovery, 36; *77 Dream Songs*, 35
Bidart, Frank, 15, **239–41**;
"Confessional," 239, 240; "Elegy,"
239; "Ellen West," 239; *In the Western
Night: Collected Poems: 1965–1990*, 239
Biko, Steve, 51
biomythography, 74, 117–18
Bishop, Elizabeth, 1, 12, **17–22**, 37, 53,
58, 148, 164, 235, 262; "At the
Fishhouses," 18; "Burglar of
Babylon, The," 18; *Cold Spring, A*, 17;
Complete Poems, 17; *Geography III*, 17,
18, 20; "In the Waiting Room,"
19–20; "Large Bad Picture," 18;
"Man Moth," 19; "Miracle for
Breakfast, A," 18; "Moose, The,"
20–21; *North & South*, 17; "One Art,"
17, 18; "Pink Dog," 21; "Poem," 18;
Questions of Travel, 17; "Roosters,"
18, 21; "Visits to St. Elizabeth," 18
black aesthetics, 49, 250–51, 259
black arts movement, 247, 248, 273,
274, 315
Blackburn, Paul, 100
Black Fire, 316
Black Mountain College, 73, 315

Black Mountain poets, 64, 69, 99, 100
Black Mountain Review, 99, 123
Blackmur, Richard, 31
black nationalism, 251, 266
Black Panthers, 266
Black Poets, The, 315
Blackwood, Caroline, 15, 16
Blake, William, 26, 75, 76
Blakely II, Henry, 46
Blazer, Robin, 68
Blok, Alexander, 209
Bloom, Harold, 149, 150
Blumenthal, Michael, 195, 319
Bly, Robert, 28, 65, 74, **104–8**, 123, 133,
195, 282; "Afterthoughts," 105; *Eight
Stages of Translation, The*, 107; "Form
that is Neither In nor Out," 108;
"Leaping Up into Political Poetry,"
106; "Looking for Dragon Smoke,"
107; "Lute of Three Loudnesses,
The," 105; "Man Writes to a Part of
Himself, A," 106; *Morning Poems*,
108; *Selected Poems*, 105
Boch, Otto, 41
Bogan, Louise, 144
Bonnefoy, Yves, 197
Borges, Jorge Luis, 209
Bottoms, David, 323
Bourdeille, Michel de, 218
*Breadloaf Anthology of Contemporary
American Poetry*, 318–19
Breaking Silence, 313
Breslin, James: *From Modern to
Contemporary*, 2
Breslin, Paul, 276
Bridge, The, 39, 198, 231, 272
Brooks, David, 45
Brooks, Gwendolyn, 37, 38, **45–52**, 124,
163, 246, 247, 248, 260, 266, 276;
"Anniad, The," 48; *Annie Allen*, 45,
47; "ballad of chocolate Mabbie,
the," 47; "Ballad of Pearly May Lee,
The," 47; "Ballad of Rudolph Reed,
The," 48; "battle, the," 47; *Bean
Eaters, The*, 46, 48; *Beckonings*, 51;
"Beverly Hills, Chicago," 48; *Blacks*,
51; "Bronzeville Mother Loiters in
Mississippi, A," 48; "Bronzeville
Woman in a Red Hat," 48; "Chicago
Defender Sends a Man to Little
Rock, The," 48; *Family Pictures*, 51;
"Gay Chaps at the Bar," 46;
Gottschalk and the Grande Tarantelle,

Index

52; "I love these little booths at Bevenute's," 48; "In Honor of David Anderson Brooks, My Father," 45; "In the Mecca," 51; *In the Mecca*, 50; "kitchenette building," 46; "Langston Hughes," 45; "Life of Lincoln West," 51; "Lovers of the Poor," 48; *Maud Martha*, 51; "murder, the," 46; "Negro Hero," 47; "Of Robert Frost," 46; *Primer for Blacks*, 51; "Queen of the Blues," 47; *Riot*, 51; "Sermons on the Warpland," 51; *Street in Bronzesville, A*, 46; "To Those of My Sisters Who Kept Their Naturals," 51; "Wall, The," 50; "when Mrs. Martin's Booker T," 47; "Womanhood, The," 48

Brooks, Keziah, 45

Broumas, Olga, 163, 193; "Namaste," 193; *Soie Sauvage*, 193

Brown, H. Rap, 56

Brown, John, 40

Brown, Sterling, **246–47**, 249, 254, 264, 270, 271, 276; *Negro Caravan, The*, 247; "Slim in Hell," 247; "Southern Road," 247

Bruce-Novoa, Juan, 295, 296, 297, 298

Bruchac, Joseph, 278, 279, 282, 313

Brueghel, Pieter, 85

Bryant, William Cullen, 215

Buddha Bandits Down Highway 99, The, 305, 308

Bukowski, Charles, 326

Burago, José Antonio, 298

Burroughs, William, 101

Cantos, The, 15, 231

Carr, Emily, 82

Carriers of the Dream Wheel, 316

Carter, Jimmy, 143

Carver, Raymond, **241–44**; "Boat, The," 244; "Elephant," 242; "Gravy," 244; "Mail, The," 242; "Memory," 243; *New Path to the Waterfall, A*, 241; "Party, The," 242; "Projectile, The," 243; "This Morning," 243; *Ultramarine*, 242; "What the Doctor Said," 244; *Where Water Comes Together with Other Water*, 242

Cash, W. J., 141

Catholicism, 12, 36, 126, 183

Cesairé, Aimé, 271

Chan, Paul Jeffrey, 305

Chants de Maldoror, Les, 99

Chicago Seven, 75

Chicano Authors, 296

Chicano Poetry, 196

Chi-Ha, Kim, 41

Chin, Frank, 305

Chu-i, Po, 110–11

City Lights bookstore, 75

Clampitt, Amy, 133, 321

Clark, Dick, 308

Cleaver, Elridge, 259, 266

Cleveland State University Poetry Center, 123

Clifton, Lucille, **264–69**; "after kent state," 266; *Book of Light, The*, 269; "dream of foxes, a," 269; "From the Cadavers," 269; *Generations: A Memoir*, 265; *Good News about the Earth*, 265, 266; *Good Times*, 264, 265, 266; *Ordinary Woman, An*, 267; "some jesus," 267; *Terrible Stories, The*, 264, 269; *Two-Headed Woman*, 267, 268; "way it was, the," 266

Clinton, Bill, 84

Codrescu, Andrei, 123, 322, 324, 325, 326

Cold War, 304

Coleman, Wanda, 325

Coleridge, Samuel Taylor, 91

Coltrane, John, 234, 254, 275

confessional poetry, 27, 29, 114, 166, 191, 204, 293

Contemporary American Poetry, 314

Controversy of Poets, A, 315

Coolidge, Clark, 320

Cooper, Jane, 45

Corso, Gregory, 75, 321; *Elegiac Feelings American*, 75

Crane, Hart, 23, 39, 40, 62, 198, 231, 272

Crane, Stephen, 85

Creeley, Robert, 28, 64, 69, 74, **99–104**, 105, 123, 249; *Day Book, A*, 102; *Echoes*, 104; *For Love*, 74, 99, 100, 101; *Hello*, 102; "I Know a Man," 102; "Introduction to New Writing in the USA," 101; *Later*, 102; "Memory, 1930," 103; *Mirrors*, 103; "Myself," 102; *Pieces*, 102; "Place," 103; *Sense of Measure, A*, 100; *Thirty Things*, 102; "Waiting," 102; "Warning, The," 102; "Whip, The," 102; "Wicker Basket, A," 102; *Words*, 102

"Crossing Brooklyn Ferry," 198, 222

Index

Cruz, Victor Hernandez, 277
cubism, 320
Cullen, Countee, 246
Cummings, E. E., 1, 23, 39, 94, 211, 325

Dacey, Philip, 321
Dadaists, 92
Daniels, Kate, 108
Davidson, Donald, 6, 138
Davidson, Michael, 68, 157
Davie, Donald, 215
Davies, Sir John: "Orchestra," 25
Davis, Miles, 248, 254, 273, 275, 308
Davison, Peter, 237
Dawson, Fielding, 99
de Kooning, Willem, 3, 28, 90
"Delight in Disorder," 195
de Prima, Diane, **191**; "Loba," 191;
    Selected Poems: 1956–75, 191
Des Pres, Terence, 83, 133, 134, 136
Dices or Black Bones, 316
Dickens, Charles, 109
Dickey, James, 7, 71, 105, **138–43**; "At
    Darien Bridge," 138; "Buckdancer's
    Choice," 138–39; *Buckdancer's Choice*,
    138; "Chenille," 138, 139; "Cherrylog
    Road," 138; *Deliverance*, 138, 141;
    "Encounter in Cage Country," 140;
    "Falling," 142; "Firebombing," 142;
    "Heaven of Animals, The," 140; "In
    the Mountain Tent," 138, 140; *In the
    Stone*, 138; "May Day Sermon," 139,
    141, 142; "Owl King, The," 140; "Salt
    Marsh," 138, 140; "Sharks Parlor,
    The," 138; "Sheep Child, The," 140;
    "Slave Quarters," 138, 141, 142;
    "Springer Mountain," 138, 140;
    Strength of Fields, The, 143; *Whole
    Motion, The: Collected Poems,
    1945–1992*, 143
Dickinson, Emily, 153, 264, 278, 280
Dine, Mark, 27
Direction of Poetry, The, 317, 322, 325
Dobyns, Stephen, 319
Dolittle, Hilda, 64, 163, 191
Donogue, Denis, 203
Dorn, Ed, 99
Dos Passos, John, 40
Doty, George, 110
Dove, Rita, 319
Du Bois, W. E. B, 254
Ducasse, Isidore, 99
Duchamp, Marcel, 92

Dunbar, Paul Lawrence, 45
Duncan, Robert, 37, 64, **68–72**, 249, 315;
    "African Elegy, An," 72; *Bending the
    Bow*, 70; *Fictive Certainties*, 70;
    "Homosexual in Society, The," 72; "I
    Am a Most Fleshy Man," 72;
    "Multiversity Passage, The," 71;
    "My Mother Would Be a
    Falconress," 71; "Often I am
    Permitted to Return to a Meadow,"
    69, 70; *Opening of the Field, The*, 69;
    "Poem Beginning with a Line by
    Pindar," 70; "Santa Cruz
    Propositions," 72; "Structure of
    Rime," 70
Dylan, Bob, 77

Ear to the Ground, An, 328
Eberhart, Richard, 76
Edel, Leon, 276
Edwards, Jonathan, 10
Eichmann, Adolf, 169
Eliot, T. S., 1, 11, 27, 61, 73, 76, 84, 92,
    93, 94, 100, 104, 123, 196, 208, 219,
    222, 231, 249, 275
Ellison, Ralph, 54, 274
Emerson, Ralph Waldo, 40, 124, 149
Epstein, Joseph, 323
Equi, Elaine, 327
Ernst, Max, 92
ethnopoetics, 316
Evans, Mari, 49
Evers, Medgar, 50, 250, 263, 269
Everson, William, **124–29**, 132; "Black
    Hills," 128; "Canticle to the
    Waterbirds, A," 126; *Crooked Lines of
    God, The*, 128; *Man-Fate*, 127; *Naked
    Heart*, 128; *Residual Years, The*, 126;
    River Root, 127; *Rose of Solitude, The*,
    127; "Scout, The," 128; "Tendril in
    the Mesh," 127; "Time to Mourn, A,"
    128; *Veritable Years, The*, 126; "Vow,
    The," 125
existentialism, 281
Expansive Poetry, 322
Exquisite Corpse, 123

Fabilli, Mary, 126
Fallen from the Symboled World, 322
Fanon, Franz, 257
fascism, 40
Faulkner, William, 141
Feirstein, Frederick, 322

Index

feminism, 41, 42, 43, 48, 82, 170, 176, 179, 194, 195, 267, 303, 311
Ferlinghetti, Lawrence, 75, 100, 127
"Fern Hill," 8
Fiedler, Leslie, 7
Field, Edward, 317
Fifties, 123
Fitzgerald, F. Scott, 225
Flaubert, Gustav, 12
Ford, Ford Maddox, 10
Ford, Henry, 40
formalist poets, 148, 191
Four Quartets, 219
Franco, Francisco, 41
Frausto, Thomas Ybarra, 296
Freud, Sigmund, 184
Friedman, Norman, 112
Frost, Robert, 1, 6, 7, 9, 17, 46, 58, 132, 146, 148, 149, 154
Fugitive, 6, 122, 138
Fugitive poets, 6, 138

Gallagher, Tess, 241
Gelpi, Albert, 126
Geography of Poets, A, 317
Georgia Review, 123
Gibbons, Reginald, 223
Gibbs, Willard, 40
Gibson, Kenneth, 253
Gillespie, Dizzy, 248
Ginsberg, Allen, 12, 73, **75–79**, 89, 93, 100, 104, 108, 123, 124, 127, 196, 206, 249, 319, 321; *Collected Poems*, 77; "Contest of the Bards," 78; *Cosmopolitan Greetings*, 78; *Fall of America, The*, 75, 78; "Father Death," 78; *Howl*, 76–77; *Howl and Other Poems*, 73, 75; "Improvisation in Beijing," 78; "Kaddish," 76, 78; "Kraj Majales," 78; *Mind Breaths*, 78; *Planet News*, 123; "Please Master," 78; *Plutonian Ode*, 75; "Poem of These States," 78; "Put Down Your Cigarette Rag," 79; "Siesta in Xbalba," 78; "Supermarket in California, A," 78; "Wales Visitation," 78; *White Shroud*, 78; "Wichita Vortex Sutra," 78
Gioia, Dana, 148, 321, 324
Giovanni, Nikki, 248
Glück, Louise, 163, **192–93**, 319; *Ararat*, 193; *Descending Figure*, 192; "Elms," 193; *Firstborn*, 192; *House on the*

Marshlands, The, 192; *Triumph of Achilles, The*, 193
Goebbels, Joseph, 230
Goldbarth, Albert, 319
Gonzales, Rodolpho, **294–95**, **301**; *I Am Joaquin*, 294
Goodman, Mitchell, 63
Graham, Jorie, 319, 326, 327
Grahn, Judy, 191; "Woman is Talking to Death, A," 191; *Work of a Common Woman, The*, 191
Great Depression, 1, 23
Gregg, Linda, 327
Guest, Barbara, 315
Gunn, Thom, 72

Hacker, Marilyn, 163, **191–92**; *Going Back to the River*, 191; *Love, Death, and the Changing of the Seasons*, 192; *Presentation Piece*, 191
Haines, John, 122
Hall, Donald, 105, 108, 196, 197, **215–19**, 314, 315, 323, 326, 327; "Barnyards," 217; "Build a House," 218; "Day I Was Older, The," 217; *Day I Was Older, The*, 216; "Days, The," 216, 217; "Eating the Pig," 216; "Four Classics Texts," 218; *Happy Man, The*, 217; *Kicking the Leaves*, 215–16; "Maple Syrup," 217; "Men Driving Cars," 217; "Merle Bascom's .22," 217; "My Son, My Executioner," 216; *One Day, The*, 216, 218; "Shrubs Burned Away," 217, 218; "Sisters," 217–18; "To a Waterfowl," 215; *Writing Well*, 215
Hamer, Fannie Lou, 178
Hardwick, Elizabeth, 13, 15
Hardy, Thomas, 132
Harlem Gallery, 276
Harlem Renaissance, 38, 45, 122, 245, 246, 271
Harper, Michael, 247, 272, **273–76**; "Blue Ruth: America," 275; "Brother John," 274; "Clark's Way West: Another Version," 274; *Dear John, Dear Coltrane*, 274; "Debridement," 275; *Healing Song for the Inner Ear*, 274, 276; "High Modes: Vision as Ritual: Confirmation," 275; *History Is Your Own Heartbeat*, 275; *Images of Kin*, 275, 276; *Photographs: Negatives: History as Apple Tree*, 274; "24th

Index

Harper, Michael (*continued*)
  Avenue: City of Roses:
  Anesthesia:2," 275
*Harper's Anthology of Twentieth-Century
  Native American Poetry,* 316
Harris, Marie, 328
Harris, William J., 248
Hart, Jane, 40
*Harvard Book of Contemporary American
  Poetry, The,* 318, 319
Hass, Robert, 109, **237–39**; *Field Guide,*
  237; "Heroic Simile," 237; *Human
  Wishes,* 237; "On Squaw Peak,"
  238–39; *Praise,* 237; "Privilege of
  Being," 238; "Santa Barbara Road,"
  237–38; *Twentieth-Century Pleasures,*
  237
Hatcher, John, 54
Hawkins, Bobby Louise, 102
Hawkins, Coleman, 234
Hawthorne, Nathaniel, 4, 11
Hayden, Robert, 37, 38, **52–58**, 246, 274;
  "Ballad of Remembrance," 55; *Ballad
  of Remembrance, A,* 52; "Ballad of Sue
  Ellen Westerfield, The," 52; "Elegies
  for Paradise Valley," 53; "For A
  Young Artist," 57; "Letter from
  Phyllis Wheatley," 55; "Middle
  Passage," 55–56; "Monet's
  Waterlilies," 53; "Night Blooming
  Cereus, The," 55; "Night, Death,
  Mississippi," 55; "Nine-Pointed
  Star," 54–55; "Stars," 54; "Tattooed
  Man, The," 54; "Those Winter
  Sundays," 54; "Whipping, The," 53
Hayden, Sue, 52
Hayden, William, 52
Hayden's Ferry Review, 123
Hecht, Anthony, 166
Hejinian, Lyn, 320
Herrick, Robert, 195
Highton, Penelope, 102
Hiroshima, 1, 201, 292, 293, 307, 311
Hitler, Adolf, 62, 72, 230
Hoagland, Everett, 316
Hoffman, Hans, 3
Holiday, Billy, 90, 308, 309
Holman, Bobm, 277
Holmes, John, 143, 165
Holocaust, 1, 40, 147, 169, 199, 230
Homer, 70, 231, 237
homosexual poetry, 72, 78
Hongo, Garrett Kaouri, 305

Hopper, Edward, 213
Horan, Robert, 61
House Un-American Activities
  Committee, 40
Howe, Florence, 44, 316
Hughes, Langston, 6, 45, 46, 52, 246,
  254, 260, 262, 264, 266, 271; *Weary
  Blues,* 46
Hughes, Ted, 85, 86, 119
Hugo, Richard, 123
Hurston, Zora Neale, 276

Ignatow, David, 105, 106, 124
I'll Take My Stand, 138
Inada, Lawson Fusao, **305–9**, 310;
  "Bandstand," 308; *Before the War:
  Poems as They Happened,* 305–6; *Big
  Aiiieeeee!, The,* 305, 309;
  "Concentration Constellation," 307;
  "Countries of War," 308; *Drawing the
  Line,* 309; "From Our Album," 306;
  "Inada Report, The," 308; "I Told
  You So," 305; "Jazz," 308; "Journey,
  The," 308; "Legends from Camp,"
  307; *Legends from Camp,* 307, 308, 309;
  "Plucking Out a Rhythm," 306;
  "Report from the New Country,"
  307; "Right on 99," 305
"In Dreams Begin Responsibilities,"
  186
In the American Tree, 320

James, Henry, 276
Jarman, Mark, 319
Jarrell, Randall, 1, **6–9**, 10, 18, 23, 31, 37,
  135, 219; *Complete Poems, The,* 8;
  "Death of the Ball Turrett Gunner,
  The," 7; "Losses," 7; *Lost World, The,*
  8; *Pictures from an Institution,* 6;
  Poetry and the Age, 6, 44; *Sad Heart at
  the Supermarket, A,* 6; *Third Book of
  Criticism, The,* 6; "Woman at the
  Washington Zoo, The," 8
Jauss, David, 321
Jeffers, Robinson, 23, 26, 122, 124, 205,
  208, 299
Jesus, 40, 231
Jimenez, Juan Ramon, 104
Johnson, James Weldon, 45, 246
Johnson, Lyndon, 14, 72
Johnson, Magic, 273
Jones, Angel, 62
Jones, Leroi. *See* Baraka, Amiri

Index

Jones, Richard, 108
Jones, Rodney, 327
Jordan, June, 108
Jordan, Michael, 273
Joyce, James, 249
Juarroz, Roberto, 209
Juhasz, Suzanne, 164
Justice, Donald, 3, 4, 6, 321

Kabir, 107
Kalstone, David, 232
Kandinsky, Wassily, 92
Kantorowicz, Ernest, 68
Karenga, Ron, 253
Keats, John, 69, 211
Kees, Weldon, 3–6, 8, 23, 37, 219;
"Aspects," 5; *Collected Poems of
Weldon Kees, The*, 3; *Fall of the
Magicians, The*, 3, 4; "Fugue," 4; *Last
Man, The*, 3; "1926," 5; "Place of
Execution," 4; *Poems: 1947–1954*, 3, 4;
"Salvo for Hans Hoffman," 5;
"Travels in North America," 4–5;
"Turtle," 5
Kelly, Robert, 315
Kennedy, John F., 250
Kennedy, Robert, 14, 56
Kennedy, X. J., 321
Kenner, Hugh, 86
Kenny, Maurice, 248
Kenyon Review, 72
Kerouac, Jack, 127
Kerr, Clark, 71
Kertesz, Louise, 39
Kesey, Ken, 75
Kim, Elaine H., 306, 308
King, Martin Luther, Jr., 51, 56, 263
Kingston, Maxine Hong, 310
Kinnell, Galway, 154, 196, 197–202, 327;
"Avenue Bearing the Initial of Christ
into the New World, The," 197,
198–99; "Bear, The," 197, 199–200;
Body Rags, 197; *Book of Nightmares,
The*, 197, 200–201, 202; "Cellist,
The," 202; "First Day of the Future,
The," 201; *Flower Herding on Mount
Monadnock*, 197; "Fundamental
Project of Technology, The," 201, 319;
"Holy Shit," 202; *Imperfect Thirst*,
197, 202; "Lastness," 200; *Mortal
Acts, Mortal Words*, 197, 201; "On the
Oregon Coast," 201; *Past, The*, 197;
"Porcupine, The," 197, 199;

"Rapture," 202; "Road Between Here
and There, The," 201; *Selected Poems*,
197; "Under the Maud Moon," 197,
200; *What a Kingdom It Was*, 197;
"When One Has Lived a Long Time
Alone," 202; *When One Has Lived a
Long Time Alone*, 197, 202
Kirby, David, 220
Kierkegaard, Søren, 225
Kizer, Carolyn, 123
Klee, Paul, 92
Kline, Franz, 28, 90
Knight, Etheridge, 66, 257, 259–64, 265,
321; "Belly Song," 262, 264; *Belly
Song*, 262; *Black Voices from Prison*,
260, 262; *Born of a Woman*, 259, 262;
"Con / Tin / U / Way / Shun
Blues," 262; *Essential Etheridge
Knight, The*, 264; "Feeling, Fucked
Up," 262; "Hard Rock Returns to
Prison from the Hospital for the
Criminally Insane," 260; "Idea of
Ancestry, The," 263; "It Was A Funky
Deal," 262; *Poems from Prison*, 260;
"Report To the Mother, 262; "Upon
Your Leaving," 261–62; "Violent
Space, The," 261; "Warden Said to
Me the Other Day, The," 261; "Wasp
Woman, A," 263
Koch, Kenneth, 124, 249
Kollwitz, Käthe, 40
Komunyakaa, Yusef, 327
Koolish, Lynda, 177
Korean War, 135, 138, 259
Kowit, Steve, 324
Kroll, Judith, 86
Kumin, Maxine, 143–49, 165, 166;
"Address to the Angels," 147;
"Amsterdam Poem, The," 147;
Connecting the Dots, 148;
"Continuum: A Love Poem," 145;
"Custodian," 146; "Encounter in
August," 146; "Envelope of Almost
Infinity," 144; "Heaven as Anus,"
147; "Hermit Poems, The," 145;
House, Bridge, Fountain, Gate, 145; "In
the Pea Patch," 146; "January 25th,"
145; "Lines Written in the Library of
Congress After the Cleanth Brooks
Lecture," 147; *Long Approach, The*,
147; *Looking for Luck*, 148; "My Great
Grandfather: A Message Long
Overdue," 144; "Nightmare," 144;

Kumin, Maxine (*continued*)
  Nightmare Factory, The, 145; *Nurture,*
  146; *Our Ground Time Here Will Be
  Brief,* 146; "Pasture Poems," 145;
  "Pawnbroker, The," 144; "Summer
  of the Watergate Hearings, The,"
  147; "Tribal Poems, The," 144; *Up
  Country,* 145; "Vealers, The," 146
Kumin, Victor, 143
Kunitz, Solomon, 27
Kunitz, Stanley, 1, **26–31**, 37, 154;
  "Father and Son," 29; "Haley's
  Comet," 31; "Hemorrhage, The," 28;
  "In a Strange House," 28; *Intellectual
  Things,* 26, 28, 29; *Kind of Order, A
  Kind of Folly, A,* 27; "Layers, The,"
  28, 30; "My Mother's Pears," 31;
  *Next to Last Things: New Poems and
  Essays,* 27; "Old Cracked Tune," 27;
  Passing Through: The Later Poems, 31;
  Passport to War, 28, 29; *Selected Poems:
  1928–58,* 30; *Testing-Tree, The,* 30
Kunitz, Yetta, 27
Kurosawa, Akira, 237

Laing, R. D., 34
Language Poetry, 320, 324, 325
language poets, 318
Lau, Alan Chong, 305
Lawrence, D. H., 158
Lea, Sidney, 318
Leary, Paris, 315
Leaves of Grass, 317
Lee, Don. *See* Madhubuti, Haki
Lehman, David, 326, 327
Leithauser, Brad, 321
Lenin, 253
Leong, George, 312
lesbian, 82, 174, 178, 191, 302
Levertov, Beatrice, 62–63, 315
Levertov, Denise, 37, 38, 40, 44, 45,
  62–68, 69, 72, 105, 268, 315; "Ache of
  Marriage, The," 65; "Age of Terror,
  The," 67; "Altars in the Street, The,"
  65; "Calvary Path, A," 67; *Candles in
  Babylon,* 67; "Death in Mexico," 63;
  Door in the Hive, A, 67; "El Salvador:
  Requiem and Invocation," 67;
  "Evening Train," 67; *Evening Train,*
  67; *Freeing of the Dust, The,* 63;
  "Hypocrite Women," 65; "In
  Memory of Muriel Rukeyser," 67;
  "Lamentation, A," 66; *Light Up the
  Cave,* 63; "Matins," 65; "90th Year,
  The," 63; "Olga Poems," 66; "On the
  Function of the Line," 64;
  "Pleasures," 65; *Poet in the World,
  The,* 63; "Primary Wonder," 67;
  Relearning the Alphabet, 66; *Sands of
  the Well,* 67; *Sorrow Dance, The,*
  65–66; "Time Past, A," 65; *To Stay
  Alive,* 66; "Two Variations," 65;
  "Wedding Ring," 65; "What It Could
  Be," 67; "What Were They Like?" 65
Levine, Philip, 133, 196, **209–15**, 224,
  327; "Asking," 213; *Bread of Time,
  The: Toward an Autobiography,* 214;
  "Cutting Edge, The," 211; "Letters
  for the Dead," 213; "My Father with
  Cigarette Twelve Years Before the
  Nazis Could Break His Heart," 214;
  "My Mother with Purse the Summer
  They Murdered the Spanish Poet,"
  214; "My Son and I," 214; *Names of
  the Lost, The,* 214; "1933," 213–14;
  1933, 213; "One for the Rose," 212;
  On the Edge, 209; "Poem Circling
  Hamtramck, Michigan, All Night in
  Search of You, The," 213; "Silent in
  America," 212; *Simple Truth, The,* 214;
  "They Feed They Lion," 211; *They
  Feed They Lion,* 211; "Walk With
  Thomas Jefferson, A," 214; *Walk With
  Thomas Jefferson, A,* 214; *What Work
  Is,* 209, 214
Lewis and Clark, 274
Lillabularo, 233
Lincoln, Abraham, 70
Logan, John, 105
Lorca, Federico Garcia, 104, 107, 211,
  249
Lorde, Audre, 42, 163, 165, **174–79**, 181,
  269; *Black Unicorn,* 177; *Cancer
  Journals, The,* 178; "Cell," 178; *Chosen
  Poems,* 176; "Death Dance for a
  Poet," 177; *Marvelous Arithmetics of
  Distance, The,* 179; "Need," 176;
  "125th Street and Abomey," 177; *Our
  Dead behind Us,* 178; "Poetry is Not a
  Luxury," 174; *Sister Outsider,* 174; "To
  the Poet Who Happens to be Black
  and the Black Poet Who Happens to
  be a Woman," 178; "Uses of the
  Erotic: The Erotic as Power," 174;
  "Woman Thing, The," 175
"Louie, El" 296

Index

"Love Song of J. Alfred Prufrock, The," 196
Lowell, Amy, 163, 325
Lowell, Harriet Winslow, 13
Lowell, James Russell, 9
Lowell, Robert, 1, 2, 6, 8, **9–17**, 18, 37, 87, 115, 123, 129, 133, 166, 208, 231, 239, 319; "Beyond the Alps," 12; "Children of Light," 10–11; "Colloquy at Black Rock," 12; *Day by Day*, 15–16; *Dolphin, The*, 15, 16; "Epilogue," 16; "Fall 1961," 14; *For Lizzie and Harriet*, 15; "For the Union Dead," 14; *For the Union Dead*, 14; *History*, 15; "In Memory of Arthur Winslow," 11; "July in Washington," 14; *Land of Unlikeness*, 10; *Life Studies*, 9, 12–14; *Lord Weary's Castle*, 10; "Man and Wife," 13; "Memories of West Street and Lepke," 13; "Mouth of the Hudson, The," 14; "91 Revere Street," 9, 13; *Notebook*, 15; *Notebook 1967–68*, 14; "Quaker Graveyard in Nantucket, The," 11; "Rebellion," 12; "Skunk Hour," 13; "To Peter Taylor on the Feast of the Epiphany," 11; "Unwanted," 16; "Waking in the Blue," 13
Lowell, Robert Sheridan, 15
LSD, 75

Machado, Antonio, 104, 107
MacLeish, Archibald, 94
Madhubuti, Haki, 51, 248, 255, 260, 264
Mailer, Norman, 14
Maine Woods, 147
Major, Clarence, 316
Malcolm X, 50, 251, 252, 255, 259, 260, 262, 262, 266
Mandela, Nelson, 52
Mandela, Winnie, 52, 268
Mandelstam, Osip, 209
Mann, Thomas, 40
"Man With the Blue Guitar, The," 306
Mao Tse Tung, 253
Marble Faun, The, 4
Marquez, Gabriel Garcia, 57; "A Very Old Man with Enormous Wings," 57
Marvell, Andrew, 195
Marx, Karl, 253
Masters, Edgar Lee, 182
Matthews, William, **233–35**; *Broken Syllables*, 233; *Curiosities*, 234; *Flood*, 234; "Happy Childhood, A," 234; *Happy Childhood, Forseeable Futures*, 234; "Moving Again," 234; *Rising and Falling*, 234; *Ruining the New Road*, 233; *Sleek for the Long Flight*, 234; "Spring Snow," 234; *Sticks and Stones*, 234

Maverick Poets, The, 324, 325
Maximus Poems, The, 254
McCarthy, Eugene, 14
McCarthy, Joseph, 60
McCarthyism, 2, 40, 135
McDowell, Robert, 324
McGrath, Thomas, 124, **133–38**, 153; "Beyond the Red River," 135; "Bread of This World, The; Praises III," 136; "Dreams of Wild Horses, The," 135; *Letter to an Imaginary Friend*, 136–37; *Movie at the End of the World*, 136; "Seekers, The," 134; *Selected Poems*, 133, 136; "Topography of History, The," 134; "Two Songs From 'The Hunted Revolutionaries,'" 135; "Up the Dark Valley," 134
McKay, Claude, 246
Melhem, D. H., 51
Melville, Herman, 39, 40, 101
men's movement, 106
Merrill, James, 18, **230–32**, 319; "Angel," 232; *Book of Ephraim, The*, 230–31; *Changing Light at Sandover, The*, 230; "Farewell Performance," 232; *Inner Room, The*, 231; *Scattering of Salts, A*, 230; *Selected Poems: 1946–1985*, 231
Merwin, W. S., 105, 122, 196, 197, **203–9**, 221, 222, 233; "Berryman," 208–9; "Chord," 207; *Drunk in the Furnace, The*, 205; "Exercise," 203; "Finally," 205; "For a Coming Extinction," 207; "Gift," 208; "Horizon of Rooms, The," 208; "Last One, The," 207; "Losing a Language," 207; "Lost Originals, The," 207; *Mask for Janus, A*, 204; *Opening the Hand*, 206; *Rain in the Trees, The*, 204, 207; *Selected Poems*, 203, 204; *Selected Translations*, 209; "St. Vincents," 208
Messerli, Doug, 321
Meyers, Jack, 323
Middlebrook, Diane, 166
Millay, Edna St. Vincent, 163

Miller, Adam, 316
Milton, John, 13, 76
Mind of the South, The, 141
minimalism, 74, 101
Mirikitani, Janice, **309–13**; *Awake in the River*, 312; *Ayumi: A Japanese American Anthology*, 309; "Breaking Silence," 312; "Breaking Tradition," 312; "Canto a Neruda," 311; "Certain Kind of Madness, A," 311; "Crazy Alice," 310; "Firepot," 309; "For My Father," 310; "Japs," 310; "Looking for a Poem," 311; "Lullabye," 310; "Ms.," 311; "Prisons of Silence," 312; "Question Is, The," 311; *Shedding Silence*, 312; "Song for You—for Cecil," 311; *Third-World Woman*, 309; *Time to Greez: Incantations from the Third World*, 309; "We, the dangerous," 311
modernism, 2, 45, 68, 73, 74, 91, 105, 108, 125, 196, 197, 237, 241, 248, 276, 290, 291, 318
Mohammed, 231
Molesworth, Charles, 200
Moliére, 61
Momaday, N. Scott, **277–80**, 290; "Abstract: Old Woman in a Room," 280; *Ancient Child*, 280; *Angle of Geese and Other Poems*, 278; "Bear, The," 280; "Before an Old Painting of the Crucifixion," 279; "Delight Song of Tsoai-talee, The," 279; "Gourd Dancer, The," 279; *Gourd Dancer, The*, 278; *House Made of Dawn*, 277; *In the Presence of the Sun*, 280; *Way to Rainy Mountain, The*, 277
Monet, Claude, 53
Monk, Thelonious, 254, 309
Montaigne, Michel de, 218
Montoya, José, 296
Mooney, Tom, 39
Moore, Marianne, 6, 19, 58, 163, 184
Moraga, Cherrie, 303
Morrow Anthology of Younger American Poets, The, 323
Mother Theresa, 230
Motherwell, Robert, 3, 92
Ms magazine, 267
Muhammad, Elijah, 257

Nagasaki, 1
Naked Lunch, 101

Neal, Larry, 251, 316
Neidecker, Lorine, 264
neoformalism, 62, 105, 192, 318, 321–22, 324, 325
Neruda, Pablo, 67, 107, 211, 271, 311
New American Poetry, The, 314, 322
New American Poets of the 80s, The, 323
New Black Poetry, The, 316
New Criticism, 1, 10
New York action painters, 69, 90, 92
New York Poets, 315
Niatum, Duane, 316
Nijinsky, Vaslav, 239, 241
Nims, John Frederick, 321
Nine Black Poets, 316
No More Masks: An Anthology of Poetry by Women, 44, 316
Nuyorican poetry, 277

O'Brian, Edward J., *Best Short Stories, 1941*, 3
O'Connell, Beatrice, 25
Odyssey, The, 33
O'Hara, Frank, 73, 74, 76, **89–93**, 104, 124, 249; "Autobiographia Literaria," 91; *Collected Poems of Frank O'Hara, The*, 89–93; "Day Lady Died, The," 90; "Memorial Day, 1950," 91, 93
Olds, Sharon, 45, 163, **184–90**, 191; "After 37 Years, My Mother Apologizes for My Childhood," 188; "Blue Dress, The," 188; "Chute, The," 187; *Dead and the Living, The*, 185, 189; "Death of Marilyn Monroe, The," 189; "Exact Moment of His Death, The," 188; "Fate," 187; *Father, The*, 185, 188; *Gold Cell, The*, 185, 186, 187, 188; "Ideal Father, The," 187; "I Go Back to May 1937," 186; "Late Poem to My Father," 188; "Looking at my Father," 187; "Reading You," 187; "Satan Says," 185; *Satan Says*, 185, 186; "Sign of Saturn, The," 187; "Sisters of Sexual Treasure, The," 186; *Wellspring, The*, 185, 190
Oliver, Mary, 139, 140, **154–56**; *American Primitive*, 154, 155; "Barn, The," 155; "Blackleaf Swamp," 156; "Farm Country," 155; *House of Light*, 155; "Indonesia," 155; "Learning About the Indians," 155; "Morning in a New Land," 154; *New and Selected Poems*, 156; *Night Traveller, The*, 154;

Index

No Voyage and Other Poems, 154;
"River Styx, The," 155; *River Styx, Ohio, and Other Poems, The*, 154, 155; "Singapore," 155; *Sleeping in the Forest*, 154; "Spring," 156; "Swans on the River Ayr," 154; "Tecumseh," 155; *Twelve Moons*, 154; "University Hospital, Boston," 155; "White Owl Flies Into and Our of the Field," 156; *White Pine*, 156; "Wild Geese, The," 156; "Winter Sleep," 156
Olson, Charles, 16, 28, 73, 74, 93, 99, 100, 127, 137, 254, 321
Onthebus, 123
Oppenheimer, J. Robert, 291
organic verse, 38, 64–65
Orr, Gregory, 28
Ortiz, Simon, **282–90**; *After and Before the Lightning*, 288; *Fight Back*, 286; *From Sand Creek*, 286, 287; *Going for the Rain*, 284, 285; *Good Journey, A*, 285; "It Was that Indian," 286; "My Father's Song," 284; "Relocation," 285; "San Diego Poem, A," 285; "Song, Poetry and Language—Expression and Perception," 284; "Story of How a Wall Stands, A," 284; *Woven Stone*, 284
Ostriker, Alicia Suskin, 148, 164, **190**; *Dream of Springtime, A*, 190; *Green Age*, 190; *Imaginary Lover, The*, 190; *Woman under the Surface, A*, 190; *Writing Like a Woman*, 190

Pack, Robert, 314, 318
pantheism, 125, 128
Parini, Jay, 318
Parker, Charlie, 254, 309
Parks, Rosa, 178
Parmigianino, Francesco, 96
Parra, Nicholas, 209
Paterson, 118, 254
Paul, Sherman, 102
Peabody, Josephine, 163
Perloff, Marjorie, 321
Personism, 93
Peters, Robert, 83, 204
Picasso, Pablo, 91, 92
Piercy, Marge, 42, 163, 164, **179–84**, 209; "ark of consequence, The," 184; *Available Light*, 181, 183; "Burial by Salt," 183; "Chuppah," 182; *Circles on the Water: Selected Poems*, 180, 181;

"Crow babies," 184; "Death of a doe on Chequesset Neck," 184; "Doing it Differently," 180; *Early Ripening*, 179; "For Mars and her children returning in March," 184; "I see the sign and tremble," 183; "Joy Road and Livernois," 182; *Mars and Her Children*, 184; "My Mother's Body," 182; *My Mother's Body*, 181, 182; *Stone, Paper, Knife*, 181; *What Are Big Girls Made Of?*, 184; *Woman on the Edge of Time*, 179
Pietri, Pedro, 277
Pilgrim's Progress, 33
Pinsky, Robert, 153, **235–37**, 319; "Ceremony for Any Beginning," 235; *Explanation of America, An*, 236; *Figured Wheel, New and Collected Poems, 1966–1996*, 236; *History of My Heart*, 236; "Poem about People," 235; "Sadness and Happiness," 236; *Sadness and Happiness*, 235, 236; *Want Bone, The*, 236
Pisan Cantos, The, 104
Plath, Sylvia, 31, 59, 74, **84–89**, 93, 115, 123, 163, 166, 174, 184, 193, 291, 293; *Ariel*, 85, 86; "Childless Woman," 88; *Collected Poems*, 84, 86, 87, 88; *Colossus, The*, 74, 84, 86; *Crossing the Water*, 86; "Cut," 88; "Daddy," 88–89; "Edge," 88; "Lady Lazarus," 87–88; "Lorelei," 88; "Manor Garden, The," 84; "Two Views of a Cadaver Room," 84; *Winter Trees*, 85, 86
Plato, 231
Platonic mysticism, 69
Ploughshares, 123
Poe, Edgar Allan, 58, 59, 76
Poetry, 122
Poetry Northwest, 123
Pollitt, Katha, 321
Pollock, Jackson, 3, 90, 92, 152
populism, 134
Poulson, Edwa, 125
Pound, Ezra, 15, 18, 62, 70, 73, 75, 76, 77, 91, 92, 93, 100, 104, 104, 123, 150, 161, 196, 208, 231, 249
Powell, Bud, 234, 309
Prairie Schooner, The, 3
"Prayer for My Daughter," 4
Prelude, The, 25
projective verse, 16, 44, 64, 69, 99–100

Prunty, Wyatt, 322
Puritanism, 142

Quasha, George, 316

Rabearivelo, Jean Joseph, 271
racism, 38, 47, 48, 56–57, 174, 179, 252, 254, 274, 308
Rahv, Philip, 314
Randall, Dudley, 51, 260, 315
Ransom, John Crowe, 1, 2, 6, 10, 11, 12, 72, 108, 138
Read, Herbert, 63
regionalism, 128, 131, 138, 148
Revolution of the Word, 316
Rexroth, Kenneth, 68, 127, 196, 211
Rich, Adrienne, 21, 43, 44, 73, **79–84**, 89, 133, 163, 164, 175, 179, 181, 194, 206, 210, 227, 292, 315, 319; *Atlas of the Difficult World, An*, 84; "Burning of Paper Instead of Children, The," 80; "Cartographies of Silence," 81; *Change of World, A*, 73, 79; "Contradictions: Tracking Poems," 82; *Dark Fields of the Republic, Poems 1991–1995*, 84; "Demon Lover, The," 80; "Diving into the Wreck," 43; "Five O'Clock, Beacon Hill," 80; "Images, The," 82; "Images for Godard," 81; *Leaflets*, 80; "Planetarium," 80; "Sources," 82; "Stepping Backward," 80; *Time's Power*, 83; "Unsaid Word, An," 80; "Unsounded," 80; "What Ghosts Can Say," 80; *Will to Change, The*, 80; *Your Native Land, Your Life*, 82
Richards, I. A., 165
Richman, Robert, 317, 321, 322
Rickson, Susanna, 127
Rilke, Rainer Maria, 63, 70, 107
Rimbaud, Arthur, 168
Robinett, Jane, 109
Robinson, Edwin A., 5
Roethke, Theodore, 1, **22–26**, 31, 33, 37, 108, 123, 154, 196; "Cuttings," 24; *Far Field, The*, 26; "Four for Sir John Davies," 25; "I Know a Woman," 25; *Lost Son and Other Poems, The*, 24; "Meditations of an Old Woman," 26; "North American Sequence," 26; "Open House," 23; *Praise to the End*, 24, 25; *Waking, The*, 25; "What Can I Tell My Bones," 26; *Words for the Wind*, 25

Rolling Stones, 77
romanticism, 131
Rose, Wendy, 165, **290–93**; *Academic Squaw*, 292; *Builder Kachina: A Home-Going Cycle*, 290; "Child Held, Child Broken," 293; "Excavation at Santa Barbara Mission," 293; "Fifty Thousand Songs," 293; *Going to War with All My Relatives*, 292; *Halfbreed Chronicles and Other Poems, The*, 291; "If I Am Too Brown Or Too White For You," 291; "Neon Scars," 291; "No One Is As Lost As This Indian Woman," 293; *Now Poof She Is Gone*, 293; "Orphan Song," 293; "Three Thousand Dollar Death Song," 292
Rothenberg, Jerome, 316
Roussel, Raymond, 94
Rukeyser, Muriel, 37, 38, **39–45**, 52, 57, 65, 67, 163; "Ajanta," 42; *Beast in View*, 42; *Breaking Open*, 41; *Collected Poems*, 40, 45; "Delta Poems," 41; "Despisals," 43; "Don Baty," 41; "Letter to the Front," 41; *Life of Poetry, The*, 39, 44; "Night Flight: New York," 39; "Nine Poems for the Unborn Child," 42; "Open the Gates," 42; "Poem as Mask, The," 43; "Poem out of Childhood," 39; "Speed of Darkness, The," 43; *Speed of Darkness*, 41; "Theory of Flight, The," 39; *Theory of Flight*, 39; "Welcome From War," 41
Rumi, 107
Ryder, Albert Pinkerton, 40

Sacco and Vanzetti trial, 39
Salter, Mary Jo, 321
Sanchez, Sonia, 165, **255–59**, 260, 261, 263; "After Saturday Night Comes Sunday," 257; "After the Fifth Day," 257; "Bluebirdbluebirdthrumywindow," 257; *Blues Book for Blue Black Magical Women, A*, 257; "Catch the Fire," 258; "Depression," 257; *HOMEGIRLS AND HANDGRENADES*, 257; *I've Been a Woman*, 257; "Letter to Dr. Martin Luther King, A," 258; *Love Poems*, 257; "Love Song for Spelman, A," 258; "Love Song #3," 259; "Poem for Some Women," 259; "Reflections After the June 12th March for

Disarmament," 257; *Under a Soprano Sky*, 258; *We a BaddDDD People*, 256; *Wounded in the House of a Friend*, 258

San Diego Museum of Contemporary Art, 270

San Francisco Poetry Renaissance, 68, 124, 127, 315

San Jose State University Poetry Center, 123

Saroyan, William, 306

Schwartz, Delmore, 31, 186, 219

Scottsboro Nine, 39, 40

Seale, Bobby, 266

sexism, 174, 254, 298, 302

Sexton, Anne, 85, 109, 115, 144, 145, 163, 164, **165–74**, 193; *All My Pretty Ones*, 166; "Ambition Bird, The," 173; *Awful Rowing toward God, The*, 174; *Book of Folly, The*, 173; "Breast, The," 169; "Cinderella," 172; *Death Notebooks, The*, 174; "Death of the Fathers, The," 173; "Eighteen Days Without You," 171; "Flee on Your Donkey," 168; "For My Lover, Returning to His Wife," 171; "Hansel and Gretel," 172; "In Celebration of My Uterus," 170–71; "Jesus Papers, The," 173–74; "Killing the Spring," 173; "Little Red Riding Hood," 172; "Live," 169; *Live or Die*, 167, 169, 171; *Love Poems*, 170, 171; "Menstruation at Forty," 169; "Operation, The," 166; "Rapunzel," 172; "Ringing the Bells," 166; "Rumplestilskin," 172; "Silence, The," 173; "Sleeping Beauty," 172; *To Bedlam and Part Way Back*, 166; *Transformations*, 164, 172; "Twelve Dancing Princesses," 172; "Wanting to Die," 169; "You All Know the Story of The Other Woman," 171

Shaku, Assta, 178

Sheffey, Asa, 52

Sheffey, Ruth, 52

Silko, Leslie Marmon, **288–90**; *Almanac of the Dead, The*, 290; *Ceremony*, 288, 289; *Delicacy and Strength of Lace, The*, 290; "It was summertime," 289; *Laguna Woman*, 288; "Long time ago," 289; "One time," 289; "Prayer to the Pacific," 289; *Storyteller*, 289; "Storyteller's Escape, The," 288

Silliman, Ron, 320, 321

Simic, Charles, 123, **232–33**; "Description," 233; *Dismantling the Silence*, 232; "Navigator," 233; *Return to a Place Lit by a Glass of Milk*, 232; "Spoons with Realistic Dead Flies on Them," 233; "Suitcase Strapped with a Rope, A," 233; "Toy Factory," 233

Simpson, Louis, 105, 314

"Sinners in the Hands of an Angry God," 10

Smart, Christopher: "Jubliate Agno," 52

Smith, Dave, 323

Smith, John, 32

Snodgrass, W. D., 12, 109, 123, 166, **229–30**; *After Experience*, 229; "Füehrer Bunker, The," 230; "Heart's Needle," 12; *Heart's Needle*, 166, 229; *In Radical Pursuit*, 230

Snyder, Gary, 100, 123, 127, 139, 146, 153, **156–62**, 315, 319; "Anasazi," 159; "Axe Handles," 161–62; *Axe Handles*, 161; "By Frazier Creek Falls," 160; "Facts," 159; "Mother Earth: Her Whales," 159; *Mountains and Rivers Without End*, 162; *Myths and Texts*, 158; "Plain Talk," 159; "Soy Sauce," 161; *Turtle Island*, 158, 159

Soares, Lota de Macedo, 17

Sojourner Truth, 54, 267

"Song of Myself," 34, 43

"Sonny's Blues," 262

Southern Review, 6

Spanish Civil War, 40, 41, 63

Spanos, William, 100

Spears, Monroe, 140

Speck, Richard, 308

Spicer, Jack, 68

Spoon River Anthology, 182

Stade, George, 85

Stafford, Jean, 10

Stafford, William, 122, 123, 124, 127, **129–33**; "Across Kansas, 130; "At the Un-National Monument Along the Canadian Border," 132; "BiFocal," 131; *Darkness Around Us is Deep, The*, 133; *Down in My Heart*, 132; "Earth Dweller," 131; "Elegy, 130; "Heard Under a Town Sign at the Beach," 131; "Listening," 129; *Rescued Year, The*, 130; "Thanksgiving for My Father, A," 130; "Travelling Through the Dark," 132; "Watching the Jet Planes Dive," 132; *West of Your City*,

Index

Stafford, William (*continued*)
133; "Whispered into the Ground,"
131; *Writing the Australian Crawl*, 133;
You Must Revise Your Life, 133
Stalin, Joseph, 1, 72
Starbuck, George, 144, 166
Stark, Inez Cunningham, 46
Stark, John, 9
Steele, Timothy, 321
Stein, Gertrude, 92, 163, 231, 320
Stevens, Wallace, 1, 15, 58, 69, 92, 93,
94, 149, 150, 151, 152, 208, 231, 232,
235, 306
"Stopping by the Woods on a Snowy
Evening," 132
Strand, Mark, 18, 196, 197, **219–23**, 233;
Continuous Life, The, 219, 221, 222,
223; *Dark Harbor*, 219, 223; "Elegy for
My Father," 221; "Keeping Things
Whole," 220; *Late Hour, The*, 219;
Monument, The, 219, 222; "My
Death," 221; "My Life," 221; "My
Life by Somebody Else," 221; *Selected
Poems*, 219; "Sleeping with One Eye
Open," 219; *Sleeping with One Eye
Open*, 219
*Strong Measures: Contemporary American
Poetry in Traditional Forms*, 321, 322
surrealism, 74, 94, 123, 220, 232, 277,
281, 282

Tannlund, Rose Moreno, 127
Tartuffe, 61
Tate, Allen., 1, 6, 10, 11, 12, 138
Taylor, Peter, 10, 16
Teasdale, Sara, 163
Technicians of the Sacred, 316
Terry, Lucy, 246
"Thieves of Language, The: Women
Poets and Revisionist Mythmaking,"
43
Thomas, Dylan, 8, 137, 138, 211
Thoreau, Henry David, 24, 131, 147,
149, 154, 156
Thornbury, Charles, 35
Tibetan Buddhism, 76
Till, Emmett, 49
"To His Coy Mistress," 195
Tolson, Melvin B., 247, 276
Tomlinson, Charles, 123, 321
Toomer, Jean, 245, 247
"Tradition and the Individual Talent,"
100

Troupe, Quincy, **269–73**; *American Rag*,
270; *Avalanche*, 272–73; "Blues for
Delmar Dosie," 270; *Giant Talk: An
Anthology of Third World Writing*, 270;
Inside Story of TV's "Roots," The, 270;
"Looking at Both Sides of a
Question," 273; *Miles: The
Autobiography*, 270; "Ode to John
Coltrane," 272; "Poem for My
Friends," 273; "River Rhythm
Town," 271; "River Town Packin
House Blues," 270; *Skulls along the
River*, 270; *Snake-Back Solos*, 271;
Soundings, 270; "Stillness," 273;
"Three Old Black Ladies Standing
on Bus Stop Corners," 273; "Today's
Subway Ride," 272; "Up Sun South
of Alaska," 271; *Watts Poets*, 270
Tubman, Harriet, 267
Tuckerman, Frederick Goddard, 278
Turner, Nat, 56
Tutu, Bishop Desmond, 228

University of Iowa Writer's Workshop,
123

Vallejo, César, 107
Veblen, Thorstein, 40
Vendler, Helen, 318, 325
Vietnam, 14, 40, 41, 56, 65, 71, 78, 106,
308, 311
Villon, Francois, 197

Wakoski, Diane, 74, **115–21**, 155, 164;
"Archeology of Movies and Books,
The," 120; *Collected Greed, 1–13, The*,
118; *Emerald Ice*, 117, 118; "Father of
My Country, The," 116; *Greed*, 118,
119; "Ice Eagle, The," 117; "I Have
Had to Learn to Live With My Face,"
117; *Medea the Sorceress*, 116, 120, 121;
"Moneylight," 120; "Smudging,"
117; "Water Element Song for Sylvia,
The," 119
Walcott, Derek, 123
Waldman, Anne, **190–91**; "Fast Talking
Woman," 190–91; *Helping the
Dreamer: New and Selected Poems*, 190
Walker, Alice, 45
Walker, Margaret, 257
Waller, Fats, 308
Warren, Robert Penn, 6
Washington, Mary Helen, 262

Index

Waste Land, The, 5, 84, 231
Weingarten, Roger, 323
Welch, James, 123, **280–82**, 290;
    "Christmas Comes to Moccasin
    Flat," 282; "Harlem, Montana: Just
    Off the Reservation," 281; "Magic
    Fox," 282; "Man from Washington,
    The," 281; *Riding the Earthboy,* 40, 280
West, Ellen, 239
Whalen, Phillip, 249
Wheatley, Phyllis, 55–56, 246
White, Herbert, 239, 240
Whiteman, Roberta Hill, 273
Whitman, Walt, 3, 6, 23, 25, 26, 34, 39,
    40, 52, 62, 70, 75, 76, 122, 124, 138,
    149, 152, 162, 198, 208, 211, 222, 245,
    268, 317, 325, 326, 328
Wilbur, Richard, 37, 38, **58–62**, 322;
    "Advice to a Prophet," 60;
    "Beautiful Changes, The," 58;
    "Cottage Street, 1953," 60; "Dubious
    Night, A," 58; "For the Student
    Strikers," 60; "Juggler," 58; *Love
    Calls Us to the Things of This World,*
    61; "Love Calls Us to the Things of
    This World," 58; "October Maples,
    Portland," 58; "On Freedom's
    Ground," 60; "On The Marginal
    Way," 58; "Poetry's Debt to Poetry,"
    61; *Responses, Prose Pieces:
    1953–1976,* 61; "Speech for the
    Repeal of the McCarron Act," 60;
    "Undead, The," 58; "World Without
    Objects Is a Sensible Emptiness,
    A," 58
Williams, C. K., 166, 196, 197, **223–29**;
    "Cave, The," 224; "Color of Time,
    The," 226–27; *Flesh and Blood,* 228;
    "From My Window," 226; "Gas
    Station, The," 226; "Gift, The," 226; *I
    Am the Bitter Name,* 223; "It is This
    Way with Men," 225; "Last Deaths,
    The," 225; "Normality," 229;
    "Sanctity, The," 224; *Tar,* 226; "To
    Market," 224; *With Ignorance,* 223
Williams, Robert, 250
Williams, Roger, 274
Williams, W. C., 1, 6, 7, 12, 14, 64, 76,
    77, 100, 115, 118, 124, 127, 137, 196,
    214, 235, 236, 249, 254, 325
Winslow, Arthur, 11
Winslow, Edward, 9
Winslow, John, 11

Winslow, Mary, 11
Winslow, Warren, 11
Winthrop, John, 274
women's poetry, 163–64, 179
Wong, Shawn Hsu, 305
Wordsworth, William, 6, 8, 22, 25, 196,
    240
*World Split Open, The: Four Centuries of
    Women Poets in England and America,
    1552–1950,* 44
World War I, 20
World War II, 7, 14, 33, 47, 58, 68, 132,
    135, 138, 150, 232, 288, 294, 306
Wright, James, 28, 74, 104, **108–15**, 154,
    282; "Above San Ferino," 109; *Above
    the River: The Complete Poems,* 109;
    "As I Step over a Puddle at the End
    of Winter, I Think of an Ancient
    Chinese Governor," 110; "At the
    Executed Murderer's Grave,"
    109–10; "Blessing, A," 112–13;
    Branch Will Not Break, The, 110, 115;
    "Fear is What Quickens Me," 112;
    "Gambling in Stateline, Nevada,"
    109; "Goodbye to the Poetry of
    Calcium," 111; *Green Wall, The,* 110;
    "In Memory of a Spanish Poet," 112;
    "In Response to a Rumor that the
    Oldest Whorehouse in Wheeling,
    West Virginia, Has Been
    Condemned," 109; "Jewel, The," 111;
    "Lying in a Hammock at William
    Duffy's Farm in Pine Island,
    Minnesota," 111; "Many of Our
    Waters," 113; "Old WPA Swimming
    Pool in Martin's Ferry, Ohio, The,"
    114–15; "Poem Written Under an
    Archway in a Discontinued Railroad
    Station, Fargo, A," 109; "Poor
    Washed Up by Chicago Winter,
    The," 109; *Shall We Gather at the
    River,* 110, 115; "Small Grove in Torri
    Del Benaco, A," 109; "Spring
    Images," 112; *This Journey,* 115; *To a
    Blossoming Pear Tree,* 115; *Two
    Citizens,* 115; "Two Hangovers," 111;
    "Variations on a Poem by a Black
    Child," 113; "Winter, Basoano del
    Grappa," 109
Wright, Jay, 247, 276
Wright, Richard, 46, 254
Wright brothers, 40
W. S. Merwin: Essays on the Poetry, 203

Yeats, William Butler, 4, 25, 26, 94, 196, 231
Young, Lester, 234, 309

Zamora, Bernice, 295, **298–300**, 302; "Living in Aztlan," 299; "Notes from a Chicano Coed," 300; "Penitents," 299; "Pico Blanco," 299; "Restless Serpent," 298; *Restless Serpent*, 298, 300; "Sonnet, Freely Adapted," 299; "So Not To Be Mottled," 299
Zen Buddhism, 157, 160
Zukofsky, Louis, 100
Zweig, Paul, 228

· *A Note on the Authors* ·

Fred Moramarco is editor of *Poetry International,* an annual poetry journal published at San Diego State University where he also teaches American Literature. His poems and essays on contemporary poetry have appeared in a wide range of books and periodicals. He is co-editor, with Al Zolynas, of *Men of Our Time: An Anthology of Male Poetry in Contemporary America,* and co-author, with Alan Shucard and William Sullivan, of *Modern American Poetry, 1865–1950.*

William Sullivan is a professor of English and Coordinator of American Studies at Keene State College in New Hampshire. With Alan Shucard and Fred Moramarco, he co-authored *Modern American Poetry, 1865–1950.*